Layering and Directionality

Advances in Optimality Theory
Editors: Armin Mester, University of California, Santa Cruz, and Vieri Samek-Lodovici, University College London

Optimality Theory is an exciting new approach to linguistic analysis that originated in phonology but was soon taken up in syntax, morphology, and other fields of linguistics. Optimality Theory presents a clear vision of the universal properties underlying the vast surface typological variety in the world's languages. Cross-linguistic differences once relegated to idiosyncratic language-specific rules can now be understood as the result of different priority rankings among universal, but violable constraints on grammar.

Advances in Optimality Theory is designed to stimulate and promote research in this provocative new framework. It provides a central outlet for the best new work by both established and younger scholars in this rapidly moving field. The series includes studies with a broad typological focus, studies dedicated to the detailed analysis of individual languages, and studies on the nature of Optimality Theory itself. The series publishes theoretical work in the form of monographs and coherent edited collections as well as pedagogical texts and reference texts that promote the dissemination of Optimality Theory.

Published:

Optimality Theory, Phonological Acquisition and Disorders
Edited by Daniel A. Dinnsen and Judith A. Gierut

Modeling Ungrammaticality in Optimality Theory
Edited by Curt Rice and Sylvia Blaho

Phonological Argumentation
Essays in Evidence and Motivation
Edited by Steve Parker

Hidden Generalizations
Phonological Opacity in Optimality Theory
John J. McCarthy

Conflicts in Interpretation
Petra Hendriks, Helen de Hoop, Irene Krämer, Henriëtte de Swart and Joost Zwarts

The Phonology of Contrast
Anna Łubowicz

Prosody Matters
Essays in Honor of Elisabeth Selkirk
Edited by Toni Borowsky, Shigeto Kawahara, Takahito Shinya and Mariko Sugahara

Blocking and Complementarity in Phonological Theory
Eric Baković

Linguistic Derivations and Filtering
Minimalism and Optimality Theory
Edited by Hans Broekhuis and Ralf Vogel

Understanding Allomorphy
Perspectives from Optimality Theory
Edited by Eulàlia Bonet, Maria-Rosa Lloret and Joan Mascaró

Layering and Directionality

Metrical Stress in Optimality Theory

Brett Hyde

SHEFFIELD UK BRISTOL CT

Published by Equinox Publishing Ltd.
UK: Office 415, The Workstation, 15 Paternoster Row, Sheffield, South Yorkshire S1 2BX
USA: ISD, 70 Enterprise Drive, Bristol, CT 06010

www.equinoxpub.com/home/

First published 2016

British Library Cataloguing-in-Publication Data

A catalogue record for this book is available from the British Library.
ISBN-13 978 1 84553 089 1 (hardback)

Library of Congress Cataloging-in-Publication Data
Hyde, Brett.
Layering and directionality: metrical stress in optimality theory / Brett Hyde.
pages cm. – (Advances in Optimality Theory)
Includes bibliographical references and index.
ISBN 978-1-84553-089-1 (hb)
1. Optimality theory (Linguistics) 2. Generative grammar. I. Title.
P158.42.H93 2015
414–dc23

2014039973

Typeset by S.J.I. Service, New Delhi
Printed and bound by Lightning Source Inc. (La Vergne, TN), Lightning Source UK Ltd. (Milton Keynes), Lightning Source AU Pty. (Scoresby, Victoria).

Contents

Dedication

To my friends in the Philosophy Department at Washington University. During the time this book was written, the faculty included the following.

Santiago Amaya
Anne Margaret Baxley
Eric Brown
Carl Craver
Emily Crookston
Dennis DesChene
John Doris
Julia Driver
Frederick Eberhardt
Claude Evans
John Heil
Philipp Koralus
Charlie Kurth
Ron Mallon
Mark Rollins
Gillian Russell
Thomas Sattig
Elizabeth Schechter
Roy Sorenson
Shannon Spaulding
Brandon Towl
Christopher "Kit" Wellman

Preface

I had not planned to write a book during the time of my probationary appointment as assistant professor at Washington University. Towards the end of this period, however, Kit Wellman, my department chair, suggested that it might be the right time for a book. At first, I was not convinced. The results of my research program on metrical stress theory had been published, and continued to be published, gradually, in an article-length format, and I was reasonably content with this approach. He made a compelling argument however, pointing out that a book-length work might be a key point in the case for my continued employment. I eventually agreed.

As I looked back over the results of the research program that I had been focused on for a little over a decade, I realized that a book would provide a much needed opportunity to integrate components of a theory that, to that point, had only been presented separately and to revise earlier proposals in light of more recent results. In particular, it was an opportunity to revise the Weak Bracketing approach to metrical stress theory, originally presented in 'A restrictive theory of metrical stress', a *Phonology* article published in 2002, in light of the proposal for Relation-Specific Alignment, originally presented in 'Alignment constraints', an article published in *Natural Language and Linguistic Theory* in 2012. The whole of Chapter 2 and the first part of Chapter 6 are modified and extended versions of the article on alignment constraints. Chapter 5 presents the revised version of the Weak Bracketing approach.

It was also an opportunity to strengthen the case for the Weak Bracketing approach in light of results connected to the Odd-Parity Input Problem. The problem was discussed using the Symmetrical Alignment approach of McCarthy and Prince (1993) and the Iterative Foot Optimization approach of Pruitt (2010) as examples in 'The odd-parity input problem in metrical stress theory', published in *Phonology* in 2012. Chapter 3 is a modified version of this article. Chapter 4 examines the problem in two additional cases: the Asymmetrical Alignment account of Alber (2005) and the Rhythmic Licensing account of Kager (2005).

Many fruitful discussions with colleagues and students have contributed to the development of the key ideas. Especially valuable in the development of the Relation-Specific Alignment proposal were the contributions of two of my undergraduate students, Kenny Hofmeister and Brook Husic. The second half of Chapter 6 is based on an article that Brook and I wrote together, 'Ancient Greek accent windows'. It appeared in *Revista Letras e Letras* in 2012.

While many of the individual ideas in the book will be familiar to researchers in the field of metrical stress theory, then, these ideas have been integrated and extended, and the consequences of their integration and extension explored, in a way that was not possible in earlier presentations. It has been a valuable exercise for me to try to forge the various pieces into a single theory, and I hope that other researchers in the field will find it a valuable contribution, as well.

Acknowledgments

Many people have contributed to this book in a number of ways. As editor, Armin Mester was instrumental in helping me get the book off the ground. Eric Bakovic and Alan Prince offered numerous helpful comments on the original draft. Over the years, I have had many fruitful discussions on key ideas with a number of colleagues, students, and teachers. These include Akin Akinlabi, Birgit Alber, Eric Bakovic, Laura Benua, Stuart Davis, Paul de Lacy, Ben Hermans, Kenny Hofmeister, Paula Houghton, Brook Husic, Ed Keer, John McCarthy, Bethany McCord, Nicole Nelson, Joe Pater, Mario Pellicciaro, Alan Prince, Katherine Pruitt, Cordula Simon, and Bruce Tesar.

I am grateful for the generosity of the Philosophy Department at Washington University, both for providing me with a home where I can teach and pursue my research program in general and for their support in writing this book in particular. Dave Balota and Roddy Roedigger in the Psychology Department have gone out of their way to support me in this and many other projects.

Finally, and most importantly, I am grateful for the support of my wife, Haydee, and my daughters, Maria and Sofia. They have been incredibly patient with me and with the time I spend thinking about metrical stress theory.

1 Introduction

In metrical stress theory, the prosodic hierarchy, the metrical grid, and the devices that establish directional parsing effects are closely intertwined. The metrical grid (Liberman and Prince 1977, Prince 1983) is the structure that represents stress patterns. The locations of stressed positions on the grid are constrained by the positions of categories in the prosodic hierarchy (Selkirk 1984, Nespor and Vogel 1986). Both the metrical grid and the prosodic hierarchy are manipulated by constraints, such as alignment constraints (McCarthy and Prince 1993a, Crowhurst and Hewitt 1995) that establish directional orientations within these structures. Assumptions about the representations affect the behavior of the constraints, and the particular formulation of the constraints influences the ultimate configuration of the representations.

This book examines the representations and constraints central to the theory of metrical stress, and the interactions between them, in the context of the constraint-based global evaluation procedure of Optimality Theory (OT; Prince and Smolensky 1993/2004). OT presents unique challenges. It insists that an output be defined through the interaction of simple requirements that have been realized as individual constraints rather than combined into the much more powerful rules characteristic of serial approaches. In general, it takes multiple constraints to do the work of a single rule, but the task is made even more difficult in that OT places a severe limit on the possible relationships between its simple requirements. The single relationship allowed between two constraints is ranking; the satisfaction of one simple requirement always takes precedence over the satisfaction of the other. There is no corresponding restriction on the relationship between simple requirements when they are combined into the rules characteristic of serial approaches; the relationships or non-relationships can be stipulated on a rule-by-rule basis.[1]

1 Though individual rules are often equivalent to several ranked constraints, the chunking of principles into separate rules and the subsequent ordering of those rules both establish relationships between principles that go far beyond the simple ranking relationship available in Optimality Theory.

Despite their intimate relationship, discussion in the OT literature has focused almost exclusively on the formulation of the constraints and has largely ignored assumptions about the representations. In a sense, this is understandable. Given the unique challenges of OT, the restriction to simple principles with a single mode of interaction, the literature quite naturally focused on identifying the relevant principles and formulating them into appropriate constraints. On the other hand, the result has been an approach to the problems of metrical stress theory is conspicuously lopsided. For example, there have been several significant proposals in the OT literature addressing the constraints that produce directional parsing effects. These include Symmetrical Alignment (McCarthy and Prince 1993a, Crowhurst and Hewitt 1995), Asymmetrical Alignment (Alber 2005), and Rhythmic Licensing (Kager 2001, 2005). In contrast, there has been almost no discussion of prosodic or metrical structure. The last substantive discussion of prosodic structure, Itô and Mester's (1992) Weak Layering proposal, roughly coincides with the advent of OT.

To better understand the significance of assumptions about prosodic structure, consider the different issues that arise when parsing an even number of syllables and an odd number of syllables. Dividing an even-parity string into binary feet is relatively straightforward. Every syllable can be included in a disyllabic foot so that no syllable is left over. There are no irregularities in prosodic layering and no indications of the influence of directional parsing.

(1) Even-parity string
(σσ)(σσ)(σσ)

In contrast, dividing an odd-parity string into binary feet is not so simple. There is always an odd, leftover syllable that must be handled differently than the others, and choices about prosodic layering and parsing directionality determine how the syllable is treated. The examples in (2) and (3) illustrate the possibilities for irregular layering available under the standard Weak Layering (Itô and Mester 1992) approach. The syllable can be parsed as monosyllabic foot, as in (2), or it can be left unfooted and incorporated directly into the prosodic word, as in (3).

(2) Leftover syllable parsed as a monosyllabic foot
a. (σσ)(σσ)(σσ)(σ) b. (σ)(σσ)(σσ)(σσ)

(3) Leftover syllable remains unparsed
a. (σσ)(σσ)(σσ) σ b. σ (σσ)(σσ)(σσ)

The location of the layering irregularity – the monosyllabic foot in (2) and the unfooted syllable in (3) – indicates the influence of directional parsing. In (2a) and (3a), it appears as if parsing has proceeded from left to right with the leftover syllable being stranded at the right edge. In (2b) and (3b), it appears as if parsing has proceeded from right to left with the leftover syllable being stranded at the left edge.

The nature and position of irregular layering is of central interest in metrical stress theory because layering irregularities often translate into departures from perfect binary alternation on the metrical grid and are thus responsible for much of the variation that we see among individual stress patterns. To illustrate, an unparsed syllable is always a stressless syllable, and its location within an odd-parity forms determines whether the form exhibits perfect binary alternation or contains a lapse (adjacent stressless syllables). When an unparsed syllable occurs at the left edge in a trochaic pattern or at the right edge in an iambic pattern, it occurs next to the stressed syllable of the only adjacent foot. The result in both cases is perfect binary alternation.

(4) Minimal alternation

a.	Trochaic	b.	Iambic
	(σ́σ)(σ́σ)(σ́σ)		(σσ́)(σσ́)(σσ́)
	σ(σ́σ)(σ́σ)(σ́σ)		(σσ́)(σσ́)(σσ́)σ

Both versions of the pattern are attested.[2] The trochaic version, (4a), has stress on every even-numbered syllable counting from the right, a pattern found in Nengone (Tryon 1967).

(5) Nengone forms (Tryon 1967)

a.	ˌačaˈkaze	'sorcerer'
b.	waˌčaruˈwiwi	'eel'

The mirror image iambic version, (4b), has stress on every even-numbered syllable from the left, a pattern found in Araucanian (Echeverria and Contreras 1965).

2 In labeling a pattern "attested", I mean only that one or more languages have been described in the literature as having the pattern. In labeling a pattern "unattested", I mean that no language has been described in the literature as exhibiting the pattern. In other words, I am trying to outline the facts as we know them while acknowledging that the facts as we know them might change, either through discovery of new languages or reevaluation of familiar languages.

(6) Araucanian forms (Echeverria and Contreras 1965)

a. eˈlumuˌyu 'give us'

b. eˈluaˌenew 'he will give me'

When the position of the unparsed syllable is switched to the opposite edge, however, to the right edge in the trochaic pattern and the left edge in the iambic pattern, the unparsed syllable occurs next to the stressless syllable of the adjacent foot. The result is a peripheral lapse.

(7) Peripheral lapse

a. Trochaic	b. Iambic
(σ́σ)(σ́σ)(σ́σ)	(σσ́)(σσ́)(σσ́)
(σ́σ)(σ́σ)(σ́σ)σ	σ(σσ́)(σσ́)(σσ́)

In this case, only one of the patterns is attested. The trochaic pattern, (7a), stresses every odd-numbered syllable from the left except the final syllable, a pattern found in Pintupi (Hansen and Hansen 1969).

(8) Pintupi forms (Hansen and Hansen 1969)

a. ˈtjamuˌlimpaˌtjunku 'our relation'

b. ˈt̪il̪iˌřiŋuˌlampatju 'the fire for our benefit flared up'

The iambic pattern, (7b), stresses every odd-numbered syllable from the right except the initial syllable, a pattern that is unattested.

Similarly, a monosyllabic foot is a stressed position, and its location within an odd-parity form determines whether the form maintains perfect binary alternation or contains a clash (adjacent stressed syllables). When a monosyllabic foot occurs at the right edge in a trochaic pattern or at the left edge in an iambic pattern, it occurs next to the stressless syllable of the only adjacent foot. The result is perfect binary alternation.

(9) Maximal alternation

a. Trochaic	b. Iambic
(σ́σ)(σ́σ)(σ́σ)	(σσ́)(σσ́)(σσ́)
(σ́σ)(σ́σ)(σ́σ)(σ́)	(σ́)(σσ́)(σσ́)(σσ́)

Both patterns are attested. The trochaic pattern, (9a), stresses every odd-numbered syllable from the left. The pattern can be found in Maranungku (Tryon 1970).

(10) Maranungku forms (Tryon 1970)

a. ˈyaŋarˌmata 'the Pleiades'

b. ˈlaŋkaˌrataˌti 'prawn'

The iambic pattern, (9b), stresses every odd-numbered syllable from the right, a pattern found in Suruwaha (Everett 1996).

(11) Suruwaha forms (Everett 1996)

a. daˌkuhuˈru 'to put in the fire'

b. ˌbihaˌwuhuˈra 'to fly'

When the monosyllabic foot is moved to the opposite edge, however, to the left edge in the trochaic pattern and the right edge in the iambic pattern, it is located next to the stressed syllable of the adjacent foot, creating a clash.

(12) Peripheral clash

a. Trochaic	b. Iambic
(σ́σ)(σ́σ)(σ́σ)	(σσ́)(σσ́)(σσ́)
(σ́)(σ́σ)(σ́σ)(σ́σ)	(σσ́)(σσ́)(σσ́)(σ́)

Only one of the patterns is actually attested. The trochaic pattern, (12a), stresses the initial syllable and every even-numbered syllable from the right. It can be found in Passamaquoddy (LeSourd 1993).

(13) Passamaquoddy forms (LeSourd 1993)

a. ˌwicohˌketaˈhamal 'he thinks of helping the other'

b. ˌtehˌsahkwaˌpasolˈtine 'let's walk around on top'

The iambic pattern, (12b), stresses the final syllable and every even-numbered syllable from the left. It is unattested.[3]

3 Potential examples of the (12b) pattern are less than persuasive. Gordon (2002a) cites the iambic Central Alaskan Yupik as a potential example of an iambic system with a final clash in odd-parity forms. According to Miyaoka (1985), however, the final accent is not a rhythmic stress; rather, it is a weaker boundary accent that arises only in specific phonological and morphological contexts. It has also been claimed, based on a pattern of vowel deletion, that the iambic Odawa (Kaye 1973, Piggott 1980) has final stress resulting in clash in odd-parity forms. However, final syllables are arguably always heavy in Odawa. Also, as Alber (2005) observes, deletion could fail in final position for a number of reasons unrelated to stress. It might fail, for example, because it would create undesirable consonant clusters.

I will address the typology of attested stress patterns in fuller detail below. At this stage, however, at least two points should be fairly clear. The first is that the nature of layering irregularities and their distribution both play key roles in determining the range of stress patterns that an account predicts. The second is that not every position in which a layering irregularity might appear yields an attested stress pattern. It is also appropriate to consider a third point: making a different set of layering irregularities available to the grammar may very well result in a different – and, perhaps, more accurate – range of predicted stress systems. The primary purpose of this book is to explore this possibility. The book examines each of the leading Weak Layering accounts and compares their predictions to those of an alternative, which I will refer to as *Weak Bracketing*, with less conventional structural assumptions. What we will find is that the alternative predicts a much more accurate typology.

This book is unique in the OT literature, then, in that it examines both halves of the equation. It addresses the formulation of constraints that produce directional parsing effects, but it also addresses assumptions concerning prosodic and metrical structure. In presenting the Weak Bracketing account, I defend three central proposals: the *Weak Bracketing* (Hyde 2001, 2002) approach to prosodic layering, from which the overall account takes its name, the *Optimal Mapping* (Hyde 2001, 2002) approach to the relationship between prosodic categories and the metrical grid, and the *Relation-Specific Alignment* (Hyde 2008a, 2012a) approach to parsing directionality. The book is also unique in its coverage of recent alternatives, comparing the Weak Bracketing account to Weak Layering accounts ranging from Symmetrical Alignment in standard OT to the more recent Iterative Foot Optimization (Pruitt 2008, 2010) couched within the framework of Harmonic Serialism (Prince and Smolensky 1993/2004, McCarthy 2008). The book will draw extensively on studies with a wide empirical base, particularly Hayes (1995) and Gordon (2002a), to evaluate the predictions of the accounts examined.

The Weak Bracketing approach to prosodic structure makes two significant departures from the standard Weak Layering approach: it requires that all syllables be parsed into feet, and it allows feet to overlap so that they share a syllable. There are two primary advantages to Weak Bracketing. The first is that it avoids the Odd-Parity Input Problem (Hyde 2008b, 2009a, 2012b), a set of pathological predictions that arise under Weak Layering due to the requirement that output forms be exhaustively parsed into binary feet.[4] We will see that the Odd-Parity Input Problem is so pervasive under Weak Layering that it is impossible for Weak Layering accounts to predict a reasonably accurate typology of stress patterns. Weak Bracketing avoids the problem altogether.

The second argument for Weak Bracketing emerges in conjunction with the Optimal Mapping approach to constructing the metrical grid. Optimal Mapping departs from the standard one-to-one correspondence between prosodic categories and grid entries (Selkirk 1980) in two ways: it enforces the relationship between prosodic categories and grid entries through violable constraints, resulting in the possibility of stressless feet (Selkirk 1995, Crowhurst 1996, Buckley 2009), and it allows overlapping feet to share a stress. As the book will demonstrate, the advantage that Weak Bracketing offers in conjunction with Optimal Mapping is that it is much more effective than Weak Layering in restricting the locations where alignment and other constraints can introduce clash or lapse in binary stress patterns. The result is significantly more accurate typological predictions.

The final component is Relation-Specific Alignment. The Relation-Specific Alignment formulation maintains the ability of alignment constraints to produce essential directionality effects while avoiding the problematic predictions that arise under the Generalized Alignment formulation. Though the deficiencies of Generalized Alignment have been laid at the feet of distance-sensitivity (McCarthy and Prince 1993a; Eisner 1997, McCarthy 2003, Buckley 2009) – the ability to distinguish between different degrees of misalignment – the book will demonstrate that distance-sensitivity is crucial in key situations and that problematic predictions can be avoided simply by making alignment constraints sensitive to the particular configurations in which misaligned categories occur. An additional advantage of the formulation is that it provides for a general account of trisyllabic accent windows, such as those found in Latin, Macedonian, Ancient Greek, and many other languages, a phenomenon that has not been addressed with a general analysis to this point.

In the remainder of this chapter, I outline the theoretical and empirical issues addressed. First, I introduce the three components of the Weak Bracketing approach in fuller detail and compare them to

4 In labeling a predicted pattern "pathological", I mean to indicate that the pattern is not only unattested (see note 2) but it is also sufficiently unlike patterns that are attested that it is implausible.

corresponding assumptions in Weak Layering accounts. I then address the typology of attested stress patterns that is used to evaluate the competing proposals.

1.1 Weak Layering and Weak Bracketing

Given the hierarchical organization of its most important structures, the prosodic hierarchy and the metrical grid, layering is a fundamental issue in metrical stress theory. With respect to the prosodic hierarchy, in particular, where the basic relationship between categories is one of constituency, assumptions about layering determine how lower categories can be integrated into higher categories. Layering assumptions are relevant to all levels of the prosodic hierarchy. The categories that concern us here are mora (μ), syllable (σ), foot (F), and prosodic word (ω).

(14) 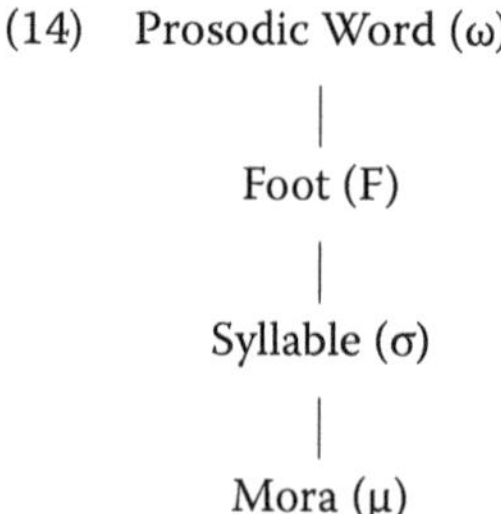

Since they determine what types of layering irregularities are allowed for dealing with the odd, leftover syllable of odd-parity strings, the area where layering and directionality issues are most closely intertwined, layering assumptions have important consequences for directionality effects.

Given a system based on binary footing, there are essentially three options for dealing with the odd, leftover syllable of an odd-parity string. The first is to leave the leftover syllable unfooted, incorporating it directly into the prosodic word, as in (15a). The second is to parse the leftover syllable as a monosyllabic foot, as in (15b). The third option is to parse the leftover syllable into a disyllabic foot that overlaps another disyllabic foot, as in (15c). (For clarity, I will switch from brackets to association lines to represent foot structure in illustrations involving overlapping feet.)

(15) Layering irregularities

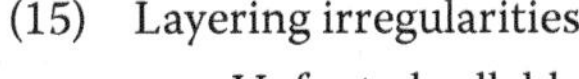

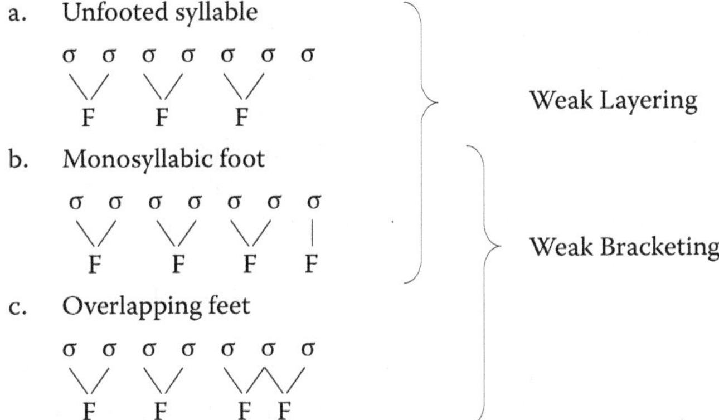

Both the Weak Layering approach and the Weak Bracketing approach restrict the layering irregularities that they allow to two of the three possibilities, but they differ in their particular choices. Weak Layering allows under-parsing and monosyllabic feet, the options in (15a,b); Weak Bracketing allows monosyllabic feet and overlapping feet, the options in (15b,c).

We can get a clearer picture of the difference between Weak Layering and Weak Bracketing in comparing the two approaches to Selkirk's (1984) Strict Layer Hypothesis. According to Nespor and Vogel (1986) and Itô and Mester (1992), the Strict Layer Hypothesis comprises the following two conditions.

(16) a. Strict Succession (adapted from Itô and Mester 1992)

Every prosodic category of level $n-1$ is immediately dominated by a prosodic category of level n (i.e. category levels are never skipped).

b. Proper Bracketing (adapted from Itô and Mester 1992)

Every prosodic category of level $n-1$ is dominated by at most one prosodic category of level n (i.e. prosodic categories of the same level may not overlap).

By requiring that all categories on one level be parsed into a category on the next level higher, the Strict Succession condition, (16a), not only tells us that every category must be parsed, it also tells us that parsing cannot skip category levels. All moras must be parsed into syllables, all syllables must be parsed into feet, all feet must be parsed into prosodic words, and so on. The effect of Strict Succession with respect to the options for irregular layering in (13) is that it prohibits the option where the odd syllable is left unfooted.

By prohibiting a category on one prosodic level from being parsed into more than one category on the next level higher, the Proper Bracketing condition, (16b), tells us that categories on the same level cannot share constituents. Two syllables may never share a mora, two feet may never share a syllable, two prosodic words may never share a foot, and so on. The effect of Proper Bracketing with respect to the irregular layering options in (15) is that it prohibits the option where the odd syllable is parsed into overlapping feet. The combined result of Strict Succession and Proper Bracketing, then, is that a monosyllabic foot is the only option for irregular layering allowed under the Strict Layer Hypothesis.

Weak Layering and Weak Bracketing are both weaker versions of the Strict Layer Hypothesis. Weak Layering retains Proper Bracketing as a non-optional requirement, but makes Strict Succession optional, either through parameterization, as in the serial account of Hayes (1995), or through its status as a violable constraint, as in the OT accounts of McCarthy and Prince (1993a), Alber (2005), and Kager (2001, 2005). As a result, it allows the two possibilities mentioned above for integrating the leftover syllable of odd-parity strings into higher prosodic structure: it can enforce Strict Succession and parse the leftover syllable as a monosyllabic foot, or it can ignore Strict Succession and leave the leftover syllable unfooted.

Weak Bracketing is essentially the opposite of Weak Layering. It retains Strict Succession as a non-optional requirement and makes Proper Bracketing optional. This is the second pair of possibilities mentioned above for dealing with leftover syllables: it can respect Proper Bracketing and parse the leftover syllable as a monosyllabic foot, or it can ignore Proper Bracketing and parse the leftover syllable into a disyllabic foot that overlaps another disyllabic foot.

In supporting the Weak Bracketing approach in the chapters that follow, I will focus on two lines of evidence. The first is that Weak Bracketing helps the theory to more effectively restrict clash and lapse in binary stress patterns. Since clash and lapse configurations are typically associated with layering irregularities, appropriate assumptions about layering are particularly important in restricting them. Under Weak Layering, if the leftover syllable of an odd-parity string is left unparsed, it creates a lapse configuration whenever it follows a trochee, as in (17a), or precedes an iamb, as in (17b).

(17) Lapse configurations

a. ...(σ́σ)σ...   b. ...σ(σσ́)...

When it is parsed as a monosyllabic foot, it creates a clash configuration whenever it follows an iamb, as in (18a), or precedes a trochee, as in (18b).

(18) Clash configurations

a. ...(σσ́)(σ́)... b. ...(σ́)(σ́σ)...

Most positions in which unparsed syllables might occur in any given form, then, are positions in which they create a lapse. In iambic systems, lapse results if an unparsed syllable occurs in initial or medial position; in trochaic systems, it occurs if an unparsed syllable occurs in medial or final position. Similarly, most positions in which monosyllabic feet can occur are positions in which they create a clash. Clash arises in iambic systems if a monosyllabic foot occurs in medial or final position; it arises in trochaic systems if a monosyllabic foot occurs in initial or medial position. As a result, Weak Layering accounts have a difficult time restricting clash and lapse to appropriate positions, so they predict more patterns with clash and lapse than are actually attested.

Under Weak Bracketing, the odd syllable of an odd-parity string can be parsed using a disyllabic foot that overlaps another disyllabic foot, and the resulting configuration can be mapped to the metrical grid in ways that avoid clash and lapse. The two feet can be stressed separately, with the middle syllable being stressless, as in (19a), or they can share a stress, with the peripheral syllables being stressless, as in (19b).

(19) Avoiding clash and Lapse

```
a.     x     x              b.         x
       x  x  x                      x  x  x
    ...σ  σ  σ...                ...σ  σ  σ...
       \/\/                         \/\/
```

Though it will be possible, of course, under the proposed approach to create stress patterns with clash and lapse, the existence of a layering irregularity that can avoid both means that they will be much harder to come by. As a result, clash and lapse will be much more limited under the Weak Bracketing approach, and it will be much easier to restrict them to attested positions.

Like the possibility of two feet sharing a syllable, the possibility of two feet sharing a stress is not an option that is allowed under conventional assumptions. Under the conventional view, feet and stress stand in a one-to-one correspondence. Each foot is associated with one and only one stress, and each stress is associated with one and only one foot. Changing the assumptions about prosodic layering, however, also requires a change in assumptions about how prosodic structure maps to the metrical grid. Though there is still a fundamental relationship between prosodic structure and grid entries, the relationship is somewhat looser than it is in conventional approaches. I address this issue in fuller detail just below.

The second line of evidence supporting Weak Bracketing is that it avoids a set of problematic predictions that I will refer to as the *Odd-Parity Input Problem* (OPIP; Hyde 2007b, 2008b, 2009a, 2012b). The OPIP arises under Weak Layering due to the parsing and minimality requirements typically implemented in OT accounts with the familiar PARSE-σ and F-BINARITY constraints. PARSE-σ requires that all syllables be footed, and F-BIN requires that all feet be either disyllabic or bimoraic.

(20) a. PARSE-σ:

Every *σ* is parsed into a *F*.

b. F-BINARITY:

Every foot is binary (either disyllabic or bimoraic).

The combined effect of the two constraints is to require exhaustive binary parsing, even in forms with an odd-number of syllables.

While it may seem impossible at first glance, there are actually three ways in which exhaustive binary parsing can be achieved for odd-parity inputs. First, if the odd-parity input contains a heavy (bimoraic) syllable in an odd-numbered position, the heavy syllable can be parsed as a monosyllabic foot with the remaining syllables parsed into disyllabic feet, as in (21a). Second, the odd-parity input can be converted into an even-parity output, either through insertion of a single syllable or deletion of a single syllable, so that each syllable in the output can be included in a disyllabic foot, as in (21b). Finally, the leftover syllable from an odd-parity input can be included in a disyllabic foot that overlaps another disyllabic foot, as in (21c).

(21) Exhaustive binary parsing for odd-parity inputs

a. Odd-numbered H foot

σσHσσσσ → σ σ H σ σ σ σ
\/ | \/ \/

b. Convert to even-parity

σσσσσσσ → σ σ σ σ σ σ σ σ *or* σ σ σ σ σ σ
\/ \/ \/ \/ \/ \/ \/

c. Overlapping feet

σσσσσσσ → σ σ σ σ σ σ σ
\/ \/ \/\/

The options in (21a,b) are the only choices available under Weak Layering, and these are the options that lead to the OPIP. The OPIP can be usefully divided into two-sub-problems. The *Odd Heavy Problem* (OHP) is a peculiar, and unattested, type of quantity-sensitivity that arises when the option in (21a) is employed. Only in odd-parity forms, a single odd-numbered heavy syllable is parsed as a monosyllabic foot. Odd-parity forms that do not contain an odd-numbered heavy syllable, and even-parity forms, are unaffected. The *Even Output Problem* (EOP) is the systematic, and unattested, conversion of odd-parity inputs to even-parity outputs. It arises when the option in (21b) is employed. In its most aggressive form, it results in languages that contain only even-parity outputs.

As we shall see, the OPIP is so pervasive under Weak Layering that it is impossible for Weak Layering accounts to predict a reasonably accurate typology of binary stress systems. One of the most important advantages of Weak Bracketing is that it avoids the problem altogether. In allowing feet to overlap, as in (21c), it allows odd-parity strings to achieve exhaustive binary parsing using only disyllabic feet. There is never a need to resort to the options in (21a) and (21b).

1.2 Mapping to the Grid

The metrical grid (Liberman and Prince 1977, Prince 1983) is a hierarchical organization of intervals of different durations that represents the relative prominence of different points in time. Points where more boundaries of different intervals coincide are more prominent than points where fewer boundaries of different intervals coincide.

```
(22) X       X       X       X
     X   X   X   X   X   X   X   X
     XXXXXXXXXXXXXXXXX
```

In the illustration in (22), the bottom level of grid entries indicates the boundaries of the shortest intervals, and the entries on higher levels indicate the boundaries of increasingly longer intervals. The coincidence of multiple boundaries forms columns of prominence. The first column, which is formed by the boundaries of three intervals, is more prominent than the third column, which is formed by the boundaries of two intervals, and the third column is more prominent than the second column, which is formed by the boundary of a single interval.

In metrical stress theory, the metrical grid represents the relative stress associated with different syllables. In the proposed account, following Kager (1993, 1995) and Hyde (2006, 2007a,b), entries on the grid's base level correspond to moras, rather than syllables, though this fact will be obscured when syllable weight is not an issue. Entries on the second level of the grid correspond to feet, indicating the positions of secondary stress. Entries on the third level correspond to prosodic words, indicating the positions of primary stress. Though there are also higher grid levels, corresponding to higher prosodic categories, these will not concern us here.

```
(23) X       X         Prosodic word level (xω)
     X   X   X   X     Foot level (xF)
     X X X X X X X X   Mora level (xμ)
```

Following Selkirk (1980), the traditional view of the relationship between prosodic categories that project to the grid and the grid entries projected is that they stand in a one-to-one correspondence. Each mora corresponds to one and only one mora-level gridmark, and each mora-level gridmark corresponds to one and only one mora; each foot corresponds to one and only one foot-level gridmark, and each foot-level gridmark corresponds to one and only one foot; and so on.

The Optimal Mapping approach departs from the traditional view in two ways. The first is that a prosodic category can fail to correspond to a grid entry. A foot, for example, may be stressed or stressless, as illustrated in (24).

```
(24) a. Stressed foot          b. Stressless foot

        x
        x  x                      x  x
        σ  σ                      σ  σ
         \/                        \/
```

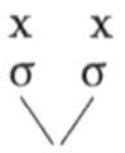

Though the traditional view holds that all feet must be stressed, stressless feet can be found in the proposals of Hayes (1987), Tyhurst (1987), Hung (1993, 1994), Selkirk (1995), Crowhurst (1996), and Buckley

(2009). The second departure, as mentioned above, is that overlapping prosodic categories may be stressed separately but they may also share a stress. In (25), for example, there is a foot-level gridmark for each foot in the overlapping configurations. In (26), however, the two feet share a foot-level gridmark.

(25) Two stresses

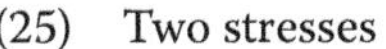

a.

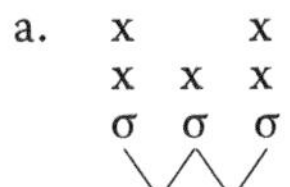

```
b.  x  x
    x  x  x
    σ  σ  σ
    \/\/\/

c.     x  x
    x  x  x
    σ  σ  σ
    \/\/\/
```

(26) Shared stress

```
   x
x  x  x
σ  σ  σ
\/\/\/
```

The mappings where feet and stress stand in the traditional one-to-one correspondence and the mappings where they do not are all made possible by the formulation of the constraints that require prosodic categories to map to the metrical grid. Since the constraints are violable, it is possible to have stressless prosodic categories when they are appropriately low-ranked. Since the constraints only require that each instance of a prosodic category be associated with a grid entry, without the additional requirement that the association be unique, it is possible for two instances of a prosodic category to share an entry, if the categories overlap. The constraint that requires feet to correspond to foot-level gridmarks is given in (27).

(27) MAP-TO-GRID
Every F has an x_F within its domain.

When MAP-TO-GRID is satisfied, each foot will be stressed. When the constraint must be violated, however, a foot may emerge without a stress. In regular layering configurations, where feet do not overlap, MAP-TO-GRID's requirement that each foot have a foot-level gridmark within its domain means that there must be a unique gridmark associated with each individual foot. In configurations where feet do overlap, however, each foot can satisfy the requirement simply by positioning a gridmark over the shared syllable, as in (26). While the constraint can also be satisfied by associating a unique gridmark with each foot, as in (25), a unique gridmark is not strictly necessary.

Though MAP-TO-GRID is the primary constraint governing the relationship between feet and stress, there are several additional constraints in the Optimal Mapping approach that refer either to the configuration of the grid itself or to the relationship between grid entries and prosodic categories. *CLASH discourages adjacent stressed syllables, INITIAL-GRIDMARK requires that the initial syllable of a prosodic word be stressed, and NON-FINALITY requires that the final syllable of a prosodic word be stressless.

(28) Additional mapping constraints

a. *CLASH (Adapted from Prince 1983)

For any two entries on level $n + 1$ of the metrical grid, there is an intervening entry on level n.

b. INITIAL-GRIDMARK (Prince 1983, Hyde 2003)

An x_F occurs over the leftmost σ of every ω.

c. NON-FINALITY (Prince and Smolensky 1993/2004, Hyde 2003):

No x_F occurs over the rightmost σ of a ω.

To provide an initial picture of the role that the Optimal Mapping constraints and the structures in (24–26) play in creating individual stress patterns, we can consider some basic cases where clash is present, where lapse is present, and where clash and lapse are both avoided. Though we shall see in Chapter 5 that additional factors play a role in avoiding lapse, MAP-TO-GRID's prohibition against stressless feet serves as the primary safeguard against lapse configurations. The *CLASH constraint is the primary safeguard against clash configurations. The asymmetrical INITIAL-GRIDMARK and NONFINALITY are the constraints responsible for introducing clash and lapse in appropriate positions.

In general, patterns that avoid clash and lapse will use overlapping feet that share a stress, as in (26), to parse the odd syllable of odd-parity forms, or they will use overlapping feet with separated stresses, as in (25a). These configurations allow MAP-TO-GRID and *CLASH to be satisfied simultaneously. The trochaic Nengone pattern, for example, where stress occurs on every even-numbered syllable counting from the right, would have a gridmark-sharing configuration at the left edge in its odd-parity forms.

(29) Gridmark sharing in Nengone

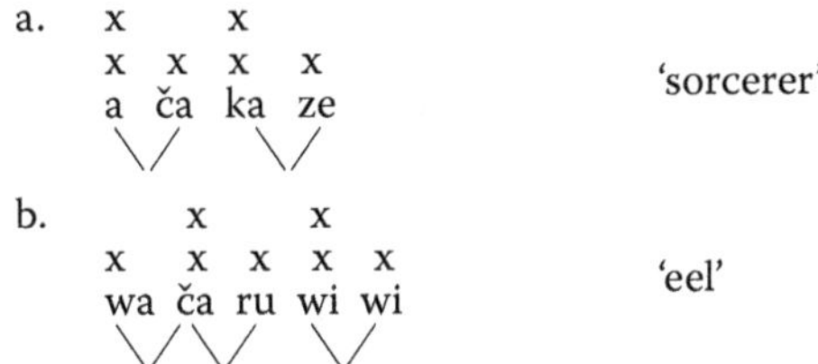

The trochaic Maranungku pattern, where stress occurs on every odd-numbered syllable counting from the left, would have a separated gridmark configuration at the right edge in its odd-parity forms.

(30) Separated gridmarks in Maranungku

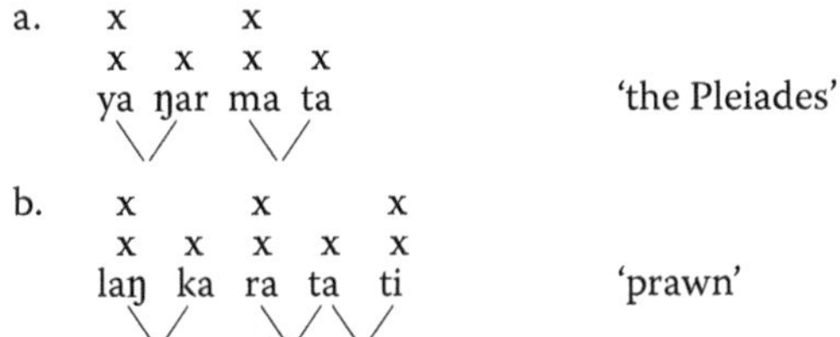

In (29), the gridmark-sharing configuration produces a pattern where each form contains the minimum number of stresses possible without creating a lapse. In (30), the separated gridmark configuration produces a pattern where each form contains the maximum number of stresses possible without creating a clash.

Patterns with clash are obtained using separately stressed overlapping feet where the stresses are adjacent, as in (25b,c). In the Passamaquoddy pattern, for example, where stress occurs on the initial syllable and every even-numbered syllable counting from the right, an adjacent stress configuration would occur at the left edge in odd-parity forms.

(31) Adjacent stresses in Passamaquoddy

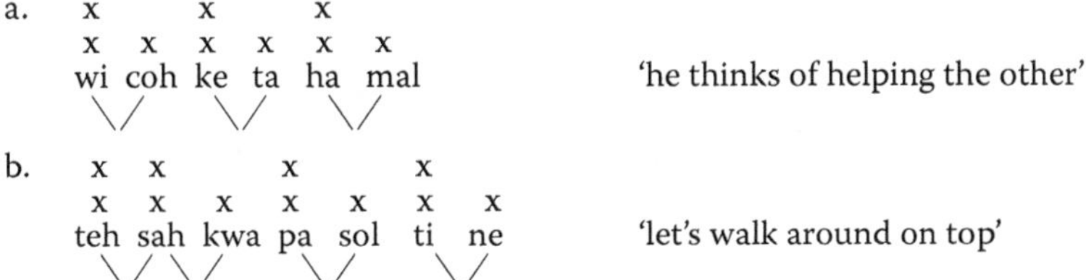

The Passamaquoddy pattern in (31) can be thought of as a variation on the Nengone pattern in (29). The adjacent stresses arise because INITIAL-GRIDMARK and MAP-TO-GRID both dominate *CLASH. It is more important both that the initial syllable be stressed and that every foot be stressed than it is that clash be avoided.

Patterns that tolerate lapse typically arise due to the presence of a stressless foot. In Garawa (Furby 1974), for example, stress occurs on the initial syllable and every even-numbered syllable counting from the right, except the peninitial syllable. The pattern emerges when the foot immediately following the initial stress is stressless in odd-parity forms.

(32) Stressless foot in Garawa

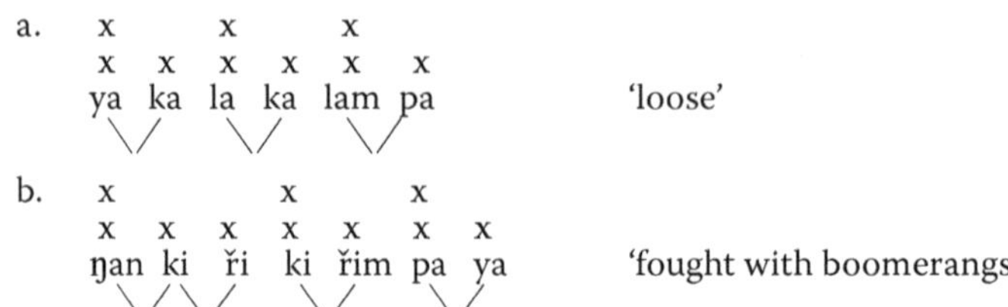

Like the Passamaquoddy pattern, the Garawa pattern can also be thought of as a variation on the Nengone pattern. In this case, however, INITIAL-GRIDMARK and *CLASH must both dominate MAP-TO-GRID. The second foot of odd-parity forms is left stressless because it is more important to stress the initial syllable while avoiding clash than it is to stress every foot.

Stressless feet can also emerge due to NON-FINALITY. Consider Pintupi, where stress occurs on every odd-numbered syllable counting from the left, except the final syllable. The desired pattern emerges when the final foot of an odd-parity form is left stressless.

(33) Stressless foot in Pintupi

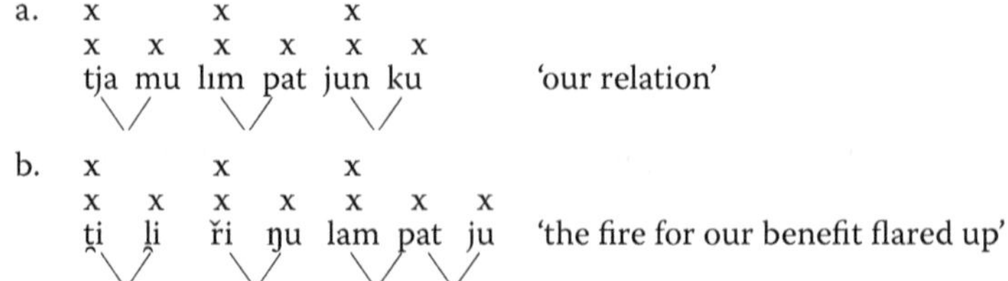

The Pintupi pattern can be thought of as a variation on the Maranungku pattern in (30) where the final foot is left stressless in odd-parity forms in order to avoid stressing the final syllable. In this case, NON-FINALITY must dominate MAP-TO-GRID.

The picture that emerges from the examples above is one where the differences between individual stress patterns are not completely determined by the positions of regular footing and irregular footing. Instead, they are determined both by the positions of regular and irregular footing and by the way in which these structures map to the metrical grid. The positions of the regular and irregular feet in (29, 31, 32) are the same, but the stress patterns are different, the differences being due to interactions between requirements that all feet be stressed (MAP-TO-GRID), that the initial syllable be stressed (INITIAL-GRIDMARK), and that clash be avoided (*CLASH). Similarly, regular and irregular feet are positioned in the same way in (30, 33), but two different stress patterns emerge. In this case, the differences are due to interactions between requirements that all feet be stressed (MAP-TO-GRID) and that the final syllable be stressless (NON-FINALITY).

While the way in which both regular and irregular footing maps to the grid will be responsible for much of the variation in individual stress patterns, mapping possibilities and prosodic layering are closely connected, so it will still be necessary to effectively restrict the position of layering irregularities. In the Weak Bracketing account, as in many earlier accounts, alignment constraints are primarily responsible for positioning layering irregularities. We turn next to the alignment formulation.

1.3 Generalized Alignment and Relation-Specific Alignment

When confronting the issue of parsing directionality, the OT literature has focused either on the advantages of alignment constraints or on alternatives that are intended to remedy alignment's perceived deficiencies. To frame the issues more clearly, it is helpful to consider the original formulation of Generalized Alignment (McCarthy and Prince 1993a). In (34), *ACat1* and *ACat2* are the categories whose edges are being aligned, and *Edge1* and *Edge2* are the relevant edge specifications. The *Edge1* (right or left) of every *ACat1* is required to coincide with the *Edge2* (right or left) of some *ACat2*. *SCat*, the 'separator' category, becomes relevant when the coincidence requirement is not met. When the relevant edges of *ACat1* and *ACat2* fail to coincide, each intervening instance of *SCat* incurs a violation.

(34) Generalized Alignment formulation

Align (*ACat1, Edge1, ACat2, Edge2, SCat*)

The *Edge1* of every *ACat1* coincides with the *Edge2* of some *ACat2*. Assess a violation mark for every *SCat* that intervenes between edges that fail to coincide.

Objections to the Generalized Alignment formulation have focused on its *distance-sensitivity*, its ability to distinguish between different degrees of misalignment. The objections take two forms. The first is that distance-sensitivity is simply unnecessary. Kager (2001, 2005) and McCarthy (2003) argue, for example, that the range of attested stress patterns can be obtained simply by licensing clash and lapse in appropriate positions. As we shall see in Chapter 2, however, distance-sensitivity is crucial in key cases.

Perhaps a more serious challenge to distance-sensitivity arises from a pathological prediction, first identified by Eisner (1997; see also Buckley 2009), which I will refer to as the *Midpoint Pathology*. Under the Generalized Alignment formulation, when multiple instances of a category whose positions are fixed are aligned with a single instance of a category whose position is not fixed, the result can be that the mobile category is drawn towards the center of the form. For example, the constraint in (34) aligns the left edges of syllables with the left edge of a foot.

(34) Align (σ, L, F, L, σ)

The left edge of every syllable coincides with the left edge of some foot. Assess a violation mark for each syllable intervening between misaligned edges.

In forms that have a single foot within a prosodic word, as in (35), Align (σ, L) has the effect of drawing the foot's left edge just to the left of the medial syllable. The result is uncontroversially pathological. In (35), *p* denotes a violation mark derived from a misaligned syllable that precedes the foot, *f* a violation mark from a misaligned syllable that follows the foot, and *c* a violation mark from a misaligned syllable contained within the foot.

(35)

	ALIGN (σ, L)
a. [(σσ)σσσσσ]	c ff fff ffff fff!ff fffff
b. [σ(σσ)σσσσ]	p c ff fff ffff ff!fff
c. [σσ(σσ)σσσ]	pp p c ff fff ffff!
☞ d. [σσσ(σσ)σσ]	ppp pp p c ff fff
e. [σσσσ(σσ)σ]	pppp ppp pp p c ff!
f. [σσσσσ(σσ)]	ppppp pppp ppp p!p p c

ALIGN (σ, L) can produce this result because every misaligned left syllable edge incurs a number of violations proportional to its degree of misalignment, and the fewest violations are incurred overall when an equal number of misaligned left syllable edges occur on either side of the left foot edge.

Though distance-sensitivity is necessary for the Midpoint Pathology to emerge, it is not the only necessary condition. The pathology could not arise without alignment constraints also being *relation-general,* without them having the ability to assess violations regardless of the configuration in which the misaligned categories occur. In (35), for example, violations are assessed whether a misaligned syllable precedes the foot, follows the foot, or is contained within the foot. If alignment constraints only assessed violations for one of these configurations in particular, the Midpoint Pathology would be avoided.

As we shall see in fuller detail in Chapter 2, Relation-Specific Alignment (Hyde 2008a, 2012a) makes it possible to maintain distance-sensitivity while avoiding the effects of the Midpoint Pathology. In the Relation-Specific Alignment approach, alignment constraints have two components, separated by a slash, as in (36). The set of categories to the left of the slash is prohibited from occurring in the configuration of misalignment indicated to the right of the slash. The prohibited configuration of misalignment is one where a separator category, *SCat,* intervenes between an edge of the first aligned category, *ACat1,* and an edge of the second aligned category, *ACat2.* Because (36a), for example, prohibits *SCat* from intervening between the left edges of *ACat1* and *ACat2,* it requires alignment of left edges. Importantly, however, it only requires alignment when *ACat1* contains *ACat2.* Similarly, because (36b) prohibits *SCat* from intervening between the right edges of *ACat1* and *ACat2,* (36b) requires alignment of right edges, but only when the first aligned category contains the second. Finally, because (36c) prohibits *ACat1* from preceding *ACat2* with *SCat* intervening, (36c) requires alignment of the right edge of *ACat1* with the left edge of *ACat2*, but only when *ACat1* precedes *ACat2*.

(36) RSA constraint schemas

a. Left-Edge: *⟨*ACat1*, *ACat2*, (*SCat*)⟩ / [… *SCat* … *ACat2* … $]_{ACat1}$

'Assess a violation mark for every ⟨*ACat1*, *ACat2*, (*SCat*)⟩ such that *SCat* precedes *ACat2* within *ACat1*.'

b. Right-edge: *⟨*ACat1*, *ACat2*, (*SCat*)⟩ / [… *ACat2* … *SCat* … $]_{ACat1}$

'Assess a violation mark for every ⟨*ACat1*, *ACat2*, (*SCat*)⟩ such that *ACat2* precedes *SCat* within *ACat1*.'

c. Opposite-edge: *⟨*ACat1*, *ACat2*, (*SCat*)⟩ / *ACat1* … *SCat* … *ACat2*

'Assess a violation mark for every ⟨*ACat1*, *ACat2*, (*SCat*)⟩ such that *ACat1* precedes *ACat2* with *SCat* intervening.'

Notice that both of the aligned categories are included in the set to the left of the slash, but the separator category is only optionally included. When an alignment constraint omits the separator category from this set, violation assessment is distance-insensitive: a single violation is assessed for each pair of misaligned categories. When the set includes the separator category, violation assessment is distance-sensitive: the number of violations assessed is equal to the number of separator categories intervening between each pair of misaligned edges.

Eliminating the Midpoint Pathology by replacing the Generalized Alignment formulation with the Relation-Specific Alignment formulation offers two advantages. The first is that it allows the theory to retain distance-sensitivity for those cases where it turns out to be crucial. The second, as we shall see in Chapter 6, is that opposite-edge Relation-Specific Alignment constraints very naturally provide a general analysis of trisyllabic and other types of accent windows.

1.4 Typological Generalizations

We turn now to the main empirical generalizations that will provide the basis for comparison of the approaches to metrical stress addressed throughout the book. The primary focus will be on the typology of *binary default patterns*, the patterns found in quantity-insensitive binary stress systems and in quantity-sensitive systems for inputs with only light syllables. Since default patterns result directly from assumptions about prosodic layering and parsing directionality, without interference from other considerations such as syllable weight or morphology, they provide the clearest cases for examining the issues that the book seeks to address.

1.4.1 Mirror Image Pairs

A long-standing observation about the typology of binary default patterns is that those that appear to be based on trochaic feet are attested in a greater variety than those that appear to be based on iambic feet (Kager 1993, Hayes 1995, van de Vijver 1998, Hyde 2002, Alber 2005, among others). While this typological imbalance is typically discussed in terms of parsing directionality – directional parsing patterns found among trochaic systems are very often absent among iambic systems – we can gain a better understanding of the disparity by considering the patterns of attestation in mirror image pairs.

In mirror image stress patterns, stressed and unstressed positions alternate in the same way, but the alternation starts from opposite edges. As examples, consider the mirror image pairs in (37) and (38). The (37a) pattern stresses every odd-numbered syllable from the left. Its mirror image, (37b), stresses every odd-numbered syllable from the right. Both patterns are attested. The (37a) pattern can be found in Maranungku (Tryon 1970) and the (37b) pattern in Suruwaha (Everett 1996).

(37) a. Trochaic: Attested b. Iambic: Attested

```
a.  x   x   x              b.    x   x   x
    σ σ σ σ σ σ                σ σ σ σ σ σ

    x   x   x   x              x   x   x   x
    σ σ σ σ σ σ σ              σ σ σ σ σ σ σ
```

The patterns in (38) differ only slightly from those in (37). In (38a), stress appears on every odd-numbered syllable from the left *except the final syllable,* resulting in a lapse at the right edge in the odd-parity form. In the mirror image, (38b), stress appears on every odd-numbered syllable from the right *except the initial syllable,* resulting in a lapse at the left edge. Only one of the patterns in this pair is actually attested, however. The (38a) pattern can be found in Pintupi (Hansen & Hansen 1969), but there appears to be no language identified as exhibiting the (38b) pattern.

(38) a. Trochaic: Attested b. Iambic: Unattested

```
a.  x   x   x              b.    x   x   x
    σ σ σ σ σ σ                σ σ σ σ σ σ

    x   x   x                      x   x   x
    σ σ σ σ σ σ σ              σ σ σ σ σ σ σ
              ‾‾‾              ‾‾‾
```

There are two advantages to considering patterns of attestation in terms of mirror image pairs like those in (37) and (38). The first is that it allows us to examine iambic-trochaic asymmetries from a more theory-neutral perspective. In general, if one member of a mirror image pair can be characterized as trochaic – most easily created with trochaic feet – then the second member can be characterized as iambic – most easily created with iambic feet. As examples, the patterns in (37) and (38) are reproduced with feet in (39) and (40), respectively, as they might be constructed under Weak Layering.

(39)	a.	Trochaic	b.	Iambic
		(όσ)(όσ)(όσ)		(σό)(σό)(σό)
		(όσ)(όσ)(όσ)(ό)		(ό)(σό)(σό)(σό)

(40)	a.	Trochaic	b.	Iambic
		(όσ)(όσ)(όσ)		(σό)(σό)(σό)
		(όσ)(όσ)(όσ)σ		σ(σό)(σό)(σό)

The ability to characterize the relevant mirror image pairs as iambic-trochaic pairs allows us to examine iambic-trochaic asymmetries from a more neutral perspective. Since mirror image pairs are not actually constructed based on any particular view of prosodic or metrical structure, or on any particular set of assumptions about the devices that produce directionality effects, the study need not make any commitment to a particular view or set of assumptions.

The second advantage of considering mirror image pairs is that it allows for comparison of patterns that are metrically similar. In mirror image pairs, both members either avoid clash and lapse altogether or they exhibit clash or lapse in corresponding positions. In (37/39), for example, neither member of the pair contains a clash or lapse. In (38/40), there is a lapse at the right edge in the odd-parity trochaic form and a corresponding lapse at the left edge in the odd-parity iambic form. In contrast, when the comparison is between iambic and trochaic stress systems created with the same directional parsing patterns, the comparison is between metrical apples and oranges. When a string of syllables is parsed into trochaic feet from right to left, as in (41a), for example, the result is a stress pattern with neither clash nor lapse. When a string of syllables is parsed into iambic feet from right to left, as in (41b), the result is lapse at the left edge in the odd-parity form.

(41) a. Right-to-left trochees
(σ́σ)(σ́σ)(σ́σ)
σ(σ́σ)(σ́σ)(σ́σ)

b. Right-to-left iambs
(σσ́)(σσ́)(σσ́)
<u>σ(σ</u>σ́)(σσ́)(σσ́)

In allowing us to compare patterns that are metrically similar, examination of mirror image pairs allows us to make generalizations based on metrical characteristics, generalizations that may not emerge otherwise. The generalizations in (42), justified in Sections 1.4.2–1.4.3 below, will be especially important in comparing competing proposals throughout the book.

(42) a. In mirror image patterns with neither clash nor lapse, both members of the pair are attested.

b. In mirror image patterns with either clash or lapse, at most one member of the pair is attested.

The generalizations in (42) tell us about the distribution of iambic-trochaic asymmetries. There are no iambic-trochaic asymmetries among patterns that avoid clash and lapse. Such patterns are always attested in mirror image pairs. The trochaic version is attested and the iambic mirror image is attested. Instead, iambic-trochaic asymmetries emerge among patterns that fail to avoid clash and lapse. If the trochaic version is attested in a mirror image pair, the iambic version is not. If the iambic version is attested, the trochaic version is not.

1.4.2 Perfect Alternation

We begin by examining the evidence for the generalization in (42a): mirror image patterns that contain neither clash nor lapse are symmetrically attested. For convenience, I will refer to patterns that contain neither clash nor lapse, patterns where stressed and unstressed syllables follow each other in perfect binary alternation, as *perfect alternation* patterns.

Only four perfect alternation patterns are possible, and they form two mirror image pairs. The first pair of patterns, which I will refer to as *minimal alternation* patterns, have the fewest stresses possible without containing a lapse. The trochaic version, (43a), stresses every even-numbered syllable counting from the right. The iambic mirror image, (43b), stresses every even-numbered syllable counting from the left.

(43) Minimal alternation patterns[5]

a. Trochaic: Attested

```
x   x   x
σ σ σ σ σ σ

  x   x   x
σ σ σ σ σ σ σ
```

b. Iambic: Attested

```
  x   x   x
σ σ σ σ σ σ

  x   x   x
σ σ σ σ σ σ σ
```

In accord with the generalization in (42a), the minimal alternation patterns form a mirror image pair, and each pattern in the pair is attested. The trochaic version can be found in Nengone (Tryon 1967) and Warao (Osborn 1966).[6]

(44) Nengone forms (Tryon 1967)

a.	ˌačaˈkaze	'sorcerer'
b.	waˌčaruˈwiwi	'eel'

The iambic version can be found in Araucanian (Echeverria and Contreras 1965).[7]

(45) Araucanian forms (Echeverria and Contreras 1965)

a.	eˈlumuˌyu	'give us'
b.	eˈluaˌenew	'he will give me'

The second pair of perfect alternation patterns are the *maximal alternation* patterns. They have the most stresses possible without creating a clash. The trochaic version, (46a), stresses every odd-numbered syllable counting from the left. The iambic mirror image, (46b), stresses every odd-numbered syllable counting from the right.

5 In a Weak Layering account, the trochaic version of minimal alternation would be created by constructing trochees from right to left and leaving leftover syllables unparsed. The iambic version would be created by constructing iambs left to right and leaving leftover syllables unparsed.

6 Gordon (2002a) lists ten additional languages that exhibit the trochaic minimal alternation pattern: Anejom (Lynch 2000), Berbice (Kouwenberg 1994), Cavineña (Key 1968), Ese Ejja (Key 1968), Larike (Laidig 1992), Malakmalak (Birk 1976), Orokolo (Brown 1986), To'aba'ita (Lichtenberk 1984), Tukang Besi (Donohue 1999), and Ura (Crowley 1998).

7 Gordon (2002a) lists two additional languages that exhibit the iambic minimal alternation pattern: Hatam (Reesink 1999) and Sirenikski (Menovshchikov 1975).

(46) Maximal alternation[8]

a. Trochaic: Attested

```
x   x   x
σ σ σ σ σ σ

x   x   x   x
σ σ σ σ σ σ σ
```

b. Iambic: Attested

```
  x   x   x
σ σ σ σ σ σ

x   x   x   x
σ σ σ σ σ σ σ
```

The maximal alternation patterns also conform to the generalization in (42a). The two patterns form a mirror image pair, and both members of the pair are attested. The trochaic version can be found in Maranungku (Tryon 1970) and Ningil (Manning and Saggers 1977).[9]

(47) Maranungku forms (Tryon 1970)

a. ˈyaŋarˌmata 'the Pleiades'

b. ˈlaŋkaˌrataˌti 'prawn'

The iambic version can be found in Suruwaha (Everett 1996), Tubatulabal (Voegelin 1935), and Weri (Boxwell and Boxwell 1966).[10]

(48) Suruwaha forms (Everett 1996)

a. daˌkuhuˈru 'to put in the fire'

b. ˌbihaˌwuhuˈra 'to fly'

1.4.3 Departures from Perfect Alternation

Since there are only four possible patterns exhibiting perfect alternation, any remaining patterns, attested or unattested, necessarily depart from perfect alternation. In examining mirror-image pairs that depart from perfect alternation, we will encounter the remaining attested binary

8 In a Weak Layering account, the trochaic version of maximal alternation would be created by constructing trochees from left to right and parsing leftover syllables as monosyllabic feet. The iambic version would be created by constructing iambs right to left and parsing leftover syllables as monosyllabic feet.

9 Gordon (2002a) lists 12 additional languages that exhibit the trochaic maximal alternation pattern: Bagandji (Hercus 1982), Czech (Kucera 1961), Hungarian (Kerek 1971), Icelandic (Árnason 1980, 1985), Livonian (Kettunen 1938), Mansi (Kálmán 1965), Murinbata (Street and Mollingin 1981), Ono (Phinnemore 1985), Panamint (Dayley 1989), Sinaugoro (Tauberschmidt 1999), Timucua (Granberry 1993), and Votic (Ariste 1968).

10 Gordon (2002a) lists four additional languages that exhibit the iambic maximal alternation pattern: Asmat (Voorhoeve 1965), Chulupi (Stell 1972), Kamayur (Saelzer 1976), and Urubú Kaapor (Kakumasu 1986).

default patterns and confirm the generalizations in (42b): mirror-image pairs that contain clash or lapse are asymmetrically attested (or symmetrically unattested).

1.4.3.1 Binary Default Patterns with Lapse

There are four clear cases where lapse is tolerated, two where it is tolerated in final position and two where it is tolerated in internal position. Lapse arises in final position in odd-parity forms in trochaic languages such as Pintupi (Hansen & Hansen 1969) and Wangkumara (McDonald & Wurm 1979).[11] As (49a) illustrates, these languages stress every odd-numbered syllable from the left except the final syllable, resulting in a lapse at the right edge in odd-parity forms. As (49b) illustrates, the iambic mirror-image stresses every odd-numbered syllable from the right except the initial syllable, resulting in a lapse at the left edge in odd-parity forms. The iambic pattern is unattested.

(49) Peripheral lapse in odd-parity forms[12]

a. Trochaic: Attested (final dactyl)

x x x
σ σ σ σ σ σ

x x x
σ σ σ σ σ $\underline{\sigma\ \sigma}$

b. Iambic: Unattested (initial anapest)

x x x
σ σ σ σ σ σ

x x x
$\underline{\sigma\ \sigma}$ σ σ σ σ σ

Example forms from Pintupi, which exhibits the pattern in (49a), are provided in (50).

(50) Pintupi forms

a. ˈtjamuˌlimpaˌtjunku — 'our relation'

b. ˈt̪il̪iˌřiŋuˌlampatju — 'the fire for our benefit flared up'

11 Gordon (2002a) lists 12 additional trochaic languages that have a final lapse in their odd-parity forms: Anguthimri (Crowley 1981), Badimaya (Dunn 1988), Bidyara/Gungabula (Breen 1973), Dalabon (Capell 1962), Dehu (Tryon 1967), Diyari (Austin 1981), Karelian (Leskinen 1984), Kate (Flierl and Strauss 1977), Pitta Pitta (Blake 1969), Tenango Otomi (Blight and Pike 1976), Wirangu (Hercus 1999), and Yingkarta (Dench 1998).

12 In a Weak Layering account, peripheral lapse would be created in the odd-parity forms of trochaic patterns by constructing trochees from left to right and leaving leftover syllables unparsed. It would be created in the odd-parity forms of iambic patterns by constructing iambs right to left and leaving leftover syllables unparsed.

Lapse arises in final position in even-parity forms in iambic languages such as Choctaw (Nicklas 1972, 1975) and Hixkaryana (Derbyshire 1985).[13] As (51b) illustrates, stress in these languages occurs on every even-numbered syllable from the left except the final syllable, producing a lapse at the right edge in even-parity forms. The trochaic mirror-image pattern is unattested. As (51a) illustrates, stress would occur on every even-numbered syllable from the right except the initial syllable, yielding a lapse at the left edge.

(51) Peripheral lapse in even-parity forms[14]

a. Trochaic: Unattested (initial lapse)

			x		x	
	<u>σ</u>	<u>σ</u>	σ	σ	σ	σ
	x		x		x	
σ	σ	σ	σ	σ	σ	σ

b. Iambic: Attested (final lapse)

	x		x			
σ	σ	σ	σ	<u>σ</u>	<u>σ</u>	
	x		x		x	
σ	σ	σ	σ	σ	σ	σ

Example forms from Choctaw, which exhibits the pattern in (51b), are provided in (52). The examples in (52) are combinations of /pisa/ 'to see', /či-/ 'you (object)', /- či / 'causative', and /-li/ 'I (subject)'.

(52) Choctaw forms

a. či'pisali

b. či'pisa'čili

An internal lapse arises near the left edge, just after the initial stress, in the odd-parity forms of trochaic languages such as Garawa (Furby 1974), Spanish (Harris 1983), Norwegian (Lorentz 1996), and Indonesian (Cohn 1989). In these languages, as illustrated in (53a), stress occurs on the initial syllable and every even-numbered syllable from the right except the peninitial syllable. The result is a lapse just to the right of the initial stress in odd-parity forms. The iambic mirror-image pattern is unattested. In the iambic version, as (53b) illustrates, stress would occur on the final syllable and every even-numbered syllable from the left except the penult, resulting in a lapse just to the left of the final stress.

13 Choctaw and Hixkaryana are both quantity-sensitive. The (51b) pattern is the pattern found in forms that contain only (underlyingly) light syllables.

14 In a Weak Layering account, peripheral lapse might be created in the even-parity forms of trochaic patterns by making initial syllables extrametrical, constructing trochees from right to left, and leaving leftover syllables unparsed. It would be created in the even-parity forms of iambic patterns by making final syllables extrametrical, constructing iambs left to right, and leaving leftover syllables unparsed.

(53) Internal lapse next to initial or final stress[15]

a. Trochaic: Attested (initial dactyl)

```
  x   x   x
σ σ σ σ σ σ

x     x   x
σ σ σ σ σ σ σ
```

b. Iambic: Unattested (final anapest)

```
  x   x   x
σ σ σ σ σ σ

  x   x     x
σ σ σ σ σ σ σ
```

Example forms from Garawa, which exhibits the pattern in (53a) are provided in (54).

(54) Garawa forms (Furby 1974)

a. ˈyakaˌlakaˌlampa 'loose'

b. ˈŋankiři̥ˌkiřimˌpaya 'fought with boomerangs'

An internal lapse arises near the right edge, just to the left of the penult, in the odd-parity forms of trochaic languages like Piro (Matteson 1965) and Polish (Rubach & Booij 1985). As (55a) illustrates, these languages stress the penult and every odd-numbered syllable from the left except the antepenult. The result is a lapse just before the penult in odd-parity forms. In the iambic mirror image, as (55b) illustrates, stress occurs on the peninitial syllable and every odd-numbered syllable from the right except the post-peninitial syllable, resulting in a lapse just after the peninitial syllable in odd-parity forms. The iambic version is unattested.

(55) Internal lapse next to penultimate or peninitial syllable[16]

a. Trochaic: Attested (final amphibrach)

```
x   x   x
σ σ σ σ σ σ

x   x     x
σ σ σ σ σ σ σ
```

b. Iambic: Unattested (initial amphibrach)

```
  x   x   x
σ σ σ σ σ σ

  x     x   x
σ σ σ σ σ σ σ
```

15 In a Weak Layering account, an internal lapse would be created after an initial stress in the odd-parity forms of trochaic patterns by constructing a single trochee at the left edge, constructing trochees from right to left, and leaving leftover syllables unparsed. It would be created before the final stress in the odd-parity forms of iambic patterns by constructing a single iamb at the right edge, constructing iambs left to right, and leaving leftover syllables unparsed.

16 In a Weak Layering account, an internal lapse would be created before the penult in the odd-parity forms of trochaic patterns by constructing a single trochee at the right edge, constructing trochees from left to right, and leaving leftover syllables unparsed. It would be created after the peninitial syllable in the odd-parity

Example forms from Piro, which exhibits the pattern in (55a), are provided in (56).

(56) Piro forms (Matteson 1965)

a. ˌpet͡šhiˌt͡šimatˈlona 'they say they stalk it'

b. ˌrusluˌnotinitˈkana 'their voices already changed'

To this point, then, we have seen that there are four attested patterns with lapse and that the mirror images of these patterns are unattested in accord with the generalization in (42b). Additional important observations that might be made in connection with lapse patterns are that lapse does not occur internally in iambic systems and it only occurs in final position in iambic systems in even-parity forms. Lapse never occurs initially, either in iambic systems or trochaic systems.

1.4.3.2 Binary Default Patterns with Clash

There are two clear cases where clash is tolerated. The first can be found in the odd-parity forms of trochaic languages such as Passamaquoddy (LeSourd 1993), Maithili (Jha 1940–1944, 1958), Biangai (Dubert and Dubert 1973), and South Conchucos Quechua (Hintz 2006).[17] As illustrated in (57a), stress in these languages occurs on the initial syllable and on every even-numbered syllable from the right, resulting in a clash at the left edge in odd-parity forms. As (57b) illustrates, stress in the iambic version would occur on the final syllable and every even-numbered syllable from the left, resulting in a clash at the right edge in even-parity forms. The iambic version is unattested.[18]

(57) Peripheral clash in odd-parity forms[19]

a. Trochaic: Attested (initial clash)

```
 x  x  x
 σ σ σ σ σ σ

x x  x  x
σ σ σ σ σ σ σ
```
(first two σ underlined)

b. Iambic: Unattested (final clash)

```
  x  x  x
σ σ σ σ σ σ

  x  x  x x
σ σ σ σ σ σ σ
```
(last two σ underlined)

forms of iambic patterns by constructing a single iamb at the left edge, constructing iambs right to left, and leaving leftover syllables unparsed.

17 The default stress pattern in Passamaquoddy can be perturbed by the presence of unstressable vowels. In Maithili, primary stress is quantity-sensitive. See Chapter 6 for discussion of Maithili primary stress.

18 See note 3.

19 In a Weak Layering account, peripheral clash would be created in the odd-parity forms of trochaic patterns by constructing trochees from right to left and parsing

Example forms from Passamaquoddy, which exhibits the pattern in (57a), are provided in (58).

(58) Passamaquoddy forms

a. ˌwicohˌketaˈhamal 'he thinks of helping the other'

b. ˌtehˌsahkwaˌpasolˈtine 'let's walk around on top'

The second clash pattern can be found in the even-parity forms of iambic languages such as Aguaruna (Payne 1990, Hung 1994), Southern Paiute (Sapir 1930), and Axininca Campa (Payne 1981). In these languages, as illustrated in (59b) stress occurs on the penult, and on every even-numbered syllable from the left that precedes the penult. The result is a clash just to the left of the final syllable in even-parity forms. In the mirror-image trochaic pattern, as (59a) illustrates, stress occurs on the peninitial syllable and every even-numbered syllable from the right that follows the peninitial syllable. A clash arises just to the right of the initial syllable in even-parity forms. The pattern is unattested.

(59) Internal clash in even-parity forms[20]

a. Trochaic: Unattested (trochaic reversal)

```
  x x   x
σ σ σ σ σ σ

  x   x   x
σ σ σ σ σ σ σ
```

b. Iambic: Attested (iambic reversal)

```
  x   x x
σ σ σ σ σ σ

  x   x   x
σ σ σ σ σ σ σ
```

Example forms from Aguaruna, which exhibits the pattern in (59b), are given in (60).

(60) Aguaruna forms

a. čaŋˈkinaˌŋuˌmina 'your basket (acc)'

b. čaŋˈkinaˌŋumiˌnaki 'only your basket (acc)'

leftover syllables as monosyllabic feet. It would be created in the odd-parity forms of iambic patterns by constructing iambs left to right and parsing leftover syllables as monosyllabic feet.

20 In a Weak Layering account, internal clash might be created in the even-parity forms of trochaic patterns by making initial syllables extrametrical, constructing trochees from right to left, and parsing leftover syllables as monosyllabic feet. It would be created in the even-parity forms of iambic patterns by making final syllable extrametrical, constructing iambs left to right, and parsing leftover syllables as monosyllabic feet.

To this point, then, we have seen that there are two attested default patterns with clash and that the mirror-images of these patterns are unattested in accord with the generalization in (42b). Before moving on, however, it is necessary to examine a mirror image pair that presents a potential counterexample to the generalization in (42b). In the secondary literature (Kager 2001, Gordon 2002a), the trochaic Goshiute Shoshone (Miller 1996) has been reported to have clash at the right edge in even-parity forms, as in (61a), and the iambic mirror image, Tauya (MacDonald 1990), to have clash at the left edge, as in (61b).

(61) a.
x x xx
$\sigma\sigma\sigma\sigma\underline{\sigma\sigma}$

x x x x
$\sigma\sigma\sigma\sigma\sigma\sigma\sigma$

b.
xx x x
$\underline{\sigma\sigma}\sigma\sigma\sigma\sigma$

x x x x
$\sigma\sigma\sigma\sigma\sigma\sigma\sigma$

While the pair potentially contradicts the generalization that mirror image pairs with clash or lapse are either asymmetrically attested or symmetrically unattested, a reexamination of the original descriptions of Goshiute Shoshone and Tauya suggests that the reports may not be correct. In fact, there is ample evidence to suggest that Goshiute Shoshone and Tauya exhibit the trochaic and iambic maximal alternation patterns, respectively, rather than patterns with clash.

From Miller's (1996) description of Goshiute Shoshone, for example, it is clear that there are significant restrictions on final stress. Final syllables are only stressed when they contain a voiced vowel (Miller 1996: 698), and final syllables with voiced vowels appear always to be heavy. In final syllables, voiced vowels are usually followed by a glottal stop plus a voiceless echo vowel (Miller 1996: 697), the additional length/segmental content likely corresponding to greater weight. The presence of the final stress necessary to produce clash in even-parity forms, then, depends on the final syllable being heavy. When the final syllable is light, the trochaic minimal alternation pattern emerges. Since it is the pattern that occurs with light syllables, trochaic maximal alternation appears to be the default.

MacDonald (1990) actually provides two descriptions of the Tauya stress pattern, both of which are supported by a pattern of vowel reduction. In the first, MacDonald (1990: 52) indicates that initial syllables are stressless in even-parity forms but that they fail to reduce just like stressed syllables.

> Stress in Tauya is by and large predictable: primary stress falls on the final syllable in a word, with secondary stress on preceding alternate syllables.

> A single unstressed vowel is optionally reduced to [ə] if it is non-initial, i.e., if it is preceded and followed by stressed syllables.

In the second description, MacDonald (1990: 84) interprets the absence of vowel reduction in initial syllables as evidence that they are always stressed, even in even-parity forms where they would participate in a clash.

> Stress in Tauya is by and large predictable: primary stress falls on the final syllable in a word, with secondary stress on preceding alternate syllables. The initial syllable in a word is never without stress; if a word is polysyllabic, the initial syllable always receives secondary stress, even if this results in adjacent stressed syllables.

Since greater resistance to vowel reduction in initial syllables is expected independently of stress (Beckman 1998), however, the case for initial stress in Tauya is not particularly strong. It is likely that Tauya is simply an example of iambic maximal alternation rather than the initial clash pattern in (64b). Vowel reduction fails to occur in initial syllables, because they are initial (and, thus, independently prominent), not because they are stressed.

In light of the lack of evidence concerning the mirror image pair in (64), I will assume that both patterns are unattested. Goshiute Shoshone and Tauya appear to be examples of common maximal alternation patterns.

1.4.4 Summary of Attested Binary Default Patterns

The most basic obligation of a theory of metrical stress is to predict the attested stress patterns. As indicated in the discussion above, I take it that there are 10 binary default patterns that the theory must account for. These are summarized in (62–64).

The first four attested patterns form symmetrically attested mirror image pairs. They are the trochaic and iambic minimal alternation patterns, (62a), and the trochaic and iambic maximal alternation patterns, (62b). The minimal and maximal alternation patterns are the four possible patterns containing neither clash nor lapse.

(62) Symmetrically attested binary default patterns

a. Minimal alternation

```
i. Trochaic              ii. Iambic

 x   x   x                   x   x   x
 σ σ σ σ σ σ               σ σ σ σ σ σ

   x   x   x                 x   x   x
 σ σ σ σ σ σ σ             σ σ σ σ σ σ σ
```

b. Maximal alternation

The next four patterns are attested trochaic patterns whose iambic mirror images are unattested. The pattern in (63a) contains a lapse in final position in odd-parity forms, the pattern in (63b) a lapse after the initial syllable, and the pattern in (63b) a lapse before the penult. The pattern in (63d) contains a clash in initial position in odd-parity forms.

(63) Asymmetrically attested patterns: trochaic version attested

a. Final dactyl (final lapse in odd-parity forms)

```
x   x   x
σ σ σ σ σ σ

x   x   x
σ σ σ σ σ σ σ
```

b. Initial dactyl (lapse after initial stress)

```
x   x   x
σ σ σ σ σ σ

x     x   x
σ σ σ σ σ σ σ
```

c. Final amphibrach (Lapse before penult)

```
x   x   x
σ σ σ σ σ σ

x   x     x
σ σ σ σ σ σ σ
```

d. Initial clash

```
  x   x   x
  σ σ σ σ σ σ

x x   x   x
σ σ σ σ σ σ σ
```

The final two patterns are attested iambic patterns whose trochaic mirror images are unattested. The pattern in (64a) contains a lapse in final position in even-parity forms, and the pattern in (64b) contains a clash before the final syllable in even-parity forms.

(64) Asymmetrically attested patterns: iambic version attested

a. Final lapse in even-parity forms

```
  x   x
σ σ σ σ σ σ

  x   x   x
σ σ σ σ σ σ σ
```

b. Iambic reversal (internal clash near right edge)

```
  x   x x
σ σ σ σ σ σ

  x   x   x
σ σ σ σ σ σ σ
```

The patterns summarized in (62–64), then, are the binary default patterns that the theory of metrical stress must predict. In comparing Weak Bracketing and the various Weak Layering proposals in the chapters that follow, the ability of the different approaches to produce these patterns will be the primary concern. It will also be important, however, that the approaches compared maintain a reasonable degree of accuracy. In other words, it will also be important that in achieving the ability to predict the attested patterns the proposals do not also predict an unreasonable number of unattested patterns.

1.5 Overview

In the chapters that follow, I address prosodic layering and parsing directionality, and the relationship between them, focusing on the types of issues outlined above.

Chapter 2 presents the Relation-Specific Alignment formulation in detail and provides evidence supporting it. The chapter demonstrates that distance-sensitive evaluation is crucial in key cases and illustrates how the approach maintains distance-sensitivity while avoiding the problematic predictions of the Generalized Alignment formulation.

Chapters 3 and 4 help to motivate the Weak Bracketing approach to prosodic structure through an examination of the Odd-Parity Input Problem. The two chapters illustrate in detail the extent of the problem under Weak Layering accounts in general. Chapter 3 focuses on Symmetrical Alignment and Iterative Foot Optimization, and Chapter 4 focuses on Asymmetrical Alignment and Rhythmic Licensing.

Chapter 5 demonstrates, first, how Weak Bracketing avoids the Odd-Parity Input Problem and, second, how it combines with Relation-Specific Alignment and Optimal Mapping to provide the foundation for an effective approach to binary default patterns. It demonstrates how the proposal restricts clash and lapse to appropriate positions and yields a more accurate typology of predicted stress patterns. This chapter also explores in detail the role of key constraints such as NON-FINALITY and INITIAL-GRIDMARK.

In Chapter 6, I present the Relation-Specific Alignment approach to trisyllabic and other accent windows and demonstrate that it provides a general account of the phenomenon where alternative proposals do not.

In Chapter 7, I summarize the main results of the previous chapters and discuss their consequences for an OT approach to metrical stress.

1.6 A Note on Tableaux

Throughout the book, one of the most important issues is how different constraints assess violation marks. Since the familiar violation tableaux are particularly well-suited to demonstrating how individual constraints assess violation marks, I will to employ them when this is the primary concern. In most other cases, however, I will switch to comparative tableaux, which are particularly well-suited to illustrating ranking arguments. Readers not yet familiar with comparative tableaux are referred to Prince (2002) for a helpful introduction.

2

Establishing Directional Orientations

Since the ability to produce directional parsing effects is crucial in both Weak Layering and Weak Bracketing approaches, it is appropriate to address the directional component of the theory first. While the primary purpose of this chapter is to address the formulation of alignment constraints, the constraints responsible for producing directional parsing effects in most Optimality Theoretic accounts, a second goal is to establish the basic predictions of two Weak Layering approaches: Symmetrical Alignment (McCarthy and Prince 1993a) and Iterative Foot Optimization (2008, 2010; see also McCarthy 2008).

I begin by examining the properties of alignment constraints under the standard Generalized Alignment (GA; McCarthy and Prince 1993a) formulation, considering both the formulation's advantages and its shortcomings. I then present the Relation-Specific Alignment (RSA; Hyde 2012a) formulation and show how it allows alignment constraints to produce their essential directional parsing effects while avoiding the problems encountered under GA. In demonstrating that RSA constraints retain the ability to produce alignment's essential directionality effects, the Symmetrical Alignment approach is the primary example employed. As Symmetrical Alignment is the standard OT account, I assume that most readers will be familiar with its basic characteristics and predictions.

After establishing the ability of RSA constraints to produce alignment's essential directionality effects while avoiding the problems encountered under GA, I then consider the importance of parallel evaluation. The primary example in this context is the Iterative Foot Optimization approach, which departs from standard OT in that it sharply restricts the role of parallelism in its evaluations. As we shall see, parallelism is crucial in allowing alignment constraints to produce the desired effects.

2.1 Generalized Alignment

The GA definition of alignment constraints has played a key role in Optimality Theoretic approaches to phonology. Perhaps more than any other type, phonological analyses have relied on GA constraints to influence the positions of phonological and morphological structures. This is especially true in metrical stress theory, where analyses have employed GA constraints to position feet (McCarthy and Prince 1993a, Kager 1994, Crowhurst and Hewitt 1995, Alber 2005), head syllables of feet (Hyde 2001, 2002), entries on the metrical grid (Gordon 2002a), and other key structures. Beyond metrical stress theory, phonological analyses have employed alignment constraints to influence the positions of features, tones, affixes, and other objects (McCarthy and Prince 1993a,b, 1994; Cole and Kisseberth 1995; Akinlabi 1996; Itô and Mester 1994; Parker 1997; Orgun and Sprouse 1999; Piñeros 2001). These are just a fraction of the possible citations.

Despite the central role that GA constraints have played in OT phonology, much of the discussion in the recent literature has focused on their deficiencies. The criticisms center on one particular characteristic: *distance-sensitivity*. GA constraints do not merely distinguish alignment from misalignment; they distinguish between different degrees of misalignment, preferring configurations where a shorter distance intervenes between misaligned edges to configurations where a greater distance intervenes. The criticisms rest on two claims: first, that distance-sensitive alignment is unnecessary (Kager 2001, McCarthy 2003, Buckley 2009) and, second, that distance-sensitive GA constraints yield pathological predictions (Eisner 1997, Buckley 2009).

Though the two claims present a substantial problem for the theory, the most difficult aspect does not arise primarily due to their particular content. It arises because they are not uniformly factual. If both claims were false, we could simply keep the GA formulation, and it could continue to play its central role. If both claims were true, we could simply abandon GA and turn to the distance-insensitive alternatives suggested by its critics. As we shall see, however, the first claim is false and the second true. Distance-sensitive alignment actually is a necessary component of the theory, but distance-sensitive GA constraints can often yield pathological predictions.

The problem requires a more inventive solution than either simply abandoning or retaining GA constraints. It requires a definition of alignment constraints that preserves distance-sensitive evaluation but that also manages to avoid the pathological predictions associated with distance-sensitivity under GA. Before introducing the proposed formulation, however, it will be helpful to consider the characteristics of GA constraints that result in the pathologies identified by Eisner (1997). As we shall see, distance-sensitivity is not the only characteristic required for the problematic predictions to emerge. It is also necessary that prohibitions against misalignment be *relation-general*: that they prohibit misalignment regardless of the configuration in which the misaligned categories occur. Section 2.1.1 discusses how relation-generality and distance-sensitivity both emerge under the GA formulation. Section 2.1.2 shows how they combine to produce pathological predictions.

2.1.1 Two Characteristics

The GA definition of alignment constraints involves five arguments. The first four specify the category edges being aligned: *ACat1* and *ACat2* are the aligned categories, and *Edge1* and *Edge2* are the relevant edges. As the formulation in (1) states, the *Edge1* of every *ACat1* must coincide with the *Edge2* of some *ACat2*. The fifth argument, *SCat*, specifies the 'separator' category, the category whose intervention between the relevant edges constitutes misalignment.[1] When misalignment occurs, a violation mark is assessed for each instance of *SCat* that intervenes between the misaligned edges.

(1) Generalized Alignment

Align (*ACat1, Edge1, ACat2, Edge2, SCat*)

The *Edge1* of every *ACat1* coincides with the *Edge2* of some *ACat2*. Assess a violation mark for every *SCat* that intervenes between edges that fail to coincide.

Though GA has several significant characteristics, the two that concern us here are relation-generality and distance-sensitivity. The former derives from the way in which GA defines alignment and the alignment requirement, the latter from the way in which GA assesses violation marks. For concreteness, relation-generality and distance sensitivity are exemplified below using Align (F, L, ω, L, σ), given in (2a).

1 As McCarthy (2003) notes, the separator category has been crucial from the earliest treatments of alignment. Though it is typically omitted from both the general formulation and individual constraints, alignment constraints have always assessed violation marks for instances of a *particular* category that intervenes between misaligned edges rather than for instances of *any* category whatsoever.

(2) a. ALIGN (F, L, ω, L, σ)

The left edge of every foot coincides with the left edge of some prosodic word. Assess a violation mark for each syllable intervening between misaligned edges.

b. ALIGN (F, R, ω, R, σ)

The right edge of every foot coincides with the right edge of some prosodic word. Assess a violation mark for each syllable intervening between misaligned edges.

In conjunction with its oppositely oriented counterpart, (2b), ALIGN (F, L) plays a central role in both Symmetrical Alignment and Iterative Foot Optimization.

First, consider GA's relation-generality. In requiring that two category edges coincide, as stated in (1), a GA constraint prohibits, in effect, *all* configurations in which they fail to coincide. The prohibition against misalignment applies whether one aligned category contains the other, for example, the first aligned category precedes the second, or the second precedes the first. It is in this sense that GA constraints are relation-general.

To illustrate, consider how ALIGN (F, L) evaluates the candidates in (3). When the foot occurs initially within the prosodic word, as in (3a), the left edges of the foot and prosodic word coincide, and the constraint is satisfied. When the foot occurs in any other position, the left edges fail to coincide, and the constraint is violated. The particular structural relationship that exists between the misaligned foot and prosodic word is of no consequence. It does not matter whether the prosodic word contains the foot, (3b), the prosodic word precedes the foot, (3c), or the foot precedes the prosodic word, (3d). Each of these configurations violates the constraint.

(3)

	ALIGN (F, L)
a. [(σσ) σσσσ]	
b. [σ (σσ) σσσ]	*
c. [σσσσ](σσ)	****
d. (σσ)[σσσσ]	**

Because Align (F, L) prohibits misalignment of left edges regardless of the configuration in which the foot and prosodic word occur, its prohibition against misalignment is relation-general. All GA constraints share this characteristic.

Now, consider how distance-sensitivity emerges in the GA approach. Constraints in the OT literature employ one of two modes of evaluation to assess violation marks. The difference between the two lies in how many violation marks can be assessed per locus of violation (LV), an LV being any instance in an output candidate of the category, feature, or configuration that the constraint prohibits. When each LV corresponds to exactly one violation mark, evaluation is *categorical*. When an LV can correspond to more than one violation mark, evaluation is *gradient*. In the GA approach, where an LV is a pair of misaligned edges, evaluation is typically gradient. As (1) states, GA does not simply assess a violation mark for each pair of misaligned edges; it assesses a violation mark for each *SCat* that intervenes between them. As a result, GA very frequently assesses multiple violation marks per LV.

GA's gradient evaluation is the source of its distance-sensitivity. Because it assesses a violation mark for each instance of *SCat* located between misaligned edges, the number of violation marks assessed is proportional to the distance between them. A greater distance results in a greater number, a lesser distance in a lesser number. Consider how ALIGN (F, L) evaluates the candidates in (4). As the foot's left edge moves further away from the left edge of the prosodic word, more syllables intervene. ALIGN (F, L) employs gradient evaluation to assess the corresponding violation marks, making the overall number of violation marks assessed proportional to the distance between the misaligned edges.

(4)

	ALIGN (F, L)
a. [(σσ)σσσσ]	
b. [σ(σσ)σσσ]	*
c. [σσ(σσ)σσ]	**
d. [σσσ(σσ)σ]	***
e. [σσσσ(σσ)]	****

Cases where distance-sensitivity is crucial are those where it is necessary to influence the position of categories that are necessarily misaligned. Such a case arises, for example, when multiple feet exhibit a general directional orientation within a prosodic word, like the general leftward orientation established by ALIGN (F, L) in (5). In each of the candidates in (5), only the first foot can actually align with the left edge of the prosodic word. The second and third feet are necessarily misaligned. ALIGN (F, L) not only insists that the alignable first foot position itself exactly at the left edge of the prosodic word, it also insists that the necessarily misaligned second and third feet position themselves as near to the left edge as possible. ALIGN (F, L)'s ability to influence the positions of the second and third feet derives from its distance-sensitivity. If it did not assess more violation marks for misaligned edges that are separated by greater distances, it could not insist that the second foot position itself two syllables away from the left edge rather than three and that the third foot position itself four syllables away rather than five.

(5)

	ALIGN (F, L)
☞ a. [(σσ)(σσ)(σσ) σ]	** ****
b. [(σσ)(σσ) σ (σσ)]	** *****!
c. [(σσ) σ (σσ)(σσ)]	*** ****!*
d. [σ (σσ)(σσ)(σσ)]	* *** ***!**

2.1.2 *The Midpoint Pathology*

As Eisner (1997) observes, GA constraints can sometimes draw an object to the center of a domain rather than one of its edges, a result that is both unexpected and uncontroversially pathological. Though Eisner, echoed by Buckley (2009), blames such *Midpoint Pathology* effects on GA's distance-sensitive assessment of violation marks, its relation-general prohibition against misalignment is also required for the problematic predictions to emerge.

To illustrate, consider again the GA constraint ALIGN (σ, L, F, L, σ), briefly discussed in Chapter 1. ALIGN (σ, L) aligns the left edge of every syllable with the left edge of some foot.

(6) ALIGN (σ, L, F, L, σ):

The left edge of every syllable coincides with the left edge of some foot. Assess a violation mark for each syllable intervening between misaligned edges.

As (7) illustrates, when there is a single foot in a form, ALIGN (σ, L) draws its left edge to the left edge of the medial syllable. The result depends on distance-sensitive evaluation, since it is necessarily misaligned syllables that determine the foot's position. The misaligned syllables draw the foot towards the center of the form because the overall distance between their left edges and the left foot edge – as reflected in the number of violation marks assessed – is shortest when it occurs in this position. The result also depends on GA's relation-generality. *Every* misaligned syllable must contribute to the overall number of violation marks, regardless of its structural relationship to the foot. In (7), *p* denotes a violation mark derived from a misaligned syllable that precedes the foot, *f* a violation mark from a misaligned syllable that follows the foot, and *c* a violation mark from a misaligned syllable contained within the foot.

(7)

	Align (σ, L)
a. [(σσ)σσσσσ]	c ff fff ffff fff!ff fffff
b. [σ(σσ)σσσσ]	p c ff fff ffff ff!fff
c. [σσ(σσ)σσσ]	pp p c ff fff ffff!
☞ d. [σσσ(σσ)σσ]	ppp pp p c ff fff
e. [σσσσ(σσ)σ]	pppp ppp pp p c ff!
f. [σσσσσ(σσ)]	ppppp pppp ppp p!p p c

A constraint that was *relation-specific* would not have yielded the same result. Unlike relation-general constraints, relation-specific constraints only prohibit misalignment when the aligned categories occur in a particular configuration. A relation-specific version of Align (σ, L) would target only misaligned syllables with a certain relationship to the foot. With its foot at the left edge, for example, (7a) incurs no *p* violation marks. If Align (σ, L) targeted only misaligned syllables that precede the foot, (7a) would be optimal. Similarly, with its foot at the right edge, (7f) incurs no *f* violation marks. If Align (σ, L) targeted only misaligned syllables that follow the foot, (7f) would be optimal. Finally, since each candidate contains a single misaligned syllable within the foot, each candidate incurs a single *c* violation mark. If Align (σ, L) targeted only misaligned syllables contained within the foot, it could not have distinguished between the different candidates, and the decision between them would have fallen to other constraints. None of these results would be problematic.

While it is true that distance-sensitivity is required for Midpoint Pathology effects to emerge, relation-generality is also required. Making prohibitions against misalignment relation-specific, then, would allow alignment constraints to avoid Midpoint Pathology effects without abandoning distance-sensitivity. This is the approach advocated here. As we shall see below, two lines of evidence offer substantial support. First, distance-sensitivity is required in the analyses of several different phenomena (Section 2.5.1), and, second, relation-specificity allows us to productively extend alignment analyses into new domains (Chapter 6). Having outlined the central issues that it is designed to address, then, we turn next to the proposed definition of alignment constraints.

2.2 Relation-Specific Alignment

Under the RSA approach, alignment constraints have two components. The two components appear in the statement of a constraint on opposite sides of a slash, as indicated in (8). To the right of the slash is the definition of the *prohibited configuration of misalignment* (PCM). Following Ellison (1995), Zoll (1996), and McCarthy (2003), RSA constraints prohibit specific configurations of misalignment directly.[2] The definition of the PCM determines the constraint's edge orientation: whether it prohibits misalignment between left edges, right edges, or opposite edges. It is also the source of the constraint's relation-specificity: it establishes the particular structural relation that must obtain between the aligned categories in order for the prohibition against misalignment to apply.

(8) *locus of violation / prohibited configuration of misalignment

To the left of the slash is the definition of a *locus of violation*. The definition of the LV determines how the constraint assesses violation marks. In particular, it determines whether the constraint is distance-insensitive or distance-sensitive.

In the discussion that follows, I focus first on the definition of the PCM, demonstrating how it establishes edge orientations and how it ensures relation-specificity. I then turn to the definition of an LV, demonstrating how distance-sensitive and distance-insensitive assessment can both be accommodated under categorical evaluation. Finally, we will see how the different types of LV and PCM permitted under RSA combine to form the proposed schemas for alignment constraints.

2.2.1 Prohibited Configurations of Misalignment

The RSA definition of a PCM involves three arguments: the aligned categories, *ACat1* and *ACat2*, and the separator category, *SCat*. The two principles determining how these arguments can be deployed are given in (9). The Basic Relations Requirement, (9a), establishes the terms in which prohibited configurations are defined. It requires that they be

2 While there is some similarity between RSA and these earlier proposals in how they define PCMs, the recognition that the PCMs result in relation-specificity, and the claim that relation-specificity is crucial to the theory of alignment, are both novel. RSA differs from the earlier proposals in other key respects, as well. It offers a more complete account, accommodating both same-edge constraints and opposite-edge constraints (the earlier proposals accommodate only the former), and it provides an explicit set of principles for constructing the necessary PCMs. It also differs from the earlier proposals in how it assesses violation marks.

defined in terms of category *containment* and *precedence*, reflecting the possible relationships between categories in phonological strings in a fairly concrete way.[3] Of the numerous possible configurations that might be defined in these terms, the Adjacency Requirement, (9b), picks out those that are prohibited by alignment constraints. In particular, by insisting that the separator category intervene between one aligned category and an adjacent edge of the other, it picks out configurations where the separator category crucially intervenes between misaligned edges.

(9) a. Basic Relations Requirement

Prohibited configurations are defined in terms of category containment and precedence.

b. Adjacency Requirement

In a PCM, the separator category must intervene between one aligned category and the adjacent edge of the other aligned category.

Under the Basic Relations Requirement and the Adjacency Requirement, the only PCMs permitted are those in (11) below. The demonstration is straightforward. Under the Basic Relations Requirement, the aligned categories must arrange themselves in one of two structural relations: one aligned category must contain the other, as in (10a), or one aligned category must precede the other, as in (10b).

(10) a. [... *ACat2* ...]$_{ACat1}$ b. *ACat1* ... *ACat2*

The Adjacency Requirement restricts the positions in which the separator category can occur in conjunction with these two configurations. When one aligned category contains the other, the separator category will only intervene between one aligned category and the adjacent edge of the other if it occurs between their left edges, as in (11a), or their right edges, as in (11b). When one aligned category precedes the other, the separator category will only intervene between one aligned category and the adjacent edge of the other if it occurs between the right edge of the first and the left edge of the second, as in (11c).

3 McCarthy (2003) uses *dominance* and *precedence* to define prohibited configurations. RSA substitutes the more flexible *containment* for *dominance* because the dominance relation is limited to categories in the same hierarchy, and the theory must be able to capture both this and the similar relationship that can arise between categories of different hierarchies. This is necessary, for example, to allow for alignment between prosodic categories and morphological categories or between prosodic categories and entries on the metrical grid.

(11)	a.	Left-edge misalignment:	*[... *SCat* ... *ACat2* ... $]_{ACat1}$
	b.	Right-edge misalignment:	*[... *ACat2* ... *SCat* ... $]_{ACat1}$
	c.	Opposite-edge misalignment:	**ACat1* ... *SCat* ... *ACat2*

The three configurations in (11), then, exhaust the options permitted under the Basic Relations Requirement and the Adjacency Requirement.[4]

Because the Adjacency Requirement always positions the separator category so that it crucially intervenes between misaligned edges, the location of the separator category determines the edge orientation of the PCMs. For example, by prohibiting *SCat* from preceding *ACat2* within *ACat1*, the (11a) schema prohibits misalignment between the left edges of *ACat1* and *ACat2*. Because the Basic Relations Requirement requires that a constraint specify in its PCM whether one aligned category contains the other or one aligned category precedes the other, the prohibition against misalignment is always relation-specific. A constraint can discourage misalignment only when the aligned categories actually occur in the relation specified. Though the (11a) schema prohibits misalignment between the left edges of *ACat1* and *ACat2*, it does so only when *ACat1* contains *ACat2*.

Similarly, by prohibiting *ACat2* from preceding *SCat* within *ACat1*, (11b) prohibits misalignment between the right edges of *ACat1* and *ACat2*, but only when *ACat1* contains *ACat2*. By prohibiting *ACat1* from preceding *ACat2* with *SCat* intervening, (11c) prohibits misalignment between the right edge of *ACat1* and the left edge of *ACat2*, but only when *ACat1* precedes *ACat2*.

To demonstrate how the schemas in (11) prohibit misalignment – and to better illustrate the relation-specific nature of their prohibitions – we can consider some examples that are a bit more concrete. In the prohibited configurations in (12), the aligned categories are *prosodic word* and *foot*, and the separator category is *syllable*.

(12)	a.	Left-edge misalignment:	$*[\ \ldots \sigma \ldots F \ldots\ ]_{\omega}$
	b.	Right-edge misalignment:	$*[\ \ldots F \ldots \sigma \ldots\ ]_{\omega}$
	c.	Opposite-edge misalignment:	$*\omega \ldots \sigma \ldots F$

By prohibiting a syllable from preceding a foot within a prosodic word, $*[\ \ldots \sigma \ldots F \ldots\ ]_{\omega}$ distinguishes between alignment and misalignment of

4 The prohibited configurations in (11) are also the only configurations where alignment is actually achievable. Same-edge alignment is only achievable when one aligned category contains the other. Opposite-edge alignment is only achievable when one aligned category precedes the other.

the left edges of feet and prosodic words, but only when the prosodic word contains the foot, as in (13a,b). It prefers a candidate where no syllable intervenes between the left edges, (13a), to a candidate where one or more syllables intervene, (13b). In contrast, when the prosodic word does not contain the foot, as in (13c,d), *[… *σ*… *F* …]$_{\omega}$ does not discourage misalignment. It offers no objection in this context even though the left edges are necessarily misaligned.

(13)

	*[… *σ*… *F* …]$_{\omega}$
a. [(σσ) σσσσ]	
b. [σ (σσ)σσσ]	*
c. [σσσ] σ (σσ)	
d. (σσ) σ [σσσ]	

Similarly, by prohibiting a foot from preceding a syllable within the prosodic word, *[… *F*… *σ* …]$_{\omega}$ discourages misalignment between the right edges of prosodic words and feet, but only when the prosodic word contains the foot. By prohibiting a prosodic word from preceding a foot with a syllable intervening, **ω* … *σ* … *F* discourages misalignment between the right edges of prosodic words and the left edges of feet, but only when the prosodic word precedes the foot.

2.2.2 Assessment of Violations

Having seen how RSA defines prohibited configurations of misalignment, we turn now to the ways in which it assesses violation marks. Two principles provide the foundation for the proposed approach. The Two Measures Requirement, (14a), addresses the types of assessment that the theory requires. It mandates that alignment constraints come in both distance-insensitive and distance-sensitive varieties. The Categoricality Hypothesis (McCarthy 2003), (14b), addresses the modes of evaluation that the theory employs to assess violation marks. It insists that the grammar rely solely on categorical evaluation. It may not resort to gradient evaluation.

(14) a. Two Measures Requirement

The definition of alignment constraints provides for both distance-insensitive assessment of violation marks and distance-sensitive assessment.

b. Categoricality Hypothesis (McCarthy 2003):

A constraint assesses no more than one violation mark per locus of violation.

At first glance, the Two Measures Requirement and the Categoricality Hypothesis seem to be incompatible. It is a straightforward matter to implement distance-insensitive assessment under categorical evaluation, but it is not as obvious how to implement distance-sensitive assessment. Distance-insensitive constraints only distinguish alignment from misalignment. If an LV is a pair of misaligned edges, as it is in GA, assessing a single violation mark for each pair is an effective way to make the needed distinction. In contrast, distance-sensitive constraints distinguish between different degrees of misalignment, and assessing a single violation mark for each pair of misaligned edges is not sufficient. It is for this reason that GA implements distance-sensitivity through gradient evaluation. It allows GA constraints to assess whatever number of violation marks is necessary in order to distinguish between different degrees of misalignment.

Despite initial appearances, the Two Measures Requirement and the Categoricality Hypothesis are not incompatible. To satisfy both at once, however, the different characteristics of distance-insensitive constraints and distance-sensitive constraints must be derived from a source other than their modes of evaluation. As it happens, it is a relatively simple matter to implement both types under categorical evaluation when LVs are appropriately defined.

In RSA, an LV is either a set of two categories – the aligned categories, *ACat1* and *ACat2* – or it is a set of three categories – *ACat1*, *ACat2*, and the separator category, *SCat*. The presence or absence of the separator category determines whether evaluation is distance-sensitive or distance-insensitive.

(15) a. Distance-insensitive constraints: ⟨*ACat1*, *ACat2*⟩

b. Distance-sensitive constraints: ⟨*ACat1*, *ACat2*, *SCat*⟩

When the definition of an LV omits the separator category, the result is a distance-insensitive constraint. A single LV derives from each instance of misaligned edges, regardless of the number of separator categories that intervene. When the definition of an LV includes the separator category, the result is a distance-sensitive constraint. The number of LVs that derive from any one instance of misaligned edges depends on the number of intervening separator categories. When multiple separator categories intervene, they help to establish multiple LVs.

Consider a constraint that aligns the right edges of a foot and a prosodic word. It would be formulated under RSA as a constraint that prohibits a syllable from following a foot within a prosodic word: $*[\ \ldots\ F\ \ldots\ \sigma\ \ldots\ ]_{\omega}$. A distance-insensitive version of the constraint would define an LV as a pair consisting of the aligned categories, *prosodic word* and *foot*: ⟨ω, *F*⟩. Because the separator category, *syllable*, is omitted, no more than one LV derives from any given misaligned foot and prosodic word, regardless of the number of intervening syllables.

To illustrate, in (16a), the foot and prosodic word align at the right edge, so there are no LVs, and no violation mark is assessed. When the foot moves one syllable away, as in (16b), so that the foot and prosodic word are misaligned, there is a single LV, $\langle \omega_A, F_\alpha \rangle$, and categorical evaluation would assess the corresponding single violation mark. Moving the foot further to the left in (16c,d), so that additional syllables intervene, fails to produce additional LVs and additional violation marks. There is a still only a single LV, $\langle \omega_A, F_\alpha \rangle$, and just a single violation mark is assessed.

(16)		$*\langle \omega, F \rangle$ / [… *F* … *σ* … $]_\omega$
	a. $[\,\sigma_1\,\sigma_2\,\sigma_3\,(\,\sigma_4\,\sigma_5\,)_\alpha\,]_A$	
	b. $[\,\sigma_1\,\sigma_2\,(\,\sigma_3\,\sigma_4\,)_\alpha\,\sigma_5\,]_A$	$\langle \omega_A, F_\alpha \rangle$
	c. $[\,\sigma_1\,(\,\sigma_2\,\sigma_3\,)_\alpha\,\sigma_4\,\sigma_5\,]_A$	$\langle \omega_A, F_\alpha \rangle$
	d. $[\,(\,\sigma_1\,\sigma_2\,)_\alpha\,\sigma_3\,\sigma_4\,\sigma_5\,]_A$	$\langle \omega_A, F_\alpha \rangle$

A distance-sensitive version of the constraint would define an LV as a triplet consisting of the aligned categories, *prosodic word* and *foot*, and the separator category, *syllable*: ⟨ω, *F*, *σ*⟩. Because the separator category is included, the number of LVs derived from any given misaligned foot and prosodic word depends on the number of intervening syllables. In (17a), for example, no syllables intervene, so there are no LVs, and no violation mark is assessed. When the foot moves one syllable away, as in (17b), there is a single LV, $\langle \omega_A, F_\alpha, \sigma_5 \rangle$, and categorical evaluation would assess a single violation mark. When the foot moves two syllables away, as in (17c), there are two LVs, $\langle \omega_A, F_\alpha, \sigma_4 \rangle$ and $\langle \omega_A, F_\alpha, \sigma_5 \rangle$, and categorical evaluation would assess a single violation mark for each. When the foot moves three syllables away, as in (17d), there are three LVs, $\langle \omega_A, F_\alpha, \sigma_3 \rangle$, $\langle \omega_A, F_\alpha, \sigma_4 \rangle$, and $\langle \omega_A, F_\alpha, \sigma_5 \rangle$, and categorical evaluation would assess a single violation mark for each.

(17)		$*\langle \omega, F, \sigma \rangle$ / [… *F* … *σ* … $]_\omega$
	a. $[\,\sigma_1\,\sigma_2\,\sigma_3\,(\,\sigma_4\,\sigma_5\,)_\alpha\,]_A$	
	b. $[\,\sigma_1\,\sigma_2\,(\,\sigma_3\,\sigma_4\,)_\alpha\,\sigma_1\,]_A$	$\langle \omega_A, F_\alpha, \sigma_5 \rangle$
	c. $[\,\sigma_1\,(\,\sigma_2\,\sigma_3\,)_\alpha\,\sigma_4\,\sigma_5\,]_A$	$\langle \omega_A, F_\alpha, \sigma_4 \rangle$, $\langle \omega_A, F_\alpha, \sigma_5 \rangle$
	d. $[\,(\,\sigma_1\,\sigma_2\,)_\alpha\,\sigma_3\,\sigma_4\,\sigma_5\,]_A$	$\langle \omega_A, F_\alpha, \sigma_3 \rangle$, $\langle \omega_A, F_\alpha, \sigma_4 \rangle$, $\langle \omega_A, F_\alpha, \sigma_5 \rangle$

Even under the limitations imposed by the Categoricality Hypothesis, then, RSA accommodates both distance-insensitive and distance-sensitive constraints. The result is significant, as the Categoricality Hypothesis has been assumed to exclude distance-sensitivity and was, as it happens, proposed for just this purpose. In general, however, categorical evaluation easily captures the effects commonly associated with gradient evaluation when the LV is appropriately defined. Note that there is nothing special about this qualification. A constraint of any type must define an LV, and the definition must be appropriate to achieve the desired effect. Given the ability of categorical evaluation to capture the effects of gradient evaluation, the Categoricality Hypothesis is adopted here primarily to eliminate a redundancy. It would be undesirable to posit two modes of evaluation – categorical and gradient – within the OT framework when only one is actually necessary.

2.2.3 Alignment Constraint Schemas

To provide an overall picture of the alignment constraints possible under RSA, we combine the two LV definitions in (15) into a single definition that indicates the separator category's optionality: ⟨*ACat1, ACat2, (SCat)*⟩. We then pair this combined definition with each of the three PCMs in (11). The result is the three schemas for alignment constraints in (18).

(18) RSA constraint schemas

a. Left-Edge: *⟨*ACat1, ACat2, (SCat)*⟩ / [... *SCat* ... *ACat2* ... $]_{ACat1}$

'Assess a violation mark for every ⟨*ACat1, ACat2, (SCat)*⟩ such that *SCat* precedes *ACat2* within *ACat1*.'

b. Right-edge: *⟨*ACat1, ACat2, (SCat)*⟩ / [... *ACat2* ... *SCat* ... $]_{ACat1}$

'Assess a violation mark for every ⟨*ACat1, ACat2, (SCat)*⟩ such that *ACat2* precedes *SCat* within *ACat1*.'

c. Opposite-edge: *⟨*ACat1, ACat2, (SCat)*⟩ / *ACat1* ... *SCat* ... *ACat2*

'Assess a violation mark for every ⟨*ACat1, ACat2, (SCat)*⟩ such that *ACat1* precedes *ACat2* with *SCat* intervening.'

The schemas in (18) prohibit the categories in the set to the left of the slash from occurring in the configuration of misalignment to the right of the slash. The set of categories to the left of the slash, the set that defines an LV, always includes the two aligned categories, *ACat1* and *ACat2*. Whether or not a constraint also includes the separator category, *SCat*, determines whether its assessment of violation marks is distance-sensitive or distance-insensitive. In the PCM to the right of the slash, the containment and precedence relations between *ACat1*, *ACat2*, and *SCat* define the particular configuration of misalignment that a schema targets. Constraints based on a given schema assess violation marks for the particular configuration targeted by that schema and no others. Finally, assessment of violation marks is always categorical. A constraint assesses a single violation mark for each LV, but it is possible for a candidate to have multiple LVs.

2.3 Essential Directionality Effects

Constraints formulated under the RSA schemas in (18) produce the same essential directionality effects as constraints formulated under the GA definition in (1). To demonstrate this ability, I will discuss alignment's essential directionality effects in general terms, contrasting them to those of iterative parsing algorithms (Halle and Vergnaud 1987, Hayes 1995), and then I will show how RSA constraints can replace GA constraints to reproduce the predictions of the standard Symmetrical Alignment approach.

In general, directionality-dictating devices like alignment and iterative parsing algorithms create one of two basic effects. In the first, they hold sway over all instances of a particular category, giving them a general directional orientation relative to instances of another category. In the second, they hold sway over just a single instance of a particular category, potentially creating an exception to a general directional orientation.

(19) Two basic directionality effects

a. Establish general directional orientations.

b. Create exceptions to general directional orientations.

As discussed in Chapter 1, Weak Layering accounts provide two options for dealing with the leftover syllable in odd-parity outputs: the leftover syllable can remain unfooted, or it can be parsed as a monosyllabic foot. The position of these irregular structures – unparsed syllable or monosyllabic foot – is the primary indication of a directional device's influence. When the device establishes a general directional orientation only, the irregular structure appears peripherally. When it also creates an exception to a general directional orientation, the irregular structure appears internally.

When the leftover syllable remains unfooted, as in (20), the position of the stray syllable is the clearest indication of a directional device's influence. General directional orientations are most obvious in simple unidirectional patterns. In (20a), the feet have all been pushed to, pulled to, or laid out from one edge of the prosodic word, and the stray syllable emerges at the opposite edge. Exceptions to general directional orientations are most conspicuous in bidirectional patterns. In (20b), one foot, the exception, anchors itself at one edge of the form; the remaining feet position themselves at the opposite edge; and the stray syllable sits in between, marking the boundary between the exceptional foot and the others.

(20) Directional orientations for feet in under-parsing systems

a. General: unidirectional	b. General + exception: bidirectional
[(σσ)(σσ)(σσ)σ]	[(σσ)σ(σσ)(σσ)]
[σ(σσ)(σσ)(σσ)]	[(σσ)(σσ)σ(σσ)]

When the leftover syllable is parsed as a monosyllabic foot, as in (21), the clearest indication of a directional device's influence is the monosyllabic foot's position. General directional orientations are most obvious in simple unidirectional patterns, as in (21a), where the disyllabic feet are strung together to one side of the prosodic word and the monosyllabic foot appears at the other. Exceptions to general directional orientations are most conspicuous in bidirectional patterns, such as those in (21b), where the monosyllable marks the boundary between two groups of disyllabic feet. One disyllabic foot (the exception) positions itself at one edge of the form; the remaining disyllabic feet are strung together at the opposite edge; and the monosyllabic foot sits in between.

(21) Directional orientations for feet in exhaustive parsing systems

a. General: unidirectional	b. General + exception: bidirectional
[(σσ)(σσ)(σσ)(σ)]	[(σσ)(σ)(σσ)(σσ)]
[(σ)(σσ)(σσ)(σσ)]	[(σσ)(σσ)(σ)(σσ)]

Though the effects described in (19) and illustrated in (20) and (21) are fairly basic, it is not the case that all directional devices produce them in the same circumstances. Differences in the ways that they establish directional orientations result in disparate abilities in different contexts, and these, in turn, lead to divergent predictions. Iterative parsing algorithms produce both effects – general directional orientations and exceptions to general directional orientations – whether instances of the specified category fail to exhaust the phonological string, as in the under-parsing patterns in (20), or actually do exhaust the phonological string, as in the exhaustive parsing patterns in (21). In contrast, alignment produces both effects only when instances of the specified category fail to exhaust the phonological string. Of the under-parsing patterns in (20), it produces both the unidirectional patterns, (20a), and the bidirectional patterns, (20b). When instances of the specified category actually do exhaust the phonological string, alignment can establish general directional orientations, but it cannot create exceptions to general directional orientations. Of the exhaustive parsing patterns in (21), it produces the unidirectional patterns, (21a), but not the bidirectional patterns, (21b).

(22) Alignment's essential directionality effects

a. When instances of the aligned category do not exhaust the string

i. Alignment establishes general directional orientations.

ii. Alignment creates exceptions to general directional orientations.

b. When instances of the aligned category do exhaust the string

Alignment establishes general directional orientations only.

The asymmetry in its ability to create exceptions to general directional orientations is one of alignment's most interesting characteristics. It is also one of its most fortunate. As it happens, the stress patterns that would emerge from the bidirectional exhaustive parsing schemes are unattested, and alignment's inability to produce them gives it an advantage over alternatives, like iterative parsing, which produce them quite naturally.

2.4 Symmetrical Alignment

To better illustrate alignment's essential directionality effects, we turn now an examination of McCarthy and Prince's (1993a) Symmetrical Alignment account. Symmetrical Alignment is a Weak Bracketing approach consisting of six constraints. The first two constraints are PARSE-σ and F-BINARITY, repeated in (23).

(23) a. PARSE-σ:

Every *σ* is parsed into a *F*.

b. F-BINARITY:

Every foot is binary (either disyllabic or bimoraic).

As mentioned in Chapter 1, the interaction between PARSE-σ and F-BIN is crucial in Weak Bracketing accounts in determining the status of the leftover syllable in odd-parity forms. The desired result of the interaction is that there are just two options for the leftover syllable: when PARSE-σ dominates F-BIN the syllable should be parsed as a monosyllabic foot; when F-BIN dominates PARSE-σ the syllable should be left unparsed.

To actually limit the grammar to these two options, however, it is necessary to assume that the maximum size of a foot is universally disyllabic. If evaluations are allowed to consider feet that are larger than disyllabic, then ternary or unbounded feet will replace monosyllabic feet when exhaustive parsing is required. To illustrate, if F-BIN assesses violations gradiently, as in (24), F-BIN will exclude unbounded feet but will not distinguish between monosyllabic feet and ternary feet, both of which depart from binarity by a single syllable. Since ternary feet allow a candidate to perform better than monosyllabic feet on constraints, like alignment, that tend to minimize the number of feet in a form, ternary feet will be preferred to monosyllabic feet.

(24)

	PARSE-σ	F-BIN	ALL-F-RIGHT
a. [(σσσσσσσ)]		**!***	
☞ b. [(σσσ)(σσ)(σσ)]		*	**** **
c. [(σσ)(σσ)(σσ)(σ)]		*	***** **!* *
d. [σ (σσ)(σσ)(σσ)]	*!		**** **

If F-BIN assesses violations categorically, as in (25), it will be unable to distinguish monosyllabic feet from ternary or unbounded feet. Since unbounded feet perform better than the others on constraints that tend to minimize the number of feet, unbounded feet will be preferred.

(25)

	PARSE-σ	F-BIN	ALL-F-RIGHT
☞ a. [(σσσσσσσ)]		*	
b. [(σσσ)(σσ)(σσ)]		*	*!*** **
c. [(σσ)(σσ)(σσ)(σ)]		*	*!**** *** *
d. [σ (σσ)(σσ)(σσ)]	*!		**** **

To limit the options for dealing with the leftover syllable of odd-parity forms to monosyllabic feet and unparsed syllables, then, it seems necessary to prevent the EVAL component of the grammar from considering candidates with feet that contain more then two syllables. I will simply assume that GEN does not produce candidates of this type.

Given this assumption, binary patterns emerge under Symmetrical Alignment whenever PARSE-σ dominates the alignment constraints, as in (26).

(26) Binary stress patterns under Symmetrical Alignment
PARSE-σ >> alignment; F-BIN

Though the ranking of F-BIN is not crucial in ensuring that *some* type of binary pattern emerges, it is crucial in determining *which* type of binary pattern emerges. If PARSE-σ dominates F-BIN, as indicated in (27), the result is exhaustive parsing. The leftover syllable of odd-parity forms is parsed as a monosyllabic foot.

(27) Exhaustive parsing under Symmetrical Alignment
PARSE-σ >> F-BIN, alignment

If F-BIN dominates PARSE-σ, as indicated in (28), the result is under-parsing. The leftover syllable of odd-parity forms remains unparsed.

(28) Under-parsing under Symmetrical Alignment
F-BIN >> PARSE-σ >> alignment

The remaining four constraints in the Symmetrical Alignment account are GA constraints requiring alignment between the edges of feet and prosodic words. These are the constraints responsible for establishing general directional orientations for feet within prosodic words and for creating exceptions to general directional orientations. The two GA constraints responsible for establishing general directional orientations are ALIGN (F, L, ω, L, σ) and ALIGN (F, R, ω, R, σ), given in (2). The two constraints responsible for creating exceptions to general directional orientations are ALIGN (ω, L, F, L, σ) and ALIGN (ω, R, F, R, σ), discussed in Section 2.5.3. Rather than rehearse in detail the predictions of the Symmetrical Alignment account when employing GA constraints, I will simply replace Symmetrical Alignment's GA constraints in the discussion that follows with RSA constraints to illustrate how RSA constraints reproduce the essential directionality effects. As we shall see, nothing is lost with the replacement.

2.4.1 Under-Parsing Systems

In any prosodic word, at most one foot can align with a given edge. Due to the intervention of that foot, and possibly others, any remaining feet are necessarily misaligned. A constraint that establishes a general directional orientation for feet, then, is a constraint that influences the position of both the alignable foot and any necessarily misaligned feet. A constraint that creates an exception to a general directional orientation is a constraint that influences the position of the alignable foot only. Under RSA, the ability to establish general directional orientations derives from distance-sensitive assessment, and the ability to create an exception to a general directional orientation derives from distance-insensitive assessment. Since alignment constraints produce both effects in under-parsing systems, we begin with under-parsing here and consider exhaustive parsing further below.

Consider the RSA constraints ALL-F-LEFT and ALL-F-RIGHT, given in (29). Both encourage same-edge alignment between feet and prosodic words. ALL-F-LEFT encourages left-edge alignment by prohibiting a syllable from preceding a foot within a prosodic word, and ALL-F-RIGHT encourages right-edge alignment by prohibiting a foot from preceding a syllable. Since they include the separator category, *syllable*, in the definition of an LV, the constraints are both distance-sensitive. The number of LVs to which any given pair of misaligned edges contributes equals the number of syllables that intervene between them.

(29) a. ALL-F-LEFT: $*\langle\omega, F, \sigma\rangle$ / $[\ \dots \sigma \dots F \dots\ ]_{\omega}$

'Assess a violation mark for every $\langle\omega, F, \sigma\rangle$ such that σ precedes F within ω.'

b. ALL-F-RIGHT: $*\langle\omega, F, \sigma\rangle$ / $[\ \dots F \dots \sigma \dots\ ]_{\omega}$

'Assess a violation mark for every $\langle\omega, F, \sigma\rangle$ such that F precedes σ within ω.'

Because they distinguish between different degrees of misalignment, ALL-F-LEFT and ALL-F-RIGHT can establish general directional orientations for feet within prosodic words. Not only can they require that alignable feet locate themselves at the appropriate edge of the prosodic word, they can also require that necessarily misaligned feet position themselves as near to the appropriate edge as possible.

Consider how ALL-F-RIGHT establishes a general rightward orientation. In (30), only the third foot can actually align with the right edge of the prosodic word. The first and second feet are necessarily misaligned. ALL-F-RIGHT insists that the third foot occur exactly at the prosodic word's right edge, but it also draws the necessarily misaligned first and second feet as far to the right as possible. It insists that the second foot occurs two syllables away from the right edge, rather than three, and it insists that the first foot occurs four syllables away, rather than five. In drawing all feet towards the right edge, ALL-F-RIGHT also has the effect of pushing the stray syllable to the left.

(30)

		ALL-F-RIGHT
	a. [(σσ)(σσ)(σσ) σ]	***** **!* *
	b. [(σσ)(σσ) σ (σσ)]	***** **!*
	c. [(σσ) σ (σσ)(σσ)]	***** **!
☞	d. [σ (σσ)(σσ)(σσ)]	**** **

In establishing general directional orientations for feet, the distance-sensitive ALL-F-LEFT and ALL-F-RIGHT produce two unidirectional parsing schemes. Since the two schemes can be implemented with either trochees or iambs, they yield four different stress patterns, three of which are attested. These are the same unidirectional under-parsing patterns predicted under Symmetrical Alignment, employing GA constraints.

(31) Unidirectional under-parsing patterns

a. F-BIN >> PARSE-σ >> ALL-F-LEFT >> ALL-F-RIGHT

i. Trochaic: Attested
(σ́σ)(σ́σ)(σ́σ)
(σ́σ)(σ́σ)(σ́σ)σ

ii. Iambic: Attested
(σσ́)(σσ́)(σσ́)
(σσ́)(σσ́)(σσ́)σ

b. F-BIN >> PARSE-σ >> ALL-F-RIGHT >> ALL-F-LEFT

i. Trochaic: Attested
(σ́σ)(σ́σ)(σ́σ)
σ(σ́σ)(σ́σ)(σ́σ)

ii. Iambic: Unattested
(σσ́)(σσ́)(σσ́)
σ(σσ́)(σσ́)(σσ́)

Now consider two additional RSA constraints, F-LEFT and F-RIGHT, given in (32). Though F-LEFT and F-RIGHT also encourage same-edge alignment between feet and prosodic words, prohibiting the same configurations of misalignment as ALL-F-LEFT and ALL-F-RIGHT, respectively, their omission of the separator category, *syllable*, from the definition of an LV means that they are distance-insensitive. The number of LVs resulting from any given pair of misaligned edges is *one*, regardless of the number of syllables that intervene.

(32) a. F-LEFT: $*\langle\omega,F\rangle$ / [...σ...F... $]_\omega$

'Assess a violation mark for every $\langle\omega, F\rangle$ such that σ precedes F within ω.'

b. F-RIGHT: $*\langle\omega,F\rangle$ / [...F...σ... $]_\omega$

'Assess a violation mark for every $\langle\omega, F\rangle$ such that F precedes σ within ω.'

Because F-LEFT and F-RIGHT only distinguish between alignment and misalignment, rather than different degrees of misalignment, they can require that the alignable foot locate itself at the appropriate edge of the prosodic word but not that necessarily misaligned feet position themselves as near as possible. Their ability to influence the position of a single foot in this fashion allows them to establish an exception to a general directional orientation.

Consider how a high-ranked F-LEFT creates an exception to the general rightward orientation established by a lower-ranked ALL-F-RIGHT. In (33), the first foot can align with the prosodic word's left edge, but the second and third feet are necessarily misaligned. F-LEFT insists that the first foot occur at the left edge, but it cannot insist that the remaining feet occur as near as possible. The second foot contributes to a single LV whether it is two syllables away or three, and the third foot contributes to a single LV whether it is four syllables away or five. It is left to the distance-sensitive ALL-F-RIGHT, then, to determine the position of the second and third feet. ALL-F-RIGHT draws both towards the right edge, so that the stray syllable separates the initial foot from the others.

(33)

	F-LEFT	ALL-F-RIGHT
a. [(σσ)(σσ)(σσ) σ]	* *	***** ***! *
b. [(σσ)(σσ) σ (σσ)]	* *	***** ***!
☞ c. [(σσ) σ (σσ)(σσ)]	* *	***** **
d. [σ (σσ)(σσ)(σσ)]	* * *!	**** **

In creating exceptions to general directional orientations, F-LEFT and F-RIGHT help to produce two bidirectional parsing patterns. Whether implemented with trochaic footing (attested) or iambic footing (unattested), bidirectional parsing schemes always yield stress patterns with an internal lapse in odd-parity forms. These are the same bidirectional patterns predicted under Symmetrical Alignment, using GA constraints.[5],[6]

(34) Bidirectional under-parsing patterns

a. F-BIN >> PARSE-σ >> F-LEFT >> ALL-F-RIGHT

i. Trochaic: Attested	ii. Iambic: Unattested
(σ́σ)(σ́σ)(σ́σ)	(σσ́)(σσ́)(σσ́)
(σ́σ)σ(σ́σ)(σ́σ)	(σσ́)σ(σσ́)(σσ́)

b. F-BIN >> PARSE-σ >> F-RIGHT >> ALL-F-LEFT

i. Trochaic: Attested	ii. Iambic: Unattested
(σ́σ)(σ́σ)(σ́σ)	(σσ́)(σσ́)(σσ́)
(σ́σ)(σ́σ)σ(σ́σ)	(σσ́)(σσ́)σ(σσ́)

Internal lapse patterns are significant not only because they illustrate both of alignment's essential directionality effects but also because they present a clear case where the alternative Rhythmic Licensing (Kager 2001, 2005) approach cannot effectively replicate the effects of distance-sensitive alignment. I address this point in Section 2.5.1.

2.4.2 Exhaustive Parsing Systems

Alignment's influence on the position of monosyllabic feet differs in two ways from its influence on the position of stray syllables. The first

5 When employing RSA constraints to create binary patterns in Weak Layering approaches, PARSE-σ must dominate the alignment constraints that create exceptions to general directional orientations, as well as those that establish general directional orientations. Because F-LEFT and F-RIGHT assess a violation for each misaligned foot, ranking one or both of them above PARSE-σ would prevent regular disyllabic parsing. The result might be a single disyllabic foot at the left or right edge or a form with no feet at all. This is not the case when employing GA constraints. Under the GA formulation, the constraints that create exceptions to general directional orientations only assess a violation mark for a single foot, the foot closest to the designated edge. They do not conflict with PARSE-σ, so their ranking with respect to PARSE-σ is not crucial. See Section 2.5.3 for discussion of a related issue.

6 Distance-sensitive alignment can also establish exceptions to general directional orientations, if the exception happens to be a sub-category of the category being aligned. For example, it might create a bidirectional parsing pattern by aligning a head foot in one direction and aligning feet generally in the opposite direction. This would suffice to create bidirectional patterns where the head foot is the isolated foot but not bidirectional patterns where a non-head foot is the isolated foot. This ability plays a key role in Alber's (2005) Asymmetrical Alignment account, examined in Chapter 4.

difference can be seen most clearly in unidirectional patterns. Where the distance-sensitive constraints prefer that stray syllables occur as far as possible from the designated edge, they prefer that monosyllabic feet occur as near as possible (Crowhurst and Hewitt 1995). The reason for the divergent preferences is fairly straightforward. Since it is feet that are being aligned, a stray syllable does not contribute to the assessment of violation marks through its own misalignment; it contributes only through its intervention between a foot and the designated edge of the prosodic word. Positioning a stray syllable as far from the designated edge as possible gives it less opportunity to intervene between the edge and a foot. In contrast, a foot contributes to the assessment of violation marks both through its own misalignment and through the intervention of its constituent syllables. Although a foot's size is irrelevant to the number of violation marks assessed due to its own misalignment – feet incur the same number of violation marks for the same degree of misalignment regardless of their size – a larger foot contributes to the assessment of more violation marks through the intervention of its constituent syllables than a smaller foot. In other words, a larger foot's intervention leaves its fellow feet further from the designated edge than a smaller foot's intervention. It is better to have smaller feet intervening between larger feet and the designated edge, then, than to have larger feet intervening between smaller feet and the designated edge.

RSA's distance-sensitive constraints have this same effect. For example, as (35) illustrates, ALL-F-LEFT is best satisfied when the monosyllabic foot occurs at the prosodic word's left edge with the disyllabic feet following. When the monosyllabic foot is the first foot, as in (35d), each foot in the form is as close as it can be to the left edge. Moving the monosyllabic foot one position to the right, as in (35c), so that a disyllabic foot is first and the monosyllabic foot second, simply means that the second foot is one syllable further from the left edge and participates in an additional LV. Moving the monosyllable one position further, as in (35b), so that the first two feet are disyllabic, means that the third foot is also one syllable further away. Moving the monosyllable foot into fourth position, as in (35a), means that the fourth foot is one syllable further away as well.

(35)

	ALL-F-LEFT
a. [(σσ)(σσ)(σσ) (σ)]	** **** ****!**
b. [(σσ)(σσ) (σ) (σσ)]	** **** ****!*
c. [(σσ) (σ) (σσ)(σσ)]	** *** *****!
☞ d. [(σ) (σσ)(σσ)(σσ)]	* *** *****

When ALL-F-LEFT and ALL-F-RIGHT establish general directional orientations in exhaustive parsing systems, the result is two different unidirectional parsing schemes. When implemented with both iambic feet and trochaic feet, the general directional orientations yield four stress patterns, three of which are attested. These are the same four unidirectional exhaustive parsing patterns that Symmetrical Alignment predicts with the corresponding GA constraints.

(36) Unidirectional exhaustive parsing patterns

a. PARSE-σ >> F-BIN; PARSE-σ >> ALL-F-LEFT >> ALL-F-RIGHT

i. Trochaic: Attested	ii. Iambic: Attested
(σ́σ)(σ́σ)(σ́σ)	(σσ́)(σσ́)(σσ́)
(σ́)(σ́σ)(σ́σ)(σ́σ)	(σ́)(σσ́)(σσ́)(σσ́)

b. PARSE-σ >> F-BIN; PARSE-σ >> ALL-F-RIGHT >> ALL-F-LEFT

i. Trochaic: Attested	ii. Iambic: Unattested
(σ́σ)(σ́σ)(σ́σ)	(σσ́)(σσ́)(σσ́)
(σ́σ)(σ́σ)(σ́σ)(σ́)	(σσ́)(σσ́)(σσ́)(σ́)

The second difference in exhaustive parsing systems is that alignment loses its ability to create exceptions to general directional orientations. RSA constraints are no different in this respect. Since edgemost feet *necessarily* occur at their corresponding edges of the prosodic word when parsing is exhaustive, the distance-insensitive F-LEFT and F-RIGHT cannot distinguish between the various candidates and, therefore, cannot create an exception to a general directional orientation. Since exhaustive parsing candidates tie on F-LEFT and F-RIGHT, regardless of the position of the monosyllabic foot, it is left to the distance-sensitive ALL-F-LEFT and ALL-F-RIGHT to determine the monosyllabic foot's position. It emerges at the left edge when ALL-F-LEFT is higher-ranked, and it emerges at the right edge when ALL-F-RIGHT is higher-ranked.

As the comparative tableaux in (37) and (38) indicate, the two candidates that locate the monosyllabic foot peripherally harmonically bound candidates that locate it medially. If ALL-F-LEFT is higher-ranked in (37) and (38), the (b) candidates are optimal, and the monosyllabic foot appears at the left edge. If ALL-F-RIGHT is higher-ranked, the (a) candidates are optimal, and the monosyllabic foot appears at the right edge.

(37)

	F-LEFT	F-RIGHT	ALL-F-L	ALL-F-R
w. [(σσ)(σσ) (σ) (σσ)]	3	3	11	10
a. [(σσ)(σσ)(σσ) (σ)]	3	3	12 W	9 L
b. [(σ) (σσ)(σσ)(σσ)]	3	3	9 L	12 W

(38)

	F-Left	F-Right	All-F-L	All-F-R
w. [(σσ) (σ) (σσ)(σσ)]	3	3	10	11
a. [(σσ)(σσ)(σσ) (σ)]	3	3	12 W	9 L
b. [(σ) (σσ)(σσ)(σσ)]	3	3	9 L	12 W

Like GA constraints, then, RSA constraints cannot produce the bidirectional parsing schemes exhibited by the harmonically bounded candidates (37w) and (38w). If implemented with both iambic and trochaic footing, these schemes would yield the four patterns in (39), the most striking feature of which is the internal clash created by the monosyllabic foot in odd-parity forms.

(39) Bidirectional exhaustive parsing patterns (not predicted under Symmetrical Alignment)

a. i. Trochaic: Unattested
(σ́σ)(σ́σ)(σ́σ)
(σ́σ)(σ́)(σ́σ)(σ́σ)

ii. Iambic: Unattested
(σσ́)(σσ́)(σσ́)
(σσ́)(σ́)(σσ́)(σσ́)

b. i. Trochaic: Unattested
(σ́σ)(σ́σ)(σ́σ)
(σ́σ)(σ́σ)(σ́)(σ́σ)

ii. Iambic: Unattested
(σσ́)(σσ́)(σσ́)
(σσ́)(σσ́)(σ́)(σσ́)

Since none of the internal clash patterns are attested, alignment's inability to produce them gives it an important advantage over accounts relying on iterative foot construction, which actually does produce them. The failure to appreciate that the standard OT account represents a substantial improvement over serial accounts in this respect has likely furthered proposals to implement the alignment analysis in the framework of Harmonic Serialism (Prince and Smolensky 1993/2004, McCarthy 2007), where alignment's advantage in this context is effectively relinquished. I address this point in Section 2.6. (See Hyde 2008b for discussion of how the internal clash patterns arise in earlier serial accounts such as that presented in Hayes 1995.)

2.4.3 Summary of Symmetrical Alignment's Predictions

To this point, we have seen that the RSA constraints produce the same essential directionality effects as GA constraints and that nothing is lost in replacing GA constraints with RSA constraints in the Symmetrical Alignment approach. Before proceeding, it will be helpful to summarize the predictions of the Symmetrical Alignment account so that they may be more easily compared with the predictions of the accounts to be discussed further below.

In summarizing the basic binary default patterns predicted under Symmetrical Alignment, the tables in (40) and (41) organize the predicted patterns into mirror-image pairs for ease of comparison with the typology established in Chapter 1. As (40) indicates, Symmetrical Alignment produces the four possible perfect alternation patterns, each of which is attested. Symmetrical Alignment, then, captures the generalization that perfect alternation patterns are symmetrically attested.

(40) Perfect alternation patterns predicted under Symmetrical Alignment

a. Minimal Alternation

i. Trochaic: Attested	ii. Iambic: Attested
(σ́σ)(σ́σ)(σ́σ)	(σσ́)(σσ́)(σσ́)
σ(σ́σ)(σ́σ)(σ́σ)	(σσ́)(σσ́)(σσ́)σ

b. Maximal alternation

i. Trochaic: Attested	ii. Iambic: Attested
(σ́σ)(σ́σ)(σ́σ)	(σσ́)(σσ́)(σσ́)
(σ́σ)(σ́σ)(σ́σ)(σ́)	(σ́)(σσ́)(σσ́)(σσ́)

As (41) indicates, Symmetrical Alignment also produces four mirror-image pairs, eight patterns total, that depart from perfect alternation. While the trochaic versions of these patterns are attested, the iambic versions are not. Symmetrical Alignment, then, fails to capture the generalization that patterns that depart from perfect alternation are asymmetrically attested.

(41) Departures from perfect alternation

a. Peripheral clash in odd-parity forms

i. Trochaic: Attested	ii. Iambic: Unattested
(σ́σ)(σ́σ)(σ́σ)	(σσ́)(σσ́)(σσ́)
(σ́)(σ́σ)(σ́σ)(σ́σ)	(σσ́)(σσ́)(σσ́)(σ́)

b. Peripheral lapse (final dactyl and initial anapest)

i. Trochaic: Attested	ii. Iambic: Unattested
(σ́σ)(σ́σ)(σ́σ)	(σσ́)(σσ́)(σσ́)
(σ́σ)(σ́σ)(σ́σ)σ	σ(σσ́)(σσ́)(σσ́)

c. Internal lapse (initial dactyl and final anapest)

i. Trochaic: Attested	ii. Iambic: Unattested
(σ́σ)(σ́σ)(σ́σ)	(σσ́)(σσ́)(σσ́)
(σ́σ)σ(σ́σ)(σ́σ)	(σσ́)(σσ́)σ(σσ́)

d. Internal lapse (final amphibrach and initial amphibrach)

i. Trochaic: Attested	ii. Iambic: Unattested
(σ́σ)(σ́σ)(σ́σ)	(σσ́)(σσ́)(σσ́)
(σ́σ)(σ́σ)σ(σ́σ)	(σσ́)σ(σσ́)(σσ́)

Overall, then, the Symmetrical Alignment approach predicts 12 binary default patterns, eight of which are attested. Note that the constraints included in the discussion above are not capable of producing additional attested patterns that depart from perfect alternation, such as the final lapse in even-parity forms in iambic languages such as Choctaw and Hixkaryana and the internal lapse in even-parity forms found in iambic languages such as Aguaruna, Southern Paiute, and Axininca Campa. These additional patterns require an additional constraint, NON-FINALITY, which prohibits stress on prosodic word-final syllables.

2.5 Advantages of Relation-Specific Alignment

Having seen that nothing is lost in the Symmetrical Alignment account by replacing GA constraints with RSA constraints, we now consider in fuller detail the evidence supporting the RSA approach. We begin with evidence for the crucial role of distance-sensitivity. Further below, we consider RSA's ability to avoid Midpoint Pathology effects and its use of distance-insensitive constraints to create exceptions to general directional orientations.

2.5.1 Maintaining Distance-Sensitivity

As McCarthy (2003) points out, the strongest evidence for distance-sensitive alignment comes from cases where the grammar must fix the position of categories that are necessarily misaligned. Since distance-insensitive constraints have no influence over the position of these categories, the grammar must employ distance-sensitive constraints in such cases, if equally successful alternatives cannot be found. Rhythmic Licensing (Kager 2001, 2005; Buckley 2009) is an attempt to provide just such an alternative in the context of binary stress systems.

Like the RSA implementation of the Symmetrical Alignment account discussed above, Rhythmic Licensing often employs distance-insensitive alignment constraints to fix the positions of alignable feet. To fix the positions of feet that are necessarily misaligned, however, Rhythmic Licensing replaces Symmetrical Alignment's distance-sensitive constraints with constraints that either prohibit lapse or license it in certain positions. Because both accounts have the use of distant-insensitive constraints in common, diverging only in the use of distance-sensitive constraints, we can gauge the relative effectiveness of distance-sensitive alignment and its most plausible alternative fairly directly.

Since I take it to be uncontroversial that prohibiting lapse or licensing it at prosodic word edges can be an effective method for producing simple unidirectional patterns, I limit my attention here to the crucial case of bidirectional patterns. Rhythmic Licensing produces bidirectional patterns by manipulating the position of the lapse that arises in odd-parity forms rather than the position of the feet themselves. It creates an internal lapse and then fixes its position in such a way that the stray syllable separates the appropriate edgemost foot from its companions.

Whether or not a lapse emerges in an odd-parity form and whether or not it emerges internally both depend on the positions of the peripheral feet. To create an internal lapse, the leftmost foot must occur at the left edge, and the rightmost foot at the right edge. Since the peripheral feet are actually alignable, it is a simple matter to locate them in these positions using distance-insensitive alignment constraints. Once the positions of the peripheral feet are fixed and an internal lapse established, Rhythmic Licensing fixes the position of medial feet by licensing the internal lapse in an appropriate position. Since the position of the lapse cannot be appropriately constrained by licensing it at an edge of the prosodic word, Kager takes the primary stress to be the licensor in this context.[7]

(42) LAPSE-AT-PEAK

If lapse occurs, it must be adjacent to the peak (primary stress).

If the initial foot is the head foot, LAPSE-AT-PEAK requires the stray syllable to follow, as in (43a), so that the lapse occurs next to the primary stress. This separates the initial foot from any remaining feet. If the final foot is the head foot, LAPSE-AT-PEAK requires the stray syllable to precede, as in (43b). This separates the final foot from the others.

7 Kager (2001) proposes to license lapse only next to the primary stress. To address the criticism of Alber (2005), however, that such an approach yields several unwanted predictions, Kager (2005) proposes to prohibit lapse between secondary stresses. The particular formulation involved in ensuring that the lapse occurs next to the primary stress need not concern us here.

(43) Bidirectional under-parsing patterns under Rhythmic Licensing

a. Head foot leftmost

i. Trochaic: Garawa-type	ii. Iambic: Unattested
(σ́σ)(σ̀σ)(σ̀σ)	(σσ́)(σσ̀)(σσ̀)
(σ́σ)σ(σ̀σ)(σ̀σ)	(σσ́)σ(σσ̀)(σσ̀)

b. Head foot rightmost

i. Trochaic: Piro-type	ii. Iambic: Unattested
(σ̀σ)(σ̀σ)(σ́σ)	(σσ̀)(σσ̀)(σσ́)
(σ̀σ)(σ̀σ)σ(σ́σ)	(σσ̀)(σσ̀)σ(σσ́)

Where the standard alignment account predicts that an internal lapse might occur next to a primary stress or between secondary stresses, Rhythmic Licensing predicts that it always occurs next to the primary stress. Rhythmic Licensing's adequacy as a replacement for distance-sensitive alignment depends, then, on whether or not this narrower range is sufficient to account for the internal lapse languages that are actually attested. This does not appear to be the case.

Proponents might offer two lines of defense for the assertion that lapse only arises next to a primary stress. The first, of course, is simply to deny the existence of patterns where it arises between secondary stresses. This is an impossible position to maintain given the number of prima facie counterexamples. Internal lapse between secondary stresses can be found in the initial dactyl patterns of Indonesian (Cohn 1989), Norwegian (Lorentz 1996), Spanish (Harris 1983), and, possibly, Brazilian Portuguese (Abaurre et al. 2001).[8] The second line of defense is to attribute lapse between secondary stresses to factors beyond the basic stress algorithm itself, either to morphological considerations or, perhaps, to the influence of a donor language's stress pattern.[9]

Consider the case of Spanish, where there are two potential opportunities for morphology to influence the stress pattern. It might be influenced by suffixation in the lexical phonology or by the presence of clitics in the post-lexical phonology. Citing Ladd and Roca (1986), Kager (2001) asserts that the latter option is the source of the Spanish initial dactyl. Initial dactyls, he claims, arise only when a word that would otherwise

8 Though Abaurre et al. (2001) explicitly compare Brazilian Portuguese initial dactyls to Spanish initial dactyls, they do not provide forms long enough to confirm that the lapse can occur between secondary stresses.

9 In Indonesian, forms long enough to contain initial dactyls are typically borrowings. Kager (2001) speculates that the initial dactyls arise under the influence of the donor language's (Dutch's) stress pattern.

have initial secondary stress occurs after a clitic (e.g. *èl constantìnopléño*; cf. *cònstantìnopléño*).

Counterexamples are not difficult to find, as initial dactyls frequently appear word-internally, unaccompanied by clitics. In forms long enough to support three stressed syllables, such as those in (44), the lapse occurs between secondary stresses.[10]

(44) Initial dactyls in Spanish

a. bùrocratìzación
b. gràmaticàlidád
c. màtematìcidád
d. nàturalìzación
e. ràcionalìzación

Though clitics are not the source of initial dactyls in Spanish – at least not in the forms in (44) – it is still possible that initial dactyls are the result of suffixation. Under such an analysis, earlier applications of the stress algorithm to base forms prevent free reapplication of the algorithm to suffixed forms. When a suffix is added, the algorithm applies to the suffix (and, often, to adjacent unparsed portions of the base), but the base's original stress pattern is essentially preserved. This frequently results in a pattern that is different than the one that would have emerged had the algorithm applied to the entire word at once. In the Spanish case, the claim would be that it just happens to result in initial dactyls whenever an odd number of syllables precedes the primary stress.

There appear to be no concrete proposals based on this possibility, making it difficult to assess fully, but there is ample evidence suggesting that it is incorrect. First, as Harris notes, the initial dactyl pattern emerges in words that have no relevant internal structure, such as the toponyms *Tègucigálpa, Tròmpipendécuaro,* and *Tlàtlauquìtepéc.* (In *Tlàtlauquìtepéc,* the adjacent /a/ and /u/ are heterosyllabic: *Tlà.tla.u.quì.te.péc.*) *Tlàtlauquìtepéc* is especially significant, as its lapse occurs between secondary stresses. Second, as Harris and Roca both note, suffixed forms do *not* preserve the stress pattern of base forms, the unique exception to this rule being those with the adverbial suffix *–mente.* For

10 According to Harris (1983), Harris, Spanish has two stress patterns: a unidirectional 'rhetorical' pattern where secondary stresses occur on alternate syllables preceding the primary stress, and a bidirectional 'colloquial' pattern that results in initial dactyls in odd-parity forms. The forms in (44), as well as the toponyms in the second paragraph below, are examples of the latter. They were either confirmed or supplied by native speakers from Mexico City and surrounding areas. Ladd and Roca's (1986) analysis seems to focus exclusively on the rhetorical pattern, ignoring the colloquial pattern.

example, the stress pattern of *burócrata* is preserved in *buròcrataménte*, and that of *nàturál* is preserved in *nàturàlménte*. In contrast, the stress pattern is not preserved between *nàturál* and *nàturalísta*, between *burócrata*, *bùrocràtizár*, and *bùrocratìzación*, or between *màtemático* and *màtematìcidád*.[11] Finally, the Spanish initial dactyl pattern appears to be entirely predictable given a form's length and the position of its primary stress, and distance-sensitive alignment provides a transparent analysis given just these factors. Introducing suffixation as an additional crucial factor would only render the analysis opaque and more complex. Such an analysis appears to be unworkable in any case. (For discussion of why a Transderivational Faithfulness account cannot be used to obtain the initial dactyl pattern necessary for Spanish, see Hyde and McCord 2012.)

The existence of Spanish and the other initial dactyl patterns demonstrates that Rhythmic Licensing is inadequate as a replacement for distance-sensitive alignment in the context of binary default patterns. Based on her examination of a related problem in left-oriented moraic trochee languages, Alber (2005) also concludes that Rhythmic Licensing is inadequate. The problem arises in forms where the placement of heavy syllables isolates an odd-parity string of light syllables. The feet used to parse these odd-parity strings exhibit a clear leftward orientation, as in (45a), but Rhythmic Licensing constraints discourage the clash and lapse configurations that result, preferring rightward orientation, as in (45b). Since Rhythmic Licensing constraints cannot promote the necessary leftward orientation, Rhythmic Licensing does not offer a viable alternative to alignment in this context. (See Alber 2005 for a more thorough discussion.)

(45)		a.	Leftward orientation	b.	Rightward orientation
	Initial		[(ĹL) L (H́) ...		[L (ĹL)(H́) ...
	Medial		... (H́)(ĹL) L (H́) ...		... (H́) L (ĹL)(H́) ...
	Final		... (H́)(ĹL) L]		... (H́) L (ĹL)]

Though alignment is clearly capable of producing the necessary leftward orientation, note that it is the final two cases of (45a), in particular, that demonstrate the need for distance-sensitivity. Since the feet used to

11 Ladd and Roca (1986) argue that primary stress is lexical and secondary stress post-lexical. Suffixation directly affects the position of primary stress, then, but not the position of secondary stress. The grammar does not position secondary stresses until after suffixation is already complete.

parse the light syllables are necessarily misaligned in these cases, only distance-sensitive constraints can draw them leftward.

We find additional support for distance-sensitivity in foot extrametricality and related effects, where a head foot has a rightward orientation but is necessarily misaligned because it cannot be the rightmost foot. Since it is necessarily misaligned, only distance-sensitive alignment can locate it in the appropriate position.[12] Consider, for example, the foot extrametricality effects in Paumari (Everett 2003) and Banawá (Buller, Buller, and Everett 1993; Everett 1996, 1997). In forms long enough to contain two stresses, the primary stress is always the penultimate stress.

(46) Foot extrametricality in Paumari

a.	kabáhakì	'to get rained on'
b.	àhakábarà	'dew'
c.	athànarárikì	'sticky consistency'
d.	bikànathàrarávinì	'to cave in, to fall apart quickly'

(47) Foot extrametricality in Banawá

a.	abárikò	'moon'
b.	mètuwásimà	'find them'
c.	tìnarífabùne	'you are going to work'

Since the primary stress is always the penultimate stress, it is clear that the head foot has a rightward orientation, but it also clear that there is another foot further to the right. Since the head foot is not the final foot, it is necessarily misaligned and must be coerced into penultimate position by a distance-sensitive alignment constraint.

Though they do not conform exactly to the traditional foot extrametricality pattern, other languages exhibit similar effects. In Buriat and

12 McCarthy (2003) points out that many of the languages traditionally cited as examples of foot extrametricality are not completely convincing. Though a right-oriented primary stress is set back the appropriate distance from the right edge of the word, there is no evidence that it is actually followed by a secondary stress, the clearest indication of an extrametrical foot. Of the potential cases discussed by Hayes (1995), for example, Bedouin Arabic (Blanc 1970), Cayuga (Chafe 1977, Foster 1982, Michelson 1988), Delaware (Goddard 1979, 1982), and Palestinian Arabic (Kenstowicz and Abdul-Karim 1980, Kenstowicz 1983) fall short in this respect, though Piggott (1983) does note the presence of post-tonic secondary stresses in the case of Ojibwa. Languages described in the more recent literature, however, such as those discussed here, do have the post-tonic secondary stresses necessary to make the strongest case possible.

Khalka Mongolian (Walker 1997), stress occurs on the initial syllable and every heavy syllable. The rightmost stress is primary, unless it occupies the final syllable, in which case the penultimate stress is primary.

(48) Buriat forms

a.	H̀H́LLL	tàːrúːlagdaxa	'to be adapted to'
b.	L̀H̀H́L	nàmàːtúːlxa	'to cause to be covered with leaves'
c.	L̀H́LH̀	xùdáːlingdàː	'to the husband's parents' (collective)
d.	H̀LH́H̀	xỳːxengéːrèː	'by one's own girl'

(49) Khalka forms

a.	H̀H́LL	bàegúːlagdax	'to be organized'
b.	L̀H̀H́L	xø̀ndɪ̀ːrýːlen	'to separate' (modal)
c.	H̀H́LH̀	bàigúːllagàːr	'by means of the organization'
d.	L̀H̀H́LH̀	ùlàːnbáːtaràːs	'Ulaanbaatar' (ablative)

Primary stress exhibits a clear rightward orientation in both languages, then, but it is not always the final stress. In situations where it is not, only distance-sensitive alignment can distinguish among the various nonfinal positions in which it might occur and ensure that it occurs in the rightmost.

2.5.2 Avoiding the Midpoint Pathology

To this point, we have seen that RSA successfully replicates GA's essential directionality effects, and we have seen that there is substantial evidence that distance-sensitivity must be maintained. In this part of the discussion, I will show how RSA constraints avoid Eisner's (1997) Midpoint Pathology without abandoning distance-sensitivity. As noted above, alignment constraints must have two properties to be susceptible to the Midpoint Pathology: they must be distance-sensitive, and they must be relation-general. Since GA constraints have both of these properties, they are susceptible to Midpoint Pathology effects. In contrast, RSA constraints do not have both properties. Although they can be distance-sensitive, they are always relation-specific. It is their relation-specificity that makes them immune to the Midpoint Pathology.

Recall from Section 2.1.2 the effects of the GA constraint Align (σ, L, F, L, σ), which aligns the left edge of every syllable with the left edge of a foot. In forms with just a single foot, Align (σ, L)'s combination of distance-sensitivity and relation-generality draws the left edge of the foot to the left edge of the medial syllable. As the tableau in (7), repeated in (50), illustrates, medial position is optimal because it minimizes the overall distance between the left foot edge and the left edges of *all* misaligned syllables. In (50) and (52) below, *p* denotes a violation mark derived from a misaligned syllable that precedes the foot, *f* a violation mark from a misaligned syllable that follows the foot, and *c* a violation mark from a misaligned syllable contained within the foot.

(50)

	ALIGN (σ, L)
a. [(σσ)σσσσσ]	c ff fff ffff fff!ff fffff
b. [σ(σσ)σσσσ]	p c ff fff ffff ff!fff
c. [σσ(σσ)σσσ]	pp p c ff fff ffff!
☞ d. [σσσ(σσ)σσ]	ppp pp p c ff fff
e. [σσσσ(σσ)σ]	pppp ppp pp p c ff!
f. [σσσσσ(σσ)]	ppppp pppp ppp p!p p c

Now consider how a left-edge alignment constraint like ALIGN (σ, L) would have to be formulated under RSA. The prohibited configuration in RSA's left-edge alignment schema, (18a), is one where the separator category precedes one aligned category within the other aligned category. To require left-edge alignment between syllables and feet, then, the prohibited configuration would be one where a syllable (the separator category) precedes another syllable (one aligned category) within a foot (the other aligned category). Including the separator category, *syllable*, in the definition of an LV makes the constraint distance-sensitive. The result is given in (51).

(51) ALL-σ-LEFT: $*\langle F, \sigma, \sigma \rangle$ / $[\ \ldots\ \sigma\ \ldots\ \sigma\ \ldots\ ]_F$

'Assess a violation mark for every $\langle F, \sigma, \sigma \rangle$ such that σ precedes σ within F.'

Though it is like ALIGN (σ, L) in its distance-sensitivity and its promotion of alignment between the left edges of syllables and feet, ALL-σ-LEFT cannot draw a foot to medial position. The difference is the crucial containment relationship specified in its PCM. ALL-σ-LEFT prohibits left-edge misalignment only when the syllable is contained within the foot, not when it either precedes or follows it. As (52) illustrates, since it only assesses violations for misaligned syllables contained within the foot, ALL-σ-LEFT assesses the same number of violation marks regardless of the foot's location. It has no influence at all over where the foot will ultimately appear.

(52)

	All-σ-Left
☞ a. [(σσ)σσσσσ]	c
☞ b. [σ(σσ)σσσσ]	c
☞ c. [σσ(σσ)σσσ]	c
☞ d. [σσσ(σσ)σσ]	c
☞ e. [σσσσ(σσ)σ]	c
☞ f. [σσσσσ(σσ)]	c

While the outcome leaves the position of the foot undecided, leaving the question to be settled by other constraints, an individual constraint's failure to arrive at a unique output is hardly pathological, or even problematic. In fact, this possibility is a necessary aspect of the OT framework.

While it is crucial that the theory avoid pathological predictions, the Midpoint Pathology is not merely a peripheral phenomenon manufacturing curiosities of over-generation like the one illustrated in (7)/(50). The Midpoint Pathology is so pervasive under GA that it actually prevents it from producing its essential directionality effects consistently, resulting in significant cases of under-generation. Consider again the GA constraints responsible in the Symmetrical Alignment account for establishing general directional orientations for feet within prosodic words: Align (F, L) and Align (F, R), given in (2) above. In exemplifying analyses in the literature, Align (F, L) and Align (F, R) are most often shown evaluating forms that contain a single prosodic word. In such forms, the two constraints establish the general directional orientations necessary for producing an appropriate range of directional parsing schemes. Align (F, L) establishes a general leftward orientation and Align (F, R) a general rightward orientation. The difficulty arises when the constraints evaluate forms that contain multiple prosodic words.

It is often the case that the left or right word edge nearest a foot does not belong to the prosodic word that actually contains that foot. Given this situation and the fact that Align (F, L) and Align (F, R) do not restrict their alignment requirements to feet and prosodic words that occur in a containment relationship, a candidate can often perform better by positioning a foot closer to the relevant edge of an *adjacent* prosodic word. As a result, optimal candidates are often those that seem to draw feet in both directions away from a central position, producing a different kind of Midpoint Pathology effect.

In (53), Align (F, L) draws the feet of the first prosodic word in two different directions. Rather than drawing all three feet towards the left edge of the first prosodic word, as in (53a), it draws the first two feet towards the left edge of the first and the third foot towards the left edge of the second, as in (53b). The third foot actually incurs fewer violations when evaluated with respect to the left edge of the second prosodic word. In (53), (55), and (56), *c* denotes a violation mark arising from evaluation of a foot with respect to the prosodic word that contains it and *f* a violation mark arising from evaluation with respect to a prosodic word that follows it.

(53)

		Align (F, L)
a.	[(σσ)(σσ)(σσ)σ] [(σσ)(σσ)(σσ)σ]	[cc ccc!c][cc cccc]
☞ b.	[(σσ)(σσ)σ(σσ)] [(σσ)(σσ)(σσ) σ]	[cc ff][cc cccc]

In general, Align (F, L) produces the expected left-oriented unidirectional pattern in final prosodic words, but it produces an unusual type of bidirectional pattern in nonfinal prosodic words. The effect varies, however, depending on the number of syllables that the nonfinal prosodic word contains. In nonfinal three-syllable prosodic words, the effect fails to emerge. In larger nonfinal prosodic words, the effect emerges in slightly different ways. In those that have an odd-number of feet (those with $4n + 3$ syllables), all feet to the right of the medial foot orient themselves towards the left edge of the following prosodic word, as in (54b). In those that have an even-number of feet (those with $4n + 5$ syllables), all but the leftmost of the final half must orient themselves towards the left edge of the following prosodic word. The position of the leftmost of the final half is actually left undetermined. It would have to be fixed by other, lower-ranked constraints.

(54) Effects of Align (F, L) in nonfinal prosodic words

a. 3 syllables

[σσσ] [σσ... → [(σσ)σ] [(σσ)...

b. 4n + 3 syllables ($n \geq 1$)

[σσσσσσσ] [σσ... → [(σσ)(σσ)σ(σσ)] [(σσ)...

[σσσσσσσσσσσ] [σσ... → [(σσ)(σσ)(σσ)σ(σσ)(σσ)] [(σσ)...

c. 4n + 5 syllables

[σσσσσ] [σσ... → [(σσ)(σσ)σ] [(σσ)...
or [(σσ)σ(σσ)] [(σσ)...

[σσσσσσσσσ] [σσ... → [(σσ)(σσ)(σσ)σ(σσ)] [(σσ)...
or [(σσ)(σσ)σ(σσ)(σσ)] [(σσ)...

The tableau in (55) illustrates the reason for the indeterminacy in (54c), using a nonfinal nine-syllable prosodic word. Since the third foot is equally well-aligned whether it is drawn towards the left edge of its own prosodic word, (55a), or the prosodic word that follows, (55b), ALIGN (F, L) cannot distinguish between the two positions. It allows either option.[13]

(55)		ALIGN (F, L)
☞ a.	[(σσ)(σσ)(σσ)σ(σσ)] [(σσ) ...	[cc cccc ff][...
☞ b.	[(σσ)(σσ)σ(σσ)(σσ)] [(σσ) ...	[cc ffff ff][...

The corresponding RSA constraints are not susceptible to this problem. Since ALL-F-LEFT and ALL-F-RIGHT only prohibit misalignment between feet and the prosodic words that contain them, a candidate can never improve its performance by orienting one or more of its feet towards the relevant edge of an adjacent prosodic word. Consider in (56) the effects of ALL-F-LEFT when evaluating multiple prosodic words. All three feet in the first prosodic word orient themselves towards the left edge of the first prosodic word, and all three feet in the second prosodic word orient themselves towards the left edge of the second. ALL-F-LEFT produces the expected unidirectional pattern, and no Midpoint Pathology effects emerge.

(56)		ALL-F-LEFT
☞ a.	[(σσ)(σσ)(σσ)σ] [(σσ)(σσ)(σσ)σ]	[cc cccc][cc cccc]
b.	[(σσ)(σσ)σ(σσ)] [(σσ)(σσ)(σσ)σ]	[cc ccccc!][cc cccc]

By avoiding Midpoint Pathology effects, RSA constraints establish the desired general directional orientations for feet, even in forms containing multiple prosodic words. As a result, they establish general directional orientations more reliably than GA itself.

2.5.3 Alignment Requirements and Parsing Requirements

Before concluding the discussion of directional parsing effects, it is important to note that the RSA approach to creating exceptions to general directional orientations differs from the GA approach. Where RSA employs distance-insensitive evaluation, GA employs existential

13 ALIGN (F, R) would produce a right-oriented unidirectional pattern in initial prosodic words and an unattested type of bidirectional pattern in noninitial prosodic words. I omit the additional tableaux.

quantification. The divergence is significant enough that it necessitates a revised analysis for dual stress systems, as discussed below, but it also has certain theoretical advantages.

As we saw in Section 2.1.1, ALIGN (F, L) and ALIGN (F, R) are the GA constraints that establish general directional orientations for feet within prosodic words. Since they have universal quantification over the *foot* category, their alignment requirements apply to all feet. ALIGN (F, L) draws them towards the left edge of the prosodic word, and ALIGN (F, R) draws them towards the right edge. The GA constraints that create exceptions to general directional orientations are ALIGN (ω, L, F, L, σ) and ALIGN (ω, R, F, R, σ), given in (49). Since they have existential quantification over the *foot* category, their alignment requirements need only apply to the single foot which can best satisfy them, the foot that is actually alignable.

(57) a. ALIGN (ω, L, F, L, σ)

The left edge of every prosodic word coincides with the left edge of some foot. Assess a violation mark for each syllable intervening between misaligned edges.

b. ALIGN (ω, R, F, R, σ)

The right edge of every prosodic word coincides with the right edge of some foot. Assess a violation mark for each syllable intervening between misaligned edges.

While the existential quantifier allows GA to create exceptions to general directional orientations, it also makes alignment constraints unnecessarily complex and violation assessment less straightforward. GA constraints are more complex because they not only require alignment, but they also often require parsing. Because *ACat2* is existentially quantified in the general definition, an instance of *ACat2* must be present in the output if an instance of *ACat1* is present. A GA constraint, then, can actually be violated in two ways: misalignment of category instances that are present in the output or the absence of an instance of the existentially quantified category.

Compare the demands of ALIGN (ω, L) with those of its RSA counterpart, F-LEFT. In (58), the two constraints evaluate a form with a single misaligned foot and a form with no feet. Both constraints assess violation marks for the misaligned foot. Although the distance-sensitive ALIGN (ω, L) assesses multiple violation marks where the distance-insensitive F-LEFT assesses only one, the important point in this context is simply that misalignment of existing categories runs afoul of both constraints. This is not the situation for the candidate where feet are absent. ALIGN (ω, L) – which requires some foot to be present, given the presence of the prosodic word – assesses a single violation mark. F-LEFT, which does not require a foot to be present, is vacuously satisfied.

(58)

	ALIGN (ω, L)	F-LEFT
a. [σσσσσσσ]	*	
b. [σσσσ(σσ)σ]	****	*

Where RSA constraints are simple prohibitions against misalignment, then, GA constraints require both alignment and parsing. The greater complexity is undesirable for two reasons. The first is that it is simply unnecessary. Consider the case of dual stress patterns, the case that is typically cited to demonstrate the usefulness of GA's parsing requirement. The usual situation in dual stress patterns is that found in Chimalapa Zoque (Knudson 1975), where one stress appears on the initial syllable and another on the penultimate, suggesting the presence of two trochaic feet.

(59) Chimalapa Zoque

a. wɨ̀ti hukúti — 'big fire'
b. mìnsukkéʔtpa — 'they are coming again'
c. wìtuʔpaynɨ́ksɨ — 'he is coming and going'
d. mìnsukkeʔtpaʔɨ́ttɨ — 'they were going to come again'

To produce such a pattern, the standard alignment account allows a constraint like ALIGN (F, L), which establishes a general leftward orientation for feet, to be dominated by a constraint like ALIGN (ω, R), which creates an exception for the rightmost. It then ranks both above PARSE-σ. The result, as (60) illustrates, is similar to the bidirectional patterns discussed above, but it lacks medial feet. Notice that ALIGN (ω, R) plays two distinct roles in this situation. First, in excluding a completely unparsed candidate, (60e), ALIGN (ω, R)'s parsing requirement insists that the output form contain at least one foot. Second, in excluding candidates where the final foot is misaligned, as in (60d), ALIGN (ω, R)'s alignment requirement anchors a single foot at the right edge. The decision between the remaining candidates falls to ALIGN (F, L) and PARSE-σ. ALIGN (F, L) excludes candidates with medial feet, such as (60c), but the lower-ranked PARSE-σ can still insist that a single foot occur at the left edge. It excludes the single stress pattern, (60b), in favor of the dual pattern, (60a).

(60)

	ALIGN (ω, R)	ALIGN (F, L)	PARSE-σ
☞ a. [(σ́σ)σσσ(σ́σ)]		*****	***
b. [σσσσσ(σ́σ)]		*****	****!*
c. [(σ́σ)(σ́σ)σ(σ́σ)]		** ****!*	*
d. [(σ́σ)σσσσσ]	*!****		*****
e. [σσσσσσσ]	*!		*******

At first glance, it might seem as if RSA is unable to reproduce these results. The RSA constraints corresponding to ALIGN (ω, R) and ALIGN (F, L) are F-RIGHT and ALL-F-LEFT respectively. Without the alignment-internal parsing requirement, the high-ranked F-RIGHT and ALL-F-LEFT would conspire to prevent any foot at all from appearing in the output. As Birgit Alber (personal communication) points out, however, the key is to recognize that one of the feet in a dual stress pattern is necessarily the head foot. A head foot can be required independently of feet in general, and it can be positioned independently. To produce the Chimalapa Zoque pattern, we require the presence of a head foot with the HEAD-FOOT constraint, (61a), and we use the RSA constraint HEAD-F-RIGHT, (61b), to align it with the right edge.

(61) a. HEAD-FOOT

Every prosodic word has a head foot.

b. HEAD-F-RIGHT: $*\langle \omega, F_{HD}, \sigma \rangle$ / $[\ \dots F_{HD} \dots \sigma \dots\ ]_{\omega}$

'Assess a violation mark for every $\langle \omega, F_{HD}, \sigma \rangle$ such that F_{HD} precedes σ within ω.'

As (62) illustrates, the combination of HEAD-FOOT and HEAD-F-RIGHT has the same effect as GA's ALIGN (ω, R). HEAD-FOOT excludes the footless candidate (62e), and HEAD-FOOT-RIGHT excludes the candidate where the head foot fails to position itself at the right edge, (62d). With the head foot in final position, ALL-F-LEFT excludes candidates with medial feet, such as (62c), but PARSE-σ is able to insist that an initial foot appear, excluding (62b) in favor of (62a).

(62)

	HD-FOOT	HD-F-R	ALL-F-L	PARSE-σ
☞ a. [(σ̀σ)σσσ(σ́σ)]			*****	***
b. [σσσσσ(σ́σ)]			*****	****!*
c. [(σ̀σ)(σ̀σ)σ(σ́σ)]			** ****!*	*
d. [(σ́σ)σσσσσ]		*!****		*****
e. [σσσσσσσ]	*!			*******

Parsing requirements and alignment requirements work just as well, then, when separate and related by ranking as they do when combined into a single complex constraint.

The second reason to avoid combining an alignment requirement with a parsing requirement in the same constraint is that it undermines the very strong position that OT takes on the way that linguistic principles interact with each other. One of the most interesting aspects of OT is its assertion that linguistic principles are implemented as simple constraints and that each principle/constraint relates to every other principle/constraint in one way and one way only: ranking. By including both in a single constraint, GA stipulates a non-ranking interaction between an alignment requirement and a parsing requirement, weakening the framework's theoretical position. In decoupling the alignment requirement from the parsing requirement, RSA helps to maintain the stronger position.

2.6 Iterative Foot Optimization

Having seen that nothing is lost when RSA constraints replace GA constraints in the Symmetrical Alignment account, and that RSA constraints actually have several advantages over GA constraints, we turn now to the Iterative Foot Optimization account of Pruitt (2008, 2010; see also McCarthy 2008). The examination of Iterative Foot Optimization at this point has two purposes. The first is to demonstrate that parallel evaluation is necessary for alignment constraints to produce their essential directionality effects. Though I will continue to employ RSA constraints in the discussion below, the results in this context are the same as those that would be obtained with GA constraints. The second is to provide an initial picture of the basic typology predicted under Iterative Foot Optimization, which we examine in fuller detail in Chapter 3.

Iterative Foot Optimization adopts the same Weak Layering assumptions as Symmetrical Alignment and utilizes the same set of constraints. PARSE-σ requires that syllables be parsed into feet, F-BIN requires that feet be disyllabic, and alignment constraints orient feet towards one edge or the other of the prosodic word. Because Iterative Foot Optimization is implemented within Harmonic Serialism, however, the constraints do not evaluate all possible output candidates in a single step, as they would in standard OT. Instead, they perform a series of evaluations on smaller, derivationally-related candidate sets.

In the first evaluation, the constraints consider the subset of candidates that differ in at most one respect from the input, selecting an optimal output from among them. The output then becomes the input to the next evaluation. The constraints consider the subsets of candidates with at most a single difference from the new input and arrive at a new output. The new output then becomes the input, and the process is repeated until the optimal output is the faithful candidate. For Iterative Foot Optimization, this essentially means that feet are added one at a time, and there is an evaluation after each addition to determine the foot's size and position.

Like Symmetrical Alignment, Iterative Foot Optimization predicts the unidirectional patterns in (63, 64), but there are slight differences in the crucial rankings involved. When the under-parsing ranking F-BIN >> PARSE-σ creates a stray syllable in odd-parity forms, as in (63), the alignment constraints locate the stray syllable just as they do in Symmetrical Alignment. ALL-F-LEFT pushes it to the right edge, and ALL-F-RIGHT pushes it to the left edge.

(63) Unidirectional under-parsing patterns under Iterative Foot Optimization

a. F-BIN >> PARSE-σ >> ALL-F-LEFT >> ALL-F-RIGHT

i. Trochaic: Attested	ii. Iambic: Attested
(σ́σ)(σ́σ)(σ́σ)	(σσ́)(σσ́)(σσ́)
(σ́σ)(σ́σ)(σ́σ)σ	(σσ́)(σσ́)(σσ́)σ

b. F-BIN >> PARSE-σ >> ALL-F-RIGHT >> ALL-F-LEFT

i. Trochaic: Attested	ii. Iambic: Unattested
(σ́σ)(σ́σ)(σ́σ)	(σσ́)(σσ́)(σσ́)
σ(σ́σ)(σ́σ)(σ́σ)	σ(σσ́)(σσ́)(σσ́)

When the exhaustive parsing ranking PARSE-σ >> F-BIN creates a monosyllabic foot in odd-parity forms, as in (64), however, the effect of the alignment constraints appears to be different than it is in Symmetrical Alignment. ALL-F-LEFT appears to push the monosyllabic foot to the right edge, just as it would a stray syllable, and ALL-F-RIGHT appears to push the monosyllabic foot to the left edge, just as it would a stray syllable.

(64) Unidirectional Exhaustive Patterns under Iterative Foot Optimization

a. PARSE-σ >> F-BIN; PARSE-σ >> ALL-F-LEFT >> ALL-F-RIGHT

i. Trochaic: Attested
(σ́σ)(σ́σ)(σ́σ)
(σ́σ)(σ́σ)(σ́σ)(σ́)

ii. Iambic: Unattested
(σσ́)(σσ́)(σσ́)
(σσ́)(σσ́)(σσ́)(σ́)

b. PARSE-σ >> F-BIN; PARSE-σ >> ALL-F-RIGHT >> ALL-F-LEFT

i. Trochaic: Attested
(σ́σ)(σ́σ)(σ́σ)
(σ́)(σ́σ)(σ́σ)(σ́σ)

ii. Iambic: Attested
(σσ́)(σσ́)(σσ́)
(σ́)(σσ́)(σσ́)(σσ́)

At first glance, then, alignment seems to have a more uniform effect on unparsed syllables and monosyllabic feet under Harmonic Serialism than it does under standard OT, pushing both away from the designated edge of alignment. A more careful examination, however, reveals that this is not truly the case. Under Iterative Foot Optimization, syllables are parsed one foot at a time and there is an evaluation after each foot is added to determine its size and position. For example, the left-oriented under-parsing pattern of (63a) is the result of the four-step derivation in (65). In the first step, at most a single foot is added to the input form to produce candidates for evaluation. F-BIN and PARSE-σ ensure that the output contains a foot and that it is disyllabic. ALL-F-LEFT draws it to the left edge of the prosodic word, pushing any stray syllables to the right. In the second and third steps, F-BIN and PARSE-σ again ensure that a disyllabic foot is added, and ALL-F-LEFT locates it next to the foot constructed in the previous step, pushing any stray syllables to the right. In the final step, the ranking F-BIN >> PARSE-σ ensures that leftover syllable – the final syllable, in this case – remains unparsed.

(65)

σσσσσσσ	Ft-Bin	Parse-Syll	All-Feet-L
☞ w. (σσ)σσσσσ		5	
a. (σ)σσσσσσ	1 W	6 W	
b. σσσσσ(σσ)		5	5 W
c. σσσσσσσ		7 W	

▶ (σσ)σσσσσ	Ft-Bin	Parse-Syll	All-Feet-L
☞ w. (σσ)(σσ)σσσ		3	2
a. (σσ)(σ)σσσσ	1 W	4 W	2
b. (σσ)σσσ(σσ)		3	5 W
c. (σσ)σσσσσ		5 W	L

▶ (σσ)(σσ)σσσ	Ft-Bin	Parse-Syll	All-Feet-L
☞ w. (σσ)(σσ)(σσ)σ		1	6
a. (σσ)(σσ)(σ)σσ	1 W	2 W	6
b. (σσ)(σσ)σ(σσ)		1	7 W
c. (σσ)(σσ)σσσ		3 W	2 L

▶ (σσ)(σσ)(σσ)σ	Ft-Bin	Parse-Syll	All-Feet-L
☞ w. (σσ)(σσ)(σσ)σ		1	6
l. (σσ)(σσ)(σσ)(σ)	1 W	L	12 W

The left-oriented exhaustive parsing pattern of (64a) arises from the derivation in (66), whose first three steps are identical to those in (65). In each of the first three steps, Parse-σ and F-Bin create a disyllabic foot, and All-F-Left draws it as close to the left edge as possible, pushing any stray syllables to the right. As in (65), this leaves just the final syllable unparsed at the end of the third step. The difference is in the fourth step. In (66), the ranking Parse-σ >> F-Bin ensures that the leftover syllable is parsed as a monosyllabic foot.

(66)

σσσσσσσ	Parse-Syll	Ft-Bin	All-Feet-L
☞ w. (σσ)σσσσσ	5		
a. (σ)σσσσσσ	W 6	W 1	
b. σσσσσ(σσ)	5		W 5
c. σσσσσσσ	W 7		

(σσ)σσσσσ	Parse-Syll	Ft-Bin	All-Feet-L
☞ w. (σσ)(σσ)σσσ	3		2
a. (σσ)(σ)σσσσ	W 4	W 1	2
b. (σσ)σσσ(σσ)	3		W 5
c. (σσ)σσσσσ	W 5		L

(σσ)(σσ)σσσ	Parse-Syll	Ft-Bin	All-Feet-L
☞ w. (σσ)(σσ)(σσ)σ	1		6
a. (σσ)(σσ)(σ)σσ	W 2	W 1	6
b. (σσ)(σσ)σ(σσ)	1		W 7
c. (σσ)(σσ)σσσ	W 3		L 2

(σσ)(σσ)(σσ)σ	Parse-Syll	Ft-Bin	All-Feet-L
☞ w. (σσ)(σσ)(σσ)(σ)		1	12
l. (σσ)(σσ)(σσ)σ	W 1	L	L 6

In comparing the derivations in (65, 66) we can see that alignment's effects on unparsed syllables and monosyllabic feet have not really changed at all from those in Symmetrical Alignment. The difference in Iterative Foot Optimization is that alignment never actually influences the positions of monosyllabic feet directly. In the first three steps in both derivations, ALL-F-LEFT draws a disyllabic foot to the left and pushes the unparsed syllables to the right. In the final step, when the position of the leftover syllable has already been determined – it is final, in this case – alignment has no influence. It is not until this point, however, that the ultimate parsing status of the leftover syllable is decided. In (65), the leftover syllable remains unparsed; in (66), it is parsed as a monosyllabic foot. The unparsed syllable and the monosyllabic foot both end up in the same position, then, but only because alignment is actually positioning unparsed syllables in both cases. It is an important point to note because it is also the reason that Iterative Foot Optimization predicts four additional unattested patterns.

In addition to the eight unidirectional patterns in (63, 64), Iterative Foot Optimization predicts the eight bidirectional patterns in (67, 68). Although its bidirectional patterns emerge under rankings similar to those employed in Symmetrical Alignment, Iterative Foot Optimization not only produces bidirectional patterns in under-parsing systems, it also produces bidirectional patterns in exhaustive parsing systems. Since the exhaustive parsing versions are all unattested, this is not a desirable result.

When the under-parsing ranking F-BIN >> PARSE-σ creates a stray syllable in odd-parity forms, as in (67), F-LEFT and F-RIGHT can create exceptions to general directional orientations much as they do in Symmetrical Alignment. The ranking F-LEFT >> ALL-F-RIGHT positions the stray syllable just to the right of the initial foot, as (67a), and the ranking F-RIGHT >> ALL-F-LEFT positions it just to the left of the final foot, as in (67b).

(67) Bidirectional Under-parsing Patterns under Iterative Foot Optimization

a. F-BIN >> PARSE-σ >> F-LEFT >> ALL-F-RIGHT

i. Trochaic: Attested	ii. Iambic: Unattested
(σ́σ)(σ́σ)(σ́σ)	(σσ́)(σσ́)(σσ́)
(σ́σ)σ(σ́σ)(σ́σ)	(σσ́)σ(σσ́)(σσ́)

b. F-BIN >> PARSE-σ >> F-RIGHT >> ALL-F-LEFT

i. Trochaic: Attested
(σ́σ)(σ́σ)(σ́σ)
(σ́σ)(σ́σ)σ(σ́σ)

ii. Iambic: Unattested
(σσ́)(σσ́)(σσ́)
(σσ́)(σσ́)σ(σσ́)

Similar patterns emerge, with a monosyllabic foot replacing the stray syllable, under the exhaustive parsing ranking PARSE-σ >> F-BIN. The ranking F-LEFT >> ALL-F-RIGHT positions the monosyllabic foot just to the right of the initial foot, as in (68a), and the ranking F-RIGHT >> ALL-F-LEFT positions it just to the left of the final foot, as in (68b).

(68) Bidirectional Exhaustive Parsing Patterns under Iterative Foot Optimization

a. PARSE-σ >> F-BIN; PARSE-σ >> F-LEFT >> ALL-F-RIGHT

i. Trochaic: Unattested
(σ́σ)(σ́σ)(σ́σ)
(σ́σ)(σ́)(σ́σ)(σ́σ)

ii. Iambic: Unattested
(σσ́)(σσ́)(σσ́)
(σσ́)(σ́)(σσ́)(σσ́)

b. PARSE-σ >> F-BIN; PARSE-σ >> F-RIGHT >> ALL-F-LEFT

i. Trochaic: Unattested
(σ́σ)(σ́σ)(σ́σ)
(σ́σ)(σ́σ)(σ́)(σ́σ)

ii. Iambic: Unattested
(σσ́)(σσ́)(σσ́)
(σσ́)(σσ́)(σ́)(σσ́)

To get a better understanding of why Iterative Foot Optimization predicts bidirectional parsing patterns in both under-parsing and exhaustive parsing systems, we can consider the derivations responsible for the under-parsing pattern of (67a) in (69) and the exhaustive parsing pattern of (68a) in (70). In the first step in the under-parsing derivation in (69), F-BIN and PARSE-σ ensure that a disyllabic foot is added to the input form. F-LEFT draws it to the prosodic word's left edge, pushing the unparsed syllables to the right. In the second step, a second disyllabic foot is added. In this case, however, ALL-F-RIGHT draws it to the right edge, pushing the unparsed syllables towards the initial foot. In third step, a final disyllabic foot is added, and ALL-F-RIGHT positions it just to the left of the final foot, leaving only the post-peninitial syllable unparsed. In the final step, the ranking F-BIN >> PARSE-σ ensures that the post-peninitial syllable remains unfooted.

(69)

σσσσσσσ	F-Bin	Parse-σ	F-Left	All-F-R
☞ w. (σσ)σσσσσ		5		5
a. (σ)σσσσσσ	W 1	W 6		W 6
b. σσσσσ(σσ)		5	W 1	L
c. σσσσσσσ		W 7		L

▶ (σσ)σσσσσ	F-Bin	Parse-σ	F-Left	All-F-R
☞ w. (σσ)σσσ(σσ)		3	1	5
a. (σσ)σσσσ(σ)	W 1	W 4	1	5
b. (σσ)(σσ)σσσ		3	1	W 8
c. (σσ)σσσσσ		W 5	L	5

▶ (σσ)σσσ(σσ)	F-Bin	Parse-σ	F-Left	All-F-R
☞ w. (σσ)σ(σσ)(σσ)		1	2	7
a. (σσ)σσ(σ)(σσ)	W 1	W 2	2	7
b. (σσ)(σσ)σ(σσ)		1	2	W 8
c. (σσ)σσσ(σσ)		W 3	L 1	L 5

▶ (σσ)σ(σσ)(σσ)	F-Bin	Parse-σ	F-Left	All-F-R
☞ w. (σσ)σ(σσ)(σσ)		1	2	7
l. (σσ)(σ)(σσ)(σσ)	W 1	L	W 3	W 11

Under the exhaustive parsing ranking in (70), the first three steps of the derivation are identical to those under the under-parsing ranking in (69). Notice that in each of these steps the alignment constraints are determining the relative positions of disyllabic feet and unparsed syllables. At no point do they influence the position of a monosyllabic foot directly. In the final step, once the position of the leftover syllable has already been determined, the ranking Parse-σ >> F-Bin converts the leftover syllable – once again, the post-peninitial syllable – into a monosyllabic foot.

(70)

σσσσσσσ	Parse-σ	F-Bin	F-Left	All-F-R
☞ w. (σσ)σσσσσ	5			5
a. (σ)σσσσσσ	W 6	W 1		W 6
b. σσσσσ(σσ)	5		W 1	L
c. σσσσσσσ	W 7			L

(σσ)σσσσσ	Parse-σ	F-Bin	F-Left	All-F-R
☞ w. (σσ)σσσ(σσ)	3		1	5
a. (σσ)σσσσ(σ)	W 4	W 1	1	5
b. (σσ)(σσ)σσσ	3		1	W 8
c. (σσ)σσσσσ	W 5		L	5

(σσ)σσσ(σσ)	Parse-σ	F-Bin	F-Left	All-F-R
☞ w. (σσ)σ(σσ)(σσ)	1		2	7
a. (σσ)σσ(σ)(σσ)	W 2	W 1	2	7
b. (σσ)(σσ)σ(σσ)	1		2	W 8
c. (σσ)σσσ(σσ)	W 3		L	L 5

(σσ)σ(σσ)(σσ)	Parse-σ	F-Bin	F-Left	All-F-R
☞ w. (σσ)(σ)(σσ)(σσ)		1	3	11
l. (σσ)σ(σσ)(σσ)	W 1	L	L 2	L 7

Since it is the only difference between Symmetrical Alignment and Iterative Foot Optimization, the latter's serialism is easily identifiable as the source of the four additional bidirectional patterns. The connection is not difficult to make. In Symmetrical Alignment, parallel evaluation determines a leftover syllable's position and parsing status *simultaneously*. A leftover syllable that ultimately emerges as an unparsed syllable is positioned as an unparsed syllable, and a leftover syllable that ultimately emerges as a monosyllabic foot is positioned as a monosyllabic foot. Since alignment can locate monosyllabic feet in only a subset of the positions in which it can locate unparsed syllables, Symmetrical Alignment predicts fewer exhaustive parsing patterns than under-parsing patterns. In particular, it predicts both unidirectional and bidirectional under-parsing patterns but only unidirectional exhaustive parsing patterns.

In Iterative Foot Optimization, serial evaluation determines a leftover syllable's position and its parsing status at different stages of the derivation. During the stages of the derivation in which alignment constraints determine its position, the leftover syllable is always unparsed. It is only *after* its position has been fixed that the ranking between PARSE-σ and F-BIN determines whether it will remain unparsed or be parsed as a monosyllabic foot. Since alignment never influences monosyllabic feet directly, its more stringent restrictions on the positions of monosyllabic feet are never felt, and they can occur in every position in which unparsed syllables occur. Not only do unidirectional patterns with unparsed syllables have corresponding patterns with monosyllabic feet in the same position, then, but bidirectional patterns with unparsed syllables also have corresponding patterns with monosyllabic feet in the same position.

2.7 Summary of Iterative Foot Optimization's Predictions

The basic binary default patterns predicted under Iterative Foot Optimization are summarized in the tables in (71–73). The patterns are organized into mirror-image pairs for ease of comparison with the typology established in Chapter 1. As (71) indicates, Iterative Foot Optimization produces the four possible perfect alternation patterns, each of which is attested. Like Symmetrical Alignment, then, Iterative Foot Optimization captures the generalization that perfect alternation patterns are symmetrically attested.

(71) Perfect alternation patterns predicted under Iterative Foot Optimization

a. Minimal Alternation

i. Trochaic: Attested	ii. Iambic: Attested
(σ́σ)(σ́σ)(σ́σ)	(σσ́)(σσ́)(σσ́)
σ(σ́σ)(σ́σ)(σ́σ)	(σσ́)(σσ́)(σσ́)σ

b. Maximal alternation

i. Trochaic: Attested	ii. Iambic: Attested
(σ́σ)(σ́σ)(σ́σ)	(σσ́)(σσ́)(σσ́)
(σ́σ)(σ́σ)(σ́σ)(σ́)	(σ́)(σσ́)(σσ́)(σσ́)

As (72) and (73) indicate, Iterative Foot Optimization also produces six mirror-image pairs, 12 patterns total, that depart from perfect alternation. Like Symmetrical Alignment, then, Iterative Foot Optimization fails to capture the generalization that patterns that depart from perfect alternation are asymmetrically attested or symmetrically unattested. The patterns in (72) are under-parsing patterns that depart from perfect alternation. The patterns in (73) are exhaustive parsing patterns.

(72) Under-parsing departures from perfect alternation

a. Peripheral lapse (final dactyl and initial anapest)

i. Trochaic: Attested	ii. Iambic: Unattested
(σ́σ)(σ́σ)(σ́σ)	(σσ́)(σσ́)(σσ́)
(σ́σ)(σ́σ)(σ́σ)σ	σ(σσ́)(σσ́)(σσ́)

b. Internal lapse (initial dactyl and final anapest)

i. Trochaic: Attested	ii. Iambic: Unattested
(σ́σ)(σ́σ)(σ́σ)	(σσ́)(σσ́)(σσ́)
(σ́σ)σ(σ́σ)(σ́σ)	(σσ́)(σσ́)σ(σσ́)

c. Internal lapse (final amphibrach and initial amphibrach)

i. Trochaic: Attested	ii. Iambic: Unattested
(σ́σ)(σ́σ)(σ́σ)	(σσ́)(σσ́)(σσ́)
(σ́σ)(σ́σ)σ(σ́σ)	(σσ́)σ(σσ́)(σσ́)

(73) Exhaustive parsing departures from perfect alternation

a. Peripheral clash in odd-parity forms

i. Trochaic: Attested	ii. Iambic: Unattested
(σ́σ)(σ́σ)(σ́σ)	(σσ́)(σσ́)(σσ́)
(σ́)(σ́σ)(σ́σ)(σ́σ)	(σσ́)(σσ́)(σσ́)(σ́)

b. Internal clash adjacent to penultimate or peninitial syllable

i. Trochaic: Unattested
(σ́σ)(σ́σ)(σ́σ)
(σ́σ)(σ́)(σ́σ)(σ́σ)

ii. Iambic: Unattested
(σσ́)(σσ́)(σσ́)
(σσ́)(σσ́)(σ́)(σσ́)

c. Internal clash adjacent to initial or final syllable

i. Trochaic: Unattested
(σ́σ)(σ́σ)(σ́σ)
(σ́σ)(σ́σ)(σ́)(σ́σ)

ii. Iambic: Unattested
(σσ́)(σσ́)(σσ́)
(σσ́)(σ́)(σσ́)(σσ́)

Overall, then, Iterative Foot Optimization predicts 16 binary default patterns, eight of which are attested. It predicts the same eight attested patterns predicted by Symmetrical Alignment, but it predicts four more unattested patterns.

2.8 Summary

We have seen that Relation-Specific Alignment constraints successfully reproduce Generalized Alignment's essential directionality effects by exploiting the different types of influence that distance-sensitive and distance-insensitive constraints have over the position of category instances. Because they can influence the positions of both alignable instances and instances that are necessarily misaligned, distance-sensitive constraints can establish general directional orientations. Because they influence the position of alignable instances only, distance-insensitive constraints can only create exceptions to general directional orientations.

An empirical advantage of RSA's relation-specificity, is that it allows RSA to avoid Midpoint Pathology effects without abandoning distance-sensitivity and losing the ability to produce essential directionality effects. In fact, in avoiding Midpoint Pathology effects, RSA not only escapes the Midpoint Pathology's characteristic curiosities of over-generation, it is also able to produce essential directionality effects more consistently than GA itself. In Chapter 6, we will examine a second empirical advantage: relation-specificity allows RSA to provide a general account of trisyllabic and other stress windows.

In creating exceptions to general directional orientations through distance-insensitive evaluation, RSA also has an important theoretical advantage over GA. By employing existential quantification to produce exceptions to general directional orientations, GA combines alignment and parsing requirements into a single constraint, making them unnecessarily complex and undermining OT's position that the only relationship between such basic requirements is that established by ranking. The RSA approach keeps alignment and parsing requirements separate, allowing the theory to maintain the stronger position.

Comparing the Symmetrical Alignment analysis of bidirectional under-parsing schemes to the Rhythmic Licensing analysis, we saw that Weak Layering approaches must include distance-sensitive alignment constraints in order to produce a sufficiently wide range of bidirectional patterns. They cannot be replaced by constraints that license rhythmic irregularities near prominent structures. Languages with foot extrametricality and similar effects also support distance-sensitivity.

Comparing the predictions of Symmetrical Alignment in standard OT to those on Iterative Foot Optimization in Harmonic Serialism, we saw that alignment's ability to avoid bidirectional exhaustive parsing patterns depends on parallel evaluation. The ability is lost under the serial approach, primarily because alignment never actually has a chance to influence the position of monosyllabic feet directly.

3 Prosodic Layering

In addressing directional parsing mechanisms in the previous chapter, the primary examples employed were two Weak Layering approaches, Symmetrical Alignment (McCarthy and Prince 1993a) and Iterative Foot Optimization (Pruitt 2008, 2010). While both predicted a number of unattested patterns, the latter a significantly greater number than the former, both were reasonably successful at capturing the range of attested patterns. As is typical in most examinations of quantity-insensitive patterns in the literature, however, the predictions were obtained under an idealized condition: all syllables were treated as if they were light so that distinctions in syllable weight were not actually considered.

In this chapter and the following, we consider the effects of weight distinctions in four Weak Layering accounts: Symmetrical Alignment, Iterative Foot Optimization, Asymmetrical Alignment (Alber 2005), and Rhythmic Licensing (Kager 2001, 2005; see also McCarthy 2003 and Buckley 2009). We also consider the effects of faithfulness violations. As we shall see, under these more realistic conditions, the predictions of Weak Layering accounts are really quite different. In fact, problems arise in the predicted typologies that are so significant that Weak Layering cannot be seen as providing a reasonable foundation for the theory of metrical stress. I focus on Symmetrical Alignment and Iterative Foot Optimization in this chapter and turn to Asymmetrical Alignment and Rhythmic Licensing in Chapter 4.

3.1 Parsing and Minimality

The requirement that syllables be parsed into feet is one of the most well-motivated requirements in phonological theory. Beyond their role in helping to establish stress patterns, feet play an important part in a variety of phenomena. Asymmetries between iambic and trochaic stress systems in rhythmic lengthening, rhythmic shortening, and quantity-sensitivity would all be difficult, if not impossible, to capture in the absence of iambic and trochaic feet (Hayes 1985, 1995; Prince 1991; Kager 1993; van de Vijver 1998; Hyde 2007b; among others).[1] Feet are often crucial in defining the domains of segmental rule application (Leer 1985, Nespor and Vogel 1986, Rice 1992, Hayes 1995, Vaysman 2009, Gordon 2011, among others). Foot structure often plays a central role in capturing differences in the behavior of vowels in unstressed syllables (Kager 1989, Dresher and Lahiri 1991, Bye 1996, Hermans 2011, among others). These are just a few of the possible citations. (See Hayes 1995, Hermans 2011, and Gordon 2011 for partial summaries.)

The requirement that feet be binary – either bimoraic or disyllabic – is also well-motivated. Many languages explicitly reject feet built on a single light (monomoraic) syllable, preventing such syllables from being stressed if they cannot be paired with another, but no language explicitly rejects feet built on a single heavy (bimoraic) syllable (Prince 1980, McCarthy and Prince 1986, Hayes 1995). In languages that prohibit words containing less than two moras, the minimal word restriction is typically a straightforward consequence of a minimal foot restriction (McCarthy and Prince 1986, Hayes 1995). In many cases of reduplication, size restrictions on the reduplicant can be explained if it must contain a binary foot (McCarthy and Prince 1986).

Since the parsing and minimality requirements are both so well-motivated, it would be somewhat surprising if they were responsible for any significant shortcomings in the theory's predictions. Yet, this is exactly the situation that obtains in most recent proposals in metrical stress theory, including Symmetrical Alignment, Iterative Foot Optimization, Asymmetrical Alignment, and Rhythmic Licensing. The shortcomings arise, not because of the parsing and minimality requirements themselves, but because of the particular options that

1 One long-standing generalization that has endured particularly well is that iambic and trochaic languages exhibit different characteristics in conjunction with quantity-sensitivity: the two types resume basic binary alternations differently after encountering a heavy syllable (Hayes 1985, 1995; Kager 1993). The limitation of rhythmic shortening to trochaic languages is also well-established (Hayes 1985, 1995; Kager 1993), though it appears that a language must also be quantity-sensitive to allow rhythmic shortening (Mellander 2003). Asymmetries in rhythmic lengthening, however, appear to be finer-grained than supposed in much of the previous literature, being keyed to the presence or absence of quantity-sensitivity. Among quantity-sensitive languages, rhythmic lengthening can be found in iambic systems but not trochaic systems; among quantity-insensitive languages, it can be found in trochaic systems but not iambic systems (Mellander 2003, Hyde 2012b).

the proposals employ to satisfy the requirements for inputs with an odd number of syllables.

Together, the parsing and minimality requirements demand exhaustive parsing of syllables into binary feet. Achieving exhaustive binary parsing for even-parity inputs is a relatively simple matter. Each syllable can be grouped with an adjacent syllable to form a disyllabic foot, as in (1a), so that none is left over. Achieving exhaustive binary parsing for odd-parity inputs, however, is not so straightforward. After as many syllables are grouped into disyllabic feet as possible, there is a still a single syllable left over, as in (1b).

(1) a. Even-parity
(σσ)(σσ)(σσ)

b. Odd-parity
(σσ)(σσ)(σσ) $\underline{\sigma}$
(σσ)(σσ) $\underline{\sigma}$ (σσ)
(σσ) $\underline{\sigma}$ (σσ)(σσ)
$\underline{\sigma}$ (σσ)(σσ)(σσ)

Although they are not always obvious, there are several options for accommodating the leftover syllable of an odd-parity input in a way that achieves exhaustive binary parsing. There are essentially three possibilities. First, if the odd-parity input contains a heavy (bimoraic) syllable in an odd-numbered position, the heavy syllable can be parsed as a monosyllabic foot with the remaining syllables parsed into disyllabic feet, as in (2a). Second, the odd-parity input can be converted into an even-parity output, either through insertion of a single syllable or deletion of a single syllable, so that each syllable in the output can be included in a disyllabic foot, as in (2b). Finally, the leftover syllable from an odd-parity input can be included in a disyllabic foot that overlaps another disyllabic foot, as in (2c).

(2) Exhaustive binary parsing for odd-parity inputs

a. Odd-numbered H foot
σσHσσσσ → (σσ)(H)(σσ)(σσ)

b. Convert to even-parity
σσσσσσσ → (σσ)(σσ)(σσ)(σσ) or (σσ)(σσ)(σσ)

c. Overlapping feet
σσσσσσσ → σ σ σ σ σ σ σ
\/ \/ \/\/

While the option in (2c) is somewhat unconventional, since it involves improper bracketing, it is actually the options in (2a,b) that result in the shortcomings associated with the parsing and minimality requirements. In fact, as we shall see below, the unconventional option in (2c) is the key to avoiding these shortcomings. If the theory does not allow feet to overlap, pathological patterns emerge, and they emerge in such numbers that they dominate the predicted typology.

I will refer to the set of pathological predictions that can arise in an effort to achieve exhaustive binary parsing (without overlapping feet) as the *Odd-Parity Input Problem* (OPIP). The OPIP can be usefully divided into two sub-problems: the *Odd Heavy Problem* (OHP) arises when an odd-numbered heavy syllable is parsed as a monosyllabic foot to achieve exhaustive binary parsing, the option in (2a), and the *Even Output Problem* (EOP) arises when the odd-parity input is converted to an even-parity output to achieve exhaustive binary parsing, the option in (2b).

3.1.1 Monosyllabic feet and the Odd Heavy Problem

The first option for achieving exhaustive binary parsing for odd-parity inputs is to parse an odd-numbered heavy syllable as a monosyllabic foot, as in (3). When an odd-numbered heavy syllable is parsed as a monosyllabic foot in an odd-parity output, the substrings on either side of the heavy syllable are even-parity and can easily be divided into disyllabic feet. Since the heavy monosyllabic foot is bimoraic, it is binary like the disyllabic feet, and exhaustive binary parsing is achieved.

(3) Parsing an odd-numbered heavy syllable as a monosyllabic foot

(σσ)(σσ)(σσ)(H)

(σσ)(σσ)(H)(σσ)

(σσ)(H)(σσ)(σσ)

(H)(σσ)(σσ)(σσ)

Achieving exhaustive binary parsing in this fashion results in the Odd Heavy Problem. To give an initial characterization, the OHP is a peculiar type of quantity-sensitivity arising in what is otherwise a quantity-insensitive system. An output form will parse a single heavy syllable as a monosyllabic foot, only if it is odd-parity and only if the heavy syllable occupies an odd-numbered position in the string. The peculiar restriction arises because it is only when a heavy monosyllabic foot occurs in an odd-numbered position in an odd-parity form that it helps to achieve exhaustive binary parsing.

(4) The Odd Heavy Problem

A single heavy syllable *H* is parsed as a monosyllabic foot if and only if

a. *H* occurs in an odd-parity form

b. *H* is located in an odd-numbered position

To illustrate, in a truly quantity-insensitive system, we expect stresses to occur in the same position in all forms – regardless of the number of syllables, regardless of the presence or absence of heavy syllables, and regardless of the position in which heavy syllables occur. If stress occupies every even-numbered syllable from the right in a quantity insensitive-sensitive system, as (5) illustrates, then it occupies every even numbered syllable from the right in both even- and odd-parity forms regardless of whether or not they contain heavy syllables and regardless of the position in which heavy syllables might arise.

(5) True quantity-insensitivity

a.	Even-parity, L syllables only	(Ĺ L)(Ĺ L)(Ĺ L)
b.	Even-parity, even-numbered H syllable	(Ĺ L)(Ĺ H)(Ĺ L)
c.	Even-parity, odd-numbered H syllable	(Ĺ L)(H́ L)(Ĺ L)
d.	Odd-parity, L syllables only	L(Ĺ L)(Ĺ L)(Ĺ L)
e.	Odd-parity, even-numbered H syllable	L(Ĺ L)(H́ L)(Ĺ L)
f.	Odd-parity, odd-numbered H syllable	L(Ĺ H)(Ĺ L)(Ĺ L)

In a system afflicted with the OHP, however, stresses do not occur in the same positions in all forms. As (6a-e) illustrate, they occupy the same positions in even-parity forms, in odd-parity forms containing only light syllables, and in odd-parity forms where heavy syllables occur only in even-numbered positions. The stress pattern shifts, however, as (6f) illustrates, in odd-parity forms with odd-numbered heavy syllables.

(6) OHP-induced quantity-sensitivity

a.	Even-parity, L syllables only	(Ĺ L)(Ĺ L)(Ĺ L)
b.	Even-parity, even-numbered H syllable	(Ĺ L)(Ĺ H)(Ĺ L)
c.	Even-parity, odd-numbered H syllable	(Ĺ L)(H́ L)(Ĺ L)
d.	Odd-parity, L syllables only	L(Ĺ L)(Ĺ L)(Ĺ L)
e.	Odd-parity, even-numbered H syllable	L(Ĺ L)(H́ L)(Ĺ L)
f.	Odd-parity, odd-numbered H syllable	(Ĺ L)(H́)(Ĺ L)(Ĺ L)

In general, the OHP can alter a stress pattern in two ways, both of which are illustrated in the contrast between (6d,e) and (6f). First, the

OHP can produce exhaustive parsing in a subset of odd-parity forms – the subset with an odd-numbered heavy syllable – in systems that otherwise exhibit under-parsing. When there is no odd-numbered heavy syllable, the leftover syllable is left unparsed. When there is an odd-numbered heavy syllable, the leftover syllable is parsed as a monosyllabic foot. Second, the OHP can disrupt the effects of directional parsing. When odd-numbered heavy syllables are present in an odd-parity form, directional devices cannot position the leftover syllable in the same place that they would locate it when odd-numbered heavy syllables are absent.

There are no descriptions of patterns with either of these properties in the literature on quantity-insensitive stress (see the typology presented in Gordon 2002a, for example). This is unsurprising, since languages with these properties could hardly be classified as quantity-insensitive. There are also no descriptions of patterns with either of these properties in the literature on quantity-sensitive stress (see the typology presented in Hayes 1995, for example). To the best of my knowledge, then, there are no attested patterns where odd-parity forms alternate between under-parsing and exhaustive parsing on the basis of the absence or presence of an odd- numbered heavy syllable.[2] Also to the best of my knowledge, there are no attested patterns where odd-parity forms alternate in displaying directional parsing effects based on the presence or absence of odd-numbered heavy syllables.

3.1.2 Faithfulness violations and the Even Output Problem

The second option for achieving exhaustive binary parsing for an odd-parity input is to convert it to an even-parity output. Under this option, the length of the input string is altered in the output, either by adding a syllable, as in (7a), or deleting a syllable, as in (7b). In either case, the result is an even-parity string that can be evenly divided into disyllabic feet, and exhaustive binary parsing is achieved.

(7) Conversion to even-parity

a. Insertion option

σσσσσσσ → (σσ)(σσ)(σσ)(σσ)

b. Deletion option

σσσσσσσ → (σσ)(σσ)(σσ)

2 The exception is when the alternation is based on the weight of final syllables only, as in Wergaia (Hercus 1986). The fact that such alternations are only ever sensitive to the weight of final syllables, however, indicates that they are a non-finality effect, rather than an effect of general minimality (Hyde 2007b).

Achieving exhaustive binary parsing in this fashion results in the Even Output Problem, which arises in two forms. The less aggressive version exhibits a peculiar quantity-sensitivity that complements that of the OHP. It achieves exhaustive binary parsing for odd-parity inputs that *do not* contain odd-numbered heavy syllables by converting them to even-parity outputs. For odd-parity inputs that *do* contain odd-numbered heavy syllables, however, exhaustive binary parsing is achieved by parsing one of these syllables as a monosyllabic foot, as described in the outline of the OHP above. In this less aggressive version, then, the EOP applies just to odd-parity inputs that escape the OHP. The result is a type of language where the only odd-parity outputs are those that contain odd-numbered heavy syllables.

(8) Quantity-sensitive EOP (deletion version)

a.	Even-parity input, L syllables only	LLLLLL → (ĹL)(ĹL)(ĹL)
b.	Even-parity input, even-numbered H	LLLHLL → (ĹL)(ĹH)(ĹL)
c.	Even-parity input, odd-numbered H	LLHLLL → (ĹL)(H́L)(ĹL)
d.	Odd-parity input, L syllables only	LLLLLLL → (ĹL)(ĹL)(ĹL)
e.	Odd-parity input, even-numbered H	LLLHLLL → (ĹL)(ĹH)(ĹL)
f.	Odd-parity input, odd-numbered H	LLHLLLL → (ĹL)(H́)(ĹL)(ĹL)

A more aggressive form of the EOP arises in approaches where there is a separate syllabic minimality restriction in addition to the moraic minimality restriction (as in Hewitt 1994 and Alber 2005, for example). The ability to require that feet be at least disyllabic, rather than just bimoraic, makes the EOP quantity-insensitive. All odd-parity inputs are converted into even-parity outputs regardless of the presence or location of heavy syllables. The result is a type of language with only even-parity surface forms.

(9) Quantity-insensitive EOP (deletion version)

a.	Even-parity input, L syllables only	LLLLLL → (ĹL)(ĹL)(ĹL)
b.	Even-parity input, even-numbered H	LLLHLL → (ĹL)(ĹH)(ĹL)

c.	Even-parity input, odd-numbered H	LLHLLL → (ĹL)(H́L)(ĹL)
d.	Odd-parity input, L syllables only	LLLLLLL → (ĹL)(ĹL)(ĹL)
e.	Odd-parity input, even-numbered H	LLLHLLL → (ĹL)(ĹH)(ĹL)
f.	Odd-parity input, odd-numbered H	LLHLLLL → (ĹL)(H́L)(ĹL)

Whether it arises in its less aggressive quantity-sensitive version or its more aggressive quantity-insensitive version, the result of the EOP is an unattested language. As far as I am aware, there are no languages where the possibility of an odd-parity output depends on the presence of an odd-numbered heavy syllable as predicted under the quantity-sensitive EOP. There also appear to be no languages that allow only even-parity forms on the surface as predicted under the quantity-insensitive EOP. This is true despite the fact that parsing and minimality requirements can clearly cause faithfulness violations. They cause faithfulness violations in enforcing minimal words – insertion in Hixkaryana (Derbyshire 1985, Hayes 1995), for example – but they do not cause faithfulness violations in longer forms. (For this reason, the EOP cannot be avoided simply by assuming a universal ranking of faithfulness over parsing and minimality.)

3.1.3 A solution: improper bracketing

Allowing disyllabic feet to overlap is the final option for satisfying the parsing and minimality requirements simultaneously, and it is the only option that avoids the effects of both the OHP and the EOP. Under this option, the leftover syllable is parsed into a disyllabic foot that overlaps another disyllabic foot, as in (2c), to achieve exhaustive binary parsing. Since parsing in this fashion is insensitive to the presence or location of heavy syllables, it avoids the OHP. Since the odd-parity input remains odd-parity on the surface, it also avoids the effects of the EOP.

Whether or not pathological predictions emerge, then, depends on which of the three options the theory allows, and this depends to a great degree on the theory's assumptions concerning prosodic layering. Weak Layering approaches allow heavy syllables to be parsed as monosyllabic feet, as in (2a), and they allow adjustments in length from input to output, as in (2b). Because these are the only options for achieving exhaustive binary parsing in Weak Layering accounts, all such accounts are susceptible to the two sub-problems of the OPIP. In contrast, the Weak Bracketing approach allows these same options, but it also allows feet to overlap, as in (2c). In allowing feet to overlap, Weak Bracketing provides an option for achieving exhaustive binary parsing that does not result in either the OHP or the EOP. In providing this option, it allows the options that are the source of the OHP and the EOP to be harmonically bounded, and the OPIP simply does not arise.

3.1.4 Preview

To this point, I have outlined the characteristics of the two sub-problems of the Odd-Parity Input Problem – the Odd Heavy Problem and the Even Output Problem – and I have established their connection to the well-motivated parsing and minimality requirements. We turn now to a more detailed examination of the issues raised above. In Section 3.2, we see how the parsing and minimality requirements lead to the OPIP under standard Optimality Theoretic Weak Layering accounts, examining the effects of the OPIP on the typology predicted by Symmetrical Alignment. (We examine the effects of the OPIP on the more recent Asymmetrical Alignment and Rhythmic Licensing in Chapter 4.) In Section 3.3, I address the possibility of avoiding the OPIP through Iterative Foot Optimization. Though the effects of the OPIP are a bit different, Iterative Foot Optimization cannot avoid the OPIP as long as it retains the structural assumptions of Weak Layering. We examine the ability of the Weak Bracketing account to avoid the OPIP and to produce the desired range of quantity-insensitive stress patterns in Chapter 5.

3.2 The OPIP in Symmetrical Alignment

The Weak Layering approach to prosodic layering makes two options available for accommodating the leftover syllable in odd-parity outputs: the leftover syllable can remain unparsed, or it can be parsed as a monosyllabic foot. In OT Weak Layering accounts, the option that is selected for a particular language depends on the relative importance of the parsing and minimality requirements, as determined by the ranking of Parse-σ and F-Bin, the two constraints that implement those requirements. Under the idealization that all syllables can be treated as if they were light, typical in the OT literature on quantity-insensitive stress patterns, Parse-σ and F-Bin are always in conflict in the competition between odd-parity output candidates. If F-Bin dominates Parse-σ, the leftover syllable in an odd-parity form remains unparsed. If Parse-σ dominates F-Bin, however, the leftover syllable is parsed as a monosyllabic foot. As we saw in Chapter 2, the conflict that arises under this idealized condition is crucial in allowing Weak Layering accounts like Symmetrical Alignment and Iterative Foot Optimization to predict a reasonable range of binary default patterns.

We turn our attention now to Symmetrical Alignment's predictions when differences in syllable weight are taken into account. Under these more realistic conditions, the crucial conflict between PARSE-σ and F-BIN is lost for odd-parity outputs that contain an odd-numbered heavy syllable. The peculiar quantity-sensitivity of the OHP emerges as a result, and it infects the predicted typology to such a degree that Symmetrical Alignment cannot possibly predict a reasonably accurate typology of quantity-insensitive stress patterns.

3.2.1 Symmetrical Alignment and the Odd Heavy Problem

When the effects of syllable weight are actually considered, all Weak Layering accounts appear to exhibit the effects of the Odd Heavy Problem. Depending on the devices used to produce the effects of directional parsing, however, the particular manifestation of the OHP varies from account to account. The particular version of the OHP that arises under Symmetrical Alignment is described in (10).

(10) The OHP in Symmetrical Alignment

A heavy syllable *H* is parsed as a monosyllabic foot *iff*

a. *H* occurs in an odd-parity form; *and*
b. *H* is odd-numbered; *and*
c. *H* is the heavy syllable conforming to (a,b) that is closest to the preferred edge of general foot alignment.

In the Symmetrical Alignment version of the OHP, a heavy syllable can be parsed as a monosyllabic foot in *any* odd-numbered position, but the alignment constraints, ALL-F-LEFT and ALL-F-RIGHT, decide among them when multiple options are available. When ALL-F-LEFT is higher-ranked, the leftmost odd-numbered heavy syllable is parsed as a monosyllabic foot. When ALL-F-RIGHT is higher-ranked, the rightmost is parsed as a monosyllabic foot.

(11) OHP varieties under Symmetrical Alignment

a. ALL-F-LEFT >> ALL-F-RIGHT

The leftmost odd-numbered heavy syllable is parsed as a monosyllabic foot.

b. ALL-F-RIGHT >> ALL-F-LEFT

The rightmost odd-numbered heavy syllable is parsed as a monosyllabic foot.

The reason that ALL-F-LEFT and ALL-F-RIGHT alone are responsible for determining the position of the heavy monosyllabic foot is that a monosyllabic foot always results in exhaustive parsing. Recall from Chapter 2 that the other two alignment constraints, F-LEFT and F-RIGHT, lose their influence under Symmetrical Alignment when parsing is exhaustive.

OHP effects emerge in the Symmetrical Alignment account whenever PARSE-σ and F-BIN both dominate ALL-F-LEFT and ALL-F-RIGHT. Since PARSE-σ and F-BIN must both dominate the alignment constraints to produce under-parsing patterns, under-parsing patterns always emerge with OHP effects. Since it is not necessary for F-BIN to dominate the alignment constraints to produce an exhaustive parsing pattern, however, exhaustive parsing patterns can emerge with or without OHP effects.[3]

(12) a. Under-parsing with OHP effects
F-BIN >> PARSE-σ >> ALL-F-LEFT, ALL-F-RIGHT
b. Exhaustive parsing with OHP effects
PARSE-σ >> F-BIN >> ALL-F-LEFT, ALL-F-RIGHT
c. Exhaustive parsing without OHP effects
i. PARSE-σ >> ALL-F-LEFT >> F-BIN, ALL-F-RIGHT
ii. PARSE-σ >> ALL-F-RIGHT >> F-BIN, ALL-F-LEFT

To illustrate how the OHP emerges in under-parsing patterns, consider first the unidirectional under-parsing ranking F-BIN >> PARSE-σ >> ALL-F-LEFT. In odd-parity forms containing only light syllables, it produces the basic odd-parity parsing pattern in (13), where the final syllable is left unparsed.

(13) F-BIN >> PARSE-σ >> ALL-F-LEFT
(LL)(LL)(LL)L

In forms containing odd-numbered heavy syllables, however, as (14) indicates, the same ranking parses one as monosyllabic foot, giving

3 There is a discrepancy between the predictions presented in Hyde 2012b, where it was claimed that Symmetrical Alignment cannot produce binary patterns free of the OHP, and those presented here, where it is claimed that exhaustive parsing patterns can emerge free of the OHP. The discrepancy is due to the assumption made here that feet have a universal disyllabic maximum, allowing for exhaustive parsing patterns to emerge without the requirement that F-BIN dominate the alignment constraints. (See Chapter 2.)

preference to the leftmost when more than one is available. The higher-ranking F-BIN and PARSE-σ insist that one of the odd-numbered heavy syllables be parsed as a monosyllabic foot even if this results in additional violations of the lower-ranked ALL-F-LEFT. ALL-F-LEFT can only ensure that the monosyllabic foot is constructed using the leftmost odd-numbered heavy syllable.

(14)

LLHLHLL	F-BIN	PARSE-σ	ALL-F-LEFT
☞ w. (LL)(H)(LH)(LL)			10
a. (LL)(HL)(H)(LL)			W 11
b. (LL)(HL)(HL)L		W 1	L 6
c. (L)(LH)(LH)(LL)	W 1		L 9

The first thing to notice in a comparison of (13) and (14) is that under-parsing rankings produce an alternation between under-parsing and exhaustive parsing based on the weight of odd-numbered syllables. If the odd-numbered syllables are all light, as in (13), an under-parsing pattern emerges. When one or more of the odd-numbered syllables is heavy, as in (14), an exhaustive parsing pattern emerges. The second thing to notice is that the monosyllabic foot in (14) may or may not appear in the same position as the unparsed syllable in (13). It is constructed on the leftmost odd-numbered heavy syllable, and any odd-numbered heavy syllable might end up being the leftmost, depending on the position of the others. The result, then, is a perturbation of the basic directional parsing pattern.

Now consider the ranking PARSE-σ >> F-BIN >> ALL-F-LEFT, an exhaustive parsing ranking that exhibits the effects of the OHP. In odd-parity forms containing only light syllables, it produces the basic odd-parity parsing pattern in (15), where the initial syllable is parsed as a monosyllabic foot.

(15) PARSE-σ >> F-BIN >> ALL-F-LEFT
(L)(LL)(LL)(LL)

In forms containing odd-numbered heavy syllables, however, as in (16), the same ranking parses one as a monosyllabic foot, giving preference to the leftmost when more than one is available. Though the ranking between F-BIN and PARSE-σ is reversed, the result is the same as that for the under-parsing ranking discussed just above. F-BIN and PARSE-σ insist that one of the odd-numbered heavy syllables be parsed as a monosyllabic foot even if it results in additional alignment violations. ALL-F-LEFT can only ensure that the monosyllabic foot is constructed using the leftmost odd-numbered heavy syllable.

(16)	LLHLHLL	PARSE-σ	F-BIN	ALL-F-LEFT
	☞ w. (LL)(H)(LH)(LL)			10
	a. (LL)(HL)(H)(LL)			W 11
	b. (LL)(HL)(HL)L	W 1		L 6
	c. (L)(LH)(LH)(LL)		W 1	L 9

Although there is no alternation between under-parsing and exhaustive parsing under an exhaustive parsing ranking, the perturbations of the basic directional parsing pattern reveal the influence of the OHP. Any odd-numbered heavy syllable may be parsed as monosyllabic foot. It need not be initial, the position of the monosyllabic foot in (15). It only needs to be the leftmost of the odd-numbered heavy syllables present in the form.

Finally, consider the ranking PARSE-σ >> ALL-F-LEFT >> F-BIN, an exhaustive parsing ranking that does not exhibit the effects of the OHP. In odd-parity forms containing only light syllables, it produces the basic odd-parity parsing pattern in (17), where the initial syllable is parsed as a monosyllabic foot.

(17) PARSE-σ >> ALL-F-LEFT >> F-BIN
(L)(LL)(LL)(LL)

As illustrated in (18), the same pattern emerges in forms that contain odd-numbered heavy syllables. In this case, though the high-ranking ranking PARSE-σ still insists that parsing be exhaustive, the lower ranked F-BIN cannot insist that the necessary monosyllabic foot be constructed on a heavy syllable. Since ALL-F-LEFT is higher ranked, it ensures that the monosyllabic foot be constructed on the leftmost syllable, regardless of its weight.

(18)

LLHLHLL	Parse-σ	All-F-Left	F-Bin
☞ w. (L)(LH)(LH)(LL)		9	1
a. (LL)(H)(LH)(LL)		10 W	L
b. (LL)(HL)(H)(LL)		11 W	L
c. (LL)(HL)(HL)L	1 W	6 L	L

When we consider the potential effects of heavy syllables, then, we can see that each of the eight under-parsing patterns predicted by Symmetrical Alignment exhibits the unattested quantity-sensitivity associated with the OHP. In the summaries in (19) and (20), the first form given with each ranking is an odd-parity form with all light syllables. This form illustrates the basic pattern that the ranking produces when odd-numbered heavy syllables are absent. The second form contains two odd-numbered heavy syllables. It illustrates the OHP effects that emerge when odd-numbered heavy syllables are present. It indicates that parsing is exhaustive, and it indicates whether the leftmost or the rightmost odd-numbered heavy syllable is parsed as a monosyllabic foot.

(19) Unidirectional under-parsing patterns with OHP effects

a. F-Bin >> Parse-σ >> All-F-Left >> All-F-Right, F-Right; Parse-σ >> F-Left

i.	Trochaic: Unattested	ii.	Iambic: Unattested
	(ĹL)(ĹL)(ĹL)L		(LĹ)(LĹ)(LĹ)L
	(ĹL)(H́)(ĹH)(ĹL)		(LĹ)(H́)(LH́)(LĹ)

b. F-Bin >> Parse-σ >> All-F-Right >> All-F-Left, F-Left; Parse-σ >> F-Right

i.	Trochaic: Unattested	ii.	Iambic: Unattested
	L(ĹL)(ĹL)(ĹL)		L(LĹ)(LĹ)(LĹ)
	(ĹL)(H́L)(H́)(ĹL)		(LĹ)(HĹ)(H́)(LĹ)

(20) Bidirectional under-parsing patterns with OHP effects

a. F-Bin >> Parse-σ >> F-Left >> All-F-Right >> All-F-Left; Parse-σ >> F-Right

i.	Trochaic: Unattested	ii.	Iambic: Unattested
	(ĹL)L(ĹL)(ĹL)		(LĹ)L(LĹ)(LĹ)
	(ĹL)(H́L)(H́)(ĹL)		(LĹ)(HĹ)(H́)(LĹ)

b. F-Bin >> Parse-σ >> F-Right >> All-F-Left >> All-F-Right; Parse-σ >> F-Left

i. Trochaic: Unattested
(ĹL)(ĹL)L(ĹL)
(ĹL)(H́)(ĹH)(ĹL)

ii. Iambic: Unattested
(LĹ)(LĹ)L(LĹ)
(LĹ)(H́)(LH́)(LĹ)

Since exhaustive parsing patterns can emerge with or without OHP effects, the number of exhaustive parsing patterns predicted under Symmetrical Alignment is doubled. Symmetrical Alignment predicts four exhaustive parsing patterns accompanied by OHP effects, none of which is attested, and four patterns unaccompanied by OHP effects, three of which are attested.

(21) Exhaustive parsing patterns with OHP effects

a. Parse-σ >> F-Bin >> All-F-Left >> All-F-Right; Parse-σ >> F-Left, F-Right

i. Trochaic: Unattested
(Ĺ)(ĹL)(ĹL)(ĹL)
(ĹL)(H́)(ĹH)(ĹL)

ii. Iambic: Unattested
(Ĺ)(LĹ)(LĹ)(LĹ)
(LĹ)(H́)(LH́)(LĹ)

b. Parse-σ >> F-Bin >> All-F-Right >> All-F-Left; Parse-σ >> F-Left, F-Right

i. Trochaic: Unattested
(ĹL)(ĹL)(ĹL)(Ĺ)
(ĹL)(H́L)(H́)(ĹL)

ii. Iambic: Unattested
(LĹ)(LĹ)(LĹ)(Ĺ)
(LĹ)(HĹ)(H́)(LĹ)

(22) Exhaustive parsing patterns without OHP effects

a. Parse-σ >> All-F-Left >> F-Bin, All-F-Right; Parse-σ >> F-Left, F-Right

i. Trochaic: Attested
(Ĺ)(ĹL)(ĹL)(ĹL)
(Ĺ)(ĹH)(ĹH)(ĹL)

ii. Iambic: Unattested
(Ĺ)(LĹ)(LĹ)(LĹ)
(Ĺ)(LH́)(LH́)(LĹ)

b. Parse-σ >> All-F-Right >> F-Bin, All-F-Left; Parse-σ >> F-Left, F-Right

i. Trochaic: Attested
(ĹL)(ĹL)(ĹL)(Ĺ)
(ĹL)(H́L)(H́L)(Ĺ)

ii. Iambic: Unattested
(LĹ)(LĹ)(LĹ)(Ĺ)
(LĹ)(HĹ)(HĹ)(Ĺ)

When we consider the potential effects of heavy syllables, then, Symmetrical Alignment has significant problems of both under-generation and over-generation. It fails to produce a single attested quantity-insensitive under-parsing pattern, and it produces 12 unattested quantity-sensitive patterns.

3.2.2 Symmetrical Alignment and the Even Output Problem

Having examined the effects of the Odd Heavy Problem in the Symmetrical Alignment account, we turn now to the effects of the Even Output Problem, the prediction that odd-parity inputs can be converted to even-parity outputs to achieve exhaustive binary parsing. Recall that the EOP comes in two versions and that which versions are possible under a given approach depends on the particular formulation of the minimality requirement.

The quantity-sensitive version, but not the quantity-insensitive version, arises when the only minimality requirement in the grammar is a bimoraic minimality requirement, as in the standard definition of F-BIN. In the quantity-sensitive version, the EOP arises only under rankings that also produce OHP effects, but it affects only those particular odd-parity inputs that escape the OHP, odd-parity inputs without odd-numbered heavy syllables. The result is a language where the only odd-parity surface forms are those that contain odd-numbered heavy syllables.

The quantity-insensitive version of the EOP arises, in addition to the quantity-sensitive version, when the grammar contains a separate disyllabic minimality requirement, distinct from the bimoraic minimality requirement, as in the F-MINIMALITY constraints in (23).

(23) Foot Minimality constraints (Hewitt 1994)

a. F-MINIMALITY-μ:
   Every *F* contains at least two *μ*.

b. F-MINIMALITY-σ:
   Every *F* contains at least two *σ*.

In cases where the syllabic minimality requirement is enforced, the only way to achieve exhaustive binary parsing is to add or subtract a single syllable from the odd-parity input, converting it to an even-parity output. The result is a language with only even-parity surface forms.[4]

3.2.2.1 Symmetrical Alignment and the QS EOP

Under the standard formulation of F-BIN, the quantity-sensitive version of the EOP arises in Weak Layering accounts in a subset of the rankings that produce the OHP. As discussed in Section 3.2.1, the emergence of the OHP depends on the ranking of both PARSE-σ and F-BIN above ALL-F-LEFT and ALL-F-RIGHT. Whether or not the EOP emerges in

4 As we shall see in Section 3.3, some exceptions to this rule arise under Iterative Foot Optimization.

conjunction with the OHP depends on the ranking of two additional constraints, the faithfulness constraints, Max and Dep, given in (24).[5]

(24) Faithfulness constraints

a. Max: Every σ in the input is present in the output.

b. Dep: Every σ in the output is present in the input.

As (25) indicates, the insertion version of the QS EOP arises when Max, Parse-σ, and F-Bin all dominate Dep. The deletion version arises when Dep, Parse-σ, and F-Bin all dominate Max.

(25) QS EOP rankings

a. Insertion version

Max, Parse-σ >> All-F-Left, All-F-Right, F-Left, F-Right, Dep;
F-Bin >> All-F-Left, All-F-Right, Dep

b. Deletion version

Dep, Parse-σ, F-Bin >> Max >> All-F-Left, All-F-Right, F-Left, F-Right

Consider the ranking for the insertion version. As (26) demonstrates, using dominant leftward alignment, odd-parity inputs with odd-numbered heavy syllables still result in outputs that exhibit OHP effects. A single odd-numbered heavy syllable, in this case the leftmost, is parsed as a monosyllabic foot. There is no need to violate faithfulness to achieve exhaustive binary parsing.

(26)

LLLLHLL	Parse-σ	F-Bin	Max	Dep	All-F-Left
☞ w. (LL)(H)(LH)(LL)					10
a. (LL)(HL)(H)(LL)					W 11
c. (LL)(HL)(HL)(LL)				W 1	W 12
b. (LL)(HL)(HL)			W 1		L 6
d. (L)(LH)(LH)(LL)		W 1			L 9
e. (LL)(HL)(HL)L	W 1				L 6

5 The ranking of Max is crucial in the production of binary stress patterns generally. If any one of the alignment constraints dominates Max, alignment will compel deletion of syllables until the point where a single foot remains.

For all other odd-parity inputs, however, DEP will be violated and a single syllable inserted to achieve exhaustive binary parsing on the surface. In (27), the odd-parity input contains no odd-numbered heavy syllables. PARSE-σ and F-BIN exclude the faithful candidates, (27b) and (27c), because they must either leave a syllable unparsed or parse a light syllable as monosyllabic foot. Since the higher-ranked MAX excludes the candidate, (27a), where a single syllable has been subtracted from the odd-parity input, the optimal candidate is the one that achieves exhaustive binary parsing by inserting a single syllable at the expense of the lower-ranked DEP.

(27)

LLLLLLL	PARSE-σ	F-BIN	MAX	DEP	ALL-F-LEFT
☞ w. (LL)(LL)(LL)(LL)				1	12
a. (LL)(LL)(LL)			W 1	L	L 6
b. (L)(LL)(LL)(LL)		W 1		L	L 9
c. (LL)(LL)(LL)L	W 1			L	L 6

The results are similar when the rankings of the faithfulness constraints are reversed so that PARSE-σ, F-BIN, and DEP all dominate MAX. For odd-parity inputs with odd-numbered heavy syllables, one of the odd-numbered heavy syllables is parsed as a monosyllabic foot. For odd-parity inputs without odd-numbered heavy syllables, however, the low-ranked MAX is violated and a single syllable is be deleted to achieve exhaustive binary parsing on the surface. I omit the additional tableaux.

In addition to the 16 patterns in (19–22), then, which emerge without the OHP or exhibit the effects of the OHP only, Symmetrical Alignment predicts eight patterns where the quantity-sensitive EOP emerges alongside the OHP. The combined OHP + quantity-sensitive EOP patterns make sensitivity to the weight of odd-numbered heavy syllables conspicuous in a new way. This time, it is conspicuous in an alternation between odd- and even-parity outputs. When an odd-numbered heavy syllable is present, the output for an odd-parity input is still odd-parity. When no odd-numbered heavy syllable is present, however, the output is even-parity.

For each language in the summaries in (28) and (29), there are two example outputs for odd-parity inputs. The first indicates which odd-numbered heavy syllable, the leftmost or the rightmost, is parsed as a monosyllabic foot when one or more is available. The second indicates whether a syllable is added or subtracted when no odd-numbered heavy syllable is available.

(28) OHP + quantity-sensitive EOP (insertion version)

a. MAX, PARSE-σ, F-BIN >> ALL-F-LEFT, ALL-F-RIGHT, DEP; ALL-F-LEFT >> ALL-F-RIGHT

i. Trochaic: Unattested	ii. Iambic: Unattested
LLHLHLL → (ĹL)(H́)(ĹH)(ĹL)	LLHLHLL → (LĹ)(H́)(LH́)(LĹ)
LLLLLLL → (ĹL)(ĹL)(ĹL)(ĹL)	LLLLLLL → (LĹ)(LĹ)(LĹ)(LĹ)

b. MAX, PARSE-σ, F-BIN >> ALL-F-LEFT, ALL-F-RIGHT, DEP; ALL-F-RIGHT >> ALL-F-LEFT

i. Trochaic: Unattested	ii. Iambic: Unattested
LLHLHLL → (ĹL)(H́L)(H́)(ĹL)	LLHLHLL → (LĹ)(HĹ)(H́)(LĹ)
LLLLLLL → (ĹL)(ĹL)(ĹL)(ĹL)	LLLLLLL → (LĹ)(LĹ)(LĹ)(LĹ)

(29) OHP + quantity-sensitive EOP (deletion version)

a. DEP, PARSE-σ, F-BIN >> MAX >> ALL-F-LEFT >> ALL-F-RIGHT

i. Trochaic: Unattested	ii. Iambic: Unattested
LLHLHLL → (ĹL)(H́)(ĹH)(ĹL)	LLHLHLL → (LĹ)(H́)(LH́)(LĹ)
LLLLLLL → (ĹL)(ĹL)(ĹL)	LLLLLLL → (LĹ)(LĹ)(LĹ)

b. DEP, PARSE-σ, F-BIN >> MAX >> ALL-F-RIGHT >> ALL-F-LEFT

i. Trochaic: Unattested	ii. Iambic: Unattested
LLHLHLL → (ĹL)(H́L)(H́)(ĹL)	LLHLHLL → (LĹ)(HĹ)(H́)(LĹ)
LLLLLLL → (ĹL)(ĹL)(ĹL)	LLLLLLL → (LĹ)(LĹ)(LĹ)

3.2.2.2 Symmetrical Alignment and the quantity-insensitive EOP

We turn now to the idea that the F-BIN constraint should be split into two constraints, one that establishes a disyllabic minimal foot and one that establishes a bimoraic minimal foot, as in (23). The advantage of a separate syllabic minimality requirement is that it would solve Symmetrical Alignment's under-generation problem. Symmetrical Alignment would be able to produce the quantity-insensitive under-parsing patterns that it fails to produce under the standard F-BIN formulation. As (30) and (31) indicate, all that would be required is for F-MIN-σ to replace F-BIN in its position above PARSE-σ in under-parsing rankings. The same under-parsing configuration would emerge for an odd-parity form whether or not it contained odd-numbered heavy syllables. (The ranking of F-MIN-μ is not be crucial in this context.)

(30) Unidirectional under-parsing patterns without OHP effects

a. F-MIN-σ >> PARSE-σ >> ALL-F-LEFT >> ALL-F-RIGHT, F-RIGHT; PARSE-σ >> F-LEFT; F-MIN-μ

i. Trochaic: Attested	ii. Iambic: Attested
(ĹL)(ĹL)(ĹL)L	(LĹ)(LĹ)(LĹ)L
(ĹL)(H́L)(H́L)L	(LĹ)(HĹ)(HĹ)L

b. F-MIN-σ >> PARSE-σ >> ALL-F-RIGHT >> ALL-F-LEFT, F-LEFT; PARSE-σ >> F-RIGHT; F-MIN-μ

i. Trochaic: Attested	ii. Iambic: Unattested
L(ĹL)(ĹL)(ĹL)	L(LĹ)(LĹ)(LĹ)
L(ĹH)(ĹH)(ĹL)	L(LH́)(LH́)(LĹ)

(31) Bidirectional under-parsing patterns without OHP effects

a. F-MIN-σ >> PARSE-σ >> F-LEFT >> ALL-F-RIGHT >> ALL-F-LEFT; PARSE-σ >> F-RIGHT; F-MIN-μ

i. Trochaic: Attested	ii. Iambic: Unattested
(ĹL)L(ĹL)(ĹL)	(LĹ)L(LĹ)(LĹ)
(ĹL)H(ĹH)(ĹL)	(LĹ)H(LH́)(LĹ)

b. F-MIN-σ >> PARSE-σ >> F-RIGHT >> ALL-F-LEFT >> ALL-F-RIGHT; PARSE-σ >> F-LEFT; F-MIN-μ

i. Trochaic: Attested	ii. Iambic: Unattested
(ĹL)(ĹL)L(ĹL)	(LĹ)(LĹ)L(LĹ)
(ĹL)(H́L)H(ĹL)	(LĹ)(HĹ)H(LĹ)

The primary disadvantage of a separate syllabic minimality restriction is that it not only fails to address the over-generation problem but it actually makes matters worse by introducing the quantity-insensitive version of the EOP. As (32), indicates, the insertion version of the QI EOP emerges when MAX, PARSE-σ, and F-MIN-σ all dominate DEP. The deletion version emerges when DEP, PARSE-σ, and F-MIN-σ all dominate MAX. In either case, the result is a language with only even-parity outputs.

(32) QI EOP rankings

a. Insertion version

Max, Parse-σ >> All-F-Left, All-F-Right, F-Left, F-Right, Dep; F-Min-σ >> All-F-Left, All-F-Right, Dep; F-Min-μ

b. Deletion version

Dep, Parse-σ, F-Min-σ >> Max >> All-F-Left, All-F-Right, F-Left, F-Right; F-Min-μ

Consider, for example, the ranking for the insertion version. As (33) demonstrates, using dominant leftward alignment, a single syllable is added to odd-parity inputs even in those cases where they contain an odd-numbered heavy syllable. Since parsing an odd-numbered heavy syllable as a monosyllabic foot, as in candidates (33b) and (33c), does nothing to help these candidates to meet F-Min-σ's requirement that all feet be disyllabic, a syllable is added at the expense of Dep to achieve exhaustive binary parsing on the surface.

(33)

LLLLHLL	Parse-σ	F-Min-σ	Max	Dep	All-F-Left
☞ w. (LL)(HL)(HL)(LL)				1	12
a. (LL)(HL)(HL)			W 1	L	L 6
b. (LL)(H)(LH)(LL)		W 1		L	L 10
c. (LL)(HL)(H)(LL)		W 1		L	L 11
d. (L)(LH)(LH)(LL)		W 1		L	L 9
e. (LL)(HL)(HL)L	W 1			L	L 6

The results are similar when the rankings of the faithfulness constraints are reversed so that Parse-σ, F-Min-σ, and Dep all dominate Max. Whether or not an odd-parity input contains odd-numbered heavy syllables, the low-ranked Max is violated and a single syllable is deleted to achieve exhaustive binary parsing on the surface. The result is a language with only even-parity forms on the surface. I omit the additional tableau.

The QI EOP patterns predicted under Symmetrical Alignment are summarized in (34) and (35). For each of the patterns, there are two example outputs for odd-parity inputs. Regardless of the presence or absence of odd-numbered heavy syllables in the inputs, the outputs are even-parity.

(34) Quantity-insensitive EOP (deletion version)

a. Trochaic: Unattested

LLHLHLL → (ĹL)(H́L)(H́L)

LLLLLLL → (ĹL)(ĹL)(ĹL)

b. Iambic: Unattested

LLHLHLL → (LĹ)(HĹ)(HĹ)

LLLLLLL → (LĹ)(LĹ)(LĹ)

(35) Quantity-insensitive EOP (insertion version)

a. Trochaic: Unattested

LLHLHLL →
(ĹL)(H́L)(H́L)(ĹL)

LLLLLLL →
(ĹL)(ĹL)(ĹL)(ĹL)

b. Iambic: Unattested

LLHLHLL →
(LĹ)(HĹ)(HĹ)(LĹ)

LLLLLLL →
(LĹ)(LĹ)(LĹ)(LĹ)

The QI EOP, of course, is a prediction *added* to the OHP and QS EOP when the minimality requirement is split into separate moraic and syllabic restrictions; it does not supplant the OHP or the QS EOP. Because the disyllabic minimality requirement could not simply replace the well-motivated bimoraic minimality requirement, the latter would still be present in the constraint set, potentially influencing the outcome even when it is relatively low-ranked.

As (36a) indicates, the effects of the OHP emerge in under-parsing patterns, unaccompanied by the QS EOP, when MAX, DEP, and F-MIN-μ all dominate PARSE-σ, and PARSE-σ dominates F-MIN- σ. As (36b) indicates, the OHP emerges in exhaustive parsing patterns when MAX, DEP, and PARSE-σ all dominate both F-MIN-μ and F-MIN-σ.

(36) OHP effects in isolation

a. Under-parsing patterns (*Summarized in (19, 20) above*)

MAX, DEP, F-MIN-μ >> PARSE-σ >> ALL-F-LEFT, ALL-F-RIGHT, F-LEFT, F-RIGHT,F-MIN-σ

b. Exhaustive parsing patterns (*Summarized in (21) above*)

MAX, PARSE-σ >> ALL-F-LEFT, ALL-F-RIGHT, F-LEFT, F-RIGHT, F-MIN-μ, F-MIN-σ; DEP >>F-MIN-μ >> ALL-F-LEFT, ALL-F-RIGHT; DEP >> F-MIN-σ

The OHP arises in conjunction with the insertion version of the QS EOP, as (37a) indicates, when PARSE-σ, F-MIN-μ, and MAX all dominate DEP and F-MIN-σ, and DEP, ALL-F-LEFT, or ALL-F-RIGHT dominates

F-MIN-σ. The OHP arises in conjunction with the deletion version of the QS EOP when DEP, PARSE-σ, and F-MIN-μ all dominate MAX, and MAX dominates F-MIN-σ.

(37) OHP + quantity-sensitive EOP

a. Insertion version *(Summarized in (28) above)*

i MAX, PARSE-σ >> ALL-F-LEFT, ALL-F-RIGHT, F-LEFT, F-RIGHT, DEP; F-MIN-μ >> ALL-F-LEFT, ALL-F-RIGHT, DEP; DEP >> F-MIN-σ

ii. MAX, PARSE-σ >> ALL-F-LEFT, ALL-F-RIGHT, F-LEFT, F-RIGHT, DEP; F-MIN-μ >> ALL-F-LEFT, ALL-F-RIGHT, DEP; ALL-F-LEFT >> F-MIN- σ

iii. MAX, PARSE-σ >> ALL-F-LEFT, ALL-F-RIGHT, F-LEFT, F-RIGHT, DEP; F-MIN-μ >> ALL-F-LEFT, ALL-F-RIGHT, DEP; ALL-F-RIGHT >> F-MIN- σ

b. Deletion version *(Summarized in (29) above)*

DEP, PARSE-σ, F-MIN-μ >> MAX >> ALL-F-LEFT, ALL-F-RIGHT, F-LEFT, F-RIGHT, F-MIN- σ

Before moving on, a final reason that a separate syllabic minimality requirement is not a viable solution to the issues addressed here is that it is not particularly well motivated. In Hewitt's (1994) account, for example, F-MIN-σ is conspicuous for standing around with nothing to do. This should not be surprising. As Hayes (1995) notes, quantity-insensitive languages that allow bimoraic syllables seem never to categorically prohibit heavy monosyllabic feet. Even in those cases where the minimal word is disyllabic, rather than bimoraic, it can be accounted for with a bimoraic minimal foot, an extrametricality/non-finality effect, or a combination of the two.

3.2.3 Interim Summary

In Chapter 2, we saw that Symmetrical Alignment predicts a reasonable range of quantity-insensitive binary stress patterns, though it has a significant over-generation problem, when the effects of syllable weight are not actually considered. We saw in the discussion above, however, that when the effects of syllable weight are considered Symmetrical Alignment manifests the effects of both the OHP and the EOP. The effects were so pervasive under the standard F-BIN formulation that Symmetrical Alignment could not predict a single attested quantity-insensitive under-parsing pattern, resulting in both a substantial under-generation problem and an even more substantial over-generation problem. While the addition of a separate syllabic minimality requirement addressed the under-generation problem, it only exacerbated the over-generation problem.

3.3 The OPIP in Iterative Foot Optimization

We next examine Iterative Foot Optimization, as it has recently been argued that Iterative Foot Optimization addresses many of the issues associated with the OPIP (Pruitt 2008, 2010). In carefully examining the predictions of Iterative Foot Optimization, however, we can see that this is really not the case. Though Iterative Foot Optimization manifests the effects of the OPIP differently, it manifests them just as thoroughly as other Weak Bracketing approaches.

3.3.1 Iterative Foot Optimization and the OHP

The idea that Iterative Foot Optimization avoids the OHP turns out to be mistaken. Iterative Foot Optimization exhibits the characteristic quantity-sensitivity described in (38a,b) but with the additional restriction given in (38c). To be parsed as a monosyllabic foot, a heavy syllable must be the last syllable in the course of the derivation to have its parsing status settled.

(38) The Odd Heavy Problem in Iterative Foot Optimization

A heavy syllable *H* is parsed as a monosyllabic foot *iff*

a. *H* occurs in an odd-parity form; *and*

b. *H* is odd-numbered; *and*

c. *H* is the last syllable in the derivation to have its parsing status settled.

In the derivation of an odd-parity form under Iterative Foot Optimization, there are four syllables which might be the last to have their parsing status addressed – the initial, the post-peninitial, the antepenult, and the ultima – depending on the preferences of the alignment constraints. This means that the OHP has four distinct types under Iterative Foot Optimization, rather than the two distinct types that it has under Symmetrical Alignment.

As (39) indicates, when ALL-F-LEFT is the highest-ranked alignment constraint, the ultima is the last addressed, so only the ultima can be parsed as a monosyllabic foot. When ALL-F-RIGHT is the highest-ranked, the initial syllable is the last addressed, so only the initial syllable can be parsed as a monosyllabic foot. The post-peninitial syllable is the last to be disposed of when F-LEFT dominates ALL-F-RIGHT, so only the post-peninitial syllable can form a monosyllabic foot. Finally, the antepenultimate is the last addressed when F-RIGHT dominates ALL-F-LEFT, so only the antepenult can form a monosyllabic foot.

(39) OHP varieties under Iterative Foot Optimization

a. ALL-F-LEFT

If the ultima is heavy, it is parsed as a monosyllabic foot.

b. ALL-F-RIGHT

If the initial syllable is heavy, it is parsed as a monosyllabic foot.

c. F-LEFT >> ALL-F-RIGHT

If the post-peninitial syllable is heavy, it is parsed as a monosyllabic foot.

d. F-RIGHT >> ALL-F-LEFT

If the antepenult is heavy, it is parsed as a monosyllabic foot.

To illustrate, consider under-parsing rankings, the rankings where F-BIN dominates PARSE-σ. In odd-parity forms with a light final syllable, the ranking F-BIN >> PARSE- SYLL >> ALL-F-LEFT produces the unidirectional parsing pattern in (40), where the final syllable remains unparsed.

(40) F-BIN >> PARSE-σ >> ALL-F-LEFT

(LL)(LL)(LL)L

As (41) illustrates, however, in odd-parity forms with a heavy final syllable, the final syllable is parsed as a monosyllabic foot. In examining the different steps of the derivation in (41), and in those that follow, notice that it is never advantageous to parse a heavy syllable as monosyllabic foot unless the heavy syllable is the only syllable left unparsed. In the first step in (41), there is the choice of creating a disyllabic foot or a heavy monosyllabic foot, but there is no advantage to constructing the latter *at this point.* Both satisfy F-BIN and ALL-F-LEFT. Because a disyllabic foot allows one more syllable to be parsed, reducing the number of PARSE-σ violations, a disyllabic foot is selected. Only in the last step, where the rightmost syllable alone remains unparsed and a disyllabic foot cannot be constructed, does it become advantageous to parse a heavy syllable as a monosyllabic foot. It is only here, then, where we see the OHP's quantity-sensitivity emerge. If the final syllable had been light, as in (40), it would not have been advantageous to parse it as a monosyllabic foot.

(41)

HLLLLLH	F-Bin	Parse-σ	All-F-Left
☞ w. (HL)LLLLH		5	
a. (H)LLLLLH		W 6	
b. HLLLL(LH)		5	W 5
c. HLLLLLH		W 7	

(HL)LLLLH	F-Bin	Parse-σ	All-F-Left
☞ w. (HL)(LL)LLH		3	2
a. (HL)(L)LLLH	W 1	W 4	2
b. (HL)LLL(LH)		3	W 5
c. (HL)LLLLH		W 5	L

(HL)(LL)LLH	F-Bin	Parse-σ	All-F-Left
☞ w. (HL)(LL)(LL)H		1	6
a. (HL)(LL)(L)LH	W 1	W 2	6
b. (HL)(LL)L(LH)		1	W 7
c. (HL)(LL)LLH		W 3	L 2

(HL)(LL)(LL)H	F-Bin	Parse-σ	All-F-Left
☞ w. (HL)(LL)(LL)(H)			12
l. (HL)(LL)(LL)H		W 1	L 6

Though both exhibit the effects of the OHP, the output for the input and under-parsing ranking in (41) is different in Iterative Foot Optimization than it is in Symmetrical Alignment. In Symmetrical Alignment, we would see both an alternation between under-parsing and exhaustive parsing and a perturbation of the basic directional parsing pattern. In Symmetrical Alignment, the leftmost heavy syllable – the initial syllable, given the input in (41) – would be parsed as a monosyllabic foot, rather than the final syllable. In Iterative Foot Optimization, we see only the alternation between under-parsing and exhaustive parsing. There is no perturbation of the basic directional parsing pattern. The monosyllabic foot in (41) occurs in the same position – final position – as the unparsed syllable in (40).

The difference arises due to the different derivational perspectives of the two approaches. The ability of odd-numbered heavy syllables to perturb parsing directionality in Symmetrical Alignment can be traced to the equal consideration given to *all* odd-numbered heavy syllables for parsing as a monosyllabic foot. The equal consideration is a direct consequence of Symmetrical Alignment's parallelism. Symmetrical Alignment evaluations simultaneously consider *all* output candidates with monosyllabic feet constructed on heavy syllables, not just candidates with monosyllabic feet in the position where the leftover syllable normally occurs in the basic pattern. While this allows appropriately positioned odd-numbered heavy syllables to perturb the basic pattern, it also limits the specific OHP types under Symmetrical Alignment to two: one where the leftmost odd-numbered heavy syllable is parsed as a monosyllabic foot, and one where the rightmost is parsed as a monosyllabic foot.

In contrast, the serial Iterative Foot Optimization does not compare all possible surface forms to see whether or not it would be advantageous to construct a heavy monosyllabic foot in a position other than the one in which the leftover syllable occurs in the basic pattern. It *first* determines where the leftover syllable will appear, and *then* it decides whether or not it would be advantageous to construct a monosyllabic foot *in that position.* While this prevents heavy syllables from perturbing basic directional parsing patterns, it also has the effect of doubling the specific OHP types under Iterative Foot Optimization to four: one for each position where the leftover syllable might appear in the basic pattern of an odd-parity form.

In the next several examples, we see the effects of the OHP under the remaining under-parsing rankings. The results are similar to those in (40) and (41). In odd-parity forms with a light initial syllable, the ranking F-Bin >> Parse-σ >> All-F-Right produces a parsing pattern where the initial syllable is left unparsed, as in (42a). In odd-parity forms with a heavy initial syllable, however, the same ranking parses the initial syllable as a monosyllabic foot, as in (42b).

(42) F-Bin >> Parse- Syll >> All-F-Right

a. Lσσσσσσ → L(σσ)(σσ)(σσ)

b. Hσσσσσσ → (H)(σσ)(σσ)(σσ)

Next consider the ranking F-Bin >> Parse-σ >> F-Right >> All-F-Left. In odd-parity forms with a light antepenult, the ranking produces a parsing pattern where the antepenult is unfooted, as in (43a). In odd-parity forms with a heavy antepenult, however, the same ranking parses the antepenult as a monosyllabic foot, as in (43b).

(43) F-Bin >> Parse- Syll >> F-Right >> All-F-Left

a. σσσσLσσ → (σσ)(σσ)L(σσ)

b. σσσσHσσ → (σσ)(σσ)(H)(σσ)

Finally, consider the ranking F-Bin >> Parse-σ >> F-Left >> All-F-Right. In odd-parity forms with a light post-peninitial syllable, the ranking produces a parsing pattern where the post-peninitial syllable is left unparsed, as in (44a). In odd-parity forms with a heavy post-peninitial syllable, however, the same ranking parses the post-peninitial syllable as a monosyllabic foot, as in (44b).

(44) F-Bin >> Parse- Syll >> F-Left >> All-F-Right

a. σσLσσσσ → (σσ)L(σσ)(σσ)

b. σσHσσσσ → (σσ)(H)(σσ)(σσ)

When we consider the effects of heavy syllables, then, we see that the OHP also emerges under Iterative Foot Optimization. In each of the 16 binary patterns that Iterative Foot Optimization predicts, an odd-numbered heavy syllable will be parsed as a monosyllabic foot if it is the last syllable in the derivation to have its parsing status settled. In the summaries in (45–48), the first odd-parity form illustrates the basic pattern produced by each ranking. The second form illustrates the effects of the OHP. It indicates the position of the last syllable addressed by the derivation, the syllable that, if heavy, will be parsed as a monosyllabic foot.

As a result of the OHP, Iterative Foot Optimization fails to predict a single quantity-insensitive under-parsing parsing pattern. In their place, Iterative Foot Optimization predicts the eight quantity-sensitive patterns in (45) and (46). Only one of these patterns is actually attested: quantity-sensitivity limited to final syllables can be found in Wergaia (Hercus 1986). (The fact that this type of quantity-sensitivity is attested only in final syllables indicates that it is a non-finality effect rather than a more general minimality effect. See Hyde 2007b, for discussion.)

(45) Unidirectional under-parsing patterns predicted by Iterative Foot Optimization

a. F-BIN >> PARSE-σ >> ALL-F-LEFT >> ALL-F-RIGHT, F-RIGHT; PARSE-σ >> F-LEFT

i. Trochaic: Attested	ii. Iambic: Unattested
(σ́σ)(σ́σ)(σ́σ)L	(σσ́)(σσ́)(σσ́)L
(σ́σ)(σ́σ)(σ́σ)(H́)	(σσ́)(σσ́)(σσ́)(H́)

b. F-BIN >> PARSE-σ >> ALL-F-RIGHT >> ALL-F-LEFT, F-LEFT; PARSE-σ >> F-RIGHT

i. Trochaic: Unattested	ii. Iambic: Unattested
L(σ́σ)(σ́σ)(σ́σ)	L(σσ́)(σσ́)(σσ́)
(H́)(σ́σ)(σ́σ)(σ́σ)	(H́)(σσ́)(σσ́)(σσ́)

(46) Bidirectional under-parsing patterns predicted by Iterative Foot Optimization

a. F-BIN >> PARSE-σ >> F-LEFT >> ALL-F-RIGHT >> ALL-F-LEFT; PARSE-σ >> F-RIGHT

i. Trochaic: Unattested	ii. Iambic: Unattested
(σ́σ)L(σ́σ)(σ́σ)	(σσ́)L(σσ́)(σσ́)
(σ́σ)(H́)(σ́σ)(σ́σ)	(σσ́)(H́)(σσ́)(σσ́)

b. F-BIN >> PARSE-σ >> F-RIGHT >> ALL-F-LEFT >> ALL-F-RIGHT; PARSE-σ >> F-LEFT

i. Trochaic: Unattested	ii. Iambic: Unattested
(σ́σ)(σ́σ)L(σ́σ)	(σσ́)(σσ́)L(σσ́)
(σ́σ)(σ́σ)(H́)(σ́σ)	(σσ́)(σσ́)(H́)(σσ́)

As indicated in (47) and (48), the quantity-sensitivity of the OHP is obscured in exhaustive parsing patterns. The same syllable will be parsed as a monosyllabic foot whether it is heavy or light. This being the case, Iterative Foot Optimization is able to produce three attested quantity-insensitive patterns: (47ai), (47aii), and (47bi). The remaining five patterns are unattested.

(47) Unidirectional exhaustive parsing patterns predicted by Iterative Foot Optimization

a. PARSE-σ >> ALL-F-RIGHT >> ALL-F-LEFT, F-LEFT; PARSE-σ >> F-BIN, F-RIGHT

i. Trochaic: Attested	ii. Iambic: Attested
(Ĺ)(σ́σ)(σ́σ)(σ́σ)	(Ĺ)(σσ́)(σσ́)(σσ́)
(H́)(σ́σ)(σ́σ)(σ́σ)	(H́)(σσ́)(σσ́)(σσ́)

b. PARSE-σ >> ALL-F-LEFT >> ALL-F-RIGHT, F-RIGHT; PARSE-σ >> F-BIN, F-LEFT

i. Trochaic: Attested	ii. Iambic: Unattested
(σ́σ)(σ́σ)(σ́σ)(Ĺ)	(σσ́)(σσ́)(σσ́)(Ĺ)
(σ́σ)(σ́σ)(σ́σ)(H́)	(σσ́)(σσ́)(σσ́)(H́)

(48) Bidirectional exhaustive parsing patterns under Iterative Foot Optimization

a. PARSE-σ >> F-LEFT >> ALL-F-RIGHT >> ALL-F-LEFT; PARSE-σ >> F-BIN, F-RIGHT

i. Trochaic: Unattested	ii. Iambic: Unattested
(σ́σ)(Ĺ)(σ́σ)(σ́σ)	(σσ́)(Ĺ)(σσ́)(σσ́)
(σ́σ)(H́)(σ́σ)(σ́σ)	(σσ́)(H́)(σσ́)(σσ́)

b. PARSE-σ >> F-RIGHT >> ALL-F-LEFT >> ALL-F-RIGHT; PARSE-σ >> F-BIN, F-LEFT

i. Trochaic: Unattested	ii. Iambic: Unattested
(σ́σ)(σ́σ)(Ĺ)(σ́σ)	(σσ́)(σσ́)(Ĺ)(σσ́)
(σ́σ)(σ́σ)(H́)(σ́σ)	(σσ́)(σσ́)(H́)(σσ́)

The OHP, then, contributes to the deterioration of Iterative Foot Optimization's predictions in two ways. The first is that it exacerbates Iterative Foot Optimization's over-generation problem. Over-generation in Iterative Foot Optimization was already substantial, given the predicted, but unattested, bidirectional exhaustive parsing patterns, and the prediction of eight unattested OHP patterns only makes matters worse. The second is that the OHP gives Iterative Foot Optimization a substantial under-generation problem. Like Symmetrical Alignment, under the standard definition of F-BIN, Iterative Foot Optimization cannot produce a single quantity-insensitive under-parsing system.

Since it emerges under both parallelism and serialism, neither derivational perspective can be the source of the OHP. Since Iterative Foot Optimization and Symmetrical Alignment place different additional restrictions on the position of heavy monosyllabic feet in their particular versions of the OHP, however, their derivational perspectives clearly do play a role in how the OHP is manifested.

3.3.2 Iterative Foot Optimization and the quantity-sensitive EOP

As in Symmetrical Alignment, the quantity-sensitive EOP only applies in Iterative Foot Optimization to odd-parity forms that escape the OHP. Under Iterative Foot Optimization, however, the quantity-sensitive EOP results in twice as many unattested patterns. The reason is simply that the EOP can accompany twice as many specific manifestations of the OHP. In Symmetrical Alignment, the OHP has only two types: one that selects the leftmost odd-numbered heavy syllable for parsing as a monosyllabic foot and one that selects the rightmost. In Iterative Foot Optimization, the OHP has four types: one that selects a heavy initial syllable, one that selects a heavy post-peninitial syllable, one that selects a heavy antepenult, and one that selects a heavy ultima. Each of these four types can be combined with both the insertion and deletion varieties of the quantity-sensitive EOP.

Iterative Foot Optimization's deletion version of the quantity-sensitive EOP arises in rankings where PARSE-σ and F-BIN both dominate MAX and MAX dominates the alignment constraints. The ranking of DEP is not crucial.

(49) OHP + quantity-sensitive EOP (deletion version)

PARSE-σ, F-BIN >> MAX >> ALL-F-LEFT, ALL-F-RIGHT, F-LEFT, F-RIGHT; DEP

To illustrate, consider the effects of the ranking (with rightward alignment) in (50) and (51) at the point in the derivation where the parsing status of the leftover syllable is determined. As (50) illustrates, the OHP, rather than the EOP, emerges in forms with an appropriately positioned heavy syllable – in this case, the initial syllable.

(50) ...

H(LL)(LL)(LL)	PARSE-σ	F-BIN	MAX	ALL-F-RIGHT
☞ w. (H)(LL)(LL)(LL)				W 12
a. (LL)(LL)(LL)			W 1	L 6
b. H(LL)(LL)(LL)	W 1			L 6

As (51) illustrates, however, a syllable is deleted in forms that lack an appropriately positioned heavy syllable. If the leftover syllable remains unparsed, it violates the high-ranked PARSE-σ. If the leftover syllable is parsed a monosyllabic foot, it violates the high-ranked F-BIN. In the end, deleting the leftover syllable is the best option, as it satisfies F-BIN and PARSE-σ simultaneously.

(51) ...

L(LL)(LL)(LL)	PARSE-σ	F-BIN	MAX	ALL-F-RIGHT
☞ w. (LL)(LL)(LL)			1	6
a. L(LL)(LL)(LL)	W 1		L	6
b. (L)(LL)(LL)(LL)		W 1	L	W 12

The reason that the ranking of DEP is not crucial in this context is that the high-ranking PARSE-σ and F-BIN both discourage syllable insertion in the final step. Adding another stray syllable would increase the violations of the high-ranked PARSE-σ. Adding a syllable to an existing disyllabic foot (making the foot ternary) would create a violation of F-BIN. It is impossible to create a new foot to accommodate the inserted syllable, as in (52), because a candidate can have only one difference from the input. A new syllable and a new foot represent two differences. There is simply no advantage to be gained, then, from a DEP violation.

(52) Impossible mapping

L(LL)(LL)(LL) → (LL)(LL)(LL)(LL)

It is only advantageous to insert a syllable when it can be added to an existing monosyllabic foot, and this circumstance helps to determine the rankings under which the insertion version of the quantity-sensitive EOP emerges. The last unparsed syllable of an odd-parity form will only be parsed as a monosyllabic foot when PARSE-σ and MAX both dominate F-BIN and F-BIN dominates DEP. In unidirectional patterns, F-BIN must also dominate either ALL-F-LEFT or ALL-F-RIGHT, ALL-F-LEFT in systems with rightward alignment and ALL-F-RIGHT in systems with leftward alignment. In bidirectional patterns, F-BIN must dominate both.

(53) OHP + quantity-sensitive EOP (insertion version)

a. Unidirectional Patterns only

i. MAX, PARSE-σ >> ALL-F-RIGHT >> F-BIN >> ALL-F-LEFT, DEP; MAX, PARSE-σ >> F-LEFT, F-RIGHT

ii. MAX, PARSE-σ >> ALL-F-LEFT >> F-BIN >> ALL-F-RIGHT, DEP; MAX, PARSE-σ >> F-LEFT, F-RIGHT

b. Unidirectional or Bidirectional patterns

MAX, PARSE-σ >> F-BIN >> ALL-F-LEFT, ALL-F-RIGHT, DEP; MAX, PARSE-σ >> F-LEFT, F-RIGHT

The tableaux in (54) and (55) illustrate the effects of the ranking (with rightward alignment) starting at the point in the derivation where the parsing status of the leftover syllable is determined. As (54) illustrates, the OHP, rather than the EOP, emerges in forms with an appropriately positioned heavy syllable – once again, the initial syllable.

(54) ...

H(LL)(LL)(LL)	PARSE-σ	MAX	F-BIN	DEP
☞ w. (H)(LL)(LL)(LL)				
a. HL(LL)(LL)(LL)	W 2			W 1
b. (LL)(LL)(LL)		W 1		
c. H(LL)(LL)(LL)	W 1			

As (55) illustrates, a syllable is inserted in forms that lack an appropriately positioned heavy syllable. At the point where only the parsing status of the leftover syllable remains to be determined, the leftover syllable cannot be left unparsed without violating the high-ranked PARSE-σ, and it cannot be deleted without violating the high-ranked MAX. To satisfy both, it is parsed as a monosyllabic foot at the expense of F-BIN. This result allows for an additional step, and the ranking F-BIN >> DEP ensures that a single syllable is added to the monosyllabic foot, making the foot disyllabic and the overall form even-parity.

(55) ...

L(LL)(LL)(LL)	PARSE-σ	MAX	F-BIN	DEP
☞ w. (L)(LL)(LL)(LL)			1	
a. L(LL)(LL)(LL)	1 W		L	
b. LL(LL)(LL)(LL)	2 W		L	
c. (LL)(LL)(LL)		1 W	L	1 W

(L)(LL)(LL)(LL)	PARSE-σ	MAX	F-BIN	DEP
☞ w. (LL)(LL)(LL)(LL)				1
l. (L)(LL)(LL)(LL)			1 W	L

In addition to the patterns summarized in (45-48), then, Iterative Foot Optimization predicts eight OHP + QS EOP deletion languages, and eight OHP + QS EOP insertion languages. The predicted OHP + QS EOP languages are summarized in (56) and (57). For each language predicted, there are two example mappings. The first indicates the type of OHP pattern that emerges from odd-parity inputs with an appropriately positioned odd-numbered heavy syllable, and the second example illustrates the type of EOP pattern that emerges from odd-parity inputs that lack such a heavy syllable.

(56) OHP + quantity-sensitive EOP (deletion version)

a. PARSE-σ, F-BIN >> MAX >> ALL-F-RIGHT >> ALL-F-LEFT, F-LEFT; MAX >> F-RIGHT; DEP

i. Trochaic: Unattested

Hσσσσσσ → (H́)(σ́σ)(σ́σ)(σ́σ)

Lσσσσσσ → (σ́σ)(σ́σ)(σ́σ)

ii. Iambic: Unattested

Hσσσσσσ → (H́)(σσ́)(σσ́)(σσ́)

Lσσσσσσ → (σσ́)(σσ́)(σσ́)

b. PARSE-σ, F-BIN >> MAX >> ALL-F-LEFT >> ALL-F-RIGHT, F-RIGHT; MAX >> F-LEFT; DEP

i. Trochaic: Unattested

σσσσσσH → (σ́σ)(σ́σ)(σ́σ)(H́)

σσσσσσL → (σ́σ)(σ́σ)(σ́σ)

ii. Iambic: Unattested

σσσσσσH → (σσ́)(σσ́)(σσ́)(H́)

σσσσσσL → (σσ́)(σσ́)(σσ́)

c. Parse-σ, F-Bin >> Max >> F-Left >> All-F-Right >> All-F-Left; Max >> F-Right; Dep

i. Trochaic: Unattested
σσHσσσσ → (σ́σ)(H́)(σ́σ)(σ́σ)
σσLσσσσ → (σ́σ)(σ́σ)(σ́σ)

ii. Iambic: Unattested
σσHσσσσ → (σσ́)(H́)(σσ́)(σσ́)
σσLσσσσ → (σσ́)(σσ́)(σσ́)

d. Parse-σ, F-Bin >> Max >> F-Right >> All-F-Left >> All-F-Right; Max >> F-Left; Dep

i. Trochaic: Unattested
σσσσHσσ → (σ́σ)(σ́σ)(H́)(σ́σ)
σσσσLσσ → (σ́σ)(σ́σ)(σ́σ)

ii. Iambic: Unattested
σσσσHσσ → (σσ́)(σσ́)(H́)(σσ́)
σσσσLσσ → (σσ́)(σσ́)(σσ́)

(57) OHP + quantity-sensitive EOP (insertion version)

a. Max, Parse-σ >> F-Bin, All-F-Right, All-F-Left, F-Left, F-Right, Dep; All-F-Right >> All-F-Left, F-Left; F-Bin >> All-F-Left, Dep

i. Trochaic: Unattested
Hσσσσσσ → (H́)(σ́σ)(σ́σ)(σ́σ)
Lσσσσσσ → (Ĺσ)(σ́σ)(σ́σ)(σ́σ)

ii. Iambic: Unattested
Hσσσσσσ → (H́)(σσ́)(σσ́)(σσ́)
Lσσσσσσ → (σĹ)(σσ́)(σσ́)(σσ́)

b. Max, Parse-σ >> F-Bin, All-F-Left, All-F-Right, F-Right, F-Left, Dep; All-F-Left >> All-F-Right, F-Right; F-Bin >> All-F-Right, Dep

i. Trochaic: Unattested
σσσσσσH → (σ́σ)(σ́σ)(σ́σ)(H́)
σσσσσσL → (σ́σ)(σ́σ)(σ́σ)(Ĺσ)

ii. Iambic: Unattested
σσσσσσH → (σσ́)(σσ́)(σσ́)(H́)
σσσσσσL → (σσ́)(σσ́)(σσ́)(σĹ)

c. Max, Parse-σ >> F-Bin, All-F-Right, All-F-Left, F-Left, F-Right, Dep; F-Bin, F-Left >> All-F-Right >> All-F-Left; F-Bin >> Dep

i. Trochaic: Unattested
σσHσσσσ → (σ́σ)(H́)(σ́σ)(σ́σ)
σσLσσσσ → (σ́σ)(Ĺσ)(σ́σ)(σ́σ)

ii. Iambic: Unattested
σσHσσσσ → (σσ́)(H́)(σσ́)(σσ́)
σσLσσσσ → (σσ́)(σĹ)(σσ́)(σσ́)

d. Max, Parse-σ >> F-Bin, All-F-Left, All-F-Right, F-Right, F-Left, Dep; F-Bin, F-Right >> All-F-Left >> All-F-Right; F-Bin >> Dep

i. Trochaic: Unattested
σσσσHσσ → (σ́σ)(σ́σ)(H́)(σ́σ)
σσσσLσσ → (σ́σ)(σ́σ)(Ĺσ)(σ́σ)

ii. Iambic: Unattested
σσσσHσσ → (σσ́)(σσ́)(H́)(σσ́)
σσσσLσσ → (σσ́)(σσ́)(σĹ)(σσ́)

Notice that the quantity-sensitivity of the OHP can be observed with exhaustive parsing rankings (Parse-σ >> F-Bin) in the context of OHP + quantity-sensitive EOP patterns, where they were obscured by the basic exhaustive parsing patterns in the predictions summarized in (47) and (48). As in Symmetrical Alignment, sensitivity to the weight of odd-numbered syllables in odd-parity forms results in an alternation between odd-parity outputs and even-parity outputs. In the context of quantity-sensitive EOP patterns, then, it is no longer the case that the last syllable addressed will be parsed as monosyllabic foot whether it is heavy or light. If it is heavy, it will be parsed as a monosyllabic foot. If it is light, it will be deleted or parsed into a disyllabic foot with an epenthetic syllable.

Before examining the possibility of splitting the minimality restriction into separate syllabic and moraic versions in Iterative Foot Optimization, and the manifestations of the quantity-insensitive EOP that would emerge as a result, I will briefly discuss how something like the QI EOP can emerge even under the standard definition of F-BIN in Iterative Foot Optimization. Although it also results in languages that only allow even-parity output forms, this case differs somewhat from the QI EOP in that it arises from an interaction between PARSE-σ, MAX, and the alignment constraints. This interesting interaction is made possible by Iterative Foot Optimization's serial component.

Under the thoroughly parallel Symmetrical Alignment, if PARSE-σ and one of the alignment constraints ranks above MAX, the result is deletion of all syllables from both even- and odd-parity inputs that cannot be contained in a single binary foot in the output. In contrast, under the serial Iterative Foot Optimization, the same ranking results in deletion of a single syllable from odd-parity inputs only.

(58) Alignment-based even-only rankings

a. PARSE-σ >> ALL-F-LEFT >> MAX; PARSE-σ >> ALL-F-RIGHT, F-LEFT, F-RIGHT; DEP, F-BIN

b. PARSE-σ >> ALL-F-RIGHT >> MAX >> ALL-F-LEFT; PARSE-σ >> F-LEFT, F-RIGHT; DEP, F-BIN

c. PARSE-σ >> F-LEFT >> MAX >> ALL-F-LEFT, ALL-F-RIGHT; PARSE-σ >> F-RIGHT; DEP, F-BIN

d. PARSE-σ >> F-RIGHT >> MAX >> ALL-F-LEFT, ALL-F-RIGHT, F-LEFT; DEP, F-BIN

As the derivation in (59) indicates, even though PARSE-σ and ALL-F-LEFT both dominate MAX, the high-ranking PARSE-σ actually prevents syllable deletion until the point where just a single syllable remains. In Iterative Foot Optimization, only a single difference is allowed between input and output, so it is not possible to delete multiple syllables in a single evaluation. Since PARSE-σ is always better satisfied when a disyllabic foot is created than when a single syllable is deleted, disyllabic parsing proceeds until just a single syllable remains. This is illustrated in the first three steps in (59). In the final step, Parse-σ does not distinguish between deleting the remaining syllable and parsing it as monosyllabic foot, so alignment is free to insist that the syllable be deleted at Max's expense. It does not matter whether the remaining syllable is light or heavy.

(59)

HLLLLLH	Parse-σ	All-F-Left	Max
☞ w. (LL)LLLLH	5		
l. LLLLLH	W 6		W 1

(LL)LLLLH	Parse-σ	All-F-Left	Max
☞ w. (LL)(LL)LLH	3	2	
l. (LL)LLLH	W 4	L	W 1

(LL)(LL)LLH	Parse-σ	All-F-Left	Max
☞ w. (LL)(LL)(LL)H	1	6	
l. (LL)(LL)LH	W 2	L 2	W 1

(LL)(LL)(LL)H	Parse-σ	All-F-Left	Max
☞ w. (LL)(LL)(LL)		6	1
l. (LL)(LL)(LL)(H)		W 12	L

3.3.3 Iterative Foot Optimization and the quantity-insensitive EOP

Under an approach where the standard F-Bin constraint is split into separate moraic and syllabic minimality requirements, Iterative Foot Optimization makes predictions similar to those of Symmetrical Alignment, but there are some important differences. Just as it does for Symmetrical Alignment, the presence of F-Min-σ in the constraint set solves the under-generation problem for Iterative Foot Optimization. Iterative Foot Optimization predicts the same range of quantity-insensitive patterns as it does under the idealized conditions discussed in Chapter 2. It predicts eight under-parsing patterns, four unidirectional and four bidirectional, and it predicts eight exhaustive parsing patterns, four unidirectional and four bidirectional. Of the 16 quantity-insensitive patterns predicted, eight are attested.

Iterative Foot Optimization's underlying over-generation problem is much more substantial than that of Symmetrical Alignment, however, and splitting the minimality restriction only makes matters worse. As it does in Symmetrical Alignment, the presence of F-MIN-μ in the constraint set means that Iterative Foot optimization still predicts languages that exhibit the OHP in isolation (summarized in (45 and (46) above) and languages that exhibit the OHP accompanied by the quantity-sensitive EOP (summarized in (56) and (57) above).

Also similar to Symmetrical Alignment, the presence of F-MIN-σ in the constraint set means that Iterative Foot Optimization suffers the effects of the quantity-insensitive EOP. There are two differences, however. The first difference is that it is possible under Iterative Foot Optimization to predict the exact position of syllable insertion and deletion. When a syllable is inserted, it is always inserted into the foot containing the last syllable to have its parsing status settled. When a syllable is deleted, it is always the last syllable to have its parsing status settled. The second difference is that Iterative Foot Optimization can combine the QI EOP with other patterns. It can combine the QI EOP with under-parsing, and it can combine the QI EOP with the QS EOP.

Rankings that conform to those in (60) or (61) result in simple quantity-insensitive EOP patterns, where languages have only even-parity forms on the surface.

(60) Quantity-insensitive EOP (deletion version)

PARSE-σ, F-MIN-σ >> MAX >> ALL-F-LEFT, ALL-F-RIGHT, F-LEFT, F-RIGHT; F-MIN-μ, DEP

(61) Quantity-insensitive EOP (insertion version)

a. Unidirectional derivations only

i. MAX, PARSE-σ >> ALL-F-RIGHT >> F-MIN-σ >> ALL-F-LEFT, DEP; MAX, PARSE-σ >> F-LEFT, F-RIGHT, F-MIN-μ

ii. MAX, PARSE-σ >> ALL-F-LEFT >> F-MIN-σ >> ALL-F-RIGHT, DEP; MAX, PARSE-σ >> F-LEFT, F-RIGHT, F-MIN-μ

b. Unidirectional or bidirectional derivations

MAX, PARSE-σ >> F-MIN-σ >> ALL-F-LEFT, ALL-F-RIGHT, DEP; MAX, PARSE-σ >> F-LEFT, F-RIGHT, F-MIN-μ

For each of the patterns summarized in (62) and (63), there are two example outputs for odd-parity inputs. Regardless of the presence or absence of odd-numbered heavy syllables in the inputs, the outputs are always even-parity.

(62) OHP + quantity-insensitive EOP (deletion version)

a. Parse-σ, F-Min-σ >> Max >> All-F-Right >> All-F-Left, F-Left; Max >> F-Right; F-Min-μ, Dep

i. Trochaic: Unattested

Hσσσσσσ → (σ́σ)(σ́σ)(σ́σ)

Lσσσσσσ → (σ́σ)(σ́σ)(σ́σ)

ii. Iambic: Unattested

Hσσσσσσ → (σσ́)(σσ́)(σσ́)

Lσσσσσσ → (σσ́)(σσ́)(σσ́)

b. Parse-σ, F-Min-σ >> Max >> All-F-Left >> All-F-Right, F-Right; Max >> F-Left; F-Min-μ, Dep

i. Trochaic: Unattested

σσσσσσH → (σ́σ)(σ́σ)(σ́σ)

σσσσσσL → (σ́σ)(σ́σ)(σ́σ)

ii. Iambic: Unattested

σσσσσσH → (σσ́)(σσ́)(σσ́)

σσσσσσL → (σσ́)(σσ́)(σσ́)

c. Parse-σ, F-Min-σ >> Max >> F-Left >> All-F-Right >> All-F-Left; Max >> F-Right; F-Min-μ, Dep

i. Trochaic: Unattested

σσHσσσσ → (σ́σ)(σ́σ)(σ́σ)

σσLσσσσ → (σ́σ)(σ́σ)(σ́σ)

ii. Iambic: Unattested

σσHσσσσ → (σσ́)(σσ́)(σσ́)

σσLσσσσ → (σσ́)(σσ́)(σσ́)

d. Parse-σ, F-Min-σ >> Max >> F-Right >> All-F-Left >> All-F-Right; Max >> F-Left; F-Min-μ, Dep

i. Trochaic: Unattested

σσσσHσσ → (σ́σ)(σ́σ)(σ́σ)

σσσσLσσ → (σ́σ)(σ́σ)(σ́σ)

ii. Iambic: Unattested

σσσσHσσ → (σσ́)(σσ́)(σσ́)

σσσσLσσ → (σσ́)(σσ́)(σσ́)

(63) OHP + quantity-insensitive EOP (insertion version)

a. Max, Parse-σ >> F-Min-σ, F-Min-μ, All-F-Right, All-F-Left, F-Left, F-Right, Dep; All-F-Right >> All-F-Left, F-Left; F-Min-σ >> All-F-Left, Dep

i. Trochaic: Unattested

Hσσσσσσ → (H́σ)(σ́σ)(σ́σ)(σ́σ)

Lσσσσσσ → (Ĺσ)(σ́σ)(σ́σ)(σ́σ)

ii. Iambic: Unattested

Hσσσσσσ → (σH́)(σσ́)(σσ́)(σσ́)

Lσσσσσσ → (σĹ)(σσ́)(σσ́)(σσ́)

b. MAX, PARSE-σ >> F-MIN-σ, F-MIN-μ, ALL-F-LEFT, ALL-F-RIGHT, F-RIGHT, F-LEFT, DEP; ALL-F-LEFT >> ALL-F-RIGHT, F-RIGHT; F-MIN-σ >> ALL-F-RIGHT, DEP

i. Trochaic: Unattested

σσσσσσH →
(σ́σ)(σ́σ)(σ́σ)(H́σ)

σσσσσσL →
(σ́σ)(σ́σ)(σ́σ)(Ĺσ)

ii. Iambic: Unattested

σσσσσσH →
(σσ́)(σσ́)(σσ́)(σH́)

σσσσσσL →
(σσ́)(σσ́)(σσ́)(σĹ)

c. MAX, PARSE-σ >> F-MIN-σ, F-MIN-μ, ALL-F-RIGHT, ALL-F-LEFT, F-LEFT, F-RIGHT, DEP; F-MIN-σ, F-LEFT >> ALL-F-RIGHT >> ALL-F-LEFT; F-MIN-σ >> DEP

i. Trochaic: Unattested

σσHσσσσ →
(σ́σ)(H́σ)(σ́σ)(σ́σ)

σσLσσσσ →
(σ́σ)(Ĺσ)(σ́σ)(σ́σ)

ii. Iambic: Unattested

σσHσσσσ →
(σσ́)(σH́)(σσ́)(σσ́)

σσLσσσσ →
(σσ́)(σĹ)(σσ́)(σσ́)

d. MAX, PARSE-σ >> F-MIN-σ, F-MIN-μ, ALL-F-LEFT, ALL-F-RIGHT, F-RIGHT, F-LEFT, DEP; F-MIN-σ, F-RIGHT >> ALL-F-LEFT >> ALL-F-RIGHT; F-MIN-σ >> DEP

i. Trochaic: Unattested

σσσσHσσ →
(σ́σ)(σ́σ)(H́σ)(σ́σ)

σσσσLσσ →
(σ́σ)(σ́σ)(Ĺσ)(σ́σ)

ii. Iambic: Unattested

σσσσHσσ →
(σσ́)(σσ́)(σH́)(σσ́)

σσσσLσσ →
(σσ́)(σσ́)(σĹ)(σσ́)

To this point, then, the pathological OPIP predictions arising under Iterative Foot Optimization with the addition of a separate syllabic minimality requirement are reasonably similar to those arising under Symmetrical Alignment under the same conditions. Iterative Foot Optimization's serialism makes it possible, however, to produce two variations that are not possible under the thoroughly parallel Symmetrical Alignment. First, rankings that conform to those in (64) combine under-parsing with the quantity-insensitive EOP. In each of these rankings, MAX and F-MIN-μ dominate PARSE-σ, PARSE-σ dominates F-MIN-σ, and F-MIN-σ dominates DEP.

(64) Under-parsing + quantity-insensitive EOP (insertion version)

a. Unidirectional patterns only

i. MAX, F-MIN-μ >> PARSE-σ >> ALL-F-RIGHT >> F-MIN-σ >> ALL-F-LEFT, DEP; PARSE-σ >> F-LEFT, F-RIGHT

ii. MAX, F-MIN-μ >> PARSE-σ >> ALL-F-LEFT >> F-MIN-σ >> ALL-F-RIGHT, DEP; PARSE-σ >> F-LEFT, F-RIGHT

b. Unidirectional or bidirectional patterns

MAX, F-MIN-μ >> PARSE-σ >> F-MIN-σ >> ALL-F-LEFT, ALL-F-RIGHT, DEP; PARSE-σ >> F-LEFT, F-RIGHT

Under the rankings in (64), odd-parity forms that lack heavy syllables in the appropriate position emerge with under-parsing patterns and remain odd-parity on the surface. Forms that do contain a heavy syllable in the appropriate position add a syllable and emerge as even-parity on the surface. The usual complementary relationship of the OHP and the EOP becomes overlapping. Rather than applying only to forms that escape the OHP, the EOP in this case applies only to forms that might otherwise have been affected by the OHP

Consider a ranking consistent with those in (64) at the point in derivation for an odd-parity input where only the parsing status of the leftover syllable remains to be determined. If the leftover syllable is light, as (65) demonstrates using a form with leftward alignment, it remains unparsed. It is not possible to parse the syllable as a monosyllabic foot to satisfy PARSE-σ, due to the higher-ranked F-MIN-μ, and it is not possible to delete a syllable to satisfy PARSE-σ, due to the higher-ranked MAX. Adding a syllable at this point only creates an additional violation of the high-ranked PARSE-σ, and a new syllable and a new foot cannot be added simultaneously. The faithful candidate with the single unparsed syllable is optimal.

(65) ...

(LL)(LL)(LL)L	MAX	F-MIN-μ	PARSE-σ	F-MIN-σ	DEP
☞ w. (LL)(LL)(LL)L			1		
a. (LL)(LL)(LL)(L)		1 W	L	1 W	
b. (LL)(LL)(LL)LL			2 W		1 W
c. (LL)(LL)(LL)	1 W		L		

If the leftover syllable is heavy, however, as in (66), the same ranking allows it to be parsed as monosyllabic foot, and this allows for an additional step. In the final step, a syllable is inserted at the expense of the low-ranked DEP to satisfy the higher ranked F-MIN-σ. The optimal output for the odd-parity input in this case is an exhaustively parsed even-parity form.

(66) ...

(LL)(LL)(LL)H	Max	F-Min-μ	Parse-σ	F-Min-σ	Dep
☞ w. (LL)(LL)(LL)(H)				1	
a. (LL)(LL)(LL)H			1 W	L	
b. (LL)(LL)(LL)HL			2 W	L	1 W
c. (LL)(LL)(LL)	1 W			L	

(LL)(LL)(LL)(H)	Max	Min-μ	Parse	Min-σ	Dep
☞ w. (LL)(LL)(LL)(HL)					1
l. (LL)(LL)(LL)(H)				1 W	L

Though forms with leftward alignment were used to illustrate in (65) and (66), the crucial rankings in (64) can combine the insertion version of the quantity-insensitive EOP with any one of Iterative Foot Optimization's basic under-parsing patterns, depending on the ranking of the alignment constraints. For each of the patterns summarized in (67), there are two example outputs for odd-parity inputs. In the first, the last syllable to have its parsing status settled is heavy. In the second, the last syllable to have its parsing status settled is light. A heavy syllable in the relevant position leads to syllable insertion, and a light syllable in the relevant position leads to under-parsing.

(67) Under-parsing + quantity-insensitive EOP (insertion version)

a. Max, F-Min-μ >> Parse-σ >> F-Min-σ, All-F-Right, All-F-Left, F-Left, F-Right, Dep; All-F-Right >> All-F-Left, F-Left; F-Min-σ >> All-F-Left, Dep

i. Trochaic: Unattested

Hσσσσσσ →
(H́σ)(σ́σ)(σ́σ)(σ́σ)

Lσσσσσσ →
L(σ́σ)(σ́σ)(σ́σ)

ii. Iambic: Unattested

Hσσσσσσ →
(σH́)(σσ́)(σσ́)(σσ́)

Lσσσσσσ →
L(σσ́)(σσ́)(σσ́)

b. MAX, F-MIN-μ >> PARSE-σ >> F-MIN-σ, ALL-F-LEFT, ALL-F-RIGHT, F-RIGHT, F-LEFT, DEP; ALL-F-LEFT >> ALL-F-RIGHT, F-RIGHT; F-MIN-σ >> ALL-F-RIGHT, DEP

i. Trochaic: Unattested	ii. Iambic: Unattested
σσσσσσH → (σ́σ)(σ́σ)(σ́σ)(H́σ)	σσσσσσH → (σσ́)(σσ́)(σσ́)(σH́)
σσσσσσL → (σ́σ)(σ́σ)(σ́σ)L	σσσσσσL → (σσ́)(σσ́)(σσ́)L

c. MAX, F-MIN-μ >> PARSE-σ >> F-MIN-σ, ALL-F-RIGHT, ALL-F-LEFT, F-LEFT, F-RIGHT, DEP; F-MIN-σ, F-LEFT >> ALL-F-RIGHT >> ALL-F-LEFT; F-MIN-σ >> DEP

i. Trochaic: Unattested	ii. Iambic: Unattested
σσHσσσσ → (σ́σ)(H́σ)(σ́σ)(σ́σ)	σσHσσσσ → (σσ́)(σH́)(σσ́)(σσ́)
σσLσσσσ → (σ́σ)L(σ́σ)(σ́σ)	σσLσσσσ → (σσ́)L(σσ́)(σσ́)

d. MAX, F-MIN-μ >> PARSE-σ >> F-MIN-σ, ALL-F-LEFT, ALL-F-RIGHT, F-RIGHT, F-LEFT, DEP; F-MIN-σ, F-RIGHT >> ALL-F-LEFT >> ALL-F-RIGHT; F-MIN-σ >> DEP

i. Trochaic: Unattested	ii. Iambic: Unattested
σσσσHσσ → (σ́σ)(σ́σ)(H́σ)(σ́σ)	σσσσHσσ → (σσ́)(σσ́)(σH́)(σσ́)
σσσσLσσ → (σ́σ)(σ́σ)L(σ́σ)	σσσσLσσ → (σσ́)(σσ́)L(σσ́)

The second variation possible under the serial Iterative Foot Optimization, but not under the thoroughly parallel Symmetrical Alignment, is one that combines the deletion version of the quantity-sensitive EOP with the insertion version of the quantity-insensitive EOP. For odd-parity inputs with a light leftover syllable, the leftover syllable is deleted. For odd-parity inputs with a heavy leftover syllable, an additional syllable is added. The result, emerging under rankings consistent with those in (68), is a language with only even-parity surface forms. In each of these rankings, PARSE-σ and F-MIN-μ dominate MAX, MAX dominates F-MIN-σ, and F-MIN-σ dominates DEP.

(68) Quantity-sensitive EOP (deletion) + quantity-insensitive EOP (insertion)
PARSE-σ, F-MIN-μ >> MAX >> F-MIN-σ >> DEP

a. Unidirectional derivations only

i. PARSE-σ, F-MIN-μ >> MAX >> ALL-F-RIGHT >> F-MIN-σ >> ALL-F-LEFT, DEP; PARSE-σ >> F-LEFT, F-RIGHT

ii. PARSE-σ, F-MIN-μ >> MAX >> ALL-F-LEFT >> F-MIN-σ >> ALL-F-RIGHT, DEP; PARSE-σ >> F-LEFT, F-RIGHT

b. Unidirectional or bidirectional derivations

PARSE-σ, F-MIN-μ >> MAX >> F-MIN-σ >> ALL-F-LEFT, ALL-F-RIGHT, DEP; PARSE-σ >> F-LEFT, F-RIGHT

Consider a ranking consistent with those in (68) at the point in derivation for an odd-parity input where only the parsing status of the leftover syllable remains to be determined. As (69) demonstrates, if the leftover syllable is light, it is deleted. The higher-ranked PARSE-σ is satisfied at the expense of the lower-ranked MAX. Note that adding a syllable only creates an additional violation of PARSE-σ, and a new syllable and new foot cannot be added simultaneously, so PARSE-σ cannot be satisfied at the expense of DEP.

(69) ...

(LL)(LL)(LL)L	PARSE-σ	F-MIN-μ	MAX	F-MIN-σ	DEP
☞ w. (LL)(LL)(LL)			1		
a. (LL)(LL)(LL)L	W 1		L		
b. (LL)(LL)(LL)(L)		W 1	L	W 1	
c. (LL)(LL)(LL)LL	W 2		L		W 1

If the leftover syllable is heavy, however, as in (70), the same ranking allows it to be parsed as monosyllabic foot, and this allows for an additional step. In the final step, a syllable is inserted at the expense of the low-ranked DEP to satisfy the higher ranked F-MIN-σ.

(70) ...

(LL)(LL)(LL)H	Parse	F-Min-μ	Max	F-Min-σ	Dep
☞ w. (LL)(LL)(LL)(H)				1	
a. (LL)(LL)(LL)H	1 W			L	
b. (LL)(LL)(LL)HL	2 W			L	1 W
c. (LL)(LL)(LL)			1 W	L	

(LL)(LL)(LL)(H)	Parse	Min-μ	Max	Min-σ	Dep
☞ w. (LL)(LL)(LL)(HL)					1
l. (LL)(LL)(LL)(H)				1 W	L

Rankings consistent with those in (68) produce eight additional patterns. For each of the patterns summarized in (71), there are two example outputs for odd-parity inputs. They illustrate the consequences of having a heavy or light syllable in the position of the last syllable to have its parsing status settled. A heavy syllable leads to syllable insertion, and a light syllable leads to syllable deletion.

(71) Quantity-sensitive EOP (deletion) + quantity-insensitive EOP (insertion)

a. Parse-σ, F-Min-μ >> Max >> F-Min-σ, All-F-Right, All-F-Left, F-Left, F-Right, Dep; All-F-Right >> All-F-Left, F-Left; F-Min-σ >> All-F-Left, Dep

i. Trochaic: Unattested

Hσσσσσσ →
(H́σ)(σ́σ)(σ́σ)(σ́σ)

Lσσσσσσ →
(σ́σ)(σ́σ)(σ́σ)

ii. Iambic: Unattested

Hσσσσσσ →
(σH́)(σσ́)(σσ́)(σσ́)

Lσσσσσσ →
(σσ́)(σσ́)(σσ́)

b. Parse-σ, F-Min-μ >> Max >> F-Min-σ, All-F-Left, All-F-Right, F-Right, F-Left, Dep; All-F-Left >> All-F-Right, F-Right; F-Min-σ >> All-F-Right, Dep

i. Trochaic: Unattested

σσσσσσH →
(σ́σ)(σ́σ)(σ́σ)(H́σ)

σσσσσσL →
(σ́σ)(σ́σ)(σ́σ)

ii. Iambic: Unattested

σσσσσσH →
(σσ́)(σσ́)(σσ́)(σH́)

σσσσσσL →
(σσ́)(σσ́)(σσ́)

c. Parse-σ, F-Min-μ >> Max >> F-Min-σ, All-F-Right, All-F-Left, F-Left, F-Right, Dep; F-Min-σ, F-Left >> All-F-Right >> All-F-Left; F-Min-σ >> Dep

i. Trochaic: Unattested

σσHσσσσ →
(σ́σ)(H́σ)(σ́σ)(σ́σ)

σσLσσσσ →
(σ́σ)(σ́σ)(σ́σ)

ii. Iambic: Unattested

σσHσσσσ →
(σσ́)(σH́)(σσ́)(σσ́)

σσLσσσσ →
(σσ́)(σσ́)(σσ́)

d. Parse-σ, F-Min-μ >> Max >> F-Min-σ, All-F-Left, All-F-Right, F-Right, F-Left, Dep; F-Min-σ, F-Right >> All-F-Left >> All-F-Right; F-Min-σ >> Dep

i. Trochaic: Unattested

σσσσHσσ →
(σ́σ)(σ́σ)(H́σ)(σ́σ)

σσσσLσσ →
(σ́σ)(σ́σ)(σ́σ)

ii. Iambic: Unattested

σσσσHσσ →
(σσ́)(σσ́)(σH́)(σσ́)

σσσσLσσ →
(σσ́)(σσ́)(σσ́)

While a separate syllabic minimality restriction solves the under-generation problem in Iterative Foot Optimization, then, it does not address its underlying over-generation problem. It also results in all the same OPIP-related predictions found in Symmetrical Alignment, plus two variations not found in Symmetrical Alignment.

3.4 Summary

In Chapter 2, we saw that Symmetrical Alignment and Iterative Foot Optimization both predict a reasonable range of binary default patterns when the effects of syllable weight are not actually considered. Both had difficulties with over-generation, though the difficulties of Iterative Foot Optimization were more significant than those of Symmetrical Alignment. The more serious over-generation problem was a direct result of the former's serialism.

As we have seen in this chapter, when the effects of syllable weight are considered, Symmetrical Alignment and Iterative Foot Optimization both exhibit the effects of the Odd-Parity Input Problem. The OPIP consists of two sub-problems: the Odd Heavy Problem, where an odd-numbered heavy syllable in an odd-parity output is parsed as a monosyllabic foot to achieve exhaustive binary parsing, and the Even Output Problem, where odd-parity inputs are converted into even-parity outputs to achieve exhaustive binary parsing.

In Section 3.2 we saw that Symmetrical Alignment manifests the effects of both the OHP and the EOP. The effects were so pervasive that Symmetrical Alignment could not produce a single attested quantity-insensitive under-parsing pattern, resulting in both a substantial under-generation problem and an even more substantial over-generation problem. While the addition of a separate syllabic minimality requirement addressed the under-generation problem, it only exacerbated the over-generation problem.

In Section 3.3, we saw that Iterative Foot Optimization also exhibits the effects of both the OHP and the EOP, though its manifests them differently than Symmetrical Alignment, resulting in both a significant under-generation problem and an even more substantial over-generation problem. While the addition of a separate syllabic minimality restriction addresses the under-generation problem in Iterative Foot Optimization, it exacerbates the over-generation problem, yielding an even greater variety of pathological predictions than Symmetrical Alignment under the same conditions.

Since the effects of the OPIP were pervasive in both Symmetrical Alignment and Iterative Foot Optimization, the discussion demonstrated as clearly as possible that neither parallelism nor serialism is the source of the difficulties. Symmetrical Alignment and Iterative Foot Optimization share the same structural assumptions and the same set of constraints. They differ only in their derivational perspective, Iterative Foot Optimization being implemented in the framework of Harmonic Serialism and Symmetrical Alignment being implemented in the framework of Optimality Theory. If the OPIP could be shown to arise in one but not the other, then the derivational perspective of the offending account would be identified as its source. Since the OPIP arises in both accounts, however, and it contributes significantly to the inadequacy of both, the source of the OPIP must be something that Symmetrical Alignment and Iterative Foot Optimization have in common, either their Weak Layering structural assumptions or their shared set of constraints.

As we shall see in Chapters 4 and 5, it is Weak Layering that is the source of the difficulties. The more recent Weak Layering accounts, Asymmetrical Alignment and Rhythmic Licensing, both employ a different set of constraints, but they also exhibit the effects of the OPIP. A Weak Bracketing approach avoids the OPIP altogether. Unlike Symmetrical Alignment, Iterative Foot Optimization, and the other Weak Layering accounts, Weak Bracketing is able to produce a reasonably accurate range of binary default patterns when the effects of syllable weight and possible breaches of faithfulness are actually considered.

4

Alternative Weak Layering Accounts

In Chapter 3, I examined the predictions of two Weak Layering approaches – Symmetrical Alignment and Iterative Foot Optimization – in light of the Odd-Parity Parsing Problem. In this chapter, I examine the predictions of two alternative Weak Layering approaches – Asymmetrical Alignment (Alber 2005) and Rhythmic Licensing (Kager 2001, 2005) – focusing in particular on the Odd Heavy Problem. I have two primary aims. The first is to assess the effectiveness of alternative methods for establishing directional orientations in the context of Weak Layering. Where Symmetrical Alignment and Iterative Foot Optimization rely on distance-sensitive foot alignment constraints to create directional parsing effects, Asymmetrical Alignment and Rhythmic Licensing rely on constraints that prohibit clash and lapse configurations. The *CLASH constraint (Prince 1983) prohibits adjacent stressed syllables, and the *LAPSE constraint (Selkirk 1984) prohibits adjacent stressless syllables.

(1) Rhythmic well-formedness constraints

a. *CLASH

Stressed syllables are not adjacent.

b. *LAPSE

Stressless syllables are not adjacent.

While Asymmetrical Alignment still supplements *CLASH and *LAPSE with a left-oriented, distance-sensitive foot alignment constraint, Rhythmic Licensing omits distance-sensitive alignment altogether.

The second aim in examining alternative approaches to directional parsing is to more firmly establish the source of the Odd-Parity Parsing Problem. In examining the predictions that arise under these alternative Weak Layering approaches, we will see that the manifestations of the OHP are still present and that they are even more exotic than they are in Weak Layering approaches where distance-sensitive alignment plays a more substantial role. This should make clear that the OPIP arises from the structural assumptions of Weak Layering rather than from specific approaches to parsing directionality. With the structural nature of the problem firmly established, we will turn in Chapter 5 to the predictions of the Weak Bracketing approach. As we shall see, the OPIP simply does not arise under the structural assumptions of Weak Bracketing.

4.1 Asymmetrical Alignment

In some respects, Asymmetrical Alignment is quite similar to Symmetrical Alignment: F-BIN, PARSE-σ, and alignment constraints all continue to play central roles. There are some important differences, however. The constraints primarily responsible for producing directional parsing effects are the rhythmic well-formedness constraints in (1) and the alignment constraints in (2).[1] Notice that Symmetrical Alignment's ALL-F-LEFT constraint is present but that its ALL-F-RIGHT constraint is missing. The gap is intended to allow Asymmetrical Alignment to avoid some of the unattested patterns predicted under Symmetrical Alignment, but it also means that *CLASH and *LAPSE must play central roles in producing directionality effects. Notice also that the constraints aligning the edges of prosodic words with feet, F_{HD}-LEFT and F_{HD}-RIGHT, refer specifically to head feet.

(2) Alignment constraints

a. ALL-F-LEFT: $*\langle\omega, F, \sigma\rangle$ / $[\ldots \sigma \ldots F \ldots]_{\omega}$

'Assess a violation mark for every $\langle\omega, F, \sigma\rangle$ such that σ precedes F within ω.'

b. F_{HD}-LEFT: $*\langle\omega, F_{HD}\rangle$ / $[\ldots\sigma\ldots F_{HD}\ldots]_{\omega}$

'Assess a violation mark for every $\langle\omega, F_{HD}\rangle$ such that σ precedes F_{HD} within ω.'

c. F_{HD}-RIGHT: $*\langle\omega, F_{HD}\rangle$ / $[\ldots F_{HD}\ldots\sigma\ldots]_{\omega}$

'Assess a violation mark for every $\langle\omega, F_{HD}\rangle$ such that F_{HD} precedes σ within ω.'

Since I have already discussed the effects of alignment in detail in Chapters 2 and 3, I begin here by outlining the effects of *CLASH and *LAPSE. While the constraints appear to be fairly simple, prohibiting

1 Alber's alignment constraints were originally formulated within the Generalized Alignment framework. They are formulated here within the Relation-Specific Alignment framework.

either adjacent stressed syllables or adjacent stressless syllables, their effects are actually fairly complex. *LAPSE promotes a certain amount of parsing, but it also has an effect on parsing directionality. *CLASH has an effect on parsing directionality, but in some contexts it actually inhibits parsing.

4.1.1 Lapse avoidance

*LAPSE has an effect on parsing that is similar to, but less stringent than, the effect of PARSE-σ. To illustrate, the forms in (3) exhibit parsing in varying degrees. The form in (3a) exhibits the type of exhaustive parsing found in the maximal alternation pattern, (3b) the type of under-parsing found in the minimal alternation patterns, and (3c) the even sparser parsing found in single stress patterns. Where PARSE-σ prefers the exhaustive parsing of (3a) to the under-parsing of (3b) and prefers the under-parsing of (3b) to the even sparser parsing of (3c), the preferences of *LAPSE are not so fine grained. *LAPSE prefers (3a) and (3b) to (3c), but it does not distinguish between the exhaustive parsing of (3a) and the under-parsing of (3b).[2]

(3)

	PARSE-σ	*LAPSE
a. (σ́)(σ́σ)(σ́σ)(σ́σ)		
b. σ(σ́σ)(σ́σ)(σ́σ)	*	
c. σσσσσ(σ́σ)	*****	****

2 While *LAPSE will typically only enforce parsing to a degree sufficient to produce under-parsing, it should be kept it mind that it can also be satisfied by exhaustive parsing and can even require exhaustive parsing in some contexts. For example, in trochaic under-parsing systems, it is only possible to avoid lapse when the unparsed syllable occurs at the left edge, as in (ic). If a high-ranked FHD-LEFT requires that the head foot occur at the left edge, however, *LAPSE can require that the leftover syllable be parsed as a monosyllabic foot, as in (ia), rather than be left unparsed in a position where it can create a lapse, as in (ib). Since the exhaustive parsing patterns created in this way – fixing the position of the head foot at the appropriate edge and then prohibiting lapse – are not unique in the predicted typology, I omit them from the discussion below.

(i)

	F_{HD}-LEFT	*LAPSE
☞ a. (σ́)(σ̀σ)(σ̀σ)(σ̀σ)		
b. (σ́σ)σ(σ̀σ)(σ̀σ)		*!
c. σ(σ́σ)(σ̀σ)(σ̀σ)	*!	

The effect of *LAPSE on parsing directionality is indirect. *LAPSE prefers that feet be distributed in such a way that there are no adjacent stressless syllables. Since the appropriate distribution depends on the type of foot used in parsing, *LAPSE's directionality effect is different for each type. In iambic under-parsing systems, lapse can only be avoided by positioning the unparsed syllable at the right edge, so *LAPSE prefers that iambic feet orient themselves towards the left, as in (4a).

(4)

	*LAPSE
☞ a. (σσ́)(σσ́)(σσ́)σ	
b. (σσ́)(σσ́)σ(σσ́)	*!
c. (σσ́)σ(σσ́)(σσ́)	*!
d. σ(σσ́)(σσ́)(σσ́)	*!

In trochaic systems, lapse can only be avoided by positioning the unparsed syllable at the left edge, so *LAPSE prefers that trochaic feet orient themselves towards the right, as in (5a).

(5)

	*LAPSE
☞ a. σ(σ́σ)(σ́σ)(σ́σ)	
b. (σ́σ)σ(σ́σ)(σ́σ)	*!
c. (σ́σ)(σ́σ)σ(σ́σ)	*!
d. (σ́σ)(σ́σ)(σ́σ)σ	*!

Note that the ability of *LAPSE to influence parsing directionality is limited to under-parsing patterns. Since it is not possible to have adjacent stressless syllables in exhaustive parsing patterns, *LAPSE is satisfied regardless of the particular directional orientation that such patterns exhibit.

4.1.2 Clash avoidance

Like *LAPSE, *CLASH affects parsing directionality indirectly. The effect of *CLASH is complementary to that of *LAPSE, however, in that it affects directionality in exhaustive parsing patterns rather than in under-parsing patterns. *CLASH prefers that feet be distributed in such a way that there are no adjacent stressed syllables, a possibility that arises only under exhaustive parsing. Since the appropriate distribution depends on whether feet are iambic or trochaic, *CLASH's directionality effect is different for the two types.

In iambic systems, clash can only be avoided by positioning the monosyllabic foot at the left edge, as in (6a).

(6)

	*CLASH
☞ a. (σ́)(σσ́)(σσ́)(σσ́)	
b. (σσ́)(σ́)(σσ́)(σσ́)	*!
c. (σσ́)(σσ́)(σ́)(σσ́)	*!
d. (σσ́)(σσ́)(σσ́)(σ́)	*!

In trochaic systems, clash can only be avoided by positioning the monosyllabic foot at the right edge, as in (7a).

(7)

	*CLASH
☞ a. (σ́σ)(σ́σ)(σ́σ)(σ́)	
b. (σ́σ)(σ́σ)(σ́)(σ́σ)	*!
c. (σ́σ)(σ́)(σ́σ)(σ́σ)	*!
d. (σ́)(σ́σ)(σ́σ)(σ́σ)	*!

Since the presence of a monosyllabic foot is necessary to create a clash in binary systems, *CLASH can have the effect of discouraging monosyllabic feet, duplicating the preferences of F-BIN in some contexts. For example, the ranking *LAPSE >> ALL-F-LEFT limits the possible outputs for trochaic odd-parity forms to the under-parsing candidate in (8a) and the exhaustive parsing candidate in (8b). Both satisfy *LAPSE, and they perform equally well on ALL-F-LEFT. In (8a), however, an unparsed syllable occurs at the left edge, avoiding clash. In (8b), a monosyllabic foot occurs at the left edge, creating a clash. When *CLASH (along with ALL-F-LEFT) dominates PARSE-σ, the monosyllabic foot of (8b) is rejected in favor of the unparsed syllable of (8a).

(8)

	*LAPSE	ALL-F-LEFT	*CLASH	PARSE-σ
☞ a. σ(σ́σ)(σ́σ)(σ́σ)		* *** *****		*
b. (σ́)(σ́σ)(σ́σ)(σ́σ)		* *** *****	*!	
c. (σ́σ)(σ́σ)(σ́σ)(σ́)		** **** ****!**		
d. (σ́σ)(σ́σ)(σ́σ)σ	*!	** ****		*

4.1.3 Rankings for binary patterns

Under the idealized condition where differences in syllable weight are not actually considered, Asymmetrical Alignment predicts a smaller range of binary default patterns than Symmetrical Alignment. In most cases, the omitted patterns are unattested. In one case, however, the omitted pattern actually is attested.

As in Symmetrical Alignment, constraints that require parsing must dominate alignment constraints that might restrict parsing in order for a binary pattern to emerge. In the case of Asymmetrical Alignment, the relevant parsing constraints are PARSE-σ and *LAPSE, and the relevant alignment constraint is ALL-F-LEFT.

(9) Rankings resulting in binary default patterns

a. PARSE-σ >> ALL-F-LEFT; *LAPSE

b. *LAPSE >> ALL-F-LEFT >> PARSE-σ

Whether or not a particular stress pattern can emerge under both (9a) and (9b) or under (9a) alone depends on the type of foot employed and the parsing pattern required.

4.1.3.1 Exhaustive parsing patterns

For exhaustive parsing patterns, where the key to parsing directionality is the position of the monosyllabic foot in odd-parity forms, the relevant directional constraints are *CLASH and ALL-F-LEFT. The two constraints have conflicting preferences in trochaic systems, so that two different trochaic patterns are possible depending on their ranking. When *CLASH dominates ALL-F-LEFT, the result is the trochaic maximal alternation pattern.

(10) Trochaic maximal alternation: Attested

a. *Pattern*

(σ́σ)(σ́σ)(σ́σ)

(σ́σ)(σ́σ)(σ́σ)(σ́)

b. *Ranking*

PARSE-σ >> F-BIN,ALL-F-LEFT; *CLASH >> ALL-F-LEFT; *LAPSE

To illustrate, ALL-F-LEFT prefers that the monosyllabic foot in an odd-parity form be located at the left edge, preceding the string of disyllabic feet, as in (11a). Since clash arises in trochaic systems whenever a monosyllabic foot precedes a trochee, however, the higher-ranked *CLASH prefers that the monosyllabic foot occur in final position, as in (11w). Clash is avoided and the maximal alternation pattern emerges as the winner.

(11)

	PARSE-σ	F-BIN	*CLASH	ALL-F-LEFT
☞ w. (σ́σ)(σ́σ)(σ́σ)(σ́)		1		12
a. (σ́)(σ́σ)(σ́σ)(σ́σ)		1	W 1	L 9
b. (σ́σ)(σ́σ)(σ́σ)σ	W 1	L		L 6
c. σ(σ́σ)(σ́σ)(σ́σ)	W 1	L		L 9

When the ranking is reversed so that ALL-F-LEFT dominates *CLASH, the result is the trochaic initial clash pattern.

(12) Trochaic initial clash: Attested

a. *Pattern*
(σ́σ)(σ́σ)(σ́σ)
(σ́)(σ́σ)(σ́σ)(σ́σ)

b. *Rankings*
i. PARSE-σ >> F-BIN, ALL-F-LEFT; ALL-F-LEFT >> *CLASH; *LAPSE
ii. *LAPSE >> ALL-F-LEFT >> PARSE-σ >> *CLASH, F-BIN

Under this ranking, as (13) illustrates, ALL-F-LEFT's preference to position the monosyllabic foot at the left edge overrides *CLASH's preference to avoid the adjacent stressed syllables that arise when a monosyllabic foot precedes a trochee. ALL-F-LEFT excludes the maximal alternation pattern in (13l), and the initial clash pattern in (13w) emerges as the winner.

(13)

	ALL-F-LEFT	*CLASH
☞ w. (σ́)(σ́σ)(σ́σ)(σ́σ)	9	1
l. (σ́σ)(σ́σ)(σ́σ)(σ́)	W 12	L

While Asymmetrical Alignment predicts two trochaic exhaustive parsing patterns, both of which are attested, it predicts only one iambic exhaustive parsing pattern. It predicts the iambic maximal alternation pattern, but it does not predict an iambic final clash pattern, the mirror image of trochaic initial clash. Since the iambic final clash pattern is unattested, this is the desired result, and it gives Asymmetrical Alignment an advantage over Symmetrical Alignment in this context.

(14) Iambic maximal alternation: Attested

a. *Pattern*

(σσ́)(σσ́)(σσ́)

(σ́)(σσ́)(σσ́)(σσ́)

b. *Ranking*

PARSE-σ >> F-BIN,ALL-F-LEFT; *CLASH, *LAPSE

In iambic systems, clash arises whenever a monosyllabic foot follows an iamb, so the monosyllabic foot must occur in initial position, as in the maximal alternation pattern in (15w), to avoid clash. Since ALL-F-LEFT also prefers that the monosyllabic foot occur in initial position, however, the maximal alternation pattern emerges whether *CLASH dominates ALL-F-LEFT or ALL-F-LEFT dominates *CLASH.

(15)

	PARSE-σ	F-BIN	ALL-F-LEFT	*CLASH
☞ w. (σ́)(σσ́)(σσ́)(σσ́)		1	9	
a. (σσ́)(σσ́)(σσ́)(σ́)		1	W 12	W 1
b. (σσ́)(σσ́)(σσ́)σ	W 1	L	L 6	
c. σ(σσ́)(σσ́)(σσ́)	W 1	L	9	

Due to the absence of a conflict between *CLASH and ALL-F-LEFT in the context of iambic systems, the iambic maximal alternation pattern, (15w), harmonically bounds the iambic final clash pattern, (15a). Both of the constraints relevant for establishing parsing directionality in this context prefer maximal alternation, so the final clash pattern cannot emerge under any ranking.

4.1.3.2 Under-parsing patterns

For under-parsing patterns, where the key to parsing directionality is the position of the unparsed syllable in odd-parity forms, the relevant directional constraints are *LAPSE, ALL-F-LEFT, and F_{HD} -RIGHT. In general, as we shall see in examining unidirectional patterns just below, *LAPSE and ALL-F-LEFT are responsible for creating general directional orientations. We shall see in examining bidirectional patterns that F_{HD} -RIGHT can create exceptions to the general leftward orientation created by ALL-F-LEFT.

4.1.3.2.1 Unidirectional patterns

As we saw above in the context of exhaustive parsing, *CLASH and ALL-F-LEFT have conflicting preferences in trochaic systems but not iambic systems. Similarly, in the context of under-parsing, *LAPSE and ALL-F-LEFT have conflicting preferences in trochaic systems but not iambic systems. As a result, Asymmetrical Alignment predicts two trochaic unidirectional under-parsing systems but only one iambic unidirectional under-parsing system.

When *LAPSE dominates ALL-F-LEFT in a trochaic system, the result is the trochaic minimal alternation pattern.

(16) Trochaic minimal alternation: Attested

a. *Pattern*

(σ́σ)(σ́σ)(σ́σ)

σ(σ́σ)(σ́σ)(σ́σ)

b. *Rankings*

i. F-BIN >> PARSE-σ; *LAPSE >> ALL-F-LEFT; *CLASH

ii. *LAPSE >> ALL-F-LEFT >> PARSE-σ >> F-BIN; *CLASH >> PARSE-σ

ALL-F-LEFT prefers that the unparsed syllable be located at the right edge, following the string of disyllabic feet, as in (17a). Since lapse arises in trochaic systems whenever an unparsed follows a trochee, however, the higher-ranked *LAPSE prefers that the unparsed syllable occur at the left edge, as in (17w). Lapse is avoided and the minimal alternation pattern emerges as the winner.

(17)

	F-BIN	PARSE-σ	*LAPSE	ALL-F-LEFT
☞ w. σ(σ́σ)(σ́σ)(σ́σ)		1		9
a. (σ́σ)(σ́σ)(σ́σ)σ		1	W 1	L 6
b. (σ́σ)(σ́σ)(σ́σ)(σ́)	W 1	L		W 12
c. (σ́)(σ́σ)(σ́σ)(σ́σ)	W 1	L		9

When the ranking between *LAPSE and ALL-F-LEFT is reversed, so that ALL-F-LEFT dominates *LAPSE, the trochaic peripheral lapse pattern emerges.

(18) Trochaic peripheral lapse (final dactyl): Attested

a. *Pattern*

(σ́σ)(σ́σ)(σ́σ)

(σ́σ)(σ́σ)(σ́σ)σ

b. *Ranking*

F-Bin >> Parse-σ >> All-F-Left >> *Lapse; *Clash

As (19) illustrates, All-F-Left's preference to position the unparsed syllable at the left edge overrides *Lapse's preference to avoid the adjacent stressless syllables that arise when an unparsed syllable follows a trochee. The higher ranked All-F-Left excludes the minimal alternation pattern, (19l), and the peripheral lapse pattern, (19w), emerges as the winner.

(19)

	All-F-Left	*Lapse
☞ w. (σ́σ)(σ́σ)(σ́σ)σ	6	1
l. σ(σ́σ)(σ́σ)(σ́σ)	W 9	L

Since the preferences of *Lapse and All-F-Left are not in conflict in iambic systems, only one unidirectional iambic under-parsing pattern is possible. Asymmetrical Alignment predicts the iambic minimal alternation pattern but not the iambic peripheral lapse pattern, the mirror image of the trochaic peripheral lapse pattern. Since iambic peripheral lapse is unattested, this is the desired result, and Asymmetrical Alignment has an advantage over Symmetrical Alignment in this context as well.

(20) Iambic minimal alternation: Attested

a. *Pattern*

(σσ́)(σσ́)(σσ́)

(σσ́)(σσ́)(σσ́)σ

b. *Rankings*

i. F-Bin >> Parse-σ >> All-F-Left; *Lapse, *Clash

ii. *Lapse >> All-F-Left >> Parse-σ; F-Bin, *Clash

In iambic systems, lapse arises whenever an unparsed syllable precedes an iamb, so the unparsed syllable must occur in final position, as in the minimal alternation pattern in (21w), to satisfy *Lapse. Since All-F-Left also prefers that the unparsed syllable occur in final position, the minimal alternation pattern emerges whether ALL-F-LEFT dominates *LAPSE or *LAPSE dominates ALL-F-LEFT.

(21)

	F-BIN	PARSE-σ	ALL-F-LEFT	*LAPSE
☞ w. (σσ́)(σσ́)(σσ́)σ		1	6	
a. σ(σσ́)(σσ́)(σσ́)		1	W 9	W 1
b. (σ́)(σσ́)(σσ́)(σσ́)	W 1	L	W 9	
c. (σσ́)(σσ́)(σσ́)(σ́)	W 1	L	W 12	

Since *LAPSE and ALL-F-LEFT both prefer minimal alternation in the context of iambic systems, the iambic minimal alternation pattern, (21w), harmonically bounds the iambic peripheral lapse pattern, (21a).

4.1.3.2.2 Bidirectional patterns

Asymmetrical Alignment produces two internal lapse patterns – one trochaic and one iambic – by anchoring the head foot at the right edge of the prosodic word and drawing all other feet to the left. F_{HD} -RIGHT is the constraint responsible for anchoring the head foot, and ALL-F-LEFT is the constraint responsible for drawing the remaining feet to the left.

Though Asymmetrical Alignment has an F_{HD} -LEFT constraint, it does not have an ALL-F-RIGHT constraint. As a result, it cannot produce patterns where the head foot is anchored at the left edge and all other feet are drawn to the right. It also cannot produce patterns where the isolated foot is a non-head foot. In general, these limitations prevent Asymmetrical Alignment from producing the full range of attested internal lapse patterns while still allowing it to produce an unattested pattern.

In the trochaic version of the internal lapse pattern, it is not only necessary that F_{HD} -RIGHT dominate ALL-F-LEFT, but it is also necessary that ALL-F-LEFT dominate *LAPSE, as indicated in (22b).

(22) Trochaic internal lapse (final amphibrach): Attested

a. *Pattern*

(σ̀σ)(σ̀σ)(σ́σ)

(σ̀σ)(σ̀σ)σ(σ́σ)

b. *Ranking*

F-Bin >> Parse-σ >> All-F-Left >> *Lapse; F_{HD}-Right >> All-F-Left; *Clash

To illustrate, each of the candidates in (23) is a trochaic under-parsing pattern. The competition between the final lapse pattern of (23b) and the internal lapse pattern of (23w) illustrates the conflict between F_{HD} -Right and All-F-Left. Candidate (23b) offers the best leftward alignment, but it fails to position the head foot at the right edge and is excluded by F_{HD} -Right. The competition between the minimal alternation pattern of (23a) and the internal lapse pattern illustrates the conflict between All-F-Left and *Lapse. Candidate (23a) avoids lapse but orients its non-head feet towards the right edge rather than the left. It is excluded by All-F-Left, and the internal lapse pattern emerges as the winner.

(23)

	F_{HD}-Right	All-F-Left	*Lapse
☞ w. (σ̀σ)(σ̀σ)σ(σ́σ)		7	1
a. σ(σ̀σ)(σ̀σ)(σ́σ)		W 9	L
b. (σ̀σ)(σ̀σ)(σ́σ)σ	W 1	L 6	1

In the iambic version, All-F-Left and *Lapse are not in conflict, so the ranking between them is not crucial.

(24) Iambic internal lapse (final anapest): Unattested

a. *Pattern*

(σσ̀)(σσ̀)(σσ́)

(σσ̀)(σσ̀)σ(σσ́)

b. *Rankings*

i. F-Bin >> Parse-σ >> All-F-Left, *Lapse; F_{HD}-Right >> All-F-Left, *Lapse; *Clash

ii. F-Bin >> *Lapse >> Parse-σ, All-F-Left; F_{HD}-Right >> *Lapse; *Clash

As (25) demonstrates, All-F-Left and *Lapse both prefer the left-oriented footing of the iambic minimal alternation pattern, (25l), so they do not conflict in this context, and the ranking between them is not crucial. The competition between the minimal alternation pattern and the internal lapse pattern (25w), however, illustrates the conflict between F_{HD} -RIGHT on one side and ALL-F-LEFT and *LAPSE on the other. Though the minimal alternation pattern avoids lapse and exhibits better leftward alignment, it fails to locate its head foot at the right edge. It is excluded by F_{HD} -RIGHT, and the internal lapse pattern emerges as the winner. Unlike the trochaic version of the internal lapse pattern, however, the iambic version is unattested.

(25)

	F_{HD}-RIGHT	ALL-F-LEFT	*LAPSE
☞ w. (σσ̀)(σσ̀)σ(σσ́)		7	1
l. (σσ̀)(σσ̀)(σσ́)σ	W 1	L 6	L

To this point Asymmetrical Alignment has had clear advantage over Symmetrical Alignment, eliminating two unattested iambic unidirectional patterns. In the case of bidirectional patterns, however, the results are mixed. Under Symmetrical Alignment, which predicts a total of eight bidirectional patterns, bidirectional patterns can be either iambic or trochaic, they can position the isolated foot at either edge of the prosodic word, and they can position the head foot at either edge of the prosodic word.[3] Under Asymmetrical Alignment, which predicts a total of two bidirectional patterns, bidirectional patterns can be either iambic or trochaic, but they must position the isolated foot at the right edge and the isolated foot must be the head foot. While Asymmetrical Alignment eliminates a number of unattested patterns, it also eliminates the attested initial dactyl patterns. In Garawa, for example, the head foot is the isolated foot, but it occurs at the left edge. In Indonesian, Norwegian, and Spanish, the isolated foot occurs at the left edge, and it is a non-head foot.

4.1.3.3 Summary of binary default patterns

Under the idealized condition where differences in syllable weight are not actually considered, Asymmetrical Alignment predicts the eight binary default patterns summarized in (26) and (27). It predicts a subset of the attested binary default patterns with a minimal amount over-generation.

3 The total of eight in this case takes into account the various positions in which primary stress might occur, a factor omitted in the discussion of Symmetrical Alignment in Chapters 2 and 3.

(26) Perfect alternation patterns predicted under Asymmetrical Alignment

a. Minimal Alternation

i. Trochaic: Attested
(σ́σ)(σ́σ)(σ́σ)
σ(σ́σ)(σ́σ)(σ́σ)

ii. Iambic: Attested
(σσ́)(σσ́)(σσ́)
(σσ́)(σσ́)(σσ́)σ

b. Maximal alternation

i. Trochaic: Attested
(σ́σ)(σ́σ)(σ́σ)
(σ́σ)(σ́σ)(σ́σ)(σ́)

ii. Iambic: Attested
(σσ́)(σσ́)(σσ́)
(σ́)(σσ́)(σσ́)(σσ́)

(27) Departures from perfect alternation

a. Trochaic Peripheral clash: Attested
(σ́σ)(σ́σ)(σ́σ)
(σ́)(σ́σ)(σ́σ)(σ́σ)

b. Trochaic Peripheral lapse (final dactyl): Attested
(σ́σ)(σ́σ)(σ́σ)
(σ́σ)(σ́σ)(σ́σ)σ

c. Iambic internal lapse (final anapest): Unattested
(σσ́)(σσ́)(σσ́)
(σσ́)(σσ́)σ(σσ́)

d. Trochaic internal lapse (final amphibrach): Attested
(σ́σ)(σ́σ)(σ́σ)
(σ́σ)(σ́σ)σ(σ́σ)

Since the patterns summarized in (26) and (27) do not reflect the effects of Parse-σ and F-Bin when heavy syllables are present, however, the predictions of Asymmetrical Alignment are actually quite different. Though Asymmetrical Alignment can produce quantity-insensitive versions of most of the patterns in (26) and (27), each of the patterns also exhibit multiple versions of the OHP.

4.2 Asymmetrical Alignment and the OHP

While clash avoidance is a well-motivated principle, the presence of *Clash in a Weak Layering approach has an unfortunate consequence: it multiplies the possible manifestations of the OHP and makes them more exotic. To illustrate the different versions of the OHP that arise under Asymmetrical Alignment, we will consider the ranking for an under-parsing pattern where *CLASH is not supposed to be crucial – the trochaic internal lapse pattern illustrated in (22) – and then observe the results when *CLASH occurs in various positions. The ranking for the trochaic internal lapse pattern is repeated in (28).

(28) Trochaic internal lapse ranking

F-BIN >> PARSE-σ >> ALL-F-LEFT >> *LAPSE; F_{HD}-RIGHT >> ALL-F-LEFT; *CLASH

If the ranking were truly quantity-insensitive, the result would be the trochaic internal lapse pattern regardless of whether or not the input contained heavy syllables. Odd-parity forms would have a single foot stranded at the right edge, all other feet would be drawn to the left, and there would be an unparsed syllable just to the left of the final foot. As we shall see below, however, the ranking always exhibits the effects of the OHP.

4.2.1 The First Version

The first version of the OHP (AA OHP1) retains the essential OHP characteristics in that footing is sensitive to the weight of odd-numbered syllables in odd-parity forms. In this version, however, heavy syllables can only be parsed as monosyllabic feet in those positions where a monosyllabic foot would not result in clash. In trochaic systems, this means that only final heavy syllables can be parsed as monosyllabic feet. In iambic systems, it means that only initial heavy syllables can be parsed as monosyllabic feet.

(29) AA OHP version 1: *CLASH,F-BIN >> PARSE-σ >> ALL-F-LEFT

A heavy syllable *H* is parsed as a monosyllabic foot *iff*

a. *H* occurs in an odd-parity form; *and*

b. *H* is odd-numbered; *and*

c. parsing *H* as a monosyllabic foot would not result in clash.

As indicated in (29), AA OHP1 arises under the ranking *CLASH, F-BIN >> PARSE-σ >> ALL-F-LEFT. Since F-BIN must dominate PARSE-σ, AA OHP1 arises only in conjunction with under-parsing rankings. When there is no odd-numbered heavy syllable in a position to avoid clash in an odd-parity form, the result is under-parsing. When there is an odd-numbered heavy syllable in a position to avoid clash, however, the result will be exhaustive parsing.

To illustrate, consider the results when *CLASH is positioned in the trochaic internal lapse ranking so that it dominates PARSE-σ. In (30), the input is an odd-parity form that has odd-numbered heavy syllables, but not in a position where clash can be avoided. Since F-BIN and PARSE-σ cannot be satisfied simultaneously in this case, without violating *CLASH, a single syllable is left unfooted, and the expected bidirectional under-parsing pattern emerges.

(30)

LLHLHLL	*CLASH	F-BIN	PARSE	F_{HD}-R	ALL-F-L
☞ w. (L̀L)(H̀L)H(ĹL)			1		7
a. (L̀L)(H̀L)(H̀L)(Ĺ)		W 1	L		W 12
b. (L̀L)(H̀)(L̀H)(ĹL)	W 1		L		W 10
c. (L̀L)(H̀L)(H̀)(ĹL)	W 1		L		W 11

In (31), however, the input is an odd-parity form that has a heavy syllable in a position to avoid clash. Parsing the heavy final syllable as a monosyllabic foot satisfies F-BIN and PARSE-σ simultaneously without violating *CLASH, and a unidirectional exhaustive parsing pattern emerges in place of the expected bidirectional under-parsing pattern.

(31)

LLHLHLH	*CLASH	F-BIN	PARSE	F_{HD}-R	ALL-F-L
☞ w. (L̀L)(H̀L)(H̀L)(H́)					12
a. (L̀L)(H̀L)H(ĹH)			W 1		L 7
b. (L̀L)(H̀)(L̀H)(ĹH)	W 1				L 10
c. (L̀L)(H̀L)(H̀)(ĹH)	W 1				L 11

The patterns that can be obtained under the ranking for AA OHP1 are summarized in (32–36). For each ranking, three examples of odd-parity forms are provided. The first, which contains only light syllables, exhibits the basic pattern. The second, which also exhibits the basic pattern, contains odd-numbered heavy syllables, but only in positions where a monosyllabic foot would result in clash. The third example contains an odd-numbered heavy syllable in the position where a monosyllabic foot can avoid clash. It is the third form that illustrates the effects of AA OHP1.

AA OHP1 can accompany both the trochaic and iambic versions of the minimal alternation patterns. Both results are unattested.

(32) Trochaic minimal alternation: AA OHP1: Unattested

a. *Pattern*

i. L(ĹL)(ĹL)(ĹL) ii. L(ĹH)(ĹH)(ĹL) iii. (ĹL)(H́L)(H́L)(H́)

b. *Ranking*

*CLASH, F-BIN >> PARSE-σ >> ALL-F-LEFT; *LAPSE >> ALL-F-LEFT

(33) Iambic minimal alternation: AA OHP1: Unattested

a. Pattern

i. (LĹ)(LĹ)(LĹ)L ii. (LĹ)(HĹ)(HĹ)L iii. (H́)(LH́)(LH́)(LĹ)

b. Ranking

*CLASH, F-BIN >> PARSE-σ >> ALL-F-LEFT; *LAPSE

AA OHP1 can also accompany the trochaic peripheral lapse pattern. In this case, however, the result is attested. Weight-based parsing for final syllables only can be found in Wergaia (Hercus 1986).

(34) Trochaic peripheral lapse: AA OHP1: Attested

a. Pattern

i. (ĹL)(ĹL)(ĹL)L ii. (ĹL)(H́L)(H́L)L iii. (ĹL)(H́L)(H́L)(H́)

b. Ranking

*CLASH, F-BIN >> PARSE-σ >> ALL-F-LEFT >> *LAPSE

Finally, both the trochaic and iambic internal lapse patterns can be accompanied by the effects of AA OHP1. The result is two unattested patterns.

(35) Trochaic internal lapse: AA OHP1: Unattested

a. *Pattern*

i. (ĹL)(ĹL)L(ĹL) ii. (ĹL)(H́L)H(ĹL) iii. (ĹL)(H́L)(H́L)(H́)

b. *Ranking*

*CLASH,F-BIN, >> PARSE-σ >> ALL-F-LEFT >> *LAPSE; F_{HD}-RIGHT >> ALL-F-LEFT

(36) Iambic internal lapse: AA OHP1: Unattested

a. *Pattern*

i. (LĹ)(LĹ)L(LĹ) ii. (LĹ)(HĹ)H(LĹ) iii. (H́)(LH́)(LH́)(LĹ)

b. *Rankings*

i. *CLASH, F-BIN >> PARSE-σ >> ALL-F-LEFT, *LAPSE; F_{HD}-RIGHT >> ALL-F-LEFT, *LAPSE

ii. *CLASH, F-BIN >> *LAPSE >> PARSE-σ, ALL-F-LEFT; F_{HD}-RIGHT >> *LAPSE

4.2.2 The Second Version

Asymmetrical Alignment's second version of the OHP (AA OHP2) is similar to the version of the OHP found under Symmetrical Alignment in that the additional restriction on the position of heavy monosyllabic feet is due to alignment. Since only the left edge can be the preferred edge of foot alignment, however, it is always the leftmost odd-numbered heavy syllable that is parsed as a monosyllabic foot.

(37) AA OHP version 2

A heavy syllable *H* is parsed as a monosyllabic foot *iff*

a. *H* occurs in an odd-parity form; *and*

b. *H* is odd-numbered; *and*

c. *H* is the heavy syllable conforming to (a,b) that is closest to the left edge.

As indicated in (38), AA OHP2 arises when F-BIN and PARSE-σ dominate ALL-F-LEFT and *CLASH. Since the ranking between F-BIN and PARSE-σ is not crucial, AA OHP2 can arise in conjunction with either under-parsing patterns or exhaustive parsing patterns. Note that in trochaic systems it is also necessary that ALL-F-LEFT dominate *CLASH. Since ALL-F-LEFT and *CLASH do not conflict in iambic systems, the ranking between the two is not crucial in iambic patterns

(38) AA OHP2 version 2 rankings

a. Trochaic systems

F-BIN, PARSE-σ >> ALL-F-LEFT >> *CLASH

b. Iambic systems

F-BIN, PARSE-σ >> ALL-F-LEFT, *CLASH

To illustrate how the second version of the OHP arises, positioning *CLASH below ALL-F-LEFT in the trochaic internal lapse ranking produces the results in (39) and (40) when odd-numbered heavy syllables are present in an odd-parity form. The high-ranking F-BIN and PARSE-σ ensure that a single odd-numbered heavy syllable is parsed as a monosyllabic foot. This is true whether one of the heavy syllables is a position to avoid clash, as in (39), or not, as in (40). ALL-F-LEFT establishes the position of the monosyllabic foot in both cases, ensuring that it is constructed over the leftmost odd-numbered heavy syllable. Since *CLASH is low-ranked, it cannot prevent clash configurations, and it plays no role in selecting the optimal candidates.

(39)

LLHLHLH	F-BIN	PARSE	F_{HD}-R	ALL-F-L	*CLASH
☞ w. (L̀L)(H̀)(L̀H)(ĹH)				10	1
a. (L̀L)(H̀L)(H̀)(ĹH)				W 11	1
b. (L̀L)(H̀L)(H̀L)(H́)				W 12	L
c. (L̀L)(H̀L)H(ĹH)		W 1		L 7	L

(40)

LLHLHLL	F-BIN	PARSE	F_{HD}-R	ALL-F-L	*CLASH
☞ w. (L̀L)(H̀)(L̀H)(ĹL)				10	1
a. (L̀L)(H̀L)(H̀)(ĹL)				W 11	1
b. (L̀L)(H̀L)H(ĹL)		W 1		L 7	L
c. (L̀L)(H̀L)(H̀L)(Ĺ)	W 1			W 12	L

The patterns that emerge under AA OHP2 are summarized in (41–47). For each ranking, three examples of odd-parity forms are provided. The first, which contains only light syllables, exhibits the basic pattern. The second and third contain odd-numbered heavy syllables. The second contains heavy syllables only in positions where clash cannot be avoided. The third has an additional heavy syllable in a position where clash can be avoided. Regardless of whether or not clash might be avoided, however, the leftmost odd-numbered heavy syllable is parsed as a monosyllabic foot, illustrating the effects of AA OHP2.

First, as (41) indicates, AA OHP2 can arise with iambic maximal alternation. Since it is crucial in obtaining the trochaic maximal alternation pattern that *CLASH dominate ALL-F-LEFT, however, AA OHP2 does not arise with the trochaic pattern.

(41) Iambic maximal alternation: AA OHP2: Unattested

a. *Pattern*

i. (Ĺ)(LĹ)(LĹ)(LĹ) ii. (LĹ)(H́)(LH́)(ĹL) iii. (H́)(LH́)(LH́)(LĹ)

b. *Ranking*

PARSE-σ >> F-BIN >> ALL-F-LEFT, *CLASH; *LAPSE

Next, as (42) and (43) indicate, both the trochaic and iambic minimal alternation patterns are susceptible to AA OHP2.

(42) Trochaic minimal alternation: AA OHP2: Unattested

a. *Pattern*

i. L(ĹL)(ĹL)(ĹL) ii. (ĹL)(H́)(ĹH)(ĹL) iii. (ĹL)(H́)(ĹH)(ĹH)

b. *Ranking*

F-BIN >> PARSE-σ >> ALL-F-LEFT >> *CLASH; *LAPSE >> ALL-F-LEFT

(43) Iambic minimal alternation: AA OHP2 Unattested

a. *Pattern*

i. (LĹ)(LĹ)(LĹ)L ii. (LĹ)(H́)(LH́)(ĹL) iii. (H́)(LH́)(LH́)(LĹ)

b. *Ranking*

F-BIN >> PARSE-σ >> ALL-F-LEFT, *CLASH; *LAPSE

Finally, AA OHP2 emerges with the trochaic peripheral clash and peripheral lapse patterns and the trochaic and iambic internal lapse patterns.

(44) Trochaic peripheral clash: AA OHP2: Unattested

a. *Pattern*

i. (Ĺ)(ĹL)(ĹL)(ĹL) ii. (ĹL)(H́)(ĹH)(ĹL) iii. (ĹL)(H́)(ĹH)(ĹH)

b. Ranking

PARSE-σ >> F-BIN >> ALL-F-LEFT >> *CLASH; *LAPSE

(45) Trochaic peripheral lapse: AA OHP2: Unattested

a. *Pattern*

i. (ĹL)(ĹL)(ĹL)L ii. (ĹL)(H́)(ĹH)(ĹL) iii. (ĹL)(H́)(ĹH)(ĹH)

b. *Ranking*

F-BIN >> PARSE-σ >> ALL-F-LEFT >> *CLASH, *LAPSE

(46) Trochaic internal lapse: AA OHP2: Unattested

a. *Pattern*

i. (ĹL)(ĹL)L(ĹL) ii. (ĹL)(H́)(ĹH)(ĹL) iii. (ĹL)(H́)(ĹH)(ĹH)

b. *Ranking*

F-Bin >> Parse-σ >> All-F-Left >> *Lapse, *Clash; F_{HD}-Right >> All-F-Left

(47) Iambic internal lapse: AA OHP2: Unattested

a. *Pattern*

i. (LĹ)(LĹ)L(LĹ) ii. (LĹ)(H́)(LH́)(ĹL) iii. (H́)(LH́)(LH́)(LĹ)

b. *Rankings*

i. F-Bin >> Parse-σ >> All-F-Left, *Clash, *Lapse; F_{HD}-Right >> All-F-Left, *Lapse

ii. F_{HD}-Right, F-Bin >> *Lapse >> Parse-σ, All-F-Left, *Clash

4.2.3 The Third Version

Asymmetrical Alignment's third version of the OHP (AA OHP3) only arises in trochaic systems, at least as a distinct pattern; in iambic systems, it is indistinguishable from the second version of the OHP. The third version is a combination of the first and second. The preference is to parse an odd-numbered heavy syllable as a monosyllabic foot in a position where it will not result in a clash configuration. If there is no heavy syllable in a position where clash can be avoided, however, the odd-numbered heavy syllable closest to the left edge will be parsed as a monosyllabic foot. As (48) indicates, the third version emerges when F-Bin and Parse-σ both dominate *Clash and *Clash dominates All-F-Left. Since the ranking between F-Bin and Parse-σ is not crucial, AA OHP3 can arise in conjunction with either under-parsing patterns or exhaustive parsing patterns.

(48) AA OHP Version 3: F-Bin, Parse-σ >> *Clash >> All-F-Left

A heavy syllable *H* is parsed as a monosyllabic foot *iff*

a. *H* occurs in an odd-parity form; *and*

b. *H* is odd-numbered; *and*

c. parsing *H* as a monosyllabic foot would not result in clash; *or*

d. if there is no heavy syllable that meets (c), *H* is the heavy syllable conforming to (a,b) that is closest to the left edge.

When *Clash is inserted into the trochaic internal lapse ranking below F-Bin and Parse-σ but above All-F-Left, the pattern exhibits the effects of AA OHP3. The input in (49) is an odd-parity form that has odd-numbered heavy syllables, but not in a position where clash can be avoided. Since the high-ranked F-Bin and Parse-σ insist on exhaustive binary parsing, the leftmost odd-numbered heavy syllable is parsed as a monosyllabic foot at the expense of *Clash.

(49)

LLHLHLL	F-Bin	Parse	F_{HD}-R	*Clash	All-F-L
☞ w. (L̀L)(H̀)(L̀H)(ĹL)				1	10
a. (L̀L)(H̀L)(H̀)(ĹL)				1	W 11
b. (L̀L)(H̀L)H(ĹL)		W 1		L	L 7
c. (L̀L)(H̀L)(H̀L)(Ĺ)	W 1			L	W 12

In (50), however, the input is an odd-parity form that has a heavy syllable in a position to avoid clash. Parsing the final heavy syllable as a monosyllabic foot satisfies F-Bin and Parse-σ simultaneously without violating *Clash. The final heavy syllable is parsed as a monosyllabic foot at the expense of All-F-Left.

(50)

LLHLHLH	F-Bin	Parse	F_{HD}-R	*Clash	All-F-L
☞ w. (L̀L)(H̀L)(H̀L)(H́)					12
a. (L̀L)(H̀L)H(ĹH)		W 1			L 7
b. (L̀L)(H̀)(L̀H)(ĹH)				W 1	L 10
c. (L̀L)(H̀L)(H̀)(ĹH)				W 1	L 11

The patterns predicted under AA OHP3 are summarized in (51–54). For each ranking, three examples of odd-parity forms are provided. The first, which contains only light syllables, exhibits the basic pattern. The effects of AA OHP3 are illustrated in the second and third examples. The second example contains odd-numbered heavy syllables but only in positions where a monosyllabic foot would result in clash. In this situation, the leftmost odd-numbered heavy syllable is parsed as a monosyllabic foot. The third example contains an odd-numbered heavy syllable in the position where a monosyllabic foot can avoid clash. In this situation, the odd-numbered heavy syllable in a position to avoid clash is parsed as a monosyllabic foot. AA OHP3 can arise in conjunction with each of Asymmetrical Alignment's basic trochaic patterns, except the peripheral clash pattern, which requires that ALL-F-LEFT dominate *CLASH.

(51) Trochaic maximal alternation: AA OHP3: Unattested

a. *Pattern*

i. (ĹL)(ĹL)(ĹL)(Ĺ) ii. (ĹL)(H́)(ĹH)(ĹL) iii. (ĹL)(H́L)(H́L)(H́)

b. *Ranking*

PARSE-σ >> F-BIN >> *CLASH >> ALL-F-LEFT; *LAPSE

(52) Trochaic minimal alternation: AA OHP3: Unattested

a. *Pattern*

i. L(ĹL)(ĹL)(ĹL) ii. (ĹL)(H́)(ĹH)(ĹL) iii. (ĹL)(H́L)(H́L)(H́)

b. *Ranking*

F-BIN >> PARSE-σ >> *CLASH >> ALL-F-LEFT; *LAPSE >> ALL-F-LEFT

(53) Trochaic peripheral lapse: AA OHP3: Unattested

a. *Pattern*

i. (ĹL)(ĹL)(ĹL)L ii. (ĹL)(H́)(ĹH)(ĹL) iii. (ĹL)(H́L)(H́L)(H́)

b. *Ranking*

F-BIN >> PARSE-σ >> *CLASH >> ALL-F-LEFT >> *LAPSE

(54) Trochaic internal lapse: AA OHP3: Unattested

a. *Pattern*

i. (ĹL)(ĹL)L(ĹL) ii. (ĹL)(H́)(ĹH)(ĹL) iii. (ĹL)(H́L)(H́L)(H́)

b. *Ranking*

F-BIN >> PARSE-σ >> *CLASH >> ALL-F-LEFT >> *LAPSE; F_{HD}-RIGHT >> ALL-F-LEFT

4.2.4 Rankings that produce patterns without the OHP

Apart from the trochaic peripheral lapse pattern, and the iambic and trochaic internal lapse patterns, each of the basic binary patterns predicted under Asymmetrical Alignment can also emerge without the OHP. The OHP fails to emerge under three types of rankings. It fails to emerge when *Clash and Parse-σ both dominate F-Bin, and it fails to emerge when All-F-Left dominates either F-Bin or Parse-σ.

As (55) and (56) indicate, both the trochaic and iambic maximal alternation patterns can emerge without the OHP. This is possible under the subset of rankings where *Clash and Parse-σ dominate F-Bin. The iambic pattern also emerges without the OHP under a ranking where All-F-Left dominates F-Bin.

(55) Trochaic maximal alternation: No OHP: Attested

a. *Pattern*

i. (ĹL)(ĹL)(ĹL)(Ĺ) ii. (ĹL)(H́L)(H́L)(Ĺ) iii. (ĹL)(H́L)(H́L)(H́)

b. *Ranking*

Parse-σ, *Clash >> All-F-Left, F-Bin; *Lapse

(56) Iambic maximal alternation: No OHP: Attested

a. *Pattern*

i. (Ĺ)(LĹ)(LĹ)(LĹ) ii. (Ĺ)(LH́)(LH́)(LĹ) iii. (H́)(LH́)(LH́)(LĹ)

b. *Rankings*

i. Parse-σ, *Clash >> F-Bin >> All-F-Left; *Lapse

ii. Parse-σ >> All-F-Left >> F-Bin; *Clash, *Lapse

As (57) and (58) indicate, the minimal alternation patterns both emerge without the OHP under rankings where All-F-Left dominates Parse-σ.

(57) Trochaic minimal alternation: No OHP: Attested

a. *Pattern*

i. L(ĹL)(ĹL)(ĹL) ii. L(ĹH)(ĹH)(ĹL) iii. L(ĹH)(ĹH)(ĹH)

b. *Rankings*

i. F-Bin, All-F-Left >> Parse-σ; *Lapse >> All-F-Left; *Clash

ii. *Lapse >> All-F-Left >> Parse-σ >> F-Bin; *Clash >> Parse-σ;

(58) Iambic minimal alternation: No OHP: Attested

a. *Pattern*

i. (LĹ)(LĹ)(LĹ)L ii. (LĹ)(HĹ)(HĹ)L iii. (HĹ)(HĹ)(HĹ)L

b. *Ranking*

*Lapse >> All-F-Left >> Parse-σ; F-Bin, *Clash;

Finally, as (59) indicates, the trochaic peripheral clash pattern emerges without the OHP under rankings where ALL-F-LEFT dominates F-BIN.

(59) Trochaic peripheral clash: No OHP: Attested

a. *Pattern*

i. (Ĺ)(ĹL)(ĹL)(ĹL) ii. (Ĺ)(ĹH)(ĹH)(ĹL) iii. (Ĺ)(ĹH)(ĹH)(ĹH)

b. *Rankings*

i. PARSE-σ >> ALL-F-LEFT >> F-BIN, *CLASH; *LAPSE

ii. *LAPSE >> ALL-F-LEFT >> PARSE-σ >> F-BIN, *CLASH;

4.2.5 Summary of Predictions

Although some of the basic patterns predicted by Asymmetrical Alignment can emerge without the OHP, each pattern can also emerge with one or more versions of the OHP. Each of the basic patterns available under Asymmetrical Alignment is listed in (60–64). For each pattern, it is indicated whether or not the pattern can emerge without the OHP and to which versions of the OHP it is susceptible.

(60) Maximal alternation patterns

a. Trochaic

No OHP (attested), AA OHP3 (unattested)

b. Iambic

No OHP (attested), AA OHP2 (unattested)

(61) Minimal alternation patterns

a. Trochaic

No OHP (attested), AA OHP1 (unattested), AA OHP2 (unattested), AA OHP3 (unattested)

b. Iambic

No OHP (attested), AA OHP1 (unattested), AA OHP2 (unattested)

(62) Trochaic peripheral clash pattern

No OHP (attested), AA OHP2 (unattested)

(63) Trochaic peripheral lapse pattern

AA OHP1 (attested), AA OHP2 (unattested), AA OHP3 (unattested)

(64) Internal lapse patterns

a. Trochaic (final amphibrach)

AA OHP1 (unattested), AA OHP2 (unattested), AA OHP3 (unattested)

b. Iambic (final anapest)

AA OHP1 (unattested), AA OHP2 (unattested)

While Asymmetrical Alignment predicts more attested quantity-insensitive patterns than Symmetrical Alignment, thus reducing the under-generation aspect of the OHP, it makes no progress on the over-generation aspect. In fact, Asymmetrical Alignment only multiplies the manifestations of the OHP and makes them more exotic.

4.3 Rhythmic Licensing

Alignment's role is reduced even further under Rhythmic Licensing. Distance-sensitive alignment is abandoned altogether, and the task of establishing directionality effects is given over almost completely to constraints that restrict clash and lapse. As in Asymmetrical Alignment, *CLASH and *LAPSE have an indirect influence on the position of layering irregularities. In exhaustive parsing systems, *CLASH restricts the position of monosyllabic feet to positions that avoid clash. In under-parsing systems, *LAPSE restricts unparsed syllables to positions that avoid lapse.

In addition to *CLASH and *LAPSE, Rhythmic Licensing employs the rhythmic well-formedness constraints in (65). LAPSE-AT-END licenses lapse configurations at the right edge of a prosodic word, and *LAPSE-IN-TROUGH prohibits lapses that that occur between secondary stresses. CLASH-AT-EDGE licenses clash configurations at either edge of the prosodic word.

(65) Additional rhythmic well-formedness constraints

a. LAPSE-AT-END:

If there is a lapse, it is adjacent to the right edge.

b. *LAPSE-IN-TROUGH:

No lapse occurs between secondary stresses.

c. CLASH-AT-EDGE:
If there is a clash, it is adjacent to the left or right edge.[4]

Of the three constraints in (65), LAPSE-AT-EDGE plays the most significant role in producing basic binary default patterns. Like *LAPSE, it enforces a certain degree of parsing, prohibiting single stress systems and certain types of under-parsing systems. It does not prohibit the same types of under-parsing systems in all contexts, however. In iambic odd-parity forms, for example, as (66) illustrates, LAPSE-AT-END has the same effect as *LAPSE: both require a left-oriented parsing pattern.

(66)

	*LAPSE	LAPSE-AT-END
a. (σσ́)(σσ́)(σσ́)σ		
b. σ(σσ́)(σσ́)(σσ́)	*	*
c. (σσ́)(σσ́)σ(σσ́)	*	*
d. (σσ́)σ(σσ́)(σσ́)	*	*

In trochaic odd-parity forms, however, as (67) illustrates, LAPSE-AT-END is less restrictive than *LAPSE. *LAPSE requires a right-oriented pattern, but LAPSE-AT-END allows either a right-oriented or left-oriented pattern. Even when LAPSE-AT-END is high-ranked in trochaic under-parsing systems, then, other constraints will play a role in determining parsing directionality.

(67)

	*LAPSE	LAPSE-AT-END
a. σ(σ́σ)(σ́σ)(σ́σ)		
b. (σ́σ)(σ́σ)(σ́σ)σ	*	
c. (σ́σ)σ(σ́σ)(σ́σ)	*	*
d. (σ́σ)(σ́σ)σ(σ́σ)	*	*

The role of *LAPSE-IN-TROUGH is limited primarily to positioning the unparsed syllable in bidirectional under-parsing systems. If the head foot is at the left edge of the prosodic word, the unparsed syllable must

4 In Kager 2001, CLASH-AT-EDGE is defined as licensing clash only at the left edge. However, Kager's tableaux indicate that CLASH-AT-EDGE is satisfied when clash occurs at either edge. Kager also posits a constraint *CLASH-AT-PEAK, which prohibits clash configurations involving a primary stress. Though it has the potential to introduce some additional wrinkles in the context of the OHP, by causing primary stress to shift positions in forms with clash, I will not consider *CLASH-AT-PEAK here.

follow the head foot, as in (68a) so that the resulting lapse does not occur between secondary stresses, as in (68b).

(68)		*Lapse-in-Trough
☞	a. (σ́σ)σ(σ̀σ)(σ̀σ)	
	b. (σ́σ)(σ̀σ)σ(σ̀σ)	*!

If the head foot is at the right edge of the prosodic word, the unparsed syllable must precede the head foot, as in (69a), so that the lapse does not occur between secondary stresses.

(69)		*Lapse-in-Trough
☞	a. (σ̀σ)(σ̀σ)σ(σ́σ)	
	b. (σ̀σ)σ(σ̀σ)(σ́σ)	*!

Though the Clash-at-Edge constraint will play an interesting role in the manifestations of the OHP under Rhythmic Licensing, it actually plays no role in producing the basic binary default patterns when differences in syllable weight are not taken into account. One limitation of constraints that restrict clash and lapse is that they cannot actually create clash and lapse. While Rhythmic Licensing employs the distance-insensitive alignment constraints F-Left and F-Right, repeated with their RSA formulations in (70), to produce lapse configurations, it does not include constraints that might be used to create clash configurations.

(70) a. F-Left: $*\langle\omega, F\rangle$ / $[\ldots\sigma\ldots F\ldots]_{\omega}$

'Assess a violation mark for every $\langle\omega, F\rangle$ such that σ precedes F within ω.'

b. F-Right: $*\langle\omega, F\rangle$ / $[\ldots F\ldots\sigma\ldots]_{\omega}$

'Assess a violation mark for every $\langle\omega, F\rangle$ such that F precedes σ within ω.'

As we shall see below, because Rhythmic Licensing does not have constraints that can introduce clash in binary default patterns, it predicts a narrower range of exhaustive parsing patterns than the other Weak Layering approaches.

4.3.1 Binary default patterns under Rhythmic Licensing

As in the other Weak Layering accounts, for a binary pattern to emerge, one of the constraints that requires parsing must dominate the alignment constraints that restrict parsing. In the case of Rhythmic Licensing, the relevant parsing constraints are PARSE-σ, *LAPSE, and LAPSE-AT-END. Ranking any one of these constraints over both F-LEFT and F-RIGHT is sufficient to ensure that *some* type of binary pattern emerges. The interactions that ultimately decide *which* type of binary pattern emerges, however, are somewhat complex. In the discussion that follows, we examine the rankings that distinguish between the different types of binary patterns under the idealized condition where differences in syllable weight are not actually considered. We begin with the exhaustive parsing patterns.

4.3.1.1 Exhaustive parsing patterns

Just as it does in other Weak Layering accounts, PARSE-σ plays a crucial role in creating exhaustive parsing patterns in Rhythmic Licensing. While *LAPSE and *LAPSE-AT-END prefer exhaustive parsing to many of the under-parsing patterns, only PARSE-σ prefers exhaustive parsing to all under-parsing patterns. In producing exhaustive parsing patterns, then, it is necessary for PARSE-σ to dominate F-BIN and at least one of the alignment constraints.

In trochaic systems, as (71) illustrates, it is necessary for PARSE-σ to dominate F-BIN and F-RIGHT to exclude the trochaic minimal alternation pattern, (71a). Ranking either PARSE-σ or *LAPSE above F-LEFT is sufficient to exclude the remaining under-parsing patterns.

(71)

	*LAPSE	PARSE-σ	F-LEFT	F-BIN	F-RIGHT
☞ w. (σ́σ)(σ́σ)(σ́σ)(σ́)			3	1	3
a. σ(σ́σ)(σ́σ)(σ́σ)		W 1	3	L	L 2
b. (σ́σ)σ(σ́σ)(σ́σ)	W 1	W 1	L 2	L	L 2
c. (σ́σ)(σ́σ)σ(σ́σ)	W 1	W 1	L 2	L	L 2
d. (σ́σ)(σ́σ)(σ́σ)σ	W 1	W 1	L 2	L	3

Note that LAPSE-AT-END cannot duplicate the effects of *LAPSE in this context. If only LAPSE-AT-END dominates F-LEFT in trochaic systems, it fails to eliminate the trochaic peripheral lapse pattern, which ultimately emerges as the winner.

(72)

	Lapse-at-End	F-Left	Parse-σ	F-Bin	F-Right
w. (σ́σ)(σ́σ)(σ́σ)(σ́)		3		1	3
a. σ(σ́σ)(σ́σ)(σ́σ)		3	W 1	L	L 2
b. (σ́σ)σ(σ́σ)(σ́σ)	W 1	L 2	W 1	L	L 2
c. (σ́σ)(σ́σ)σ(σ́σ)	W 1	L 2	W 1	L	L 2
☞ d. (σ́σ)(σ́σ)(σ́σ)σ		L 2	W 1	L	3

In iambic systems, as (73) illustrates, it is necessary for Parse-σ to dominate F-Bin and F-Left to exclude the iambic minimal alternation pattern, (73a). Ranking Parse-σ, *Lapse, or Lapse-at-End above F-Right is sufficient to exclude the remaining under-parsing patterns.

(73)

	Lpse-End	*Lpse	Prse-σ	F-Rght	F-Bin	F-Lft
☞ w. (σ́)(σσ́)(σσ́)(σσ́)				3	1	3
a. (σσ́)(σσ́)(σσ́)σ			W 1	3	L	L 2
b. (σσ́)(σσ́)σ(σσ́)	W 1	W 1	W 1	L 2	L	L 2
c. (σσ́)σ(σσ́)(σσ́)	W 1	W 1	W 1	L 2	L	L 2
d. σ(σσ́)(σσ́)(σσ́)	W 1	W 1	W 1	L 2	L	3

As mentioned above, Rhythmic Licensing predicts a narrower range of exhaustive parsing patterns than the other Weak Layering accounts. Since Rhythmic Licensing contains no distance-insensitive alignment constraints to position the monosyllabic feet that accompany exhaustive parsing in odd-parity forms, it must rely on the influence of *Clash to determine parsing directionality. Since *Clash always prefers directional configurations where clash is avoided, Rhythmic Licensing cannot produce exhaustive parsing patterns that contain a clash. It can only produce patterns where clash is absent.

In trochaic systems, *CLASH restricts monosyllabic feet to final position, since this in the only position in which clash can be avoided. Note that the ranking of *CLASH is not crucial. It just has to be present in the constraint set. The result is the trochaic maximal alternation pattern.

(74) Trochaic maximal alternation: Attested

a. *Pattern*
(σ́σ)(σ́σ)(σ́σ)
(σ́σ)(σ́σ)(σ́σ)(σ́)

b. *Rankings*

i. PARSE-σ >> F-BIN, F-LEFT, F-RIGHT; *CLASH,*LAPSE

ii. *LAPSE >> F-LEFT >> PARSE-σ >>F-BIN, F-RIGHT; *CLASH

In iambic systems, *CLASH restricts monosyllabic feet to initial position. Again, the ranking of *CLASH is not crucial. The result is iambic maximal alternation.

(75) Iambic maximal alternation: Attested

a. *Pattern*
(σσ́)(σσ́)(σσ́)
(σ́)(σσ́)(σσ́)(σσ́)

b. *Rankings*

i. PARSE-σ >> F-BIN, F-LEFT, F-RIGHT; *CLASH, *LAPSE, LAPSE-AT-END

ii. *LAPSE >> F-RIGHT >> PARSE-σ >> F-BIN, F-LEFT; *CLASH, LAPSE-AT-END

iii. LAPSE-AT-END >> F-RIGHT >> PARSE-σ >> F-BIN, F-LEFT; F-RIGHT >> *LAPSE; *CLASH

The fact that Rhythmic Licensing cannot produce binary default patterns with clash means it does not predict the trochaic peripheral clash pattern, the pattern found in Passamaquoddy, Maithili, Biangai, and South Conchucos Quechua.[5] It also means that there is very little for the CLASH-AT-EDGE constraint to do in the context of binary default patterns. As we shall see in Section 4.4, CLASH-AT-EDGE plays a key role in the different manifestations of the OHP under Rhythmic Licensing.

5 The Passamaquoddy pattern could be produced under the Rhythmic Licensing account with a nonfinality constraint that prohibits stress on final syllables. In general, however, nonfinality does not appear to play a central role in any of the OT Weak Layering accounts. At least, it does not play a central role in producing the basic binary stress patterns.

Since the presence of heavy syllables creates the potential for monosyllabic feet, and, thus, for clash configurations, CLASH-AT-EDGE is quite important in this context.

4.3.1.2 Trochaic under-parsing patterns

Rhythmic Licensing produces a broader range of under-parsing patterns, but not as broad as some of the other Weak Layering accounts. To ensure that a single syllable remains unparsed in odd-parity forms, it is sufficient for F-BIN to dominate PARSE-σ. For some patterns, however, it is also sufficient for *LAPSE or LAPSE-AT-END to dominate one of the alignment constraints and the alignment constraint, in turn, to dominate PARSE-σ. For these patterns, the alignment constraint plays much the same role as F-BIN: it prevents the leftover syllable in odd-parity outputs from being parsed.

In trochaic systems, the ranking of F-LEFT plays the key role in determining which particular under-parsing pattern emerges. If a higher ranked constraint or combination of constraints prevents F-LEFT from positioning the leftmost foot at the left edge of an odd-parity form, then the unparsed syllable will occur at the left edge, lapse will be avoided, and the minimal alternation pattern emerges. If F-LEFT is able to position the leftmost foot at the left edge, however, the unparsed syllable must occur in a position that results in lapse, and one of three patterns with lapse emerges.

There are two rankings for F-LEFT that result in trochaic minimal alternation. The first is *LAPSE >> F-LEFT, and the second is LAPSE-AT-END, F-RIGHT >> F-LEFT. Consider in (76) the effects of ranking *LAPSE above F-LEFT. If the leftmost foot occurs at the left edge in an odd-parity form the form necessarily contains a lapse. If the unparsed syllable rather than the leftmost foot occurs at the left edge, lapse is avoided. The higher-ranked *LAPSE prefers the candidate where the unparsed syllable occurs at the left edge, resulting in trochaic minimal alternation.

(76)

	*LAPSE	F-LEFT
☞ w. σ(σ́σ)(σ́σ)(σ́σ)		3
a. (σ́σ)σ(σ́σ)(σ́σ)	W 1	L 2
b. (σ́σ)(σ́σ)σ(σ́σ)	W 1	L 2
c. (σ́σ)(σ́σ)(σ́σ)σ	W 1	L 2

Ranking Lapse-at-End and F-Right above F-Left has a similar effect. Although Lapse-at-End does not prohibit lapse generally, it does prohibit lapse in initial and medial positions. By insisting that the rightmost foot be final, F-Right prevents the unparsed syllable – and therefore a lapse configuration – from occurring in final position, the only position tolerated by Lapse-at-End. The result of their combined preferences, then, is that lapse is suppressed altogether, and the minimal alternation pattern emerges.

(77)

	F-Right	Lapse-at-End	F-Left
☞ w. σ(σ́σ)(σ́σ)(σ́σ)	2		3
a. (σ́σ)σ(σ́σ)(σ́σ)	2	1 W	2 L
b. (σ́σ)(σ́σ)σ(σ́σ)	2	1 W	2 L
c. (σ́σ)(σ́σ)(σ́σ)σ	3 W		2 L

There are four distinct rankings where F-Left is dominated by a constraint or set of constraints that result in trochaic minimal alternation. In the rankings in (78bi,iii), *Lapse dominates F-Left. In the rankings in (78bii,iv), F-Right and Lapse-at-End both dominate F-Left. The vast majority of the possible under-parsing rankings are consistent with one of the rankings in (78), and, thus, result in minimal alternation in trochaic systems.

(78) Trochaic minimal alternation: Attested

a. *Pattern*

(σ́σ)(σ́σ)(σ́σ)

σ(σ́σ)(σ́σ)(σ́σ)

b. *Rankings*

i. F-Bin >> Parse-σ >> F-Right; *Lapse >> F-Left; Lapse-at-End

ii. F-Bin >> Parse-σ >> F-Right >> F-Left >> *Lapse; Lapse-at-End >> F-Left

iii. *Lapse >> F-Right >> Parse-σ; *Lapse >> F-Left; F-Bin, Lapse-at-End

iv. Lapse-at-End >> F-Right >> F-Left, Parse-σ, *Lapse; F-Bin

For a pattern with lapse to emerge in a trochaic system, F-LEFT must be sufficiently high-ranked that it can always position the leftmost foot at a form's left edge. In particular, it is necessary that F-LEFT dominate *LAPSE and either F-RIGHT or LAPSE-AT-END. The ranking between F-LEFT, F-RIGHT, and LAPSE-AT-END determines whether the lapse will be final or internal.

When F-LEFT and LAPSE-AT-END both dominate F-RIGHT, restricting lapse to the right edge is more important than locating the rightmost foot at the right edge, so the lapse will be final.

(79) Trochaic peripheral lapse: Attested

a. *Pattern*

(σ́σ)(σ́σ)(σ́σ)

(σ́σ)(σ́σ)(σ́σ)σ

b. *Rankings*

i. F-BIN >> PARSE-σ >> F-LEFT >> *LAPSE, F-RIGHT; LAPSE-AT-END >> F-RIGHT

ii. LAPSE-AT-END >> F-LEFT >> PARSE-σ, *LAPSE, F-RIGHT; F-BIN

As (80) illustrates, ranking F-LEFT above F-RIGHT (and *LAPSE), ensures that the leftmost foot occurs at the left edge rather than the unparsed syllable. This guarantees that a lapse emerges in some position. Ranking LAPSE-AT-END above F-RIGHT ensures that the lapse occurs in final position rather than medial position.

(80)

	F-LEFT	*LAPSE	LAPSE-AT-END	F-RIGHT
☞ w. (σ́σ)(σ́σ)(σ́σ)σ	2	1		3
a. (σ́σ)σ(σ́σ)(σ́σ)	2	1	W 1	L 2
b. (σ́σ)(σ́σ)σ(σ́σ)	2	1	W 1	L 2
c. σ(σ́σ)(σ́σ)(σ́σ)	W 3	L		L 2

A lapse arises internally when F-LEFT and F-RIGHT both dominate LAPSE-AT-END. Under this ranking, aligning the rightmost foot is more important than restricting lapse to the right edge of the form.

(81) Trochaic internal lapse (initial dactyl and final anapest)

a. *Pattern*

i. Head foot leftmost: Attested	ii. Head foot rightmost: Attested
(σ́σ)(σ̀σ)(σ̀σ)	(σ̀σ)(σ̀σ)(σ́σ)
(σ́σ)σ(σ̀σ)(σ̀σ)	(σ̀σ)(σ̀σ)σ(σ́σ)

b. *Ranking*

F-BIN >> PARSE-σ >> F-LEFT >> *LAPSE, LAPSE-AT-END; PARSE-σ >> F-RIGHT >> LAPSE-AT-END; *LAPSE-IN-TROUGH

As (82) illustrates, ranking F-LEFT above LAPSE-AT-END (and *LAPSE) ensures that a lapse emerges in some position rather than being absent altogether. Ranking F-RIGHT above LAPSE-AT-END ensures that the rightmost foot occurs in final position, guaranteeing that the lapse is internal.

(82)

	F-LEFT	*LAPSE	F-RIGHT	LAPSE-AT-END
☞ w1. (σ́σ)σ(σ́σ)(σ́σ)	2	1	2	1
☞ w2. (σ́σ)(σ́σ)σ(σ́σ)	2	1	2	1
a. (σ́σ)(σ́σ)(σ́σ)σ	2	1	W 3	L
b. σ(σ́σ)(σ́σ)(σ́σ)	W 3	L	2	L

The exact position of an internal lapse is determined by *LAPSE-IN-TROUGH and the position of the primary stress. If the head foot is initial, as in (81ai), the unparsed syllable occurs just to the right of the head foot. This ensures that the lapse configuration does not occur between secondary stresses. If the head foot is final, as in (81aii), the unparsed syllable occurs just to the left of the head foot. Note that the ranking of *LAPSE-IN-TROUGH is not crucial. It just has to be present in the constraint set to produce this result.

While Rhythmic Licensing does predict two trochaic internal lapse patterns, both of which are attested, it also predicts that the lapses will never occur between secondary stresses. This being the case, Rhythmic Licensing does not predict an initial dactyl pattern with initial secondary stress, the pattern found in Indonesian, Norwegian, and Spanish.

4.3.1.3 Iambic under-parsing patterns

In iambic under-parsing systems, the interactions determining whether or not a lapse emerges are slightly more complex. For lapse to be avoided altogether, so that the iambic minimal alternation pattern emerges, PARSE-σ or *LAPSE must dominate F-LEFT, and *LAPSE or LAPSE-AT-END must dominate F-RIGHT.

The domination of F-LEFT by PARSE-σ or *LAPSE is crucial to prevent lapse from arising at the right edge in even-parity forms. As (83) indicates, a high-ranking PARSE-σ or *LAPSE prevents F-LEFT from deleting a final foot, ensuring that the iambic minimal alternation pattern, rather than the iambic final lapse pattern, ultimately emerges.

(83)

	PARSE-σ	*LAPSE	F-LEFT
☞ w. (σσ́)(σσ́)(σσ́)			2
l. (σσ́)(σσ́)σσ	W 2	W 1	L 1

The domination of F-RIGHT by *LAPSE or LAPSE-AT-END is crucial to prevent an internal lapse from arising in an odd-parity form. As (84) illustrates, lapse can only arise in iambic odd-parity forms if the rightmost foot occurs in final position. Ranking *LAPSE over F-RIGHT is the most obvious way to ensure that the unparsed syllable occurs in final position and that the minimal alternation pattern emerges. While LAPSE-AT-END does not actually prohibit lapse, it does restrict any potential lapse to final position. Since iambic footing does not allow for a final lapse (without omitting one or more disyllabic feet), LAPSE-AT-END prohibits lapse in all positions in which it might actually occur in a binary pattern, and ranking LAPSE-AT-END above F-RIGHT has the same effect as ranking *LAPSE above F-RIGHT in this context.

(84)

	*LAPSE	LAPSE-AT-END	F-RIGHT
☞ w. (σσ́)(σσ́)(σσ́)σ			3
a. (σσ́)(σσ́)σ(σσ́)	W 1	W 1	L 2
b. (σσ́)σ(σσ́)(σσ́)	W 1	W 1	L 2
c. σ(σσ́)(σσ́)(σσ́)	W 1	W 1	L 2

Four distinct under-parsing rankings satisfy the conditions for the iambic minimal alternation pattern. Parse-σ dominates F-Left, and *Lapse dominates F-Right in (85bi). Parse-σ dominates F-Left, and Lapse-at-End dominates F-Right in (85bii). *Lapse dominates F-Left and F-Right in (85biii). *Lapse dominates F-Left, and Lapse-at-End dominates F-Right in (85biv). The vast majority of possible under-parsing rankings are consistent with one of the iambic minimal alternation rankings, and, thus, result in minimal alternation in iambic systems.

(85) Iambic minimal alternation: Attested

a. *Pattern*

(σσ́)(σσ́)(σσ́)

(σσ́)(σσ́)(σσ́)σ

b. *Rankings*

i. F-Bin >> Parse-σ >> F-Left; *Lapse >> F-Right; Lapse-at-End

ii. F-Bin >> Parse-σ >> F-Left; Lapse-at-End >> F-Right >> *Lapse

iii. *Lapse >> F-Left >> Parse-σ; *Lapse >> F-Right; F-Bin, Lapse-at-End

iv. Lapse-at-End >> F-Right >> *Lapse >> F-Left >> Parse-σ; F-Bin

The iambic final lapse pattern, where a lapse arises at the right edge of even-parity forms, emerges when F-Left is ranked sufficiently high to prevent parsing at the right edge but not high enough to prevent parsing of more than the final two syllables.

(86) Iambic final lapse: Attested

a. *Pattern*

(σσ́)(σσ́)σσ

(σσ́)(σσ́)(σσ́)σ

b. *Ranking*

Lapse-at-End >> F-Left >> Parse-σ, *Lapse; Lapse-at-End >> F-Right; F-Bin

As (87) illustrates, ranking F-Left above Parse-σ and *Lapse prevents the latter two constraints from insisting on exhaustive parsing, When F-Left is dominated in turn by Lapse-at-End, however, Lapse-at-End prevents feet from being omitted if the omission would result in a lapse in any position but final position. The result is that just the final foot of even-parity forms is absent, resulting in the iambic final lapse pattern.

(87)

	Lapse-at-End	F-Left	Parse-σ	*Lapse
☞ w. (σσ́)(σσ́)σσ		1	2	1
a. (σσ́)σσσσ	2 W	L	4 W	3 W
b. (σσ́)(σσ́)(σσ́)		2 W	L	L

Note that this result is only possible when GA constraints – such as those employed in Kager (2001, 2005) – are replaced by the RSA constraints employed here. If we were to replace F-Left with Align (ω, L) (see Section 2.5.3), feet misaligned with the left edge would not be penalized, there would be no reason to omit the final foot, and the result would be minimal alternation.

(88)

	Lapse-at-End	Align (ω, L)	Parse-σ
☞ w. (σσ́)(σσ́)(σσ́)			
l. (σσ́)(σσ́)σσ			2 W

The final iambic patterns produced under Rhythmic Licensing are the internal lapse patterns, which emerge under rankings where F-Right dominates *Lapse and Lapse-at-End.

(89) Iambic internal lapse (initial amphibrach and final anapest): Unattested

a. *Pattern*

i. Head foot leftmost
(σσ́)(σσ̀)(σσ̀)
(σσ́)σ(σσ̀)(σσ̀)

ii. Head foot rightmost
(σσ̀)(σσ̀)(σσ́)
(σσ̀)(σσ̀)σ(σσ́)

b. *Ranking*

F-Bin >> Parse-σ >> F-Right >> *Lapse, Lapse-at-End; Parse-σ >> F-Left; *Lapse-in-Trough

As (90) illustrates, the high-ranking F-Right prevents the unparsed syllable from occurring in final position. Lapse cannot be avoided, and an internal lapse configuration emerges. (Lapse cannot emerge initially in this context due to the uncontested demands of F-Left.)

(90)

	F-RIGHT	*LAPSE	LAPSEAT-END	F-LEFT
☞ w1. (σσ́)(σσ́)σ(σσ́)	2	1	1	2
☞ w2. (σσ́)σ(σσ́)(σσ́)	2	1	1	2
a. σ(σσ́)(σσ́)(σσ́)	2	1	1	W 3
b. (σσ́)(σσ́)(σσ́)σ	W 3	L	L	2

As in trochaic systems, the exact position of the internal lapse in iambic systems is determined by the position of the head foot and the *LAPSE-IN-TROUGH constraint. If the head foot is initial, as in (89ai), the unparsed syllable occurs just to the right of the head foot. If the head foot is final, as in (89aii), the unparsed syllable occurs just to the left of the head foot. The result is two unattested iambic patterns.

4.3.1.4 Summary of Rhythmic Licensing's binary default patterns

The patterns in (91) are the basic predictions of Rhythmic Licensing under the idealized condition where differences in syllable weight are not considered. In this context, Rhythmic Licensing predicts a subset of the attested binary default patterns with a degree of over-generation somewhat greater than Asymmetrical Alignment.

(91) Summary of predicted patterns

a. Minimal alternation

i. Trochaic: Attested
(σ́σ)(σ́σ)(σ́σ)
σ(σ́σ)(σ́σ)(σ́σ)

ii. Iambic: Attested
(σσ́)(σσ́)(σσ́)
(σσ́)(σσ́)(σσ́)σ

b. Maximal alternation

i. Trochaic: Attested
(σ́σ)(σ́σ)(σ́σ)
(σ́σ)(σ́σ)(σ́σ)(σ́)

ii. Iambic: Attested
(σσ́)(σσ́)(σσ́)
(σ́)(σσ́)(σσ́)(σσ́)

d. Trochaic peripheral lapse: Attested
(σ́σ)(σ́σ)(σ́σ)
(σ́σ)(σ́σ)(σ́σ)σ

e. Iambic final lapse: Attested
(σσ́)(σσ́)σσ
(σσ́)(σσ́)(σσ́)σ

f. Internal lapse

i. Trochaic, head foot final: Attested
(σ̀σ)(σ̀σ)(σ́σ)
(σ̀σ)(σ̀σ)σ(σ́σ)

ii. Iambic, head foot initial: Unattested
(σσ́)(σσ̀)(σσ̀)
(σσ́)σ(σσ̀)(σσ̀)

iii. Trochaic, head foot initial: Attested
(σ́σ)(σ̀σ)(σ̀σ)
(σ́σ)σ(σ̀σ)(σ̀σ)

iv. Iambic, head foot final: Unattested
(σσ̀)(σσ̀)(σσ́)
(σσ̀)(σσ̀)σ(σσ́)

Since these predictions do not take into account the effects of PARSE-σ and F-BIN when heavy syllables are present, however, the actual predictions of Rhythmic Licensing are really quite different. Although the patterns in (48) are all intended to be quantity-insensitive, most actually occur with one or more of the different manifestations of the OHP possible under Rhythmic Licensing.

4.4 The OHP in Rhythmic Licensing

When differences in syllable weight are taken into account, the patterns produced under Rhythmic Licensing frequently exhibit the effects of the OHP. In general, OHP effects emerge when F-BIN dominates either PARSE-σ or *CLASH. In trochaic systems, it is also necessary that PARSE-σ dominate F-RIGHT; in iambic systems, it is also necessary that PARSE-σ dominate F-LEFT.

(92) OHP rankings for Rhythmic Licensing

a. Trochaic systems

i. F-BIN >> PARSE-σ; PARSE-σ >> F-RIGHT; *CLASH

ii. PARSE-σ >> F-BIN >> *CLASH; PARSE-σ >> F-RIGHT;

b. Iambic Systems

i. F-BIN >> PARSE-σ; PARSE-σ >> F-LEFT; *CLASH

ii. PARSE-σ >> F-BIN >> *CLASH; PARSE-σ >> F-LEFT;

The OHP emerges in three distinct versions under Rhythmic Licensing, with the particular version that arises being determined primarily by the ranking of *CLASH and CLASH-AT-EDGE. Except for the iambic final lapse pattern, each of the basic patterns in (91) can emerge with multiple versions of the OHP. Most emerge with all three versions.

To illustrate the different versions of the OHP under Rhythmic Licensing in the discussion that follows, we will consider an underparsing pattern where the ranking of *CLASH and CLASH-AT-EDGE is not supposed to be crucial – the trochaic internal lapse pattern, head foot final – and then observe the results under various rankings of the two constraints. The ranking for the trochaic internal lapse pattern, head foot final, is repeated in (93).

(93) Trochaic internal lapse, head foot final, ranking

F-BIN >> PARSE-σ >> F-LEFT >> *LAPSE, LAPSE-AT-END; PARSE-σ >> F-RIGHT >> LAPSE-AT-END; *LAPSE-IN-TROUGH, *CLASH, CLASH-AT-EDGE

If the ranking were truly quantity-insensitive, the result would be the same stress pattern regardless of whether or not the input contained heavy syllables. Odd-parity forms would have the head foot stranded at the right edge, all other feet would be drawn to the left, and there would be an unparsed syllable just to the left of the head foot. As we shall see below, however, the ranking always exhibits the effects of the OHP.

4.4.1 The First Version

Rhythmic Licensing's first version of the OHP (RL OHP1) is the same as the first version under Asymmetrical Alignment. It arises when *CLASH and F-BIN both dominate PARSE-σ. As (94) indicates, footing is sensitive to odd-numbered heavy syllables in odd-parity forms but only when they occur in a position where a monosyllabic foot would not result in clash.

(94) RL OHP version 1

a. Ranking

*CLASH, F-BIN >> PARSE-σ

b. Description

A heavy syllable *H* is parsed as a monosyllabic foot *iff*

i. *H* occurs in an odd-parity form; *and*

ii. *H* is odd-numbered; *and*

iii. parsing *H* as a monosyllabic foot would not result in clash.

In the tableaux in (95) and (96), the ranking intended to produce the trochaic internal lapse pattern, head foot final, is assumed, but only the constraints most directly relevant to OHP effects are shown. In (95), we see the result for an odd-parity form with a peripheral heavy syllable in a position to avoid clash (final position in trochaic systems). The final syllable is parsed as a monosyllabic foot satisfying the high-ranking *CLASH, F-BIN, and PARSE-σ simultaneously. The result is an exhaustive parsing pattern rather than the expected bidirectional pattern.

(95)

HLHLHLH	*CLASH	F-BIN	PARSE-σ
☞ w. (H̀L)(H̀L)(H̀L)(H́)			
a. (H̀L)(H̀L)H(ĹH)			1 W
b. (H̀)(L̀H)(L̀H)(ĹH)	1 W		
c. (H̀L)(H̀L)(H̀)(ĹH)	1 W		
d. (H̀L)(H̀)(L̀H)(ĹH)	1 W		

In (96), we see the result for an input that has odd-numbered heavy syllables, but not in a position to avoid clash. Since the heavy syllables cannot be parsed as monosyllabic feet without violating the high-ranking *CLASH, the core constraints of the trochaic internal lapse ranking assert their preferences, and the expected bidirectional pattern emerges.

(96)

HLHLHLL	*CLASH	F-BIN	PARSE-σ
☞ w. (H̀L)(H̀L)H(ĹL)			1
a. (H̀L)(H̀L)(H̀L)(Ĺ)		1 W	L
b. (H̀)(L̀H)(L̀H)(ĹL)	1 W		L
c. (H̀L)(H̀L)(H̀)(ĹL)	1 W		L
d. (H̀L)(H̀)(L̀H)(ĹL)	1 W		L

As summarized in (97–101), RL OHP1 emerges with most of the basic binary default patterns in (91). For each pattern in (97–101), four examples of odd-parity forms are provided. The first, which contains only light syllables, exhibits the basic pattern. The second through fourth contain odd-numbered heavy syllables. The second contains heavy syllables in all odd-numbered positions, including the peripheral position where a monosyllabic foot can avoid clash. The third omits a heavy syllable in the peripheral position where a monosyllabic foot can avoid clash. The fourth contains odd-numbered heavy syllables in medial positions only. It is the second form in each case that exhibits the effects of RL OHP1.

(97) Trochaic minimal alternation: RL OHP1: Unattested

a. *Pattern*

i. L(ĹL)(ĹL)(ĹL) ii. (H́L)(H́L)(H́L)(H́)

iii. H(ĹH)(ĹH)(ĹL) iv. L(ĹH)(ĹH)(ĹL)

b. *Rankings*

i. F-Bin, *Clash >> Parse-σ >> F-Right; *Lapse >> F-Left; Clash-at-Edge

ii. F-Bin, *Clash >> Parse-σ >> F-Right >> F-Left >> F-Left >> *Lapse; Lapse-at-End >> F-Left; Clash-at-Edge

(98) Iambic minimal alternation: RL OHP1: Unattested

a. *Pattern*

i. (LĹ)(LĹ)(LĹ)L ii. (H́)(LH́)(LH́)(LH́)

iii. (LĹ)(HĹ)(HĹ)H iv. (LĹ)(HĹ)(HĹ)L

b. *Rankings*

i. F-Bin, *Clash >> Parse-σ >> F-Left; *Lapse >> F-Right; Lapse-at-End, Clash-at-Edge

ii. F-Bin, *Clash >> Parse-σ >> F-Left; Lapse-at-End >> F-Right >> *Lapse; Clash-at-Edge

(99) Trochaic peripheral lapse: RL OHP1: Attested

a. *Pattern*

i. (ĹL)(ĹL)(ĹL)L ii. (H́L)(H́L)(H́L)(H́)

iii. (H́L)(H́L)(H́L)L iv. (ĹL)(H́L)(H́L)L

b. *Ranking*

F-Bin, *Clash >> Parse-σ >> F-Left >> *Lapse, F-Right; Lapse-at-End >> F-Right; Clash-at-Edge

(100) Trochaic internal lapse: RL OHP1: Unattested

a. *Head foot leftmost pattern*

i. (ĹL)L(L̀L)(L̀L) ii. (H́L)(H̀L)(H̀L)(H̀)

iii. (H́L)H(L̀H)(L̀L) iv. (ĹL)H(L̀H)(L̀L)

b. *Head foot rightmost pattern*

i. (L̀L)(L̀L)L(ĹL) ii. (H̀L)(H̀L)(H̀L)(H́)

iii. (H̀L)(H̀L)H(ĹL) iv. (L̀L)(H̀L)H(ĹL)

c. *Ranking*

F-Bin, *Clash >> Parse-σ >> F-Left >> *Lapse, Lapse-at-End; Parse-σ >> F-Right >> Lapse-at-End; *Lapse-in-Trough; Clash-at-Edge

(101) Iambic internal lapse: RL OHP1: Unattested

a. *Head foot leftmost pattern*

i. (LĹ)L(LL̀)(LL̀) ii. (H́)(LH̀)(LH̀)(LH̀)

iii. (LĹ)H(LH̀)(LH̀) iv. (LĹ)H(LH̀)(LL̀)

b. *Head foot rightmost pattern*

i. (LL̀)(LL̀)L(LĹ) ii. (H̀)(LH̀)(LH̀)(LH́)

iii. (HL̀)(HL̀)H(LĹ) iv. (LL̀)(HL̀)H(LĹ)

c. *Ranking*

F-Bin, *Clash >> Parse-σ >> F-Right >> *Lapse, Lapse-at-End; Parse-σ >> F-Left; *Lapse-in-Trough, Clash-at-End

While RL OHP1 emerges with most of the basic binary default patterns under Rhythmic Licensing, it does not emerge with the maximal alternation patterns or the iambic final lapse pattern. The maximal alternation patterns require that Parse-σ dominate F-Bin, a ranking inconsistent with the RL OHP1 ranking. The iambic final lapse pattern avoids OHP effects altogether. Note that in the case of the trochaic peripheral lapse pattern, (99), the result of RL OHP 1 is actually an attested pattern. Quantity-sensitive parsing for final syllables only can be found in Wergaia (Hercus 1986).

4.4.2 The Second Version

Rhythmic Licensing's second version of the OHP (RL OHP2) emerges in exhaustive parsing patterns when Clash-at-Edge and Parse-σ both dominate F-Bin and F-Bin dominates *Clash, as in (102a) It emerges in under-parsing patterns when Clash-at-Edge and F-Bin dominate Parse-σ and Parse-σ dominates *Clash, as in (102b). RL OHP2 is similar to RL OHP1, but it allows heavy syllables to be parsed as monosyllabic feet in an additional position. It still prefers that monosyllabic feet be limited to heavy syllables in positions where clash can be avoided, the right edge for trochees and the left edge for iambs, but it allows a heavy syllable at the opposite edge to be parsed as a monosyllabic foot in those cases where clash cannot be avoided.

(102) RL OHP version 2

a. Ranking for exhaustive parsing systems

CLASH-AT-EDGE, PARSE-σ >> F-BIN >> *CLASH

b. Ranking for under-parsing systems

CLASH-AT-EDGE, F-BIN >> PARSE-σ >> *CLASH

c. Description

A heavy syllable *H* is parsed as a monosyllabic foot *iff*

i. *H* occurs in an odd-parity form; *and*

ii. *H* is odd-numbered; *and*

iii. parsing *H* as a monosyllabic foot would not result in clash; *or*

iv. if there is no heavy syllable that meets (iii), parsing *H* as a monosyllabic foot would result in a peripheral clash.

The tableaux in (103–105) illustrate how the effects of RL OHP2 emerge in conjunction with the trochaic internal lapse pattern, head foot final. If the input has a heavy syllable in a peripheral position that can avoid clash, as in (103), that syllable will be parsed as a monosyllabic foot. This allows for exhaustive binary footing in a way that satisfies both the low-ranked *CLASH and the high ranked CLASH-AT-EDGE.

(103)

HLHLHLH	CLASH-AT-EDGE	F-BIN	PARSE	*CLASH
☞ w. (H̀L)(H̀L)(H̀L)(H́)				
a. (H̀L)(H̀L)H(ĹH)			W 1	
b. (H̀)(L̀H)(L̀H)(ĹH)				W 1
c. (H̀L)(H̀L)(H̀)(ĹH)	W 1			W 1
d. (H̀L)(H̀)(L̀H)(ĹH)	W 1			W 1

If the input does not have a peripheral heavy syllable in a position where clash can be avoided, but it has a heavy syllable at the opposite edge, as in (104), the heavy syllable at the opposite edge will be parsed as a monosyllabic foot. While the resulting configuration violates the low-ranked *Clash, it allows exhaustive binary parsing while respecting the high-ranked Clash-at-Edge.

(104)

HLHLHLL	Clash-at-Edge	F-Bin	Parse	*Clash
☞ w. (H̀)(L̀H)(L̀H)(ĹL)				1
a. (H̀L)(H̀L)H(ĹL)			1 W	L
b. (H̀L)(H̀L)(H̀L)(Ĺ)		1 W		L
c. (H̀L)(H̀L)(H̀)(ĹL)	1 W			1
d. (H̀L)(H̀)(L̀H)(ĹL)	1 W			1

Finally, in (105), we see that an input that has only medial heavy syllables exhibits the same output pattern as an input that has only light syllables. Although the input in (105) has medial odd-numbered heavy syllables, the clash configurations that result from parsing one of them as a monosyllabic foot violate the high-ranked Clash-at-Edge.

(105)

LLHLHLL	Clash-at-Edge	F-Bin	Parse	*Clash
☞ w. (L̀L)(H̀L)H(ĹL)			1	
a. (L̀L)(H̀L)(H̀L)(Ĺ)		1 W	L	
b. (L̀)(L̀H)(L̀H)(ĹL)		1 W	L	1 W
c. (L̀L)(H̀L)(H̀)(ĹL)	1 W		L	1 W
d. (L̀L)(H̀)(L̀H)(ĹL)	1 W		L	1 W

The patterns that can emerge under the rankings for RL OHP2 are summarized in (106–112). For each ranking, four examples of odd-parity forms are provided. The first, which contains only light syllables, exhibits the basic pattern. The second and third contain peripheral odd-numbered heavy syllables, the second in a position where clash can be avoided and the third only in a position where clash cannot be avoided. The fourth contains odd-numbered heavy syllables in medial positions only. It is the second and third forms in each case that exhibit the effects of RL OHP2.

(106) Trochaic maximal alternation: RL OHP2: Unattested

a. *Pattern*

i. (ĹL)(ĹL)(ĹL)(Ĺ) ii. (H́L)(H́L)(H́L)(H́)

iii. (H́)(ĹH)(ĹH)(ĹL) iv. (ĹL)(H́L)(H́L)(Ĺ)

b. *Rankings*

i. PARSE-σ, CLASH-AT-EDGE >> F-BIN >> *CLASH; PARSE-σ >> F-LEFT, F-RIGHT; *LAPSE

ii. *LAPSE >> F-LEFT >> PARSE-σ >> F-BIN, F-RIGHT; CLASH-AT-EDGE >> F-BIN >> *CLASH

(107) Iambic maximal alternation: RL OHP2: Unattested

a. *Pattern*

i. (Ĺ)(LĹ)(LĹ)(LĹ) ii. (H́)(LH́)(LH́)(LH́)

iii. (LĹ)(HĹ)(HĹ)(H́) iv. (Ĺ)(LH́)(LH́)(LĹ)

b. *Rankings*

i. PARSE-σ, CLASH-AT-EDGE >> F-BIN >> *CLASH; PARSE-σ >> F-LEFT, F-RIGHT; *LAPSE, LAPSE-AT-END

ii. *LAPSE >> F-RIGHT >> PARSE-σ >> F-BIN, F-LEFT; CLASH-AT-EDGE >> F-BIN >> *CLASH; LAPSE-AT-END

iii. LAPSE-AT-END >> F-RIGHT >> PARSE-σ >> F-BIN, F-LEFT; CLASH-AT-EDGE >> F-BIN >> *CLASH; F-RIGHT >> *LAPSE

(108) Trochaic minimal alternation: RL OHP2: Unattested

a. *Pattern*

i. L(ĹL)(ĹL)(ĹL) ii. (H́L)(H́L)(H́L)(H́)

iii. (H́)(ĹH)(ĹH)(ĹL) iv. L(ĹH)(ĹH)(ĹL)

b. *Rankings*

i. F-BIN, CLASH-AT-EDGE >> PARSE-σ >> F-RIGHT, *CLASH; *LAPSE >> F-LEFT; LAPSE-AT-END

ii. F-BIN, *CLASH-AT-EDGE >> PARSE-σ >> F-RIGHT >> F-LEFT >> F-LEFT >> *LAPSE; PARSE-σ >> *CLASH; LAPSE-AT-END >> F-LEFT

(109) Iambic minimal alternation: RL OHP2: Unattested

a. *Pattern*

i. (LĹ)(LĹ)(LĹ)L ii. (H́)(LH́)(LH́)(LH́)

iii. (LĹ)(HĹ)(HĹ)(H́) iv. (LĹ)(HĹ)(HĹ)L

b. *Rankings*

i. F-BIN, CLASH-AT-EDGE >> PARSE-σ >> F-LEFT, *CLASH; *LAPSE >> F-RIGHT; LAPSE-AT-END

ii. F-BIN, CLASH-AT-EDGE >> PARSE-σ >> F-LEFT, *CLASH; LAPSE-AT-END >> F-RIGHT >> *LAPSE

(110) Trochaic peripheral lapse: RL OHP2: Unattested

a. *Pattern*

i. (ĹL)(ĹL)(ĹL)L   ii. (H́L)(H́L)(H́L)(H́)

iii. (H́)(ĹH)(ĹH)(ĹL)   iv. (ĹL)(H́L)(H́L)L

b. *Ranking*

F-BIN, CLASH-AT-EDGE >> PARSE-σ >> F-LEFT >> *LAPSE, F-RIGHT; LAPSE-AT-END >> F-RIGHT; PARSE-σ >> *CLASH

(111) Trochaic internal lapse: RL OHP2: Unattested

a. *Head foot leftmost pattern*

i. (ĹL)L(L̀L)(L̀L)   ii. (H́L)(H̀L)(H̀L)(H̀)

iii. (H́)(ĹH)(ĹH)(ĹL)   iv. (ĹL)H(L̀H)(L̀L)

b. *Head foot rightmost pattern*

i. (L̀L)(L̀L)L(ĹL)   ii. (H̀L)(H̀L)(H̀L)(H́)

iii. (H́)(ĹH)(ĹH)(ĹL)   iv. (L̀L)(H̀L)H(ĹL)

c. *Ranking*

F-BIN, CLASH-AT-EDGE >> PARSE-σ >> F-LEFT >> *LAPSE, LAPSE-AT-END; PARSE-σ >> F-RIGHT >> LAPSE-AT-END; PARSE-σ >> *CLASH; *LAPSE-IN-TROUGH

(112) Iambic internal lapse: RL OHP2: Unattested

a. *Head foot leftmost pattern*

i. (LĹ)L(LL̀)(LL̀)   ii. (H́)(LH̀)(LH̀)(LH̀)

iii. (LĹ)(HĹ)(HĹ)(H́)   iv. (LĹ)H(LH̀)(LL̀)

b. *Head foot rightmost pattern*

i. (LL̀)(LL̀)L(LĹ)   ii. (H̀)(LH̀)(LH̀)(LH́)

iii. (LĹ)(HĹ)(HĹ)(H́)   iv. (LL̀)(HL̀)H(LĹ)

c. *Rankings*

F-BIN, CLASH-AT-END >> PARSE-σ >> F-RIGHT >> *LAPSE, LAPSE-AT-END; PARSE-σ >> F-LEFT, *CLASH; *LAPSE-IN-TROUGH

Each of the binary patterns predicted by Rhythmic Licensing, then, except the iambic final lapse pattern, can emerge with RL OHP2. The result is always an unattested pattern.

4.4.3 *The Third Version*

Rhythmic Licensing's final version of the OHP (RL OHP3) emerges when F-BIN and PARSE-σ dominate *CLASH and CLASH-AT-EDGE, and it allows heavy monosyllabic feet in an even greater variety of positions. In this version, heavy monosyllabic feet are still preferred in peripheral position, and in the peripheral position that avoids clash, if possible. If there are no peripheral heavy syllables, however, a medial odd-numbered heavy syllable will be parsed as a monosyllabic foot.

(113) RL OHP version 3

a. Ranking

F-BIN, PARSE-σ >> *CLASH, CLASH-AT-EDGE

b. Description

A heavy syllable *H* is parsed as a monosyllabic foot *iff*

i. *H* occurs in an odd-parity form; *and*

ii. *H* is odd-numbered; *and*

iii. parsing *H* as a monosyllabic foot would not result in clash; *or*

iv. if there is no heavy syllable that meets (iii), parsing *H* as a monosyllabic foot would result in a peripheral clash; *or*

v. if there is no heavy syllable that meets (iii) or (iv), parsing *H* as a monosyllabic foot would result in a non-peripheral clash.

In (114–116), we see the results of positioning *CLASH and CLASH-AT-EDGE below F-BIN and PARSE-σ in the ranking for the trochaic internal lapse pattern, head foot final. If there is a heavy syllable in the peripheral position where a monosyllabic foot can avoid clash, as in (114), that syllable will be parsed as a monosyllabic foot.

(114)

HLHLHLH	F-BIN	PARSE	*CLASH	CLASH-AT-EDGE
☞ w. (H̀L)(H̀L)(H̀L)(H́)				
a. (H̀L)(H̀L)H(ĹH)		1 W		
b. (H̀)(L̀H)(L̀H)(ĹH)			1 W	
c. (H̀L)(H̀L)(H̀)(ĹH)			1 W	1 W
d. (H̀L)(H̀)(L̀H)(ĹH)			1 W	1 W

If no heavy syllable is in a position to avoid clash, as in (115), a heavy syllable at the opposite edge will be parsed as a monosyllabic foot.

(115)

HLHLHLL	F-Bin	Parse	*Clash	Clash-at-Edge
☞ w. (H̀)(L̀H)(L̀H)(ĹL)			1	
a. (H̀L)(H̀L)H(ĹL)		W 1	L	
b. (H̀L)(H̀L)(H̀L)(Ĺ)	W 1		L	
c. (H̀L)(H̀L)(H̀)(ĹL)			1	W 1
d. (H̀L)(H̀)(L̀H)(ĹL)			1	W 1

If there is no peripheral heavy syllable, as in (116), a medial odd-numbered heavy syllable will be parsed as a monosyllabic foot. Notice in this case, however, that when multiple medial heavy syllables are available, Rhythmic Licensing does not have the distance-sensitive alignment constraints necessary to determine which one should be parsed as a monosyllabic foot. The result is that two or more candidates tie and there is no unique optimal output.

(116)

LLHLHLL	F-Bin	Parse	*Clash	Clash-at-Edge
☞ wi. (L̀L)(H̀L)(H̀)(ĹL)			1	1
☞ wii. (L̀L)(H̀)(L̀H)(ĹL)			1	1
a. (L̀L)(H̀L)H(ĹL)		W 1	L	L
b. (L̀L)(H̀L)(H̀L)(Ĺ)	W 1		L	L
c. (L̀)(L̀H)(L̀H)(ĹL)	W 1		1	

The patterns that can emerge under the rankings for RL OHP3 are summarized in (117–123). For each pattern, four examples of odd-parity forms are provided. The first, which contains only light syllables, exhibits the basic pattern. The second and third contain peripheral odd-numbered heavy syllables, and the fourth contains odd-numbered heavy syllables in medial positions only. All forms with odd-numbered heavy syllables exhibit the effects of RL OHP3.

(117) Trochaic maximal alternation: RL OHP3: Unattested

a. *Pattern*

i. (ĹL)(ĹL)(ĹL)(Ĺ) ii. (H́L)(H́L)(H́L)(H́)

iii. (H́)(ĹH)(ĹH)(ĹL) iv. (ĹL)(H́)(ĹH)(ĹL) *or* (ĹL)(H́L)(H́)(ĹL)

b. *Rankings*

i. Parse-σ >> F-Bin >> *Clash, Clash-at-Edge; Parse-σ >> F-Left, F-Right; *Lapse

ii. *Lapse >> F-Left >> Parse-σ >> F-Bin >> *Clash, Clash-at-Edge; Parse-σ >> F-Right

(118) Iambic maximal alternation: RL OHP3: Unattested

a. *Pattern*

i. (Ĺ)(LĹ)(LĹ)(LĹ) ii. (H́)(LH́)(LH́)(LH́)

iii. (LĹ)(HĹ)(HĹ)(H́) iv. (LĹ)(H́)(LH́)(LĹ) *or* (LĹ)(HĹ)(H́)(LĹ)

b. *Rankings*

i. Parse-σ >> F-Bin >> *Clash, Clash-at-Edge; Parse-σ >> F-Left, F-Right; *Lapse, Lapse-at-End

ii. *Lapse >> F-Right >> Parse-σ >> F-Bin >> *Clash, Clash-at-Edge; Parse-σ >> F-Left; Lapse-at-End

iii. Lapse-at-End >> F-Right >> Parse-σ >> F-Bin >> *Clash, Clash-at-Edge; F-Right >> *Lapse; Parse-σ >> F-Left

(119) Trochaic minimal alternation: RL OHP3: Unattested

a. *Pattern*

i. L(ĹL)(ĹL)(ĹL) ii. (H́L)(H́L)(H́L)(H́)

iii. (H́)(ĹH)(ĹH)(ĹL) iv. (ĹL)(H́)(ĹH)(ĹL) *or* (ĹL)(H́L)(H́)(ĹL)

b. *Rankings*

i. F-Bin >> Parse-σ >> F-Right, *Clash, Clash-at-Edge; *Lapse >> F-Left; Lapse-At-End

ii. F-Bin >> Parse-σ >> F-Right >> F-Left >> F-Left >> *Lapse; Parse-σ >> *Clash, *Clash-at-Edge; Lapse-at-End >> F-Left

(120) Iambic minimal alternation: RL OHP3: Unattested

a. *Pattern*

i. (LĹ)(LĹ)(LĹ)L ii. (H́)(LH́)(LH́)(LH́)

iii. (LĹ)(HĹ)(HĹ)(H́) iv. (LĹ)(H́)(LH́)(LĹ) *or* (LĹ)(HĹ)(H́)(LĹ)

b. *Rankings*

i. F-Bin >> Parse-σ >> F-Left, *Clash, Clash-at-Edge; *Lapse >> F-Right; Lapse-at-End

ii. F-Bin >> Parse-σ >> F-Left, *Clash, Clash-at-Edge; Lapse-at-End >> F-Right >> *Lapse

(121) Trochaic peripheral lapse: RL OHP3: Unattested

a. *Pattern*

i. (ĹL)(ĹL)(ĹL)L ii. (H́L)(H́L)(H́L)(H́)

iii. (H́)(ĹH)(ĹH)(ĹL) iv. (ĹL)(H́)(ĹH)(ĹL) *or* (ĹL)(H́L)(H́)(ĹL)

b. *Ranking*

F-Bin >> Parse-σ >> F-Left >> *Lapse, F-Right; Lapse-at-End >> F-Right; Parse-σ >> *Clash, Clash-at-Edge

(122) Trochaic internal lapse: RL OHP3: Unattested

a. *Head foot leftmost pattern*

i. (ĹL)L(L̀L)(L̀L) ii. (H́L)(H̀L)(H̀L)(H̀)

iii. (H́)(ĹH)(ĹH)(ĹL) iv. (ĹL)(H́)(ĹH)(ĹL) *or* (ĹL)(H́L)(H́)(ĹL)

b. *Head foot rightmost pattern*

i. (L̀L)(L̀L)L(ĹL) ii. (H̀L)(H̀L)(H̀L)(H́)

iii. (H́)(ĹH)(ĹH)(ĹL) iv. (ĹL)(H́)(ĹH)(ĹL) *or* (ĹL)(H́L)(H́)(ĹL)

c. *Ranking*

F-Bin >> Parse-σ >> F-Left >> *Lapse, Lapse-at-End; Parse-σ >> F-Right >> Lapse-at-End; Parse-σ >> *Clash, Clash-at-Edge; *Lapse-in-Trough

(123) Iambic internal lapse: RL OHP3: Unattested

a. *Head foot leftmost pattern*

i. (LĹ)L(LL̀)(LL̀) ii. (H́)(LH̀)(LH̀)(LH̀)

iii. (LĹ)(HĹ)(HĹ)(H́) iv. (LĹ)(H́)(LH́)(LĹ) *or* (LĹ)(HĹ)(H́)(LĹ)

b. *Head foot rightmost pattern*

i. (LL̀)(LL̀)L(LĹ) ii. (H̀)(LH̀)(LH̀)(LH́)

iii. (LĹ)(HĹ)(HĹ)(H́) iv. (LĹ)(H́)(LH́)(LĹ) *or* (LĹ)(HĹ)(H́)(LĹ)

c. *Ranking*

F-BIN >> PARSE-σ >> F-RIGHT >> *LAPSE, LAPSE-AT-END; PARSE-σ >> F-LEFT, *CLASH, CLASH-AT-END; *LAPSE-IN-TROUGH

Each of the binary patterns predicted by Rhythmic Licensing, then, except for the iambic final lapse pattern, can emerge with RL OHP3, and the result is always an unattested pattern.

4.4.4 Rankings producing patterns without the OHP

Except for the trochaic and iambic internal lapse patterns, each of the basic binary patterns predicted under Rhythmic Licensing can also emerge without the OHP. The circumstances where the OHP fails to emerge vary depending on the particular basic pattern. Since the maximal alternation patterns require that PARSE-σ dominate F-BIN, for example, they cannot emerge with the OHP under the ranking for RL OHP1 in (94). They will be truly quantity-insensitive whenever *CLASH dominates F-BIN.

The RSA formulation for F-LEFT and F-RIGHT prevents the OHP from emerging in under-parsing patterns in some contexts, as well. The effects of the OHP fail to emerge in the trochaic minimal alternation pattern, for example, for the subset of the rankings where F-RIGHT dominates PARSE-σ. As (124) illustrates, a high-ranked F-RIGHT prevents the addition of the monosyllabic foot necessary for OHP effects to emerge.

(124)

HLHLHLH	*LAPSE	F-RIGHT	PARSE-σ
☞ w. H(ĹH)(ĹH)(ĹH)		2	1
a. (H́L)(H́L)(H́L)(H́)		W 3	L
b. (H́)(ĹH)(ĹH)(ĹH)		W 3	L
c. (H́L)(H́L)(H́)(ĹH)		W 3	L
d. (H́L)(H́)(ĹH)(ĹH)		W 3	L

The result in (124) depends, however, on F-RIGHT's ability to assess violations for all misaligned feet. As (125) illustrates, OHP effects would emerge under the same ranking with F-RIGHT's GA counterpart, ALIGN (ω, R) (see Section 2.5.3), which only assesses violations for the right-most misaligned foot.

(125)

HLHLHLH	*LAPSE	ALIGN (ω, R)	PARSE-σ
w. H(ĹH)(ĹH)(ĹH)			1
☞ a. (H́L)(H́L)(H́L)(H́)			L
☞ b. (H́)(ĹH)(ĹH)(ĹH)			L
☞ c. (H́L)(H́L)(H́)(ĹH)			L
☞ d. (H́L)(H́)(ĹH)(ĹH)			L

The rankings where basic binary patterns are not accompanied by OHP effects are summarized in (126–131). OHP effects fail to emerge in maximal alternation patterns when *CLASH dominates PARSE-σ.

(126) Trochaic maximal alternation: No OHP: Attested

a. *Pattern*

i. (ĹL)(ĹL)(ĹL)(Ĺ) ii. (H́L)(H́L)(H́L)(H́)

iii. (H́L)(H́L)(H́L)(Ĺ) iv. (ĹL)(H́L)(H́L)(Ĺ)

b. *Rankings*

i. PARSE-σ >> F-BIN, F-LEFT, F-RIGHT; *CLASH >> F-BIN; *LAPSE, CLASH-AT-EDGE

ii. *LAPSE >> F-LEFT >> PARSE-σ >> F-BIN, F-RIGHT; *CLASH >> F-BIN; CLASH-AT-EDGE

(127) Iambic maximal alternation: No OHP: Attested

a. *Pattern*

i. (Ĺ)(LĹ)(LĹ)(LĹ) ii. (H́)(LH́)(LH́)(LH́)

iii. (Ĺ)(LH́)(LH́)(LH́) iv. (Ĺ)(LH́)(LH́)(LĹ)

b. *Rankings*

i. PARSE-σ >> F-BIN, F-LEFT, F-RIGHT; *CLASH >> F-BIN; *LAPSE, LAPSE-AT-END, CLASH-AT-EDGE

ii. *LAPSE >> F-RIGHT >> PARSE-σ >> F-BIN, F-LEFT; *CLASH >> F-BIN; LAPSE-AT-END, CLASH-AT-EDGE

iii. LAPSE-AT-END >> F-RIGHT >> PARSE-σ >> F-BIN, F-LEFT; F-RIGHT >> *LAPSE; *CLASH >> F-BIN; CLASH-AT-EDGE

OHP effects fail to emerge in the trochaic minimal alternation pattern in the subset of rankings where F-RIGHT dominates PARSE-σ.

(128) Trochaic minimal alternation: No OHP: Attested

a. *Pattern*

i. L(ĹL)(ĹL)(ĹL) ii. H(ĹH)(ĹH)(ĹH)

iii. H(ĹH)(ĹH)(ĹL) iv. L(ĹH)(ĹH)(ĹL)

b. *Rankings*

i. *LAPSE >> F-RIGHT >> PARSE-σ; *LAPSE >> F-LEFT; F-BIN, *CLASH, LAPSE-AT-END, CLASH-AT-EDGE

ii. LAPSE-AT-END >> F-RIGHT >> PARSE-σ, *LAPSE, F-LEFT; F-BIN, *CLASH, CLASH-AT-EDGE

They fail to emerge in the iambic minimal alternation pattern in the subset of rankings where F-LEFT dominates PARSE-σ.

(129) Iambic minimal alternation: Attested

a. *Pattern*

i. (LĹ)(LĹ)(LĹ)L ii. (HĹ)(HĹ)(HĹ)H

iii. (LĹ)(HĹ)(HĹ)H iv. (LĹ)(HĹ)(HĹ)L

b. *Rankings*

i. *LAPSE >> F-LEFT >> PARSE-σ; *LAPSE >> F-RIGHT; F-BIN, *CLASH, LAPSE-AT-END, CLASH-AT-EDGE

ii. LAPSE-AT-END >> F-RIGHT >> *LAPSE >> F-LEFT >> PARSE-σ; F-BIN, *CLASH, CLASH-AT-EDGE

iii. LAPSE-AT-END >> F-LEFT >> PARSE-σ, *LAPSE; LAPSE-AT-END >> F-RIGHT; F-BIN, *CLASH, CLASH-AT-EDGE

The trochaic final lapse and iambic final lapse both avoid the OHP with the subset of rankings where F-LEFT dominates PARSE-σ and *LAPSE.

(130) Trochaic peripheral lapse: Attested

a. *Pattern*

i.	(ĹL)(ĹL)(ĹL)L	ii.	(H́L)(H́L)(H́L)H
iii.	(H́L)(H́L)(H́L)L	iv.	(ĹL)(H́L)(H́L)L

b. *Ranking*

Lapse-at-End >> F-Left >> *Lapse, F-Right; F-Left >> Parse-σ; F-Bin, *Clash, Clash-at-Edge

(131) Iambic final lapse: Attested

a. *Pattern*

i.	(LĹ)(LĹ)(LĹ)L	ii.	(HĹ)(HĹ)(HĹ)H
iii.	(LĹ)(HĹ)(HĹ)H	iv.	(LĹ)(HĹ)(HĹ)L

b. *Rankings*

Lapse-at-End >> F-Left >> Parse-σ, *Lapse; Lapse-at-End >> F-Right; F-Bin

4.4.5 Summary of Predictions

When we actually take the presence of heavy syllables into account, we get a very different picture of Rhythmic Licensing's predictions. Though the rankings are intended to be quantity-insensitive, the results are typically patterns with the peculiar type of quantity-sensitivity characteristic of the OHP. Of the ten binary default patterns predicted under Rhythmic Licensing, only the iambic final lapse pattern avoids OHP effects altogether.

The maximal patterns, both trochaic and iambic, can emerge without OHP effects, but they also emerge with RL OHP2 and RL OHP3.

(132) Maximal alternation patterns

a. Trochaic

No OHP (attested), RL OHP2 (unattested), RL OHP3 (unattested)

b. Iambic

No OHP (attested), RL OHP2 (unattested), RL OHP3 (unattested)

The minimal alternation patterns, both trochaic and iambic, can emerge without OHP effects, but they also emerge with all three versions of the OHP.

(133) Minimal alternation patterns

a. Trochaic

No OHP (attested), RL OHP1 (unattested), RL OHP2 (unattested), RL OHP3 (unattested)

b. Iambic

No OHP (attested), RL OHP1 (unattested), RL OHP2 (unattested), RL OHP3 (unattested)

The trochaic peripheral lapse pattern can emerge without the OHP, but it can also emerge with all three versions of the OHP. When it emerges with RL OHP 1, the result is an attested pattern. The iambic final lapse pattern avoids the OHP altogether.

(134) Trochaic peripheral lapse pattern

No OHP (attested), RL OHP1 (attested), RL OHP2 (unattested), RL OHP3 (unattested)

(135) Iambic final lapse pattern

No OHP (attested)

The internal lapse patterns, both trochaic and iambic, always emerge with one of the three versions of the OHP.

(136) Internal lapse patterns

a. Trochaic

RL OHP1 (unattested), RL OHP2 (unattested), RL OHP3 (unattested)

b. Iambic

RL OHP1 (unattested), RL OHP2 (unattested), RL OHP3 (unattested)

4.5 Summary

In this chapter, I examined the predictions of Asymmetrical Alignment and Rhythmic Licensing in light of the OHP. Asymmetrical Alignment and Rhythmic Licensing differ from the Symmetrical Alignment and Rhythmic Licensing approaches in relying less on distance-sensitive alignment and more on rhythmic well-formedness constraints, such as

*Clash and *Lapse, to produce directional parsing effects. We saw that the reduced role of alignment constraints in the alternative approaches leads to increasingly exotic manifestations of the OHP and, as a consequence, to an increasingly serious over-generation problem. The manifestations of the OHP are least colorful under Symmetrical Alignment and Iterative Foot Optimization, the accounts where distance-sensitive alignment plays the most substantial role. As the role of alignment is reduced in favor of restrictions on clash and lapse in Asymmetrical Alignment and Rhythmic Licensing, the manifestations of the OHP become increasingly exotic.

The chapter also illustrated in fuller detail that the structural assumptions of Weak Layering are responsible for the OPIP in whatever form it appears. As we saw in Chapter 3, the OPIP cannot be attributed to the parallelism of the OT framework. This chapter has established that the OPIP also cannot be attributed to any particular approach to directional parsing effects. At this point, then, there should be little doubt that a structural solution is required, and we can turn in Chapter 5 to the predictions of the Weak Bracketing approach. As we shall see, the OPIP simply does not arise under Weak Bracketing's structural assumptions

5 Restricting Clash and Lapse

The central assumption of the Weak Bracketing approach is that prosodic categories can overlap. This is by no means a standard assumption in metrical stress theory. Liberman (1975), Itô and Mester (1992), and Kenstowicz (1995) have all explicitly rejected overlapping prosodic categories, and neither the recent OT accounts examined in earlier chapters nor their serial predecessors have employed them.

The assumption is not really that unusual, however, as similar structures have been employed in numerous other contexts. At the featural level, an affricate's specification as both [+continuant] and [-continuant] can be seen as an instance of overlapping features (Kenstowicz 1995). At the syllable level, the segmental ambisyllabicity most often associated with gemination and flapping can be seen as an instance of overlapping syllables (Itô and Mester 1992). In morphology, haplology can be considered a case of overlap where two morphemes share a segment or string of segments (Lawrence 1997, de Lacy 1999). In syntax, the notion of multi-dominance is quite similar to the notion of overlapping prosodic categories (Starke 2001, Chomsky [2001] 2004, Chen-Main 2006). Finally, though it is outside the domain of linguistic theory, constituent overlap sometimes plays a role in theories of musical rhythm (Cooper and Meyer 1960, Lehrdahl and Jackendoff 1983). These are especially significant due to their similarity to theories of linguistic rhythm.

In this chapter, then, I examine some of the consequences of allowing prosodic categories to overlap. In particular, I examine the consequences of allowing one prosodic category – feet – to overlap in the context of the Weak Bracketing approach to metrical stress. We saw in the previous two chapters that Weak Layering accounts suffer the effects of the Odd-Parity Input Problem to such a degree that they cannot predict a reasonably accurate range of basic binary default patterns. This chapter will demonstrate how the overlapping feet tolerated under Weak Bracketing allow the theory to avoid the OPIP altogether. We will then examine the typology of binary default patterns predicted by the Weak Bracketing account.

Before proceeding, it will be useful to repeat the typological generalizations that the theory aims to account for. The first is that perfect alternation patterns are symmetrically attested in mirror-image pairs, and the second is that patterns that depart from perfect alternation are asymmetrically attested or symmetrically unattested. It is the asymmetrically attested departures from perfect alternation that form the iambic-trochaic asymmetries that have been the focus of so much of the recent literature on metrical stress theory.

(1) a. In mirror image patterns with neither clash nor lapse, both members of the pair are attested.

b. In mirror image patterns with either clash or lapse, at most one member of the pair is attested.

As I hope to frame the issue here, predicting iambic-trochaic asymmetries means confining departures from perfect alternation to appropriate positions. Clash can occur in certain positions but not in others, and lapse can occur in certain positions but not in others. To the two generalizations in (1), then, we can add a third, which we will find ample support for in the discussion that follows.

(2) Attested patterns with clash or lapse always have stress on the initial syllable, always leave the final syllable stressless, or both.

The generalization in (2) provides a clue to the reasons that arrhythmic configurations like clash or lapse arise – and, therefore, a clue to the reasons that iambic-trochaic asymmetries arise. When a clash or lapse arises, it arises near a form's left edge to accommodate an initial stressed syllable or near its right edge to accommodate a final stressless syllable. Since iambic patterns are typically incompatible with initial stress and final stresslessness, it is most often the iambic patterns that are unattested in iambic-trochaic asymmetries.

5.1 Conditions and Constraints

The Weak Bracketing account preserves a distinction between the metrical grid and the prosodic hierarchy, allowing each to maintain its own internal prominence relationships.[1] Metrical prominence is expressed

1 The separation of the metrical grid and the prosodic hierarchy in the Weak Bracket account is similar in spirit, however, if not in actual execution, to the original proposals of Liberman (1975) and Liberman and Prince (1977). It

in the relative height of grid columns. Columns of grid entries indicate stress (or, more precisely, relative degrees of stress). Prosodic prominence is expressed using a system of prosodic heads. A head is the most prominent immediate constituent of a prosodic category – for example, the head syllable of a foot. We can think of syllables that are heads as the possible locations for stress and of heads that correspond to grid columns as the actual locations of stress. While stress can only appear on head syllables, it is not the case that all head syllables will be stressed.

The formal separation of the prosodic hierarchy and the metrical grid allows the theory to refer to the two systems, and their internal prominence relationships, independently. In the Weak Bracketing account, non-violable conditions typically regulate the basic relationships between categories in the prosodic hierarchy. Forms that fail to conform to these conditions cannot be considered as output candidates. In contrast, the requirements that regulate the construction of the metrical grid are typically violable constraints. Metrical constraints compete with other constraints in the grammar to arrive at an optimal output.

5.1.1 Weak Bracketing

Assumptions about the possible relationships between prosodic categories differ in two fundamental respects in the Weak Bracketing account from corresponding assumptions in Weak Layering accounts. First, where Weak Layering accounts treat Strict Succession, repeated in (3), as a parameter or the subject of violable constraints, the Weak Bracketing account treats it as a non-violable condition.

(3) Strict Succession (adapted from Itô and Mester 1992)

Every prosodic category of level $n - 1$ is immediately dominated by a prosodic category of level n (i.e. category levels are never skipped).

Moras must be constituents of syllables, syllables must be constituents of feet, and feet must be constituents of prosodic words. In the present context, Strict Succession's most important role is to eliminate the possibility of unfooted syllables. In effect, it converts the PARSE-σ constraint of Weak Layering accounts from a violable constraint to a nonviolable

contrasts with the approach in most recent accounts, which typically follow one of two courses. They either take entries on the metrical grid to be the heads of prosodic categories, as in the bracketed grids of Halle and Vergnaud (1987) and Hayes (1995), or they reject the metrical grid altogether, making allowances to interpret the head syllables of feet as stressed (Crowhurst 1996). The latter option appears to be the typical choice in most recent OT accounts.

condition, so that forms with unfooted syllables cannot be considered as output candidates.

The requirement that prosodic categories have heads is also governed by a non-violable condition, the Headedness condition, given in (4).

(4) Headedness

For every prosodic category of level $n + 1$, there is a prosodic category of level n designated as its head.

Under the Headedness condition, all prosodic categories must have heads. Every syllable must have a head mora, every foot must have a head syllable, every prosodic word must have a head foot, and so on. Forms with prosodic categories that do not have heads cannot be considered as output candidates. In illustrations of Weak Bracketing structures in the remainder of the book, prosodic heads will be denoted with vertical association lines, and non-heads will be denoted with diagonal association lines.

The second fundamental departure from Weak Layering accounts lies in Weak Bracketing's approach to Proper Bracketing.

(5) Proper Bracketing (adapted from Itô and Mester 1992)

Every prosodic category of level $n - 1$ is dominated by at most one prosodic category of level n. (i.e. prosodic categories of the same level may not overlap).

Where Weak Layering accounts treat Proper Bracketing as a non-violable condition, the Weak Bracketing approach abandons Proper Bracketing altogether. In the present context, the most important consequence of abandoning Proper Bracketing is that it allows the grammar to consider output candidates with overlapping feet, such as the pair of overlapping trochees in (6a), the pair of overlapping iambs in (6b), or the overlapping trochee and iamb in (6c).

(6) Overlapping Feet

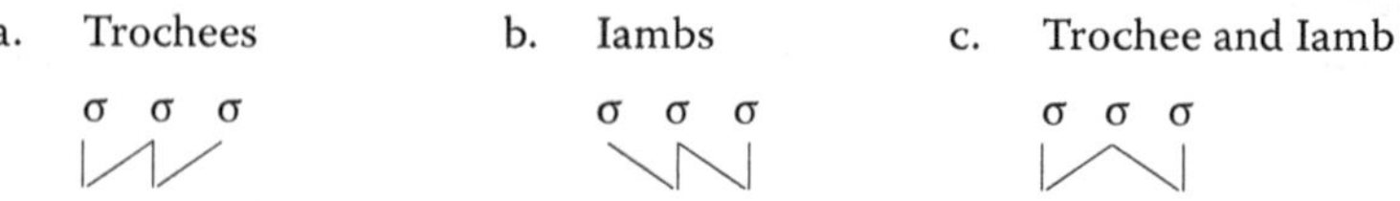

While it has no conditions or constraints that specifically prohibit overlapping categories of the types illustrated in (6), as we shall see in Section 5.1.3, Weak Bracketing's alignment constraints indirectly restrict instances of overlapping prosodic categories.

Note that abandoning Proper Bracketing does not mean that the Weak Bracketing approach tolerates every possible overlapping configuration. The non-violable Unique Head condition, given in (7), prevents prosodic categories from sharing a head.

(7) Unique Head

A constituent that is the head of one prosodic category cannot also be the head of another prosodic category (i.e. prosodic categories cannot share heads).

It prevents, for example, the configuration in (8), where an overlapping iamb and trochee share a head syllable.

(8) Excluded by the Unique Head condition

The non-violable Unique Domain condition, given in (9), insists that some part of a prosodic category be unique to that category. A prosodic category cannot share all of its constituents with other categories.

(9) Unique Domain

Every prosodic category must have at least one unique constituent. (i.e. prosodic categories cannot share all of their constituents).

For example, the Unique Domain condition excludes candidates where one foot is a subset of another foot, such as the overlapping trochee and monosyllable in (10a) or the completely overlapping trochee and iamb in (10b). It also excludes candidates where one foot is completely overlapped by two others, as in (10c).

(10) Excluded by the Unique Domain condition

Two additional non-violable conditions on prosodic structure play a significant role in the Weak Bracketing approach. These refer specifically to feet and to the head syllables of feet.

(11) a. Foot Maximum

Feet are maximally disyllabic.

b. Head Gap

For every two adjacent syllables, one must be a foot-head.

The Foot Maximum condition limits the size of feet to at most two syllables. Forms with feet that are larger than disyllabic cannot be considered as output candidates, meaning that ternary and unbounded feet are impossible in the Weak Bracketing account. The Head Gap condition limits the distance between the head syllables of feet to a single syllable. Forms that have adjacent non-head syllables cannot be considered as output candidates. The Head Gap condition is similar to Selkirk's (1984) Lapse constraint and to the more recent proposals of Kager (1994), Green (1995), and Green and Kenstowicz (1995). As formulated here, however, the Head Gap condition crucially refers to head syllables rather than to grid entries, feet, or stressed syllables.

5.1.2 Optimal Mapping

Where the relationships between prosodic categories are typically governed by non-violable conditions in the Weak Bracketing account, the relationships between prosodic categories and entries on the metrical grid are governed by violable constraints. The constraint governing the relationship between feet and stress is MAP-TO-GRID, given in (12). It requires that each foot have a stress, or foot-level grid entry, within its domain.

(12) MAP-TO-GRID

Every *F* has an x_F within its domain.

The formulation and violability of MAP-TO-GRID represents another significant departure from prevailing approaches. Following Selkirk (1980), prevailing approaches insist that feet and stress maintain a one-to-one correspondence: each foot corresponds to one and only one stress, and each stress corresponds to one and only one foot. Because MAP-TO-GRID is violable, however, it is possible that higher ranked constraints will insist that feet remain stressless, as in (13a).[2] Because MAP-TO-GRID requires only that each foot have a foot-level grid entry within it domain, and does not require that the relationship between foot and stress be unique, it is also possible for overlapping feet to share a stress, as in (13b). Since both feet in (13b) have a foot-level grid entry within their domain, both are stressed, and both satisfy MAP-TO-GRID.

2 Stressless feet, or at least the possibility of stressless feet, can be found in the proposals of Hayes 1987; Tyhurst 1987; Hung 1993, 1994; Selkirk 1995; Crowhurst 1996; and Buckley 2009.

(13) a. Stressless foot b. Gridmark sharing

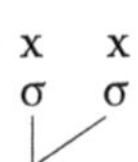

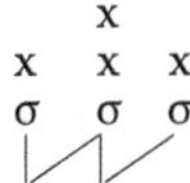

As in the case of overlapping feet, there are no conditions or constraints that directly restrict gridmark sharing, and, in this sense, the configuration is freely allowed. Although it may seem counterintuitive at this point, this situation is an important component of the Weak Bracketing account's restrictiveness. As we shall see in Sections 5.3 and 5.4, a gridmark-sharing configuration is often an alternative to configurations that result in clash or lapse. Making this alternative freely available means that it is more difficult to produce departures from perfect alternation.

MAP-TO-GRID is not the only constraint that influences how the metrical grid is constructed. The three constraints in (14) also figure prominently in the Optimal Mapping approach. *CLASH discourages adjacent stressed syllables. INITIAL-GRIDMARK requires stress on a prosodic word's initial syllable, and NON-FINALITY discourages stress on a prosodic word's final syllable.

(14) a. *CLASH

For any two entries on level $n + 1$ of the metrical grid, there is an intervening entry on level n.

b. INITIAL-GRIDMARK

An x_F occurs over the leftmost σ of every ω.

c. NON-FINALITY

No x_F occurs over the rightmost σ of a ω.

While constraints that can be thought of as having a directional orientation are typically symmetrically formulated, in that they can refer to either right edges or left edges or to initial position or final position, the formulations of INITIAL-GRIDMARK and NON-FINALITY are crucially asymmetrical.[3] In the end, the asymmetrical formulation of the two constraints is justified by the accuracy of the predicted typology, presented

3 There are several notable exceptions to the view that directional constraints are symmetrical. See Alber (2005) concerning alignment constraints, Nelson (2003) concerning anchor constraints, and Kager (2001, 2005) concerning rhythmic licensing constraints. The familiar ONSET and NOCODA constraints (Prince and Smolensky 1993/2004) are also exceptions to this view.

Section 5.3. In this case, however, there is independent justification, and I will mention it briefly. (See Hyde 2009b for a more detailed discussion.)

The asymmetrical preferences of INITIAL-GRIDMARK and NON-FINALITY, correspond to the different types of phonetic lengthening effects found in initial and final syllables. The characteristics of phonetic initial lengthening are clearly compatible with the characteristics of stressed syllables. For example, initial lengthening is often associated with longer voice onset time and onset aspiration. (See Oller 1973 and Keating et al 2003 among others.) Stressed syllables also frequently exhibit fortition, lengthening, or aspiration of the onset. (See Lieberman 1960, Beckman 1986, Gordon 2002b, among others.) In contrast, the characteristics of phonetic final lengthening are less compatible with stress. For example, final lengthening is typically associated with devoicing in the rhyme and a decline in amplitude. (See Oller 1973 and Wightman et al 1992, among others.) Stressed syllables, however, frequently exhibit increased intensity in the rhyme. (See Lieberman 1960, Beckman 1986, Gordon 2002b, among others.) Given the asymmetries in phonetic initial lengthening and phonetic final lengthening, then, it seems natural to expect a constraint like INITIAL-GRIDMARK that requires stress on initial syllables specifically and a constraint like NON-FINALITY that prohibits stress on final syllables specifically.

5.1.3 Head Syllable Alignment

As in the Symmetrical Alignment account, and other alignment-based accounts, distance-sensitive alignment constraints establish general directional orientations in the Weak Bracketing account, and distance-insensitive alignment constraints create exceptions to general directional orientations. Notice, however, that the constraints in (15) do not establish alignment relationships between the edges of prosodic words and the edges of feet as they do in Symmetrical Alignment. Instead, they establish alignment relationships between the edges of prosodic words and the edges of head syllables of feet. (See Green 1993 for a previous similar proposal.) ALL-σ_{HD}-LEFT, (15a), and ALL-σ_{HD}-RIGHT, (15b), are distance-sensitive Relation-Specific Alignment constraints that establish general directional orientations for the head syllables of feet within prosodic words. σ_{HD}-LEFT, (15c), and σ_{HD}-RIGHT, (15d), are distance-insensitive RSA constraints that create exceptions to general directional orientations for the head syllables of feet within prosodic words.

(15) a. ALL-σ_{HD}-LEFT: $*\langle\omega, \sigma_{HD}, \sigma\rangle$ / [...σ... σ_{HD}...]$_\omega$
'Assess a violation mark for every $\langle\omega, \sigma_{HD}, \sigma\rangle$ such that σ precedes σ_{HD} within ω.'

b. ALL-σ_{HD}-RIGHT: $*\langle\omega, \sigma_{HD}, \sigma\rangle$ / [... σ_{HD}...σ...]$_\omega$
'Assess a violation mark for every $\langle\omega, \sigma_{HD}, \sigma\rangle$ such that σ_{HD} precedes σ within ω.'

c. σ_{HD}-LEFT: $*\langle\omega, \sigma_{HD}\rangle$ / [...σ... σ_{HD}...]$_\omega$
'Assess a violation mark for every $\langle\omega, \sigma_{HD}\rangle$ such that σ precedes σ_{HD} within ω.'

d. σ_{HD}-RIGHT: $*\langle\omega, \sigma_{HD}\rangle$ / [... σ_{HD}...σ...]$_\omega$
'Assess a violation mark for every $\langle\omega, \sigma_{HD}\rangle$ such that σ_{HD} precedes σ within ω.'

Throughout the discussion, it will be important to keep in mind that these particular constraints refer to head syllables (syllables with vertical association lines) and not to foot-level grid entries. To help avoid any initial confusion on this point, in the discussion just below, I have omitted foot-level grid entries from the tableaux.

In general, whether distance-sensitive or distance-insensitive, the head syllable alignment constraints all have the effect of reducing structure to the minimal amount necessary to parse a form. Head syllable alignment reduces structure because it prefers a minimal number of head syllables: fewer head syllables in a prosodic word means fewer head syllables to incur alignment violations. Since head syllables and feet maintain a one-to-one correspondence, reducing the number of head syllables means reducing the number of feet involved in parsing a form.

One way to reduce the number of feet involved in parsing a form is to make them as large possible, up to the disyllabic maximum. A second is to avoid overlapping feet. In (16), σ_{HD}-RIGHT and ALL-σ_{HD}-RIGHT illustrate the structure-reducing effect of head syllable alignment. As the contrast between (16a) and (16c) illustrates, using disyllabic feet to parse a string of syllables requires fewer feet and produces fewer head syllable alignment violations than using monosyllabic feet. As a result, head syllable alignment restricts the occurrence of monosyllabic feet. It restricts the occurrence of overlapping feet for similar reasons. As the contrast between (16a) and (16b) illustrates, using overlapping feet to parse a string of syllables requires more feet and produces more head syllable alignment violations than using non-overlapping feet. In (16–18), a leftward pointing finger, "☜", in a constraint column indicates the candidate preferred by that constraint.

(16)

	σ_{HD}-RIGHT	ALL-σ_{HD}-RIGHT
a. σ σ σ σ σ σ	☞ ** (2)	☞ **** ** (6)
b. σ σ σ σ σ σ	*** (3)	**** *** * (8)
c. σ σ σ σ σ σ	***** (5)	***** **** *** ** * (15)

Head syllable alignment, then, tends to eliminate the additional structure that accompanies monosyllabic feet and overlapping feet. In even-parity forms, like those in (16), head syllable alignment eliminates such structures entirely. In odd-parity forms, head syllable alignment restricts overlapping feet and monosyllabic feet to the single occurrence necessary to parse the odd, leftover syllable.

The distance-sensitive ALL-σ_{HD}-LEFT and ALL-σ_{HD}-RIGHT establish general directional orientations for head syllables. When they are highly ranked, the general directional orientation established is sufficient to determine both foot type and footing directionality. Their influence over foot type is most easily demonstrated using even-parity forms. ALL-σ_{HD}-LEFT prefers trochaic footing, and ALL-σ_{HD}-RIGHT prefers iambic footing. In (17), the (a) candidate's trochaic footing allows it to perform better with respect to ALL-σ_{HD}-LEFT. By positioning themselves at the left edges of the individual feet, the head syllables also position themselves as near as possible to the left edge of the prosodic word. For similar reasons, the (b) candidate's iambic footing allows it to perform better with respect to ALL-σ_{HD}-RIGHT.

(17)

	ALL-σ_{HD}-LEFT	ALL-σ_{HD}-RIGHT
a. σ σ σ σ σ σ	☞ ** **** (6)	***** *** * (9)
b. σ σ σ σ σ σ	* *** ***** (9)	☞ **** ** (6)

In odd-parity forms, footing directionality also becomes an issue. ALL-σ_{HD}-LEFT and ALL-σ_{HD}-RIGHT not only restrict overlapping feet and monosyllabic feet to the single instance necessary to parse the odd, leftover syllable, they also determine the position in which the pair of overlapping feet or monosyllabic foot occurs. Alignment constraints affect the position of overlapping feet similarly to the way in which they affect the position of a monosyllabic foot (see Chapter 2). They prefer the concentration of structure that accompanies overlapping feet or a monosyllabic foot to be as near as possible to the designated edge of alignment. ALL-σ_{HD}-LEFT prefers that the pair of overlapping feet or monosyllabic foot occur at the prosodic word's left edge, as in (18a, b), and ALL-σ_{HD}-RIGHT prefers that the pair of overlapping feet or monosyllabic foot occur at the prosodic word's right edge, as in (18c, d).

(18)	σσσσσσσ	ALL-σ_{HD}-LEFT	ALL-σ_{HD}-RIGHT
	a. σ σ σ σ σ σ σ	☞ * *** ***** (9)	****** ***** *** * (15)
	b. σ σ σ σ σ σ σ	☞ * *** ***** (9)	****** ***** *** * (15)
	c. σ σ σ σ σ σ σ	* *** ***** ****** (15)	☞ ***** *** * (9)
	d. σ σ σ σ σ σ σ	* *** ***** ****** (15)	☞ ***** *** * (9)

In conjunction with their preferences respecting foot type, then, ALL-σ_{HD}-LEFT prefers footing that is both leftward and trochaic, and ALL-σ_{HD}-RIGHT prefers footing that is both rightward and iambic. Notice in (18), however, that ALL-σ_{HD}-LEFT and ALL-σ_{HD}-RIGHT do not discriminate between overlapping feet and monosyllabic feet *when they occur in the same position*. Overlapping feet at the designated edge produces the same violations as a monosyllabic foot. As we shall see in fuller detail below, however, overlapping feet are almost always preferred over monosyllabic feet due to other considerations. They are always preferred over a light monosyllable foot due to the minimality requirement, and they are preferred over a heavy monosyllabic foot when they allow for better alignment. (This is always the case when the heavy monosyllabic foot does not occur at the designated edge of alignment.) They are also preferred to monosyllabic feet in cases where a gridmark-sharing configuration would help to avoid clash or a stressless foot.

In establishing exceptions to general directional orientations, the distance-insensitive σ_{HD}-LEFT and σ_{HD}-RIGHT do not create clear conflicts in directionality like those created by distance-insensitive foot alignment constraints in the Symmetrical Alignment account, for example. This is not due to the difference in the particular object being aligned or to the possibility of allowing feet to overlap. Instead, it is due to Weak Bracketing's Head Gap condition, which prevents head syllables from being separated by more than one syllable. Once σ_{HD}-LEFT or σ_{HD}-RIGHT anchors a head syllable at the appropriate edge of a prosodic word, Head Gap limits the ability of the ALL-σ_{HD}-LEFT or ALL-σ_{HD}-RIGHT to draw the remaining head syllables in the opposite direction. Rather than a clear directional conflict, the result is that a head syllable is anchored at one edge of a form and the remaining head syllables are evenly distributed in the opposite direction.

Anchoring a head syllable at one edge and evenly distributing the remaining head syllable in the opposite direction is sufficient to determine foot-type in even-parity forms. Consider the ranking σ_{HD}-LEFT >> ALL-σ_{HD}-RIGHT in (19). Though ALL-σ_{HD}-RIGHT prefers iambic footing, as in (19b), the higher-ranked σ_{HD}-LEFT insists that the initial foot be a trochee, as in (19a,c). Since the non-violable Head Gap condition prohibits forms where head syllables occur more that one syllable apart, any non-initial feet must be trochees, as well. A form where an iamb follows a trochee (without overlap), as in (19c), cannot be considered as an output candidate. This ensures that the thoroughly trochaic (19a) emerges as the winner.

(19)

	σ_{HD}-LEFT	ALL-σ_{HD}-RIGHT
☞ a. σ σ σ σ σ σ (trochees: |/ |/ |/)	* *	***** *** * (9)
b. σ σ σ σ σ σ (iambs: \\\| \\\| \\\|)	* * *!	**** ** (5)

c. σ σ σ σ σ σ (\|/ \\\| \\\|) (not a possible candidate)

In odd-parity forms, as well, highly-ranked distance-insensitive constraints restrict the general directional orientation established by the distance-sensitive constraints. Consider the effects of ranking σ_{HD}-LEFT over ALL-σ_{HD}-RIGHT in (20). As we saw above, ALL-σ_{HD}-RIGHT prefers a configuration in odd-parity forms that results in a cluster of two head syllables at the right edge of the prosodic word. By insisting that one of head syllables occur at the left edge, however, a high-ranked σ_{HD}-LEFT combines with the Head Gap condition to prevent ALL-σ_{HD}-RIGHT from creating such a cluster. In particular, σ_{HD}-LEFT eliminates candidates, such as (20e), where the leftmost head syllable does not occur at the left edge. The Head Gap condition prevents ALL-σ_{HD}-RIGHT from drawing the remaining head syllables so far to the right that a gap of more than one syllable occurs between any two head syllables, as in (20f) and (20g). ALL-σ_{HD}-RIGHT can still ensure, however, that they are drawn far enough to the right to prevent clusters of head syllables away from the right edge, as in (20c) and (20d). Overall, the result is that the head syllables are evenly distributed throughout the prosodic word.

(20)

	σ_{HD}-LEFT	ALL-σ_{HD}-RIGHT
☞ a. σ σ σ σ σ σ σ	* * *	****** **** ** (12)
☞ b. σ σ σ σ σ σ σ	* * *	****** **** ** (12)
c. σ σ σ σ σ σ σ	* * *	****** **** ** *! (13)
d. σ σ σ σ σ σ σ	* * *	****** ***** **!* * (15)
e. σ σ σ σ σ σ σ	* * * *!	***** *** * (9)

f. σ σ σ σ σ σ σ

g. σ σ σ σ σ σ σ

(not possible candidates)

Note, however, that the distribution of head syllables created by ranking a distance-insensitive constraint over a distance-sensitive constraint is not sufficient to fully determine foot-type and footing directionality. As (21) demonstrates, the distribution of head syllables is consistent with either the right-oriented trochaic pattern in (21a) or the left-oriented iambic pattern in (21b).

(21) a. Right-oriented trochaic parsing b. Left-oriented iambic parsing

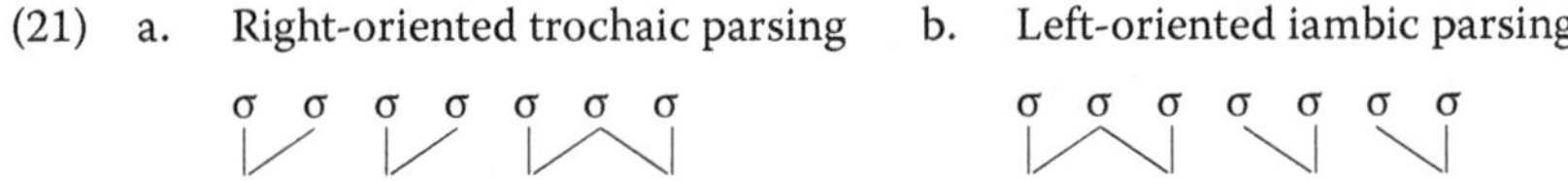

As noted in Hyde (2001), a principle of non-finality within the foot would always resolve the ambiguity in favor of the trochaic version. To avoid confusion in the discussion below, however, I will assume that the ranking σ_{HD}-LEFT >> ALL-σ_{HD}-RIGHT always results in trochaic footing in both even- and odd-parity forms and that the ranking σ_{HD}-RIGHT >> ALL-σ_{HD}-LEFT always results in iambic footing in both even- and odd-parity forms. Nothing in the discussion below turns on this particular point.[4]

4 The prediction of languages with iambic footing in even-parity forms and trochaic footing in odd-parity forms would lead us to expect that at least some of these languages would have iambic lengthening in even-parity forms but not in odd-parity forms. The expectation is difficult to assess. None of the languages with the appropriate distribution of head syllables – Suruwaha (Everett 1996), Tubatulabal (Voegelin 1935), and Weri (Boxwell and Boxwell 1966) – actually exhibits iambic lengthening in forms of any length.

In the Weak Bracketing account, then, the distance-sensitive ALL-σ_{HD}-LEFT and ALL-σ_{HD}-RIGHT establish general directional orientations for head syllables within prosodic words. In odd-parity forms, this results in a cluster of two head syllables at the designated edge of alignment and an even-distribution of head syllables away from the designated edge. When high-ranked, the distance-insensitive σ_{HD}-LEFT and σ_{HD}-RIGHT combine with the Head Gap condition to restrict the general directional orientation established by the distance-sensitive constraints. In odd-parity forms, the result is an even distribution of head syllables throughout the prosodic word. Having introduced the core components of the Weak Bracketing approach, we turn now to the approach's predictions. We begin in Section 5.2 by discussing what the Weak Bracketing approach does not predict: patterns that exhibit the effects of the Odd-Parity Input Problem. In Section 5.3, I present the predicted typology of binary default patterns.

5.2 Avoiding the Odd-Parity Input Problem

All Weak Layering Accounts – including, as we have seen, Symmetrical Alignment, Iterative Foot Optimization, Asymmetrical Alignment, and Rhythmic Licensing – exhibit the effects of the Odd-Parity Input Problem. The OPIP is a structural problem, and it must be addressed with a structural solution. The proposed alternative to Weak Layering is Weak Bracketing. As outlined above, there are two fundamental differences between the approaches. First, where Weak Layering allows under-parsing, Weak Bracketing requires exhaustive parsing. Second, where Weak Layering prohibits overlapping prosodic categories, Weak Bracketing tolerates overlapping prosodic categories.

Under Weak Bracketing, then, the two options for accommodating the leftover syllable of odd-parity outputs are to parse it as a monosyllabic foot or to parse it into a disyllabic foot that overlaps another disyllabic foot. Although both of these options are available, at least in principle, the latter has the advantage that it allows the parsing and minimality requirements to be satisfied simultaneously, regardless of the weight of the syllables involved. Since there is never a need to parse a heavy syllable as a monosyllabic foot to achieve exhaustive binary parsing, the Odd Heavy Problem simply does not emerge. Since there is never a need to convert odd-parity inputs to even-parity outputs to achieve exhaustive binary parsing, the Even Output Problem also simply does not emerge.

The possibility of overlapping disyllabic feet makes both the existence and position of heavy syllables irrelevant to a form's ability to achieve exhaustive binary parsing, a result sufficient to eliminate the OHP. As (22) illustrates, even when an odd-parity form consists of all light syllables, overlapping feet allow it to achieve exhaustive binary parsing. An overlapping configuration parses three syllables into two disyllabic feet. With an even number of syllables remaining, it is a simple matter to parse the rest of the string into disyllabic feet, as well. As a result F-Bin and Parse-σ are satisfied simultaneously. Note that leaving a syllable unparsed, as in (22b), is not actually an option under Weak Bracketing, and Parse-σ is not actually a violable constraint. Given Strict Layering, all syllables must be parsed into feet. Parse-σ and under-parsing candidates are included in (22–25) simply to show that even if the Strict Layering requirement were relaxed overlapping feet would still be optimal

(22)

LLLLLLL	F-Bin	Parse-σ
☞ w. L L L L L L L		
a. L L L L L L L	W 1	
b. L L L L L L L		W 1

As (23) and (24) demonstrate, parsing an odd-numbered heavy syllable as a monosyllabic foot, when one is available, never presents a better alternative to overlapping feet. Parse-σ and F-Bin can be satisfied simultaneously by parsing an odd-numbed heavy syllable as a monosyllabic foot, but they can also be satisfied simultaneously by parsing three syllables of any weight into two overlapping feet. Since the overlapping feet can be freely positioned by alignment and other relevant constraints without the interference of weight-based restrictions, and will be preferred to forms with a heavy monosyllabic foot as a result, syllable weight affects neither parsability nor parsing directionality. When odd-numbered heavy syllables are present, then, exactly the same pattern emerges as when they are absent.

(23)

LLHLLLL	F-BIN	PARSE-σ	ALL-σ_{HD}-LEFT
☞ w. L L H L L L L			9
a. L L H L L L L			W 10
b. L L H L L L L	W 1		9
c. L L H L L L L		W 1	L 6

(24)

LLHLLLL	F-BIN	PARSE-σ	ALL-σ_{HD}-RIGHT
☞ w. L L H L L L L			9
a. L L H L L L L			W 11
b. L L H L L L L	W 1		9
c. L L H L L L L		W 1	L 6

The OHP, then, simply does not arise under the structural assumptions of Weak Bracketing.

Similar considerations allow the Weak Bracketing approach to avoid the EOP. As (25) indicates, since overlapping feet can achieve exhaustive binary parsing for any odd-parity form, even those containing only light syllables, there is no advantage to be gained by converting an odd-parity input to an even-parity output, either through deletion or insertion. Overlapping feet allow PARSE-σ and F-BIN to be satisfied simultaneously while remaining faithful to the odd-parity input. Inserting a syllable simply creates a gratuitous DEP violation without improving performance on the parsing and minimality requirements, and deleting a syllable simply creates a gratuitous MAX violation.

(25)

LLLLLLL	F-BIN	PARSE-σ	MAX	DEP
☞ a. L L L L L L L				
b. L L L L L L L L				W 1
c. L L L L L L			W 1	

The EOP, then, also simply does not arise under the structural assumptions of Weak Bracketing. Its ability to eliminate both aspects of the OPIP gives the Weak Bracketing account a significant advantage over all Weak Layering approaches – including Symmetrical Alignment, Iterative Foot Optimization, Asymmetrical Alignment, and Rhythmic Licensing.

Under Weak Bracketing, the option of allowing disyllabic feet to overlap effectively removes the conflict between the parsing and minimality requirements that is so central to Weak Layering accounts. Overlapping feet provide a way to achieve exhaustive binary footing for any odd-parity input without making parsing sensitive to syllable weight or converting the odd-parity input into an even-parity output. This allows the theory to avoid both aspects of the OPIP – the OHP and the EOP – altogether. While this accomplishment gives the Weak Bracketing account a significant initial advantage over Weak Layering accounts, it remains to be seen whether or not the set of binary default patterns that Weak Bracketing predicts are a reasonably close match to the set of attested patterns. As it happens, the Weak Bracketing approach does predict a reasonably close match, being particularly strong in the area of iambic-trochaic asymmetries. As we shall see next, however, rather than exploiting a conflict between parsing and minimality, as in Weak Layering accounts, Weak Bracketing uses Optimal Mapping to exploit the possibility of mismatches between feet and stress to produce the desired range of binary default patterns.

5.3 Binary default patterns

Having established that it avoids the OPIP, we turn next to the typology of binary default patterns predicted by the Weak Bracketing account. In examining the typologies predicted by Weak Layering accounts in Chapters 3 and 4, the focus was primarily on the effects of the constraints used to establish parsing directionality, since these, along with foot-type, were primarily responsible for the variation seen within the predicted typologies. Under Weak Bracketing, the possible directional parsing patterns that can be produced by head alignment are much more limited. In fact, in the context of binary default patterns, they are essentially limited to the four patterns in (26–28) and (31), though some slight adjustments to the iambic pattern in (27) and the trochaic pattern in (28) do occur in particular cases.

In the left-oriented trochaic parsing pattern, the overlapping feet in odd-parity forms occur at the left edge. The ranking that produces it is fairly straightforward: ALL-σ_{HD}-LEFT must dominate both of the right-oriented alignment constraints, ALL-σ_{HD}-RIGHT and σ_{HD}-RIGHT.

(26) Trochaic left-oriented parsing

a. *Pattern*

σ σ σ σ σ σ

σ σ σ σ σ σ σ

b. *Ranking*

ALL-σ_{HD}-LEFT >> ALL-σ_{HD}-RIGHT, σ_{HD}-RIGHT

For the right-oriented iambic parsing pattern in (27), the ranking is also straightforward. ALL-σ_{HD}-RIGHT must dominate INITIAL-GRIDMARK and both of the left-oriented alignment constraints, ALL-σ_{HD}-LEFT and σ_{HD}-LEFT. In this parsing pattern, the overlapping feet in odd-parity forms occur at the right edge.

(27) Iambic right-oriented parsing

a. *Pattern*

σ σ σ σ σ σ

σ σ σ σ σ σ σ

b. *Ranking*

ALL-σ_{HD}-RIGHT >> ALL-σ_{HD}-LEFT, σ_{HD}-LEFT, INITIAL-GRIDMARK

I will refer to the trochaic parsing pattern in (28) as right-oriented, even though its general rightward orientation is restricted by an undominated σ_{HD}-LEFT or INITIAL-GRIDMARK constraint. Notice that several different rankings produce the right-oriented trochaic pattern.

(28) Trochaic right-oriented parsing

a. *Pattern*

σ σ σ σ σ σ

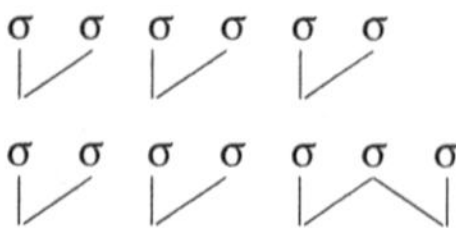

b. *Rankings*

i. σ_{HD}-Left >> All-σ_{HD}-Right, σ_{HD}-Right; All-σ_{HD}-Right >> All-σ_{HD}-Left

ii. σ_{HD}-Left >> All-σ_{HD}-Right, σ_{HD}-Right; σ_{HD}-Right >> All-σ_{HD}-Left

iii. Initial-Gridmark >> All-σ_{HD}-Right, σ_{HD}-Right; All-σ_{HD}-Right >> All-σ_{HD}-Left

iv. Initial-Gridmark >> All-σ_{HD}-Right, σ_{HD}-Right; σ_{HD}-Right >> All-σ_{HD}-Left

The greater variety of rankings is due to the ability of σ_{HD}-Right to duplicate the effects of All-σ_{HD}-Right in establishing a general rightward orientation in this context, given the effects of the Head Gap condition, and to the ability of Initial-Gridmark to duplicate the effects of σ_{HD}-Left in restricting the general rightward orientation.

To illustrate, σ_{HD}-Right is employed to duplicate the effects of establishing the desired general rightward orientation in an odd-parity form in (29). Once the high ranked σ_{HD}-Left anchors a head syllable at the left edge, excluding candidates with an unrestricted rightward orientation, such as (29c), the combination of σ_{HD}-Right and the Head Gap condition is sufficient to draw the remaining head syllables to the right. σ_{HD}-Right ensures that the final syllable is a head syllable, excluding candidates with an unrestricted leftward orientation, such as (29b). Head Gap ensures that medial head syllables are evenly distributed between the two peripheral head syllables by preventing consideration of forms, such as (29d), that have a two-syllable gap.

(29)

	σ_{HD}-Left	σ_{HD}-Right
☞ a. σ σ σ σ σ σ σ	***	***
b. σ σ σ σ σ σ σ	***	****!
c. σ σ σ σ σ σ σ	****!	***

d. σ σ σ σ σ σ σ (not a possible candidate)

Initial-Gridmark is employed to restrict the general rightward orientation in (30). Since Initial-Gridmark requires stress on initial syllables, and stressed syllables must be head syllables, it can exclude candidates, such as (30b) that do not have a head syllable at the left edge.

The lower-ranked ALL-σ_{HD}-RIGHT can then draw the remaining head syllables to the right.

(30)

	INITIAL -GRIDMARK	ALL-σ_{HD}-RIGHT
x x x x x x x x x x x ☞ a. σ σ σ σ σ σ σ		****** **** ** (12)
x x x x x x x x x x b. σ σ σ σ σ σ σ	*!	***** *** * (9)

Finally, I will refer to the parsing pattern in (31) as a left-oriented iambic parsing pattern, though the undominated σ_{HD}-RIGHT restricts the general leftward orientation. The variety of rankings that produce this pattern is due to the ability of σ_{HD}-LEFT and INITIAL-GRIDMARK in this context to duplicate the effects of ALL-σ_{HD}-LEFT in establishing the general leftward orientation.

(31) Iambic left-oriented parsing

a. *Pattern*

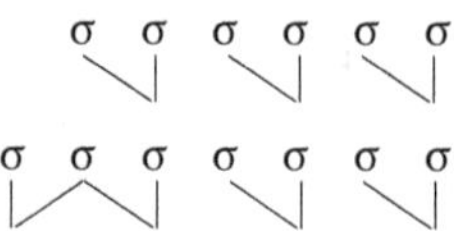

b. *Rankings*

i. σ_{HD}-RIGHT >> ALL-σ_{HD}-LEFT, σ_{HD}-LEFT, INITIAL-GRIDMARK; ALL-σ_{HD}-LEFT >> ALL-σ_{HD}-RIGHT

ii. σ_{HD}-RIGHT >> ALL-σ_{HD}-LEFT, σ_{HD}-LEFT, INITIAL-GRIDMARK; σ_{HD}-LEFT >> ALL-σ_{HD}-RIGHT

iii. σ_{HD}-RIGHT >> ALL-σ_{HD}-LEFT, σ_{HD}-LEFT, INITIAL-GRIDMARK; INITIAL-GRIDMARK >> ALL-σ_{HD}-RIGHT

Since the parsing patterns available under Weak Bracketing are so limited, most of the variation seen the typology predicted is due to interactions among the Optimal Mapping constraints. Each of the directional parsing patterns in (26–28) and (31) can map to the grid in multiple ways, yielding multiple distinct stress patterns. In discussing the predicted typology below, then, the focus will be on the interactions of the Optimal Mapping constraints. I will consider each of the parsing patterns in (26–28) and (31) in turn, beginning with the trochaic parsing pattern in (26), and examine the different mappings to the metrical grid that can arise with each.

5.3.1 Trochaic minimal alternation and its variants

As we saw in Section 5.1.3, the parsing pattern in (26) is the result of a high-ranking ALL-σ_{HD}-LEFT constraint. Under the Weak Bracketing approach, the parsing pattern can be mapped to the metrical grid in three distinct ways, as indicated in (32), yielding three distinct stress patterns. The differences between the three patterns are slight, being confined to the left edge of odd-parity forms, and they can be traced to the presence or absence of an initial stress. Omitting an initial stress, as in (32a), allows the overlapping feet at the left edge in odd-parity forms to map to the grid in a gridmark-sharing configuration, resulting in a pattern with perfect binary alternation. Maintaining an initial stress prevents the overlapping feet from mapping to the grid in a gridmark-sharing configuration, resulting in a departure from perfect binary alternation. It results in a clash, as in (32b), or a lapse, as in (32c). The clash in (32b) arises because the foot adjacent to the initial stress also contains a stress. The lapse in (32c) arises because the adjacent foot is left stressless.

(32) Binary default patterns with left-oriented trochaic parsing

a. Minimal Alternation: Attested

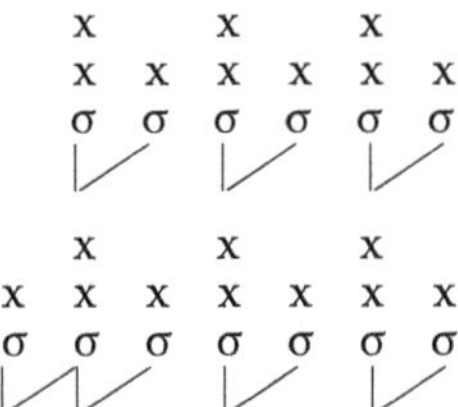

b. Initial Clash: Attested

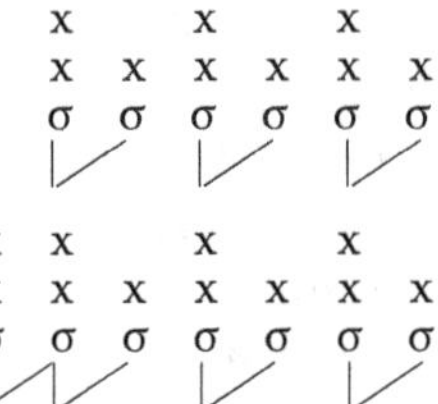

c. Initial Dactyl: Attested

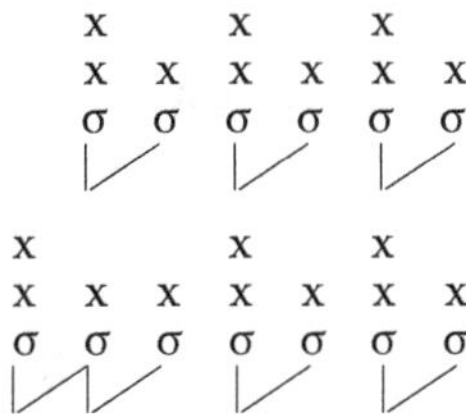

Since the different stress patterns in (32) are all built on the same parsing pattern, the head syllable alignment constraints do not play a central role in distinguishing between them. The crucial interactions in this case arise among a subset of the Optimal Mapping constraints: *Clash, Map-to-Grid, and Initial-Gridmark. Of the three constraints, Initial-Gridmark plays the key role in creating the range of trochaic patterns in (32). As (33) illustrates, the gridmark-sharing configuration of the minimal alternation pattern emerges when Initial-Gridmark ranks below *Clash and Map-to-Grid. The gridmark-sharing configuration allows the minimal alternation pattern to avoid clash, as in (33b), and stressless feet, as in (33a), simultaneously. Although the minimal alternation pattern violates Initial-Gridmark, Initial-Gridmark is not ranked highly enough to influence the outcome, and the minimal alternation pattern emerges as the winner.

(33)

	*Clash	Map-to-Grid	Initial-GM
☞ w. x x x x x x x x x x σ σ σ σ σ σ σ			1
a. x x x x x x x x x x σ σ σ σ σ σ σ		1 W	L
b. x x x x x x x x x x x σ σ σ σ σ σ σ	1 W		L

When Initial-Gridmark is high-ranked, it prevents the left-oriented trochaic parsing pattern from mapping to the grid in a perfect alternation configuration. Under a ranking where Initial-Gridmark and Map-to-Grid both dominate *Clash, as in (34), a clash emerges at the left edge in odd-parity forms. Initial-Gridmark excludes the stressless initial syllable of the gridmark-sharing configuration in the minimal alternation pattern, (34b), and Map-to-Grid excludes the stressless foot of the initial dactyl pattern, (34a). Although the initial clash pattern in (34w) violates *Clash, *Clash is low-ranked and cannot influence the outcome. The initial clash pattern emerges as the optimal candidate.

(34)

	INITIAL-GM	MAP-TO-GRID	*CLASH
☞ w. x x x x x x x x x x x σ σ σ σ σ σ σ			1
a. x x x x x x x x x x σ σ σ σ σ σ σ		W 1	L
b. x x x x x x x x x x σ σ σ σ σ σ σ	W 1		L

Finally, when *CLASH and INITIAL-GRIDMARK both dominate MAP-TO-GRID, as in (35), the second foot is left stressless in odd-parity forms, resulting in a lapse after the initial stress. *CLASH excludes the trochaic initial clash pattern, (35b), and INITIAL-GRIDMARK excludes the trochaic minimal alternation pattern, (35a). Although the initial dactyl pattern in (35w) violates MAP-TO-GRID, MAP-TO-GRID is low-ranked, and the initial dactyl pattern emerges as the optimal candidate.

(35)

	*CLASH	INITIAL-GM	MAP-TO-GRID
☞ w. x x x x x x x x x x σ σ σ σ σ σ σ			1
a. x x x x x x x x x x σ σ σ σ σ σ σ		W 1	L
b. x x x x x x x x x x x σ σ σ σ σ σ σ	W 1		L

Under the Weak Bracketing approach, then, the trochaic minimal alternation, initial clash, and initial dactyl patterns are all based on the same left-oriented trochaic parsing pattern. Given such a pattern, a conflict arises among INITIAL-GRIDMARK, MAP-TO-GRID and *CLASH. When INITIAL-GRIDMARK is low-ranked, it cannot introduce clash or lapse, and a trochaic minimal alternation pattern emerges. When INITIAL-GRIDMARK is high-ranked, it can produce clash exactly at the left edge of the prosodic word, resulting in the trochaic initial clash pattern, or it can produce lapse one syllable removed from the left edge, resulting in the trochaic initial dactyl pattern.

5.3.2 Iambic minimal alternation and its variants

We saw in Section 5.1.3 that the right-oriented iambic parsing pattern in (27) is the result of a high-ranking ALL-σ_{HD}-LEFT constraint. Under Weak Bracketing, this parsing pattern can be mapped to the metrical grid in two distinct ways, yielding two distinct stress patterns. The first is the iambic minimal alternation pattern, (36a), and the second is the iambic final lapse pattern, (36b). The difference between these two patterns is that the final syllable, and thus the final foot, is stressed in the even-parity forms of the minimal alternation pattern but the final syllable, and thus the final foot, is left stressless in the even-parity forms of the final lapse pattern. The iambic reversal pattern, (36c), is based on a parsing pattern that is nearly identical to that of (36a) and (36b). The only difference is the position of the rightmost head syllable in even-parity forms. In the iambic reversal pattern, the rightmost head syllable has been retracted from final to penultimate position.

(36) Binary default patterns with right-oriented iambic parsing

a. Minimal Alternation: Attested

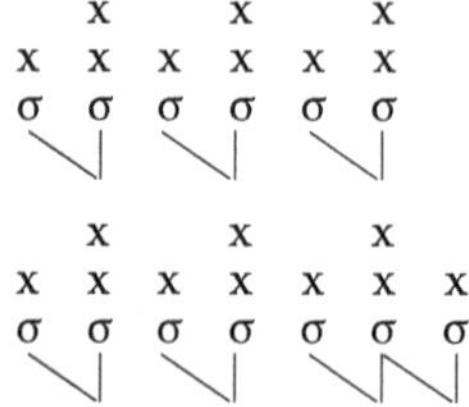

b. Final lapse: Attested

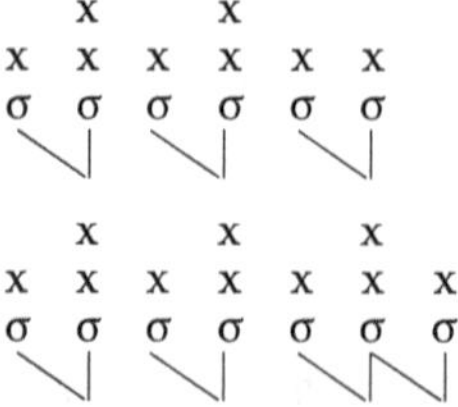

c. Reversal: Attested

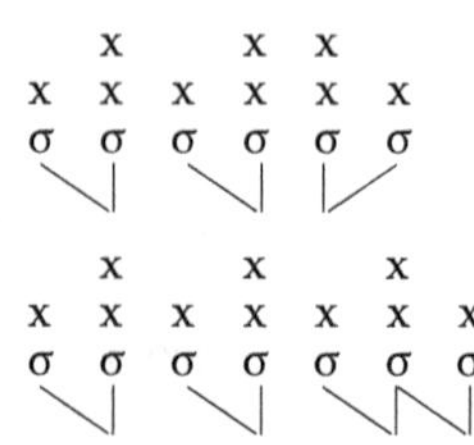

The group of iambic patterns in (36) differs from the group of trochaic patterns in (32) in two ways. The first is that the variation between the iambic patterns lies in their even-parity forms rather than their odd-parity forms, and the second is that the variations are located at the right edge rather than the left edge.

The reason for the differences between the iambic and trochaic patterns can be traced to the constraints responsible for producing them. For the trochaic patterns, the key constraint was INITIAL-GRIDMARK, a constraint that influences gridmark mapping at the left edge. Since each of the trochaic patterns accommodated an initial stress in their even-parity forms, the ranking of INITIAL-GRIDMARK had no influence over gridmark mapping in even-parity forms. Because the trochaic patterns did not all accommodate initial stress in their odd-parity forms, however, the ranking of INITIAL-GRIDMARK had a significant influence over the gridmark mapping that odd-parity forms ultimately exhibited.

For the iambic patterns in (36), the key constraint is NON-FINALITY, a constraint that influences gridmark mapping at the right edge. Since each of the iambic patterns avoids final stress in their odd-parity forms, there is no variation in the odd-parity configuration. Because the iambic patterns do not all avoid final stress in their even-parity forms, however, the ranking of NON-FINALITY has a significant influence over even-parity configurations.

For the iambic minimal alternation pattern to emerge, NON-FINALITY must be low-ranked. In particular, ALL-σ_{HD}-RIGHT and MAP-TO-GRID must both dominate NON-FINALITY. ALL-σ_{HD}-RIGHT excludes the iambic reversal candidate in (37b), where the final head syllable is pushed leftward to avoid final stress. It also excludes a candidate like (37c) which employs thoroughly trochaic footing to avoid final stress. MAP-TO-GRID excludes the final lapse candidate in (37d), where the rightmost foot is left stressless to avoid final stress. While (37w) stresses a final iambic foot, violating the low-ranked NON-FINALITY, it correctly emerges as the winner.

(37)

	ALL-σ_{HD}-R	MAP-TO-GRID	NON-FINALITY
x x x x x x x x x ☞ w. σ σ σ σ σ σ (σ σ) (σ σ) (σ σ)	6		1
x x x x x x x x a. σ σ σ σ σ σ (σ σ) (σ σ) (σ σ)	6	W 1	L
x x x x x x x x x b. σ σ σ σ σ σ (σ σ) (σ σ) (σ σ)	W 7		L
x x x x x x x x x c. σ σ σ σ σ σ (σ σ) (σ σ) (σ σ)	W 9		L

The iambic final lapse and iambic reversal patterns both require NON-FINALITY to be high-ranked. In producing the iambic final lapse pattern, the satisfaction of NON-FINALITY comes at the expense of MAP-TO-GRID. As (38) demonstrates, NON-FINALITY and ALL-σ_{HD}-RIGHT must both dominate MAP-TO-GRID to produce the desired result. NON-FINALITY excludes the minimal alternation pattern in (38a) with its stressed final iamb, and ALL-σ_{HD}-RIGHT excludes the final trochee of (38b). Although the final lapse pattern in (38w) violates MAP-TO-GRID with its stressless final iamb, MAP-TO-GRID is the lowest ranked constraint, and the final lapse pattern emerges as the winner.

(38)

	NON-FINALITY	ALL-σ_{HD}-R	MAP-TO-GRID
x x (over σ2, σ4) x x x x x x ☞ w. σ σ σ σ σ σ		6	1
x x x (over σ2, σ4, σ6) x x x x x x a. σ σ σ σ σ σ	1 W	6	L
x x x (over σ2, σ4, σ5) x x x x x x b. σ σ σ σ σ σ		7 W	L

To produce the iambic reversal pattern, NON-FINALITY and MAP-TO-GRID must both dominate ALL-σ_{HD}-RIGHT. This is sufficient to create a final trochee, avoiding the final stress of the minimal alternation pattern, (39a), and the final stressless iamb in the final lapse pattern, (39b). ALL-σ_{HD}-RIGHT, in turn, must dominate *CLASH. This ensures that the remaining feet will be iambs rather than trochees, as in (39c), preserving the iambic reversal configuration.

(39)

	NON-FIN	MAP-GRID	ALL-σ_{HD}-R	*CLASH
x x x x x x x x x ☞ w. σ σ σ σ σ σ			7	1
x x x x x x x x x a. σ σ σ σ σ σ	1 W		6 L	L
x x x x x x x x b. σ σ σ σ σ σ		1 W	6 L	L
x x x x x x x x x c. σ σ σ σ σ σ			9 W	L

In Section 5.3.1, we saw that INITIAL-GRIDMARK was crucially low-ranked in producing the odd-parity forms of trochaic minimal alternation, making it possible for a high-ranking INITIAL-GRIDMARK to produce variations on trochaic minimal alternation in odd-parity forms. In this section, we have seen a similar key role for NON-FINALITY in iambic systems. Since NON-FINALITY was crucially low-ranked in producing the even-parity forms of iambic minimal alternation, it is possible for a high-ranking NON-FINALITY constraint to produce variations on iambic minimal alternation in even-parity forms.

5.3.3 Trochaic maximal alternation and its variants

In Section 5.1.3, we saw that the right-oriented trochaic parsing pattern in (28) is the result of ranking σ_{HD}-LEFT above ALL-σ_{HD}-RIGHT. This parsing pattern can be mapped to the grid in two distinct ways. Maintaining a final stress in odd-parity forms, as in the trochaic maximal alternation pattern in (40a), allows for a pattern with perfect binary alternation. Omitting the final stress, as in the trochaic final lapse pattern in (40b), creates a final stressless foot and a departure from perfect binary alternation in the form of a final lapse. In the trochaic final amphibrach pattern in (40c), a slight modification of the parsing pattern results in a lapse before the penult. The final head syllable in odd-parity forms is pushed one syllable to the left, resulting in a gridmark-sharing configuration. Since the initial syllable of the gridmark-sharing configuration is stressless and follows another stressless syllable, the result is a lapse preceding the penult.

(40) Binary default patterns with right-oriented trochaic parsing

a. Maximal Alternation: Attested

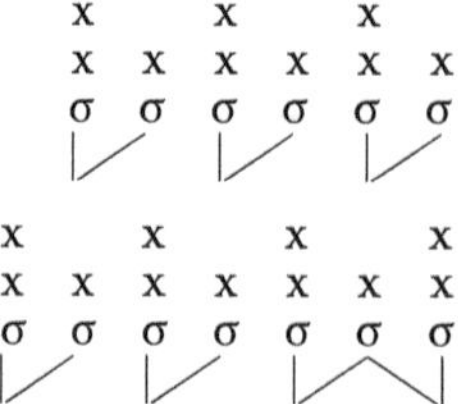

b. Final dactyl: Attested

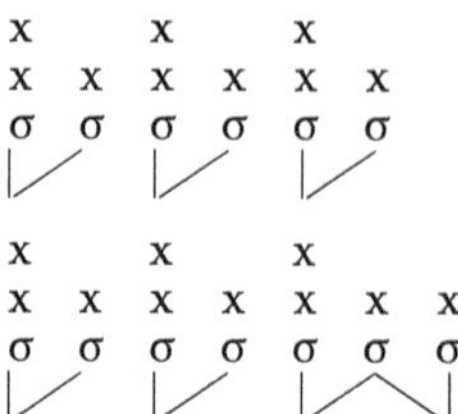

c. Final amphibrach: Attested

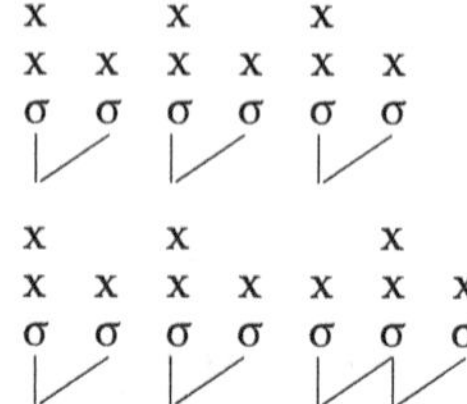

Though the differences between the three trochaic patterns in (40) arise in their odd-parity forms, they are similar to the differences between the three iambic patterns in Section 5.3.2. Preserving a final stress results in a perfect alternation pattern, and avoiding a final stress results in a departure from perfect alternation at or near the right edge. As might be expected, then, the differences in this case also arise from different rankings of NON-FINALITY.

Like the iambic minimal alternation pattern, the trochaic maximal alternation pattern arises when ALL-σ_{HD}-RIGHT and MAP-TO-GRID both dominate NON-FINALITY. ALL-σ_{HD}-RIGHT excludes the final amphibrach candidate in (41b), where the final head syllable is pushed leftward to avoid final stress. MAP-TO-GRID excludes the final lapse candidate in (41a), where the rightmost foot is left stressless to avoid final stress. While the trochaic maximal alternation pattern in (41w) stresses its final syllable in violation of NON-FINALITY, NON-FINALITY is low-ranked, and (41w) emerges as the optimal candidate.

(41)

	ALL-σ_{HD}-R	MAP-TO-GRD	NON-FINALITY
x x x x x x x x x x x ☞ w. σ σ σ σ σ σ σ	12		1
x x x x x x x x x x a. σ σ σ σ σ σ σ	12	W 1	L
x x x x x x x x x x b. σ σ σ σ σ σ σ	W 13		L

The trochaic final dactyl and final amphibrach patterns both require NON-FINALITY to be high-ranked. Like the iambic final lapse pattern, the trochaic final dactyl pattern emerges when NON-FINALITY and ALL-σ_{HD}-RIGHT both dominate MAP-TO-GRID. NON-FINALITY excludes the trochaic maximal alternation pattern in (42a) with its stressed final syllable, and ALL-σ_{HD}-RIGHT excludes the final amphibrach pattern (42b) with its retracted rightmost head syllable. Although the final dactyl pattern in (42w) violates MAP-TO-GRID with its stressless final foot, MAP-TO-GRID is the lowest ranked constraint, and (42w) is optimal.

(42)

	ALL-σ_{HD}-R	NON-FINALITY	MAP-TO-GRD
x x x x x x x x x x ☞ w. σ σ σ σ σ σ σ	12		1
x x x x x x x x x x x a. σ σ σ σ σ σ σ	12	W 1	L
x x x x x x x x x x b. σ σ σ σ σ σ σ	W 13		L

Like the iambic reversal pattern, the trochaic final amphibrach pattern requires that NON-FINALITY and MAP-TO-GRID both dominate ALL-σ_{HD}-RIGHT. Rather than resulting in a clash, however, as (43) illustrates, the retraction of the rightmost head syllable results in a gridmark-sharing configuration. (The presence of *CLASH in the constraint set is sufficient to rule out a mapping, as in (43a), that results in a clash.[5]) NON-FINALITY excludes the trochaic maximal alternation pattern, (43c), due to its final stress, and MAP-TO-GRID excludes the trochaic final dactyl pattern, (43d), which leaves its final foot stressless. The final amphibrach pattern, (43w), emerges as the optimal candidate.

(43)

	MAP-GRID	NON-FIN	ALL-σ_{HD}-R	*CLSH
x x x x x x x x x x ☞ w. σ σ σ σ σ σ σ			13	
x x x x x x x x x x x a. σ σ σ σ σ σ σ			13	1 W
x x x x x x x x x x x c. σ σ σ σ σ σ σ		1 W	12 L	
x x x x x x x x x x d. σ σ σ σ σ σ σ	1 W		12 L	

Just as NON-FINALITY allows the grammar to produce attested variations on iambic minimal alternation, then, NON-FINALITY allows the grammar to produce attested variations on trochaic maximal alternation. When NON-FINALITY is low-ranked, the trochaic maximal alternation pattern emerges. When NON-FINALITY is high-ranked, however, it can create a stressless final foot, resulting in the trochaic final dactyl pattern, or it can retract the rightmost head syllable, resulting in the trochaic final amphibrach pattern.

5 Notice that the trochaic final amphibrach pattern actually harmonically bounds (43a), a pattern produced with exhaustive bidirectional parsing under Iterative Foot Optimization (see Chapter 2). In general, such patterns are harmonically bounded and cannot be produced under Weak Bracketing. Since they are also unattested, this is the desired result.

5.3.4 Iambic maximal alternation and its variants

The final two binary default patterns predicted under Weak Bracketing are the iambic maximal alternation pattern and an unattested variation on iambic maximal alternation. We saw in Section 5.1.3 that the left-oriented iambic parsing pattern in (31) is the result of ranking σ_{HD}-Right over All-σ_{HD}-Left. When every foot in a form is mapped to the grid, this parsing pattern yields the iambic maximal alternation pattern, (44a). When the final foot is left stressless in both even- and odd-parity forms, the parsing pattern yields the unattested iambic double lapse pattern, (44b).

(44) Binary default patterns with left-oriented iambic parsing

a. Maximal Alternation: Attested b. Double lapse: Unattested

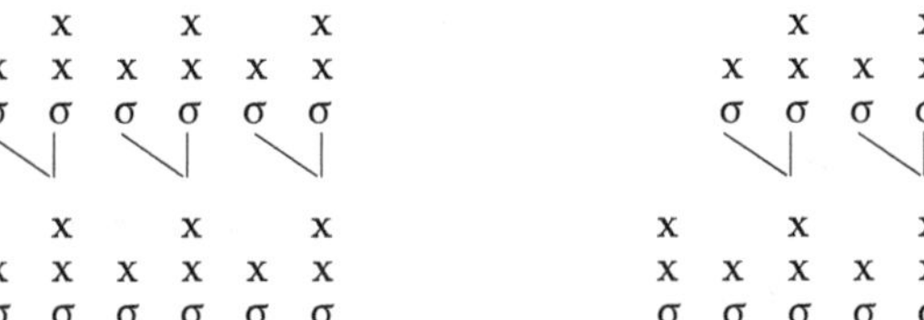

Just as it was for the groups of patterns discussed in the previous two sections, Non-Finality is the key constraint distinguishing between the iambic maximal alternation pattern and the iambic double lapse pattern. For the iambic maximal alternation pattern to emerge, Non-Finality must be low-ranked: σ_{HD}-Right and Map-to-Grid must both dominate Non-Finality. Rather than directly preventing the retraction of a final head syllable in this case, the role of σ_{HD}-Right is to exclude the left-oriented trochaic pattern, (45b), that harmonically bounds the retracted pattern, (45c). (Given the ranking σ_{HD}-Right >> All-σ_{HD}-Left, the direct consequence of violating σ_{HD}-Right is not a single retracted head syllable but the thoroughly trochaic pattern preferred by All-σ_{HD}-Left.) Map-to-Grid excludes the double lapse candidate in (45a), where the rightmost foot is left stressless to avoid final stress. While (45w) stresses a final iambic foot, violating the low-ranked Non-Finality, it correctly emerges as the winner.

(45)	σ_{HD}-R	All-σ_{HD}-L	Map-Grid	Non-Fin
x x x x x x x x x x x ☞ w. σ σ σ σ σ σ σ	3	12		1
x x x x x x x x x x a. σ σ σ σ σ σ σ	3	12	W 1	L
x x x x x x x x x x b. σ σ σ σ σ σ σ	W 4	L 9		L
x x x x x x x x x x x c. σ σ σ σ σ σ σ	W 4	L 11		L

The iambic double lapse pattern requires Non-Finality to be high-ranked. As (46) demonstrates, Non-Finality and σ_{HD}-Right must both dominate Map-to-Grid. Non-Finality excludes the iambic maximal alternation pattern in (46a) with its stressed final iamb, and σ_{HD}-Right excludes the left-oriented trochaic pattern in (46b). Although the double lapse pattern in (46w) violates Map-to-Grid, Map-to-Grid is the low-ranked, and (46w) is the optimal candidate.

(46)	σ_{HD}-Right	Non-finality	Map-to-Grid
x x x x x x x x x x ☞ w. σ σ σ σ σ σ σ	3		1
x x x x x x x x x x x a. σ σ σ σ σ σ σ	3	W 1	L
x x x x x x x x x x b. σ σ σ σ σ σ σ	W 4		L

5.3.5 Summary of predicted binary default patterns

In all, the Weak Bracketing account predicts 11 binary default patterns, ten of which are attested. As indicated in (47) and (48), Weak Bracketing predicts the trochaic minimal alternation pattern and the mirror-image iambic minimal alternation pattern. For trochaic minimal alternation, it is crucial that ALL-σ_{HD}-LEFT dominates ALL-σ_{HD}-RIGHT and σ_{HD}-RIGHT in order to establish the basic left-oriented trochaic parsing pattern, and it is crucial that *CLASH and MAP-TO-GRID dominate INITIAL-GRIDMARK in order to prevent initial stress in odd-parity forms.

(47) Trochaic minimal alternation: Attested

a. *Pattern*

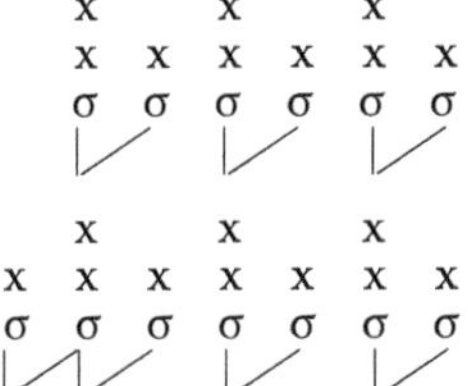

b. *Ranking*

ALL-σ_{HD}-LEFT >> ALL-σ_{HD}-RIGHT, σ_{HD}-RIGHT; ALL-σ_{HD}-LEFT, *CLASH, MAP-TO-GRID >> INITIAL-GRIDMARK

For iambic minimal alternation, ALL-σ_{HD}-RIGHT must dominate ALL-σ_{HD}-LEFT, σ_{HD}-LEFT, and INITIAL-GRIDMARK in order to establish the basic right-oriented iambic parsing pattern. ALL-σ_{HD}-RIGHT and MAP-TO-GRID must dominate NON-FINALITY to promote final stress in even-parity forms.

(48) Iambic minimal alternation: Attested

a. *Pattern*

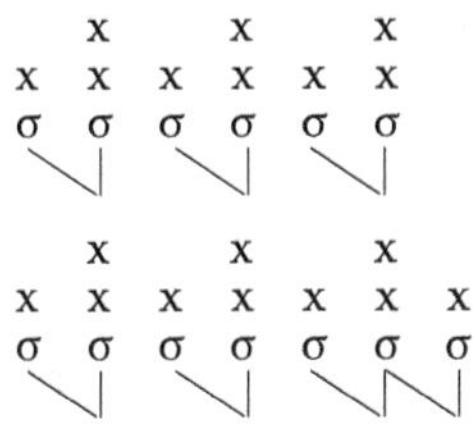

b. *Ranking*

ALL-σ_{HD}-RIGHT >> ALL-σ_{HD}-LEFT, σ_{HD}-LEFT, INITIAL-GRIDMARK; ALL-σ_{HD}-RIGHT, MAP-TO-GRID >> NON-FINALITY

As indicated in (49) and (50), Weak Bracketing also predicts the trochaic maximal alternation pattern and the mirror-image iambic maximal alternation pattern. Note that the maximal alternation patterns emerge under a greater variety of crucial rankings than the minimal alternation patterns. For trochaic systems, the greater variety is due to the ability of INITIAL-GRIDMARK to duplicate the effects of σ_{HD}-LEFT in restricting the general rightward orientation of the basic parsing pattern and to the ability of σ_{HD}-RIGHT to duplicate the effects of ALL-σ_{HD}-RIGHT in producing the general rightward orientation and in promoting final stress in odd-parity forms.

(49) Trochaic maximal alternation: Attested

a. *Pattern*

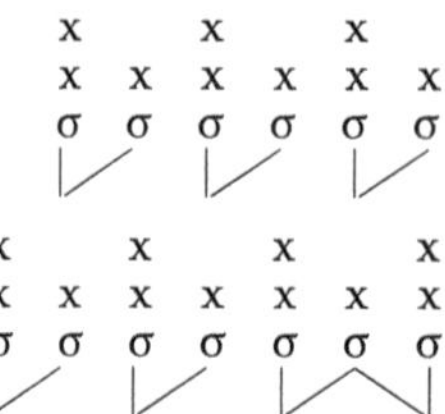

b. *Rankings*

i. σ_{HD}-LEFT >> ALL-σ_{HD}-RIGHT, σ_{HD}-RIGHT; ALL-σ_{HD}-RIGHT >> NON-FINALITY, ALL-σ_{HD}-LEFT; MAP-TO-GRID >> NON-FINALITY

ii. σ_{HD}-LEFT >> ALL-σ_{HD}-RIGHT, σ_{HD}-RIGHT; σ_{HD}-RIGHT >> NON-FINALITY, ALL-σ_{HD}-LEFT; MAP-TO-GRID >> NON-FINALITY

iii. INITIAL-GRIDMARK >> ALL-σ_{HD}-RIGHT, σ_{HD}-RIGHT; ALL-σ_{HD}-RIGHT >> NON-FINALITY, ALL-σ_{HD}-LEFT; MAP-TO-GRID >> NON-FINALITY

iv. INITIAL-GRIDMARK >> ALL-σ_{HD}-RIGHT, σ_{HD}-RIGHT; σ_{HD}-RIGHT >> NON-FINALITY, ALL-σ_{HD}-LEFT; MAP-TO-GRID >> NON-FINALITY

For iambic maximal alternation, the greater variety is due to the ability of σ_{HD}-LEFT and INITIAL-GRIDMARK both to duplicate the effects of ALL-σ_{HD}-LEFT establishing the general left-oriented iambic parsing pattern. Ranking σ_{HD}-RIGHT and MAP-TO-GRID above NON-FINALITY ensures the maintenance of final stress.

(50) Iambic maximal alternation: Attested

a. *Pattern*

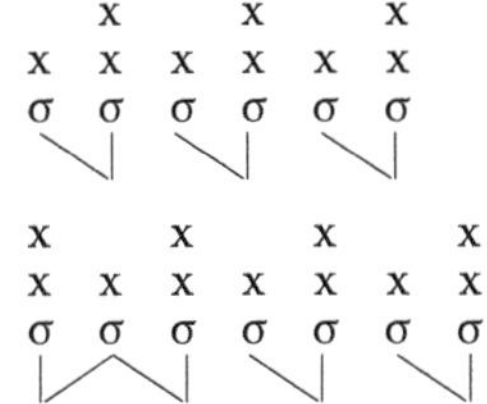

b. *Rankings*

i. σ_{HD}-RIGHT >> ALL-σ_{HD}-LEFT, σ_{HD}-LEFT, INITIAL-GRIDMARK; ALL-σ_{HD}-LEFT >> ALL-σ_{HD}-RIGHT; σ_{HD}-RIGHT, MAP-TO-GRID >> NON-FINALITY

ii. σ_{HD}-RIGHT >> ALL-σ_{HD}-LEFT, σ_{HD}-LEFT, INITIAL-GRIDMARK; σ_{HD}-LEFT >> ALL-σ_{HD}-RIGHT; σ_{HD}-RIGHT, MAP-TO-GRID >> NON-FINALITY

iii. σ_{HD}-RIGHT >> ALL-σ_{HD}-LEFT, σ_{HD}-LEFT, INITIAL-GRIDMARK; INITIAL-GRIDMARK >> ALL-σ_{HD}-RIGHT; σ_{HD}-RIGHT, MAP-TO-GRID >> NON-FINALITY

The Weak Bracketing approach, then, captures the generalization that the perfect alternation patterns are attested in mirror image pairs. It predicts both the trochaic minimal alternation pattern and the mirror-image iambic minimal alternation pattern. It also predicts both the trochaic maximal alternation pattern and the mirror image iambic maximal alternation pattern. As the summary of the remaining patterns will indicate, Weak Bracketing also captures the generalization that attested departures from perfect alternation exhibit iambic-trochaic asymmetries. If it predicts an attested iambic pattern, it fails to predict its unattested trochaic mirror image. If it predicts an attested trochaic pattern, it fails to predict its unattested iambic mirror image.

The trochaic initial clash pattern in (51) and the trochaic initial dactyl pattern in (52) are both produced under Weak Bracketing as variations on trochaic minimal alternation. Both employ the minimal alternation ranking ALL-σ_{HD}-LEFT >> ALL-σ_{HD}-RIGHT, σ_{HD}-RIGHT to establish a basic left-oriented trochaic parsing pattern. The initial clash pattern differs from the minimal alternation pattern in ranking INITIAL-GRIDMARK and MAP-TO-GRID above *CLASH in order to allow for a clash configuration to accommodate initial stress in odd-parity forms.

(51) Trochaic initial clash: Attested

a. *Pattern*

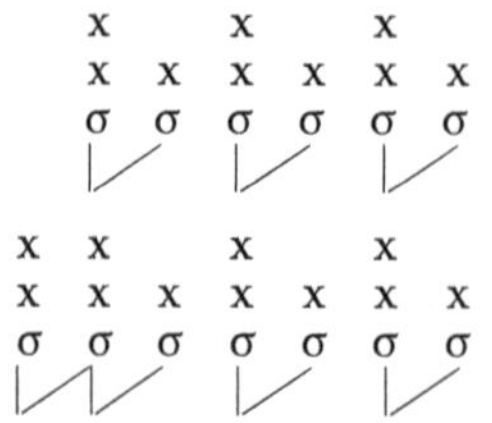

```
      x     x     x
      x  x  x  x  x  x
      σ  σ  σ  σ  σ  σ
      |/    |/    |/

   x  x     x     x
   x  x  x  x  x  x  x
   σ  σ  σ  σ  σ  σ  σ
   |/ |/    |/    |/
```

b. *Ranking*

All-σ_{Hd}-Left >> All-σ_{Hd}-Right, σ_{Hd}-Right; All-σ_{Hd}-Left, Initial-Gridmark, Map-to-Grid >> *Clash

The initial dactyl pattern differs from the minimal alternation pattern in ranking Initial-Gridmark and *Clash above Map-to-Grid in order to allow for a lapse configuration to accommodate initial stress in odd-parity forms.

(52) Trochaic initial dactyl: Attested

a. *Pattern*

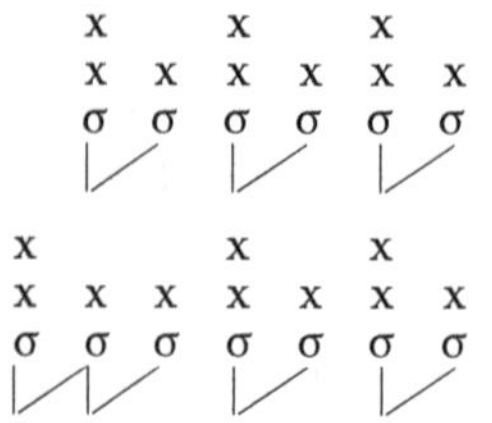

```
      x     x     x
      x  x  x  x  x  x
      σ  σ  σ  σ  σ  σ
      |/    |/    |/

   x        x     x
   x  x  x  x  x  x  x
   σ  σ  σ  σ  σ  σ  σ
   |/ |/    |/    |/
```

b. *Ranking*

All-σ_{Hd}-Left >> All-σ_{Hd}-Right, σ_{Hd}-Right; All-σ_{Hd}-Left, Initial-Gridmark, *Clash >> Map-to-Grid

The iambic final lapse pattern, (53), and the iambic reversal pattern, (54), are produced under Weak Bracketing as variations on iambic minimal alternation. Both share with minimal alternation the ranking of All-σ_{Hd}-Right above All-σ_{Hd}-Left and σ_{Hd}-Left, which establishes a basic right-oriented iambic parsing pattern. The final lapse pattern differs from the minimal alternation pattern in ranking All-σ_{Hd}-Right and Non-Finality above Map-to-Grid in order to allow the final foot to remain stressless in even-parity forms.

(53) Iambic final lapse: Attested

a. *Pattern*

```
   x       x
x  x   x   x   x   x
σ  σ   σ   σ   σ   σ

   x       x       x
x  x   x   x   x   x   x
σ  σ   σ   σ   σ   σ   σ
```

b. *Ranking*

All-σ_{HD}-Right >> All-σ_{HD}-Left, σ_{HD}-Left, Initial-Gridmark;
All-σ_{HD}-Right, Non-Finality >> Map-to-Grid

The iambic reversal pattern differs from iambic minimal alternation in ranking Non-Finality and Map-to-Grid above All-σ_{HD}-Right and *Clash. This allows the rightmost head syllable to retract by one syllable in even-parity forms.

(54) Iambic reversal: Attested

a. *Pattern*

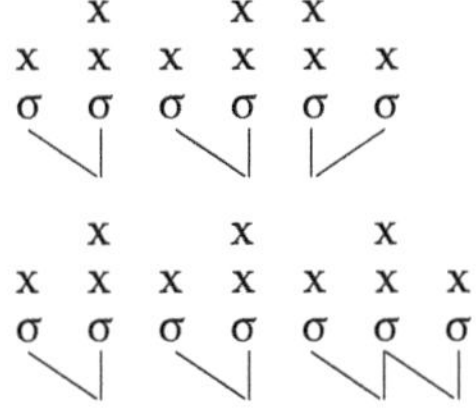

b. *Ranking*

All-σ_{HD}-Right >> All-σ_{HD}-Left, σ_{HD}-Left, Initial-Gridmark;
Non-Finality, Map-to-Grid >> All-σ_{HD}-Right >> *Clash

The trochaic final dactyl pattern, (55), and trochaic final amphibrach pattern, (56), are Non-Finality-induced variations on the trochaic maximal alternation pattern. The final dactyl pattern shares in the variety of rankings that can be employed to produce maximal alternation, but it differs in ranking All-σ_{HD}-Right or σ_{HD}-Right and Non-Finality above Map-to-Grid in order to produce a stressless final foot in odd-parity forms.

(55) Trochaic final dactyl: Attested

a. *Pattern*

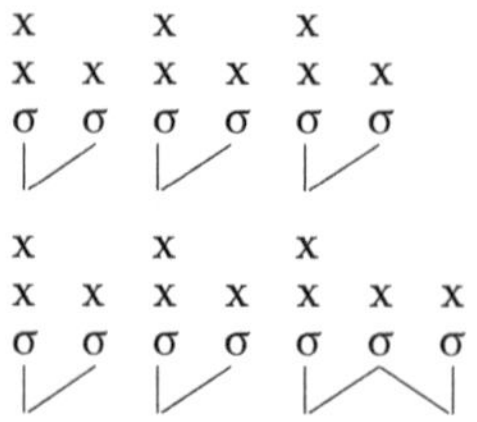

```
x     x     x
x  x  x  x  x  x
σ  σ  σ  σ  σ  σ

x     x     x
x  x  x  x  x  x  x
σ  σ  σ  σ  σ  σ  σ
```

b. *Rankings*

i. σ_{Hd}-Left >> All-σ_{Hd}-Right, σ_{Hd}-Right; All-σ_{Hd}-Right >> Map-to-Grid, All-σ_{Hd}-Left; Non-Finality >> Map-to-Grid

ii. σ_{Hd}-Left >> All-σ_{Hd}-Right, σ_{Hd}-Right; σ_{Hd}-Right >> Map-to-Grid, All-σ_{Hd}-Left; Non-Finality >> Map-to-Grid

iii. Initial-Gridmark >> All-σ_{Hd}-Right, σ_{Hd}-Right; All-σ_{Hd}-Right >> Map-to-Grid, All-σ_{Hd}-Left; Non-Finality >> Map-to-Grid

iv. Initial-Gridmark >> All-σ_{Hd}-Right, σ_{Hd}-Right; σ_{Hd}-Right >> Map-to-Grid, All-σ_{Hd}-Left; Non-Finality >> Map-to-Grid

The trochaic final amphibrach pattern is produced under fewer rankings. It differs from the maximal alternation pattern in ranking Map-to-Grid and Non-Finality above All-σ_{Hd}-Right and σ_{Hd}-Right. This allows the rightmost head syllable in odd-parity forms to retract into a gridmark-sharing configuration.

(56) Trochaic final amphibrach: Attested

a. *Pattern*

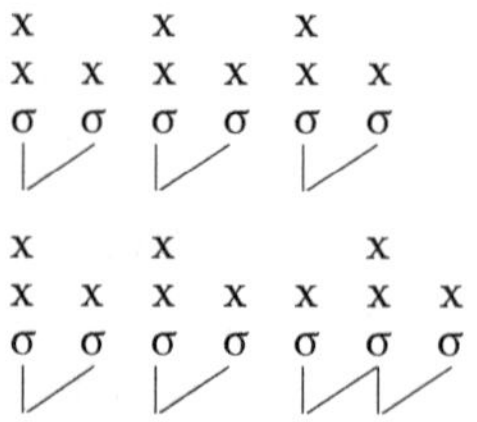

```
x     x     x
x  x  x  x  x  x
σ  σ  σ  σ  σ  σ

x     x        x
x  x  x  x  x  x  x
σ  σ  σ  σ  σ  σ  σ
```

b. *Rankings*

i. σ_{Hd}-Left, Map-to-Grid, Non-Finality >> All-σ_{Hd}-Right, σ_{Hd}-Right; All-σ_{Hd}-Right >> All-σ_{Hd}-Left

ii. Initial-Gridmark, Map-to-Grid, Non-Finality >> All-σ_{Hd}-Right, σ_{Hd}-Right; All-σ_{Hd}-Right >> All-σ_{Hd}-Left

Finally, Weak Bracketing predicts the unattested iambic double lapse pattern as a Non-Finality-induced variation on iambic maximal alternation.

(57) Iambic double lapse: Unattested

a. *Pattern*

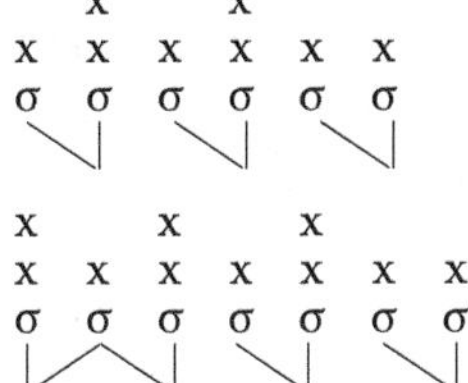

b. *Rankings*

i. σ_{HD}-Right >> All-σ_{HD}-Left, σ_{HD}-Left, Initial-Gridmark; All-σ_{HD}-Left >> All-σ_{HD}-Right; σ_{HD}-Right, Non-Finality >> Map-to-Grid

ii. σ_{HD}-Right >> All-σ_{HD}-Left, σ_{HD}-Left, Initial-Gridmark; σ_{HD}-Left >> All-σ_{HD}-Right; σ_{HD}-Right, Non-Finality >> Map-to-Grid

iii. σ_{HD}-Right >> All-σ_{HD}-Left, σ_{HD}-Left, Initial-Gridmark; Initial-Gridmark >> All-σ_{HD}-Right; σ_{HD}-Right, Non-Finality >> Map-to-Grid

Overall, then, the Weak Bracketing account predicts a very accurate typology of binary default patterns. It predicts all of the attested patterns and only one unattested pattern. Combined with Weak Bracketing's ability to avoid the Odd-Parity Input Problem, the accuracy of the predicted typology makes a strong case for the Weak Bracketing approach. One aspect of the approach that we have not examined in detail, however, is why it fails to predict the unattested mirror images of the attested departures from perfect alternation discussed above. We turn to this issue in the next section.

5.4 The unattested mirror images

In the discussion above, we saw how Initial-Gridmark and Non-Finality allow the Weak Bracketing account to introduce clash and lapse in positions that typically result in attested patterns. In this part of the discussion, we see that these same constraints do not allow the account to introduce clash and lapse in positions that result in the unattested mirror images of these patterns.

In Section 5.3.1, we saw that INITIAL-GRIDMARK allows the grammar to produce the trochaic initial clash and initial dactyl patterns as variations on the trochaic minimal alternation pattern. The unattested mirror image of the initial clash pattern is the iambic final clash pattern, (58a). Much like the initial clash pattern tolerates a clash at the left edge to accommodate an initial stress in odd-parity forms, the final clash pattern would tolerate a clash at the right edge to accommodate a final stress in odd-parity forms. The unattested mirror image of the initial dactyl pattern is the iambic final anapest pattern, (58b). Much like the initial dactyl pattern tolerates a stressless foot, and thus a lapse, near the left edge to accommodate an initial stress in odd-parity forms, the final anapest pattern would tolerate a stressless foot near the right edge to accommodate a final stress in odd-parity forms.

(58) Harmonically bounded variations on iambic minimal alternation

a. Final clash: Unattested b. Final anapest: Unattested

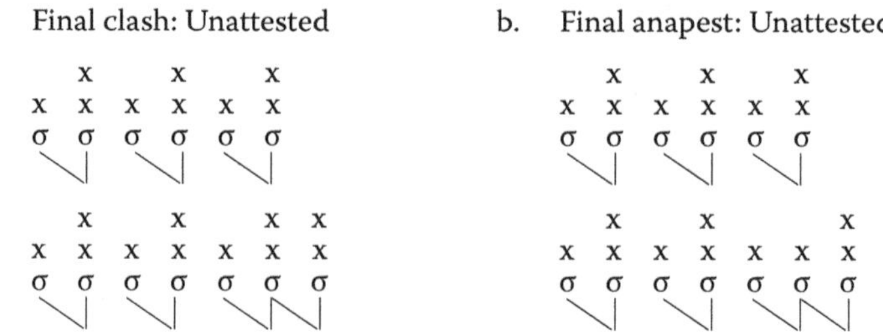

While INITIAL-GRIDMARK allows the grammar to produce the trochaic initial clash and initial dactyl patterns, it does not allow the grammar to produce their unattested iambic mirror images. The asymmetry is due to INITIAL-GRIDMARK's asymmetrical formulation. By insisting on an initial stress, a high-ranking INITIAL-GRIDMARK can create a clash or lapse near the left edge of a form, as required for the attested trochaic patterns. Because it cannot insist on a final stress, however, INITIAL-GRIDMARK cannot create a clash or lapse at the right edge of a form, as required for the unattested iambic mirror images.

As (59) demonstrates, the unattested iambic mirror images are harmonically bounded by iambic minimal alternation. Since we are now considering right-oriented iambic patterns, we can assume that ALL-σ_{HD}-RIGHT is high-ranked. Fist, the minimal alternation pattern in (59w) performs as well as the final clash pattern in (59) with respect to INITIAL-GRIDMARK and MAP-TO-GRID and better with respect to

*CLASH, so the minimal alternation pattern harmonically bounds the final clash pattern. Second, the minimal alternation pattern performs as well as the final anapest pattern in (59b) with respect to INITIAL-GRIDMARK and *CLASH and better with respect to MAP-TO-GRID, so minimal alternation harmonically bounds the final anapest pattern as well. The inability of INITIAL-GRIDMARK (or any other constraint in the Weak Bracketing account) to undermine the gridmark-sharing configuration of the iambic minimal alternation pattern is the crucial factor in producing this result.

(59)

	INITIAL-GM	MAP-TO-GRID	*CLASH
x x x x x x x x x x ☞ w. σ σ σ σ σ σ σ	1		
x x x x x x x x x x x a. σ σ σ σ σ σ σ	1		1 W
x x x x x x x x x x b. σ σ σ σ σ σ σ	1	1 W	

In Section 5.3.2, we saw that NON-FINALITY allows the grammar to produce the iambic final lapse and iambic reversal patterns as variations on iambic minimal alternation. While it allows the grammar to produce these iambic variations, it does not allow the grammar to produce their unattested trochaic mirror images. The unattested mirror image of the iambic final lapse pattern is the trochaic initial lapse pattern, (60a). Much like the final lapse pattern tolerates a stressless final foot, and thus a final lapse, to avoid final stress in even-parity forms, the initial lapse pattern would tolerate an initial stressless foot to avoid initial stress in even-parity forms. The unattested mirror image of the iambic reversal pattern is the trochaic reversal pattern, (60b). Much like the iambic reversal pattern retracts it rightmost head syllable, creating a clash near the right edge, to avoid final stress in even-parity forms, the trochaic reversal pattern would advance its leftmost head syllable to avoid initial stress in even-parity forms.

(60) Harmonically bounded variations on trochaic minimal alternation

a. Initial lapse: Unattested

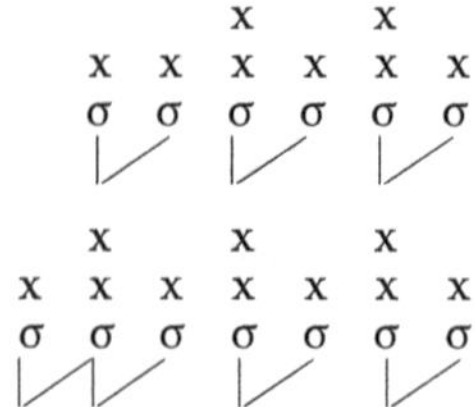

b. Reversal: Unattested

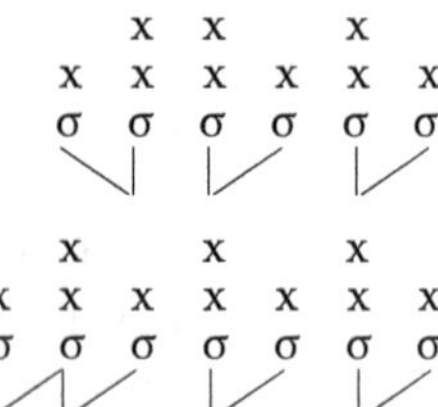

Due to its asymmetrical formulation, a high-ranking NON-FINALITY can create a lapse at the right edge or a clash near the right edge to avoid a final stress, as required for the attested iambic patterns, but it cannot create a lapse at the left edge or a clash near the left edge to avoid an initial stress, as would be required for the unattested trochaic mirror images. To illustrate, consider how trochaic minimal alternation and its potential variants perform on the most relevant constraints in (61). The minimal alternation pattern in (61w) performs as well as the initial lapse pattern in (61a) with respect to NON-FINALITY, ALL-σ_{HD}-LEFT, and *CLASH and better with respect to MAP-TO-GRID, so the minimal alternation pattern harmonically bounds the initial lapse pattern. The minimal alternation pattern performs as well the trochaic reversal pattern in (61b) with respect to NON-FINALITY and MAP-TO-GRID and better with respect to ALL-σ_{HD}-LEFT and *CLASH, so trochaic minimal alternation harmonically bounds the trochaic reversal pattern as well.

(61)

	NON-FIN	MAP-GRID	*CLASH	ALL-σ_{HD}-L
x x x x x x x x x ☞ w. σ σ σ σ σ σ				6
x x x x x x x x a. σ σ σ σ σ σ		W 1		6
x x x x x x x x x b. σ σ σ σ σ σ			W 1	W 7

As we saw in Section 5.3.3, NON-FINALITY also allows the trochaic final dactyl and final amphibrach patterns to be produced as variations on trochaic maximal alternation, but it does not allow the grammar to produce their unattested iambic mirror images. The mirror image of the trochaic final dactyl pattern is the iambic initial anapest pattern, (62a). In the final dactyl pattern, a final foot is left stressless to avoid final stress in odd-parity forms, resulting in a lapse at the right edge. Similarly, in the initial anapest pattern, an initial foot would be left stressless in odd-parity forms to avoid an initial stress. The mirror image of the trochaic final amphibrach pattern is the iambic initial amphibrach pattern, (62b). In the final amphibrach pattern, the rightmost head syllable is retracted in odd-parity forms to avoid final stress, resulting in a gridmark-sharing configuration at the right edge. Similarly, in the initial amphibrach pattern, the leftmost head syllable would be advanced to avoid initial stress in odd-parity forms.

(62) Harmonically bounded variations on iambic maximal alternation

a. Initial anapest: Unattested

```
     x   x   x
   x x x x x x
   σ σ σ σ σ σ

       x   x   x
   x x x x x x x
   σ σ σ σ σ σ σ
```

b. Initial amphibrach: Unattested

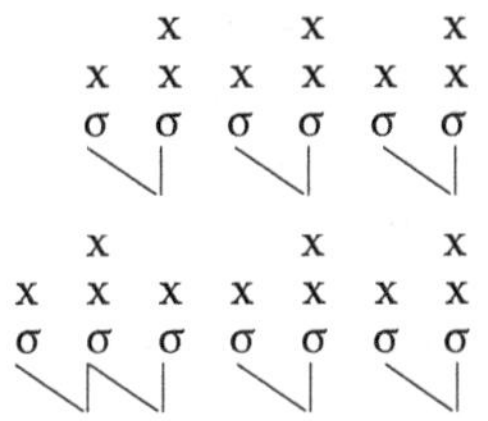

The tableau in (63) illustrates how the iambic maximal alternation, initial anapest, and initial amphibrach patterns perform on the most relevant constraints. Since the iambic maximal alternation pattern, (63w), performs as well as the initial anapest pattern, (63a), with respect to σ_{HD}-RIGHT, σ_{HD}-LEFT, ALL-σ_{HD}-LEFT, and NON-FINALITY and better with respect to MAP-TO-GRID, iambic maximal alternation harmonically bounds the initial anapest pattern. Because iambic maximal alternation performs as well as the initial amphibrach pattern in (63b) with respect to σ_{HD}-RIGHT, NON-FINALITY, and MAP-TO-GRID and better with respect to σ_{HD}-LEFT and ALL-σ_{HD}-LEFT, iambic maximal alternation also harmonically bounds the initial amphibrach pattern.

(63)

	σ_{HD}-R	σ_{HD}-L	ALL-σ_{HD}-L	N-FIN	MAP
x x x x x x x x x x x ☞ w. σ σ σ σ σ σ σ	3	3	12	1	
x x x x x x x x x x a. σ σ σ σ σ σ σ	3	3	12	1	W 1
x x x x x x x x x x b. σ σ σ σ σ σ σ	3	W 4	W 13	1	

Finally, we saw in Section 5.3.4 how NON-FINALITY allows the Weak Bracketing account to produce the unattested iambic double lapse pattern as a variation on iambic maximal alternation. The mirror image of the iambic pattern, the trochaic double lapse pattern in (64), is also unattested. In this case, however, the Weak Bracketing account is able to exclude it. In the iambic double lapse pattern, the rightmost foot is left stressless in both even- and odd-parity forms to avoid final stress. In the trochaic double lapse pattern, the leftmost foot would be left stressless in both even- and odd-parity forms to avoid initial stress.

(64) Harmonically bounded variation on trochaic maximal alternation

Double lapse: Unattested

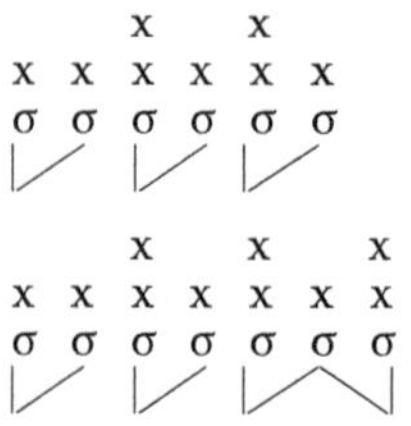

```
    x   x
x x x x x x
σ σ σ σ σ σ

    x   x   x
x x x x x x x
σ σ σ σ σ σ σ
```

While NON-FINALITY can create stressless feet at the right edge, it cannot create the stressless foot at the left edge necessary to create the trochaic double lapse pattern. As (65) illustrates, the trochaic maximal alternation pattern performs equally well on all of the most relevant constraints. It performs equally to the trochaic double lapse pattern on σ_{HD}-LEFT, NON-FINALITY, and *CLASH. Because it performs better on MAP-TO-GRID, however, the maximal alternation pattern harmonically bounds the double lapse pattern.

(65)

	σ_{HD}-LEFT	NON-FIN	*CLSH	MAP-GRID
x x x x x x x x x x x ☞ w. σ σ σ σ σ σ σ	3	1		
x x x x x x x x x x l. σ σ σ σ σ σ σ	3	1		W 1

5.5 Two additional patterns

Before moving on to the discussion of accent windows in Chapter 6, consideration of two additional patterns can give us further insight into the way that relation-specific alignment constraints insist on a minimal amount of structure. The two additional patterns are the trochaic final clash pattern in (66a) and the iambic initial clash pattern in (66b). The key characteristic of both patterns is found in their even-parity forms. Since even-parity forms can be evenly divided into disyllable feet, we would expect no more than half of their syllables to carry a stress. In (66), however, the two patterns both have an overabundance of stressed syllables in their even-parity forms.

(66) a. Trochaic final clash: Unattested b. Iambic initial clash: Unattested

a.

x x x x
x x x x x x
σ σ σ σ σ σ

x x x x
x x x x x x x
σ σ σ σ σ σ σ

b.

x x x x
x x x x x x
σ σ σ σ σ σ

x x x x
x x x x x x x
σ σ σ σ σ σ σ

Though a single example of each pattern has been presented in the literature, we saw in Chapter 1 that there is good reason to doubt that the languages presented as having the trochaic final clash and iambic initial clash pattern, Goshiute Shoshone and Tauya, respectively, actually have these stress patterns. It is more likely that they are examples of the basic trochaic and iambic maximal alternation patterns.

In any case, the formulation of the RSA constraints employed here prevents the Weak Bracketing account from producing either of the patterns in (66). As Gordon (2002a) argues, a requirement that a stress occur at both edges of a prosodic word would produce the overcrowding seen in the even-parity forms in (66). At first glance, it seems that the distance-insensitive σ_{Hd}-Left and σ_{Hd}-Right offer an indirect means to anchor a stress to both edges of a prosodic word, through anchoring a head syllable at both edges. This is not really the case, however. Anchoring head syllables at both edges of an even-parity form means that a greater number of feet will be required to parse it, and a greater number of feet, means a greater number of head syllables. Because a greater number of head syllables necessarily means a greater number of σ_{Hd}-Left and σ_{Hd}-Right violations, σ_{Hd}-Left and σ_{Hd}-Right cannot combine to anchor head syllables at both edges of an even-parity form, even when both are highly ranked.

To illustrate, consider how the patterns in (66) fare against the minimal alternation patterns with respect to σ_{Hd}-Left and σ_{Hd}-Right. In (67), where σ_{Hd}-Right is the higher ranked constraint, the iambic minimal alternation pattern performs better than either of the patterns in (66). Adding the extra head syllable necessary to accommodate both initial stress and final stress in even parity forms does not allow σ_{Hd}-Left and σ_{Hd}-Right to be satisfied simultaneously. Rather, it simply increases the number of violations for σ_{Hd}-Right. Initial-Gridmark is included in the tableaux in (67) and (68), since it can duplicate the effects of σ_{Hd}-Left in this context.

(67)

	σ_{Hd}-Right	σ_{Hd}-Left	Initial-Gridmark
☞ w. . x . x . x x x x x x x σ σ σ σ σ σ (σ σ)(σ σ)(σ σ)	2	3	1
a. x . x . x x x x x x x x σ σ σ σ σ σ (σ σ)(σ σ)(σ)(σ)	3 W	3	L
b. x x . x . x x x x x x x σ σ σ σ σ σ (σ)(σ)(σ σ)(σ σ)	3 W	3	L

The situation is similar in (68), where σ_{Hd}-Left and Initial-Gridmark are the higher-ranked constraints. In this case, however, we can see that the trochaic minimal alternation pattern actually harmonically bounds both of the patterns in (66). The extra head syllable necessary to accommodate both initial and final stress in even-parity forms does not allow σ_{Hd}-Left, σ_{Hd}-Right, and Initial-Gridmark to be satisfied simultaneously. It only increases the violations of σ_{Hd}-Left.

(68)

	σ_{Hd}-LEFT	INITIAL-GRIDMARK	σ_{Hd}-RIGHT
x . x . x . x x x x x x ☞ w. (σ σ)(σ σ)(σ σ)	2		3
x . x . x x x x x x x x a. (σ σ)(σ σ)(σ)(σ)	W 3		3
x x . x . x x x x x x x b. (σ)(σ)(σ σ)(σ σ)	W 3		3

Given the RSA formulation for the distance-insensitive alignment constraints, then, the Weak Bracketing account is unable to produce the iambic initial clash pattern or the trochaic final clash pattern. Both patterns are harmonically bounded by trochaic minimal alternation. Since the two patterns appear to be unattested at this point, this is probably a desirable result.

5.6 Summary

In this chapter, we have seen how the combination of Weak Bracketing and Optimal Mapping accomplishes two objectives: it allows the grammar to avoid the Odd-Parity Input Problem, and it predicts a reasonably accurate typology of binary default patterns. Weak Bracketing is the component of the approach that allows the grammar to avoid the OPIP. The option of allowing disyllabic feet to overlap effectively removes the conflict in odd-parity forms between the requirement that syllables be parsed into feet and the requirement that feet be minimally bimoraic. Overlapping feet provide a way to achieve exhaustive binary footing for any odd-parity input without making parsing sensitive to syllable weight or converting the odd-parity input into an even-parity output.

Optimal mapping is the component of the approach that allows the grammar to predict an accurate typology of binary default patterns. The stress patterns in the predicted typology are constructed on just four basic parsing patterns. The variation among the stress patterns lies primarily in how the basic parsing patterns map to the metrical grid. Given the possibility of gridmark sharing between overlapping feet, the Optimal Mapping constraints MAP-TO-GRID and *CLASH conspire to promote stress patterns with perfect binary alternation, patterns that contain no clash configurations and no lapse configurations.

Two additional Optimal Mapping constraints, INITIAL-GRIDMARK and NON-FINALITY, are primarily responsible for introducing clash and lapse in appropriate positions and for accounting for the iambic-trochaic asymmetries in patterns that depart from perfect alternation. Because INITIAL-GRIDMARK can introduce clash or lapse near the left edge but not the right edge, it cannot create variations on perfect alternation in mirror-image pairs. Only the version with the variation at the left edge is predicted. Similarly, because NON-FINALITY can introduce clash or lapse near the right edge but not the left edge, it cannot create variations on perfect alternation in mirror-image pairs. Only the version with the variation at the right edge is predicted.

In additional to avoiding the OPIP, then, the Weak Bracketing approach captures the key typological generalizations repeated in (69).

(69) a. In mirror image patterns with neither clash nor lapse, both members of the pair are attested.

b. In mirror image patterns with either clash or lapse, at most one member of the pair is attested.

It captures the generalization that perfect alternation patterns are symmetrically attested in mirror-image pairs, and it captures the generalization that patterns that depart from perfect alternation are asymmetrically attested or symmetrically unattested.

Given the key roles of INITIAL-GRIDMARK and NON-FINALITY in successfully predicting iambic and trochaic asymmetries, we have also found substantial support for the additional generalization repeated in (70).

(70) Attested patterns with clash or lapse always have stress on the initial syllable, always leave the final syllable stressless, or both.

Clash can occur in certain positions but not in others, and lapse can occur in certain positions but not in others. When a clash or lapse arises, it arises near a form's left edge to accommodate an initial stressed syllable or near its right edge to accommodate a final stressless syllable. Since iambic patterns are typically incompatible with initial stress and final stresslessness, it is most often the iambic patterns that are unattested in iambic-trochaic asymmetries.

6

Accent Windows

Having examined the predictions arising under the different approaches to prosodic layering in the previous three chapters, we return in this chapter to the Relation-Specific Alignment formulation and to an unexpected result that emerges in the context of opposite-edge alignment. As we saw in Chapter 2, the midpoint pathology arises in the context of same-edge alignment under the Generalized Alignment formulation. By making alignment requirements relation-specific, the RSA formulation manages to avoid the midpoint pathology while maintaining distance-sensitivity, allowing it to produce alignment's essential directionality effects. As we shall see below, the midpoint pathology also emerges under Generalized Alignment in the context of opposite-edge alignment. While the RSA formulation still manages to avoid the midpoint pathology in this context, the result is not what might be expected of opposite-edge constraints. This unexpected result, however, allows for a natural and general account of trisyllabic accent windows and similar phenomena.

Like its same-edge constraints, GA's opposite-edge constraints produce Midpoint Pathology effects because they are both distance-sensitive and relation general. Consider, for example, the opposite-edge GA constraint ALIGN (F, L, x_ω, R, σ), a constraint that requires alignment between the left edges of feet and the right edge of a primary stress.

(1) ALIGN (F, L, x_ω, R, σ)

The left edge of every foot coincides with the right edge of some primary stress. Assess a violation mark for each syllable intervening between misaligned edges.

As (2) illustrates, ALIGN (F, L, x_ω, R, σ) draws the right stress edge to the left edge of the medial foot, minimizing the overall distance between the right stress edge and the left edges of *all* misaligned feet. In (2) and (4), *p* denotes a violation mark derived from a misaligned foot that precedes the stress, *f* a violation mark from a misaligned foot that follows the stress, and *c* a violation mark from a misaligned foot that contains the stress.

(2)

	Align (F, L, x_{ω}, R, σ)
a. (σ́σ)(σσ)(σσ)(σσ)(σσ)	c f fff ffff fff!ffff
b. (σσ́)(σσ)(σσ)(σσ)(σσ)	cc ff ffff fffff!f
c. (σσ)(σ́σ)(σσ)(σσ)(σσ)	ppp c f fff fffff!
☞ d. (σσ)(σσ́)(σσ)(σσ)(σσ)	pppp cc ff ffff
e. (σσ)(σσ)(σ́σ)(σσ)(σσ)	ppppp ppp c f fff!
f. (σσ)(σσ)(σσ́)(σσ)(σσ)	pppppp pppp cc f!f
g. (σσ)(σσ)(σσ)(σ́σ)(σσ)	ppppppp ppppp p!pp c f
h. (σσ)(σσ)(σσ)(σσ́)(σσ)	pppppppp ppppp!p pppp cc
i. (σσ)(σσ)(σσ)(σσ)(σ́σ)	ppppppppp pppp!ppp ppppp ppp c
j. (σσ)(σσ)(σσ)(σσ)(σσ́)	pppppppppp ppp!ppppp pppppp pppp cc

Like its same-edge counterparts, RSA's opposite-edge constraints avoid Midpoint Pathology effects due to their relation-specificity. In the opposite-edge case, however, the remedy has some surprising consequences. Opposite-edge constraints have the effect of confining instances of one of the aligned categories to a 'window' at an edge of a form established by an instance of the other aligned category. Consider how an opposite-edge constraint like Align (F, L, x_{ω}, R, σ) would have to be formulated under RSA. In the prohibited configuration in RSA's opposite-edge alignment schema, one aligned category precedes the other with the separator category intervening. To require alignment between the right edge of a primary stress and the left edge of a foot, then, the prohibited configuration would be one where a primary stress precedes a foot with a syllable intervening. Including the separator category, *syllable*, in the definition of the locus of violation makes the constraint distance-sensitive. The result is the constraint in (3).

(3) $*\langle x_{\omega}, F, \sigma\rangle / x_{\omega} \ldots \sigma \ldots F$

'Assess a violation mark for every $\langle x_{\omega}, F, \sigma\rangle$ such that x_{ω} precedes *F* with *σ* intervening.'

Though the RSA constraint is like Align (F, L, x_{ω}, R, σ) in that it is distance-sensitive and promotes alignment between the left edges of feet and the right edge of the primary stress, it differs from its GA counterpart in being relation-specific. Where Align (F, L, x_{ω}, R, σ) prohibits misalignment whether the misaligned foot precedes, follows, or contains the primary stress, the RSA constraint prohibits misalignment only when the misaligned foot follows the stress. As (4) illustrates, the RSA constraint draws the primary stress, not to the center of the form, but to the syllable adjacent to the final foot, (4h), or to one of the two syllables that make up the final foot, (4i,j). The constraint is satisfied when the stress occurs in these positions because any misaligned foot either precedes the stress or contains it and, therefore, fails to produce violation marks. The result is that the RSA constraint confines the primary stress to a three-syllable window at the right edge.

(4)

	$*\langle x_{\omega}, F, \sigma\rangle / x_{\omega} \ldots \sigma \ldots F$
a. (σ́σ)(σσ)(σσ)(σσ)(σσ)	f! fff fffff fffffff
b. (σσ́)(σσ)(σσ)(σσ)(σσ)	f!f ffff ffffff
c. (σσ)(σ́σ)(σσ)(σσ)(σσ)	f! fff fffff
d. (σσ)(σσ́)(σσ)(σσ)(σσ)	f!f ffff
e. (σσ)(σσ)(σ́σ)(σσ)(σσ)	f! fff
f. (σσ)(σσ)(σσ́)(σσ)(σσ)	f!f
g. (σσ)(σσ)(σσ)(σ́σ)(σσ)	f!
☞ h. (σσ)(σσ)(σσ)(σσ́)(σσ)	
☞ i. (σσ)(σσ)(σσ)(σσ)(σ́σ)	
☞ j. (σσ)(σσ)(σσ)(σσ)(σσ́)	

Though the window effect is unexpected, it is not unwelcome. It is often the case that some type of phonological structure finds itself confined to a certain space at the edge of a form. The window effect provides a simple, general account in such situations. Perhaps the most familiar examples of windows are found in languages with trisyllabic stress windows, languages that confine primary stress to a form's first three syllables or a form's final three syllables. We consider such cases next in Sections 6.1–6.3. In Section 6.4, we consider a morphology-based window.

6.1 A General Approach to Trisyllabic Windows

Many languages restrict the position of accent to a three-syllable window at one edge or the other of the prosodic word. In some languages, the accent may occur on any of the syllables within the window. In others, it is clearly oriented toward the window's inner edge, preferring to occur on the innermost syllable.

Trisyllabic accent windows have three basic characteristics. The first is their size. In theories that exclude ternary feet, as most contemporary theories of metrical stress do, there is no prosodic category that regularly consists of three syllables and that, therefore, could be used to establish a trisyllabic domain directly. The proposed approach circumvents this problem by focusing on the gap between the accent and the relevant edge of the prosodic word rather than on the three-syllable domain itself. Since the maximum gap is two syllables, the standard disyllabic foot is the obvious choice to establish it. From the perspective of the proposed approach, then, a language with a trisyllabic accent window is essentially a language that insists that primary stress occur no further away from the relevant edge of the prosodic word than a single foot.

(5) Peripheral feet and the maximal gap in accent windows

Within the window

Initial	Final
(σ́σ)σσσσ	σσσσ(σσ́)
(σσ́)σσσσ	σσσσ(σ́σ)
(σσ)σ́σσσ	σσσσ́(σσ)

Outside the window

Initial	Final
(σσ)σσ́σσ	σσσ́σ(σσ)
(σσ)σσσ́σ	σσ́σσ(σσ)

The second characteristic of trisyllabic accent windows is that they can arise at either edge of the prosodic word. They arise at the left edge in Azkoitia Basque (Hualde 1998) and Kashaya (Buckley 1992, 1994). In Azkoitia Basque, for example, stress occurs on the rightmost of the first three syllables that is not also the word-final syllable.

(6) Initial accent window in Azkoitia Basque

a. óna 'good'
b. gizóna 'man'
c. katedrála 'cathedral'
d. melokótoye 'peach'
e. telebísixue 'television'

From the perspective of the proposed approach, languages with initial windows are those that confine accent to a position within or adjacent to an initial foot.

More commonly, stress windows arise at the right edge of the prosodic word, as in Macedonian, Maithili, and Pirahã (Everett and Everett 1984, Everett 1988). In the regular stress pattern of Macedonian, for example, stress prefers to occur on the leftmost of the final three syllables.

(7) Macedonian regular pattern

a.	zbór	'word'	b.	vodéničar	'miller'
	zbórot			vodeníčarot	
	zbórovi			vodeníčari	
	zboróvite			vodeničárite	

Macedonian also has an irregular pattern, however, were stress occurs on a lexically specified syllable as long as it is one of the final three. If suffixation pushes the lexically specified syllable to the left of the final three syllables, stress shifts to the antepenult by default.

(8) Macedonian irregular pattern

a.	citát	'quotation'	b.	romántik	'romantic'
	citátot			romántikot	
	citáti			romántici	
	citátite			romantícite	

From the perspective of the proposed approach, languages with final accent windows are those that confine primary stress to a position within or adjacent to a final foot.

The third characteristic of trisyllabic accent windows is that they can be either *truncated* or *full*. When a window is truncated, there are restrictions on – or outright prohibitions against – stressing the third syllable from the edge when it is heavy. The final stress windows of Latin, English, and Ancient Greek all have restrictions of this sort. In Latin, for example, the restriction can be seen in the different results for words where the penult and antepenult are both light and words where the penult and antepenult are both heavy. When both are light, as in (9a), stress appears on the antepenult, a result of Latin's preference to stress the leftmost of the final three syllables. When both are heavy, as in (9d), however, stress appears on the penult. There appear to be no languages with truncated initial windows.

(9) Truncated window in Latin

a.	LĹLH	komítium
b.	LH́H	amí:kus
c.	LH́LH	doméstikus
d.	LHH́H	mone:bá:mus

When a window is full, there are no particular restrictions on stressing third-from-the-edge syllables when they are heavy. The stress windows of Azkoitia Basque, Kashaya, Macedonian, Maithili, and Pirahã are all examples of full windows.

From the point of view of the proposed approach, whether a window is truncated or full depends on what counts as a position that is adjacent to a peripheral foot. If the accent need only occur on an adjacent syllable, the situation depicted in (5), then the window is full. If the stress must occur on the adjacent mora, however, the situation depicted in (10), then the window is truncated.

(10) Truncated accent windows

Initial	Final
Within the window	
(σ́σ).CVV.σ	σ.CVV.(σσ́)
(σσ́).CVV.σ	σ.CVV.(σ́σ)
(σσ).CV́V.σ	σ. CVV́.(σσ)
Outside the window	
(σσ).CVV́.σ	σ.CV́V.(σσ)
(σσ).CVV.σ́	σ́.CVV.(σσ)

Given the overwhelming preference when a heavy syllable is stressed for the stress to occupy the initial mora (Kager 1993, Hyde 2007a), the situation depicted in (10) helps to explain both why stress windows can be truncated in the first place and why it is only final windows that are ever actually truncated. In a language with a final window, stress would fall outside the window if it fell on the initial mora of bimoraic antepenult. This being the case, such languages take steps to avoid stress in this position. In Latin, as illustrated in (9d), stress will occupy a heavy penult instead. In trisyllabic shortening in English, a stressed bimoraic antepenult is shortened, making it monomoraic on the surface. In Ancient Greek, the accent appears over the final mora of a heavy antepenult rather than the initial. In contrast, in a language with an initial stress window, stress is still within the window when it falls on the initial mora of a heavy syllable. To fall outside the window, it would have to fall on the second mora, a circumstance that seems to be rare cross-linguistically.

The three characteristics of trisyllabic accent windows arise from a set of four opposite-edge RSA constraints: FINAL-WINDOW-σ and INITIAL-WINDOW-σ, given in (11a,b), and FINAL-WINDOW-μ and INITIAL-WINDOW-μ, given in (11c,d). The size of the accent window and the particular object confined to it are both determined by the categories being aligned. One aligned category, *head syllable*, indirectly establishes the maximal distance that can intervene between the other aligned category, *primary stress*, and the relevant edge of the prosodic word. Since the leftmost or rightmost head syllable must occur within the leftmost or rightmost foot, respectively, and the primary stress must be adjacent to it, the primary stress can occur no further from the relevant edge of the prosodic word than a single foot.

(11) a. FINAL-WINDOW-σ: $*\langle x_\omega, \sigma_{HD}, \sigma\rangle\ /x_\omega...\sigma...\sigma_{HD}$

'Assess a violation mark for every $\langle x_\omega, \sigma_{HD}, \sigma\rangle$ such that x_ω precedes σ_{HD} with σ intervening.'

b. INITIAL-WINDOW-σ: $*\langle\sigma_{HD}, x_\omega, \sigma\rangle\ /\ \sigma_{HD} \ldots \sigma \ldots x_\omega$

'Assess a violation mark for every $*\langle\sigma_{HD}, x_\omega, \sigma\rangle$ such that σ_{HD} precedes x_ω with σ intervening.'

c. FINAL-WINDOW-μ: $*\langle x_\omega, \sigma_{HD}, \mu\rangle\ /\ x_\omega \ldots \mu \ldots \sigma_{HD}$

'Assess a violation mark for every $\langle x_\omega, \sigma_{HD}, \mu\rangle$ such that x_ω precedes σ_{HD} with μ intervening.'

d. INITIAL-WINDOW-μ: $*\langle\sigma_{HD}, x_\omega, \mu\rangle\ /\ \sigma_{HD} \ldots \mu \ldots x_\omega$

'Assess a violation mark for every $*\langle\sigma_{HD}, x_\omega, \mu\rangle$ such that σ_{HD} precedes x_ω with μ intervening.'

Whether the accent window occurs at the left edge of the form or the right edge depends on the order in which the aligned categories appear in the prohibited configuration of misalignment. The FINAL-WINDOW constraints prohibit primary stress from preceding a misaligned head syllable, so they confine primary stress to the final foot or adjacent position, establishing accent windows at the right edge of the form. FINAL-WINDOW-σ is used to illustrate in (12).

(12)

	FINAL-WINDOW-σ
x x x x x x ☞ a. σ σ σ σ	
x x x x x x ☞ b. σ σ σ σ	
x x x x x x ☞ c. σ σ σ σ	
x x x x x x d. σ σ σ σ	*!

The INITIAL-WINDOW constraints prohibit feet from preceding a misaligned head syllable, so they confine primary stress to the initial foot or adjacent position, establishing accent windows at the left edge of the form. INITIAL-WINDOW-σ is used to illustrate in (13).

(13)

	INITIAL-WINDOW-σ
x x x x x x ☞ a. σ σ σ σ	
x x x x x x ☞ b. σ σ σ σ	
x x x x x x ☞ c. σ σ σ σ	
x x x x x x d. σ σ σ σ	*!

Finally, the particular separator category that a constraint specifies determines what counts as a position adjacent to a peripheral head syllable and, thus, whether the stress window is truncated or full. When the separator category is *syllable,* as it is in the INITIAL-WINDOW-σ and FINAL-WINDOW-σ constraints, the stress need only occur on the adjacent syllable to be appropriately aligned with a head syllable, as in (12) and (13), so the accent window is full. When the separator category is *mora,* however, as it is in INITIAL-WINDOW-μ and FINAL-WINDOW-μ, the stress must occur on the adjacent mora to be appropriately aligned with the peripheral head syllable, so the window is truncated. FINAL-WINDOW-μ is used to illustrate in (14).

(14)

	FINAL-WINDOW-μ
x (on final σ) x ☞ a. σ CVV σ σ	
x (on penultimate σ) x ☞ b. σ CVV σ σ	
x (on CVV) x ☞ c. σ CVV σ σ	
x (on CVV) x d. σ CVV σ σ	*!
x (on initial σ) x e. σ CVV σ σ	*!*

Although we have not explored the analyses of individual cases at this point, it should already be clear how the characteristics of trisyllabic accent windows connect to the properties of the opposite-edge alignment constraints in (11), indicating that it is indeed possible to provide a general account of the phenomenon. It should be noted, however, that the alignment account is not compatible with all approaches to metrical stress. Implicit in the analysis is the assumption that the grammar allows feet to be stressless. To establish an accent window, there must be a foot to carry the primary stress and there must be a foot to establish the maximal gap between the primary stress and relevant edge of the prosodic word. When the primary stress occurs on a window's innermost syllable, the post-peninitial syllable for initial windows and the antepenultimate syllable for final windows, the two feet are necessarily distinct. To accommodate languages where no secondary stress occurs in the gap, a typical but not a universal circumstance, it must be possible for the foot that establishes the gap to be stressless. In light of this requirement, I adopt the assumptions of the Weak Bracketing approach in examining individual cases below.

6.2 Full Windows

In this part of the discussion, we examine two cases that have full accent windows. The accent windows in Macedonian and Maithili are especially significant because they are straightforwardly obtained under the RSA approach to windows but they cannot be produced by potential alternative accounts. The inability of the alternatives to produce the Macedonian and Maithili windows demonstrates that they cannot provide a general approach.

6.2.1 Macedonian

In Macedonian, many forms exhibit a regular, predictable stress pattern, but there are also numerous cases of irregular, lexical stress. In the regular pattern, as we saw in (7), primary stress occurs on the antepenult in words longer than two syllables and on the initial syllable in shorter words. There appears to be no evidence of secondary stress. In the irregular pattern, as we saw in (8), primary stress occurs on a lexically specified syllable as long as it is also one of the final three. If suffixation pushes the stress beyond the three-syllable window, it returns to the antepenult by default.

To produce the antepenultimate stress of the regular Macedonian pattern, FINAL-WINDOW-σ creates a three-syllable window at the right edge of the word and x_ω-LEFT, given in (15), aligns the primary stress as far to the left within the window as possible.

(15) x_ω-LEFT: $*\langle\omega, x_\omega, \sigma\rangle$ / $[\ \ldots\ \sigma\ \ldots\ x_\omega\ \ldots\ ]_\omega$

'Assess a violation mark for every $\langle\omega, x_\omega, \sigma\rangle$ such that σ precedes x_ω within ω.'

As (16) illustrates, the ranking FINAL-WINDOW-σ >> x_ω-LEFT locates the primary stress just to left of a final stressless foot. FINAL-WINDOW-σ excludes (16d,e), where the primary stress fails to occur either within the final foot or adjacent to the final foot. As for the remaining competitors, x_ω-LEFT excludes (16a,b), because the stress occurs further to the left in (16w). The analysis in the tableau assumes that footing is trochaic. It should be noted, however, that the absence of a secondary stress pattern prevents us from being certain about preferred foot-type and parsing directionality.

(16)

	FINAL-WINDOW-σ	x_ω-LEFT
x (σ3) x (σ3) x x x x x ☞ w. σ σ σ σ σ (σσ)σ(σσ)		2
x (σ5) x (σ5) x x x x x a. σ σ σ σ σ (σσ)(σσ)(σ)		4 W
x (σ4) x (σ4) x x x x x b. σ σ σ σ σ σ(σσ)(σσ)		3 W
x (σ2) x (σ2) x x x x x c. σ σ σ σ σ σ(σσ)(σσ)	1 W	1 L
x (σ1) x (σ1) x x x x x d. σ σ σ σ σ σ(σσ)(σσ)	2 W	L

When we insert the constraint that requires faithfulness to a lexically stressed syllable into the ranking between FINAL-WINDOW-σ and x_ω-LEFT, the analysis also establishes the appropriate restrictions on irregular stress.

(17) IO-FAITH-x_ω

Every prosodic word-level grid entry in the input occurs in the same position in the output.

As (18) illustrates, FINAL-WINDOW-σ must dominate IO-FAITH-x_ω to prevent the stress from following the lexically specified syllable beyond the three-syllable window. FINAL-WINDOW-σ excludes the faithful candidate in such cases and, in conjunction with the low-ranked x_ω-LEFT (omitted from the tableau), returns stress to its default position over the antepenult.

(18)

σσσ́σσσ	FINAL-WINDOW-σ	IO-FAITH-x_ω

☞ w. x x (x x x) x x x x x / σ σ σ σ σ (stress on 3rd σ)
        x
        x
x x x x x
σ σ σ σ σ
		1

l.
    x
    x
x x x x x
σ σ σ σ σ
	1 W	L

As (19) illustrates, IO-FAITH-x_ω must dominate x_ω-LEFT to allow the lexically specified syllable to retain its stress when it is penultimate or final. In such cases, IO-FAITH-x_ω prevents x_ω-LEFT from pushing the stress to the left edge of the stress window.

(19)

σσσσσ́σ	IO-FAITH-x_ω	x_ω-LEFT

☞ w.
            x
            x
x x x x x
σ σ σ σ σ
		3

l.
        x
        x
x x x x x
σ σ σ σ σ
	1 W	2 L

To summarize, then, the proposed approach to opposite-edge alignment helps to establish the type of stress window appropriate for both the regular and irregular stress patterns of Macedonian. The ranking FINAL-WINDOW-σ >> x_ω-LEFT establishes the antepenultimate stress of the regular pattern, and the ranking FINAL-WINDOW-σ >> IO-FAITH-x_ω >> x_ω-LEFT confines lexical stress to a three-syllable window in the irregular pattern.

6.2.2 *Maithili*

The trochaic language Maithili (Jha 1940–1944, 1958, Hayes 1995) offers one of the clearest examples of a trisyllabic window for primary stress being accompanied by a pattern of secondary stresses.[1] The basic pattern locates stress on the initial syllable and every even-numbered syllable counting from the right, with the rightmost stress being primary. This basic pattern can be altered, however, by the preference of primary stress to occur on a heavy syllable. As (20c,d) illustrate, if the penult is heavy, it carries the primary stress, and the overall pattern is the same as if both the penult and the antepenult were light. As (20e) illustrates, however, if the penult is light and the antepenult heavy, primary stress shifts to the antepenult, leaving the penult with a secondary stress. Any secondary stress between the antepenult and the initial syllable shifts one syllable to the left.

(20) Maithili Pattern

a.	L̀ĹL	bɪ̀ndúlə̆	'a fabulous horse'
b.	H̀LĹL	bɑ̀:ɟ̆ɪtɒ́tʰɪ̆	'speak-3 FUT.'
c.	L̀L̀LH́L	dɑ̀hɪ̀nə̆bɑ́:rɪ̆	'the right one'
d.	H̀H́L	dè:kʰɑ́:rə̆	'seen'
e.	L̀L̀LH́L̀L	ɟ̆ɪmùtə̆bɑ́:hɒ̀nə̆	(proper name)

To focus on the implementation of the stress window, I will take the pattern of secondary stresses as given and consider only the most relevant possible variations in the position of primary stress. Given the pattern of secondary stresses, we can see that primary stress prefers to fall on the rightmost nonfinal heavy syllable, as long as it is one of the final three. If there is no nonfinal heavy syllable among the final three, then primary stress occurs on the rightmost nonfinal syllable.

As in Macedonian, we can use the opposite-edge alignment constraint FINAL-WINDOW-σ to produce the stress window in Maithili. The rightward orientation of the primary stress can be captured with the alignment constraint, x_{ω}-RIGHT, given in (21a), and the preference

1 Norwegian appears to be another case where a final stress window is accompanied by a pattern of secondary stresses. See Rice 2006 and Lunden 2006 for a description of the primary stress pattern and Lorentz 1996 for a description of the secondary stress pattern. The initial window of Kashaya is also accompanied by a pattern of secondary stresses.

of primary stress to fall on a heavy syllable can be captured with the STRESS-TO-WEIGHT constraint, given in (21b).[2]

(21) a. x_ω-RIGHT: $*\langle \omega, x_\omega, \sigma \rangle$ / $[\ \ldots x_\omega \ldots \sigma \ldots\ ]_\omega$

'Assess a violation mark for every $\langle \omega, x_\omega, \sigma \rangle$ such that x_ω precedes σ within ω.'

b. Stress-to-Weight

No x_ω occurs over the rightmost μ of σ.

The Maithili primary stress pattern emerges when FINAL-WINDOW-σ dominates STRESS-TO-WEIGHT and STRESS-TO-WEIGHT dominates x_ω-RIGHT.

Ranking FINAL-WINDOW-σ above STRESS-TO-WEIGHT prevents the weight of syllables that occur outside the trisyllabic window from affecting the position of primary stress. It prevents primary stress from moving to the left of the antepenult in order to satisfy the lower-ranked STRESS-TO-WEIGHT.

(22)

H̀LL̀L	FINAL-WINDOW-σ	STRESS-TO-WEIGHT
x x x x x x x ☞ w. H L L L		1
x x x x x x x l. H L L L	1 W	L

Ranking STRESS-TO-WEIGHT above x_ω-RIGHT allows the preference for primary stress to fall on a heavy syllable to overcome its basic rightward orientation. As (23) demonstrates, the higher-ranked STRESS-TO-WEIGHT prevents x_ω-RIGHT from positioning the primary stress on a light penult when a heavy antepenult is available.

2 STRESS-TO-WEIGHT is formulated here as a nonfinality constraint. If primary stress cannot occur on the final mora of a syllable, then a syllable must have at least two moras to support a primary stress. See Hyde (2007b) for arguments supporting this approach.

(23)

L̀L̀LH̀L̀L	Stress-to-Weight	x_ω-Right
x x x x x x x x x x x ☞ w. L L L H L L		2
x x x x x x x x x x x l. L L L H L L	1 W	1 L

As (24, 25) demonstrate, however, the lower-ranked x_ω-Right is able to draw primary stress onto the penult when the penult and the antepenult are both the same weight.

(24)

H̀H̀L	Stress-to-Weight	x_ω-Right
x x x x x x ☞ w. H H L		1
x x x x x x l. H H L		2 W

(25)

L̀L̀L	Stress-to-Weight	x_ω-Right
x x x x x x ☞ w. L L L	1	1
x x x x x x l. L L L	1	2 W

To summarize, then, we have seen that the proposed approach to opposite edge alignment also establishes the type of stress window appropriate for Maithili. The ranking Final-Window-σ >> Stress-to-Weight confines the primary stress to one of the final three syllables, and the ranking Stress-to-Weight >> x_ω-Right ensures that the primary stress occurs on a heavy syllable when one is present within the window.

6.2.3 Extended Lapse and Weak Local Parsing

Even though we have only examined two cases at this point, we can already see that potential alternatives cannot provide a general approach to trisyllabic windows. A nonfinality approach, used by Prince and Smolensky (1993/2004) to produce the stress window of Latin, fails to account for the restrictions on irregular stress in Macedonian. Extended lapse avoidance (Gordon 2002a, Kager 2005) and weak local parsing (Kager 1994, Green 1995, Green and Kenstowicz 1995) fail to account for the restrictions on primary stress in Maithili.

First, consider the role that F_{HD}-NONFINAL, given in (26a), might play in establishing regular antepenultimate stress.

(26) a. F_{HD}-NONFINAL (Prince and Smolensky 1993/2004)
The head foot is not final in the prosodic word.

b. F_{HD}-RIGHT: $*\langle\omega, F_{HD}, \sigma\rangle$ / $[\ldots F_{HD} \ldots \sigma \ldots]_{\omega}$
'Assess a violation mark for every $\langle\omega, F_{HD}, \sigma\rangle$ such that F_{HD} precedes σ within ω.'

When F_{HD}-NONFINAL dominates F_{HD}-RIGHT, repeated in (26b), it prevents the head foot from including the final syllable, as in (27b). Assuming that the head foot is trochaic, then, the primary stress can occur no closer to the right edge than the antepenult. By insisting that the head foot occur as close to the right edge as possible, F_{HD}-RIGHT excludes candidates, like (27a), where the primary stress occurs to the left of the antepenult. The result is the regular antepenultimate stress of Macedonian.

(27)

	F_{HD}-NONFINAL	F_{HD}-RIGHT
☞ w. σσσ(σ́σ)σ		1
a. σσ(σ́σ)σσ		2 W
b. σσσσ(σ́σ)	1 W	L

The problem arises in accounting for the irregular Macedonian pattern: attempting to use F_{HD}-NONFINAL to restrict lexical stress to a three-syllable window results in a ranking conflict. As (28) illustrates, IO-FAITH-X_{ω} must dominate F_{HD}-NONFINAL in order to allow irregular stress on the penult or the ultima.

(28)

σσσσσ́σ	IO-Faith-x_{ω}	F_{HD}-Nonfinal
☞ w. σσσσ(σ́σ)		1
l. σσσ(σ́σ)σ	1 W	L

As (29) indicates, however, when the lexically specified syllable has drifted further to the left, it is necessary to rank FHd-Nonfinal above F_{HD}-Right and to rank F_{HD}-Right above IO-Faith-x_{ω} in order to return the primary stress to its default position over the antepenult.

(29)

σσσ́σσσ	F_{HD}-Nonfinal	F_{HD}-Right	IO-Faith-x_{ω}
☞ w. σσσ(σ́σ)σ		1	1
a. σσ(σ́σ)σσ		2 W	L
b. σσσσ(σ́σ)	1 W	L	1

IO-Faith-x_{ω} must dominate F_{HD}-Nonfinal, then, so that a lexically specified stress is retained when it occurs on any of the final three syllables, but F_{HD}-Nonfinal must dominate IO-Faith-x_{ω} in order to return stress to its default location when the lexically specified syllable drifts outside the window. These conflicting ranking requirements make it impossible to implement the analysis, demonstrating that nonfinality is inadequate as a general approach to stress windows.

The demonstration that extended lapse avoidance and weak local parsing are also inadequate is even more straightforward. Some stress windows are accompanied by a pattern of secondary stresses with binary alternation. In the case of Maithili, there can even be a secondary stress within the stress window intervening between the primary stress and the right edge of the prosodic word. Since the distance between stresses and the distance between peripheral stresses and word edges is actually smaller than that allowed by extended lapse avoidance or weak local parsing, neither can be used to establish the stress window.

The extended lapse avoidance approach is the more direct of the two. *Extended-Lapse-Right simply prohibits configurations where the final three syllables of a form are all stressless.[3]

(30) *Extended-Lapse-Right

A maximum of two unstressed syllables separates the rightmost stress from the right edge of the stress domain.

3 The constraint is *Extended-Lapse-Right in Gordon (2002a) and *Final-Long-Lapse in Kager (2005).

As (31) illustrates, assuming that the primary stress is the only stress, *EXTENDED-LAPSE-RIGHT is only satisfied when the primary stress occurs over one of the final three syllables, effectively establishing a trisyllabic window.

(31)

	*EXTENDED-LAPSE-RIGHT
☞ a. σσσσσσ́	
☞ b. σσσσσ́σ	
☞ c. σσσσ́σσ	
d. σσσ́σσσ	*
e. σσ́σσσσ	*

The weak local parsing approach is less direct. WEAK-LOCAL-PARSING prohibits a form from containing adjacent stray syllables.[4]

(32) WEAK-LOCAL-PARSING

For every two adjacent syllables, one must be parsed into a foot.

As (33) illustrates, assuming that the primary stress is the only stress, the constraint can be satisfied only when the final foot occurs no more than one syllable away from the right edge. If the final foot is the head foot, WEAK-LOCAL-PARSING effectively establishes a trisyllabic window for the primary stress.

(33)

	WEAK-LOCAL-PARSING
☞ a. σ(σσ)σ(σ́σ)	
☞ b. (σσ)σ(σ́σ)σ	
c. (σσ)(σ́σ)σσ	*

The problem for such approaches arises when other considerations impose more severe restrictions on stresses or feet than those imposed by *EXTENDED-LAPSE-RIGHT or WEAK-LOCAL-PARSING. If *EXTENDED-LAPSE-RIGHT and WEAK-LOCAL-PARSING do not actually play a role in establishing the maximum distance allowed between the rightmost stress and the right edge of the word, they cannot establish a stress window.

4 WEAK-LOCAL-PARSING represents the LAPSE constraint of Green (1995) and Green and Kenstowicz (1995) and the PARSE-2 constraint of Kager (1994). Though there is a slight difference between the two constraints, both essentially insist on weak local parsing (see Hayes 1995 for discussion).

In the case of Maithili, for example, neither *Extended-Lapse-Right nor Weak-Local-Parsing can restrict the primary stress's position. Since no more than one syllable ever occurs between the rightmost stress and the end of the word, *Extended-Lapse-Right has no influence over the position of the primary stress. It is satisfied regardless of which stress is primary. Similarly, since parsing is exhaustive, Weak-Local-Parsing has no influence over the position of the primary stress.

(34)

LLLHLL	*Ex-Lapse-Right	Wk-Local-Parsing
☞ a. (L̀)(L̀L)(H̀)(ĹL)		
☞ b. (L̀)(L̀L)(H́)(L̀L)		
☞ c. (L̀)(ĹL)(H̀)(L̀L)		
☞ d. (Ĺ)(L̀L)(H̀)(L̀L)		

Since *Extended-Lapse-Right and Weak-Local-Parsing cannot effectively restrict the position of primary stress in languages that have a binary pattern of secondary stresses, neither offers a general approach to stress windows.

6.3 Truncated Windows

In this part of the discussion, we examine three different cases of truncated accent windows. English, Latin, and Ancient Greek employ different strategies for ensuring that accent occurs no further to the left than the mora adjacent to the final foot. While the discussion of the English and Latin cases will be relatively brief, the discussion of Ancient Greek will be more extensive. In addition to its trisyllabic accent window, Ancient Greek has a morphology-based accent window, which I will address in Section 6.4. Discussion of the trisyllabic window in Ancient Greek provides important background for discussion of the morphology-based window further below.

6.3.1 Trisyllabic Shortening in English

When stress falls on a heavy syllable, it appears that the preference in most languages is for stress to fall on the syllable-initial mora. The preference is well-motivated. In most languages, a syllable's most sonorous segment is associated with the initial mora, at least in cases where sonority distinctions can be made. If a language maintains a truncated accent window, however, the preference can come into conflict with the window's restrictions. Placing the accent on the initial mora of a heavy antepenult positions it outside of the window.

There are essentially three options that a language might take to avoid stressing the initial mora of a heavy antepenult: it can shift the accent to the final mora, it can shift the accent to another syllable, or it can make the antepenult light. The last option can be found in the phenomenon of trisyllabic shortening in English. In many words in English, a stressed vowel is long when penultimate or final, but it shortens when it becomes antepenultimate under suffixation. A few examples are given in (35).

(35)	a.	sərí:n ~ sərɛ́nɪti	'serene ~ serenity'
	b.	profé:n ~ profǽnɪti	'profane ~ profanity'
	c.	sé:n ~ sǽnɪti	'sane ~ sanity'
	d.	ó:mən ~ ɔ́mənəs	'omen ~ ominous'

I will assume that the accent maintains its position in suffixed forms like those in (35) due a preference for the accent to be faithful to its position in the base form. The relevant faithfulness constraint, OO-FAITH-x_ω, is given in (36a). The constraint that captures the preference for stress to fall on syllable-initial moras, FIRST-μ, is given in (36b). Rather than violating OO-FAITH-x_ω by shifting stress to another syllable or FIRST-μ by shifting stress to the final mora of the heavy antepenult, English violates, MAX-μ, given in (36c). It deletes the final mora from the heavy antepenult to allow the stress to fall within the accent window.

(36) a. OO-FAITH-x_ω

Every x_ω in the base form occurs in the same position in the derived form.

b. FIRST-μ

In a stressed σ, stress falls on the σ-initial μ.

c. MAX-μ

Every μ in the input is present in the output.

The desired result emerges when FINAL-WINDOW-μ, FIRST-μ, and OO-FAITH-x_ω all dominate MAX-μ. FINAL-WINDOW-μ excludes the candidate where stress falls on the initial mora of a heavy antepenult, as in (37c). Because a mora intervenes between the stress and the final head syllable, it falls outside the window. FIRST-μ excludes candidate (37b) where stress shifts to the final mora of the heavy antepenult, and OO-FAITH-x_ω excludes candidate (37a) where stress shifts to the penultimate syllable. Candidate (37w), which shortens the antepenult at the expense of MAX-μ to position the stress inside the window, correctly emerges as the winner.

(37)

<table>
<tr><th>σ.CV́V.σσ</th><th>FIN-WIN-μ</th><th>FIRST-μ</th><th>OO-FTH-x_{ω}</th><th>MAX-μ</th></tr>
<tr><td>x
x
x x x x
☞ w. σ CV σ σ</td><td></td><td></td><td></td><td>1</td></tr>
<tr><td>x
x
x x x x x
a. σ CVV σ σ</td><td></td><td></td><td>1 W</td><td>L</td></tr>
<tr><td>x
x
x x x x x
b. σ CVV σ σ</td><td></td><td>1 W</td><td></td><td>L</td></tr>
<tr><td>x
x
x x x x x
c. σ CVV σ σ</td><td>1 W</td><td></td><td></td><td>L</td></tr>
</table>

6.3.2 Latin

Where English shortens a heavy antepenult to bring the accent within a truncated window, Latin shifts the accent to a heavy penult, if one is available. In general, accent in Latin is left-oriented. It prefers to occur as far to the left within the accent window as possible. If the penult and the antepenult are both light, for example, as in (38a, c, f), the stress falls on the antepenult. There are two restrictions on Latin's leftward orientation, however. First, stress prefers to fall on a heavy syllable. If the antepenult is light and the penult heavy, as in (38b), stress falls on the penult. Second, as mentioned above, stress prefers to avoid a heavy antepenult. If the antepenult is heavy and the penult light, as in (38d), the preference to stress a heavy syllable is overriding, and the antepenult is stressed. If the both the antepenult and penult are heavy, however, as in (38e), the penult is stressed. Note that stress never falls on the final syllable (except in monosyllabic words). The avoidance of final stress indicates a high-ranked NON-FINALITY constraint, which need not concern us here.

(38)
a. ĹLH — símula:
b. LH́H — amí:kus
c. LĹLH — komítium
d. LH́LH — doméstikus
e. LHH́H — mone:bá:mus
f. HLĹLH — partikípium

As (39) demonstrates, to ensure that stress occupies a heavy penult in Latin, rather than a heavy antepenult, FINAL-WINDOW-μ, FIRST-μ, and MAX-μ must all dominate x_ω-LEFT. FINAL-WINDOW-μ excludes candidate (39c), where stress falls on the initial mora of the heavy antepenult, and FIRST-μ excludes candidate (39b), where stress falls on the final mora of the heavy antepenult. MAX-μ excludes candidate (39a), which shortens the antepenult so that no mora intervenes between the accent and the final head syllable. Candidate (39w), which stresses the heavy syllable at the expense of x_ω-LEFT, correctly emerges as the winner.

(39)

σ.CVV.CVV.σ	FIN-WIN-μ	FIRST-μ	MAX-μ	x_ω-LEFT
x (over 2nd V of 2nd CVV) x x xx xx x ☞ w. σ CVV CVV σ				2
x x x x xx x a. σ CV CVV σ			W 1	L 1
x (over 2nd V of 1st CVV) x x xx xx x b. σ CVV CVV σ		W 1		L 1
x (over 1st V of 1st CVV) x x xx xx x c. σ CVV CVV σ	W 1			L 1

To ensure that a heavy penult is stressed when the antepenult is light, as (40) demonstrates, it is necessary that STRESS-TO-WEIGHT dominate x_ω-LEFT. STRESS-TO-WEIGHT prevents x_ω-LEFT from drawing the stress as far to the left within the window as possible, as in (40l), in order to ensure that the stressed syllable is heavy, as in (40w).

(40)

CV.CVV.σ	STRESS-TO-WEIGHT	x_ω-LEFT
x x x xx x ☞ w. CV CVV σ		1
x x x xx x l. CV CVV σ	1 W	L

Finally, STRESS-TO-WEIGHT must also dominate FINAL-WINDOW-μ. The high-ranked STRESS-TO-WEIGHT prevents FINAL-WINDOW-μ from pushing stress to a light penult, as in (41l), when a heavy antepenult is available. Note, however, that stress never shifts to the left of the antepenult to occupy a heavy syllable. This indicates that a full stress window is also at work in Latin and that FINAL-WINDOW-σ dominates STRESS-TO-WEIGHT. FINAL-WINDOW-μ can be violated if there is no other option for stressing a heavy syllable, but FINAL-WINDOW-σ cannot.

(41)

σ.CVV.CV.σ	STRESS-TO-WEIGHT	FINAL-WINDOW-μ
x x x xx x x ☞ w. σ CVV CV σ		1
x x x xx x x l. σ CVV CV σ	1 W	L

6.3.3 Ancient Greek

The final option to avoid accenting a non-final mora in a heavy antepenultimate syllable is to shift stress to the final mora. This is the option found in Ancient Greek (AG). The analysis of the AG accent window is a bit more complex than the analyses of the cases discussed above. There are two reasons. First, the AG accent was tonal. The analysis assumes, however, following Steriade (1988), that the high tone corresponds to a word-level stress. In Section 6.4, this assumption will allow us to account for restrictions on the proximity of accents in terms of clash avoidance. To capture the connection between word-level stress and high tone, the analysis assumes that the x_ω-HIGH-TONE constraint, given in (42), is undominated. Most of the constraints responsible for positioning the AG accent are constraints that refer directly to word-level stress rather than the associated high tone.

(42) x_ω-HIGH-TONE:

Every x_ω corresponds to a high tone.

Second, the size of the AG window can vary depending on the weight of the word-final syllable. When the ultima is light, the accent may fall on the ultima, as in (43a), the penult, as in (43b,c), or the final mora of the antepenult, as in (43d-g). It may not occur further to the left than the final mora of the antepenult. (In final position, syllables with long vowels, syllables with diphthongs, and syllables closed with two consonants are heavy. In nonfinal position, only syllables with long vowels or diphthongs are heavy.) Example forms are taken from Steriade (1988).

(43)	a.	hodós	'road'
	b.	óikos	'house'
	c.	paidískos	'little child'
	d.	ánthroopos	'man'
	e.	ángelos	'messenger'
	f.	eépreiros	'continent'
	g.	poikilóstolos	'with variegated prow'

When the ultima is heavy, the window shrinks by a syllable. The accent may fall on the ultima, as in (44a,b), or the final mora of the penult, as in (44c,d). It may not occur further to the left than the final mora of the penult.

(44)	a.	boteér	'herdsman'
	b.	hodóu	'road-GEN'
	c.	patrídoon	'fatherland-GEN PLUR'
	d.	daímoon	'god-GEN PLUR'

While the accent in verb forms is typically recessive – it occurs as far to the left within the window as possible – the accent in noun forms can be either recessive or inherent. It can be located on a particular affix or on the root just before the derivational affix. Inherent accents are also subject to the window. When an inherent accent would fall outside the window, it shifts from its underlying position to the leftmost position within the window.

(45) iskhuuró tatoon → iskhuurotátoon 'the most powerful-GEN PLUR'

In terms of the RSA approach, the accent window in Ancient Greek consists of a final foot and the mora adjacent to the final foot. When the final syllable is light, the final foot is maximally disyllabic, as illustrated in (46), and the accent may occur as far to the left as the final mora of the antepenult.

(46) Ancient Greek accent window: final light syllable

Within the window

σ.CVV(σ.CV́)

σ.CVV(σ́.CV)

σ.CVV́(σ.CV)

Outside the window

σ.CV́V(σ.CV)

σ́.CVV(σ.CV)

When the final syllable is heavy, however, the final foot is monosyllabic, as illustrated in (47), and the accent may only occur as far to the left as the final mora of the penult.

(47) Ancient Greek accent window: final heavy syllable

Within the window

σ.CVV(CVV́)

σ.CVV(CV́V)

σ.CVV́(CVV)

Outside the window

σ.CV́V(CVV)

σ́.CVV(CVV)

As in English and Latin, FINAL-WINDOW-μ is responsible for establishing the accent window in AG. Since it prohibits a mora from intervening between the primary stress and a head syllable to its right, the primary stress can occur no further to the left than the mora adjacent to the head syllable of the final foot. The distance that can occur between the primary stress and the right edge of the word, then, depends on the position of the head syllable. If the head syllable of the final foot is penultimate, then two syllables can separate the primary stress from the right edge of the word. If the head syllable is ultimate, however, then only a single syllable may separate the primary stress from the right edge. The position of the head syllable is determined by the interaction of two constraints, WEIGHT-TO-HEAD, given in (48), which requires heavy syllables to be the head syllables of feet, and x_ω-LEFT, which draws primary stress as far to the left as possible.

(48) WEIGHT-TO-HEAD

Every bimoraic σ is the head syllable of a *F*.

The ranking appropriate for the AG window positions WEIGHT-TO-HEAD with FINAL-WINDOW-μ above x_ω-LEFT.

The tableau in (49) illustrates the results of the ranking for recessive forms with a light ultima: the accent window expands to its maximum size, allowing the primary stress (and its associated high tone) to fall on the antepenult. The two constraints most active in producing this result are FINAL-WINDOW-μ and x_ω-LEFT. FINAL-WINDOW-μ prevents the primary stress from occurring further to the left then the mora adjacent to the final foot. This is true whether the final foot is disyllabic, as in (49d), or monosyllabic, as in (49e). Since the ultima is light, however, there is no need to make it a head syllable to satisfy WEIGHT-TO-HEAD. This allows x_ω-LEFT not only to draw the primary stress as far to the left within the accent window as possible but also to insist that the head syllable of the final foot occur as far to the left as possible, expanding the foot that defines the gap between stress and edge to its maximum size. In other words, it not only excludes candidates (49a,b), where the primary stress occurs within the final foot rather than on the adjacent mora, but it also excludes candidate (49c), where the final foot is monosyllabic, rather than the disyllabic maximum. Candidate (49w), which minimally violates x_ω-LEFT while remaining within the largest possible accent window, emerges as the winner.

(49)

poikilostolos	WEIGHT-TO-HD	FIN-WIND-μ	x_ω-LEFT
x (lo) x (lo) xx x x x x ☞ w. poi ki lo sto los			2
x (sto) x (sto) xx x x x x a. poi ki lo sto los			3 W
x (los) x (los) xx x x x x b. poi ki lo sto los			4 W
x (sto) x (sto) xx x x x x c. poi ki lo sto los			3 W
x (ki) x (ki) xx x x x x d. poi ki lo sto los		1 W	1 L
x (lo) x (lo) xx x x x x e. poi ki lo sto los		1 W	2

The tableau in (50) illustrates the results for recessive forms with a heavy ultima: the accent window shrinks, forcing the main stress to fall on the penult. In this case, WEIGHT-TO-HEAD insists that the ultima be a head syllable. It prevents the final foot from expanding to include the penult, as in (50c), effectively restricting the maximum gap between stress and edge to a single syllable. Since the final foot must be monosyllabic, FINAL-WINDOW-μ prevents the primary stress from occurring to the left of the mora adjacent to the final syllable, as in (50b). Finally, x_ω-LEFT draws the primary stress as far to the left within the basic window as possible; it excludes candidate (50a), where the primary stress occurs within the final foot, allowing candidate (50w), where the primary stress is adjacent to the final foot, to emerge as the winner.

(50)

lipothriks	WEIGHT-TO-HD	FINAL-WINDOW-µ	x_ω-LEFT
x x x x xx ☞ w. li po thriks			1
x x x x xx a. li po thriks			2 W
x x x x xx b. li po thriks		1 W	L
x x x x xx c. li po thriks	1 W		L

Two additional constraints influence accent placement in a number of forms. The first is FIRST-µ. In AG, the preference for stress to fall on syllable-initial moras is reflected in the default position of the accent in recessive forms that are not actually long enough to contain an accent window of the largest possible size. In the form *óikos* 'house', for example, the ultima is light, and the basic window would extend through the final mora of the antepenult, if there were a sufficient number of syllables. Since *óikos* contains only two syllables, the accent can only occur as far left as the penult, and it always occupies the initial mora in such cases. Similarly, in the form *phóos* 'light', the ultima is heavy, and the basic window would extend through the final mora of the penult, if there were a sufficient number of syllables. Since *phóos* has only a single syllable, the accent must occur on the ultima, where it occupies the initial mora.

When a form with recessive accent has a sufficient number of syllables that the accent window can extend to its maximum possible size, the accent always occurs on the final mora of the syllable at the edge of the window – the final mora of the antepenult when the ultima is light and the final mora of the penult when the ultima is heavy. This indicates that the preferences of FIRST-µ are subject to those of both FINAL-WINDOW-µ and x_ω-LEFT.

Consider the form *anthroópoon* 'man-GEN PLUR' in the tableau in (51). Since the ultima is heavy, WEIGHT-TO-HEAD requires that it be a head syllable. (The tableau only contains candidates where Weight-to-Head is satisfied.) While First-μ would prefer that the primary stress move one mora to the left or one mora to the right, so it can fall on a syllable-initial mora, these options are ruled out by the Final-Window-μ and x_ω-Left. Moving the accent one mora to the left, as in candidate (51b), violates Final-Window-μ. Moving the accent one mora to the right, as in candidate (51a), incurs an extra violation of x_ω-Left. The result is accent on the final mora of the penult, as in (51w).

(51)

<table>
<tr><th>anthroopoon</th><th>Final-Window-μ</th><th>x_ω-Left</th><th>First-μ</th></tr>
<tr><td>x
x
x xx xx
☞ w. an throo poon
| | |</td><td></td><td>1</td><td>1</td></tr>
<tr><td>x
x
x xx xx
a. an throo poon
| | |</td><td></td><td>W
2</td><td>L</td></tr>
<tr><td>x
x
x xx xx
b. an throo poon
| | |</td><td>W
1</td><td>1</td><td>L</td></tr>
</table>

The final constraint that influences accent placement in AG is IO-Faith-x_ω, the constraint responsible for preserving the position of inherent accents on the surface. Since inherent accents only maintain their position when they occur inside the basic window in AG, and default to the innermost position within the window when they do not, it is necessary to rank the constraints that establish the window and its size – Final-Window-μ and Weight-to-Head – above IO-Faith-x_ω.

Consider the derivation of *iskhuurotátoon* 'the most powerful-gen plur' in (52). Candidates (52a,b) are faithful to the position of the inherent accent, which occurs over the antepenult, but are excluded by the constraints establishing the accent window. Since the ultima is heavy in this case, Weight-to-Head requires that it be a head syllable. It excludes candidate (52b), which satisfies Final-Window-μ by making the penult the head of the final foot rather than the ultima. Candidate (52a) satisfies Weight-to-Head, but it is excluded by Final-Window-μ because its accent occurs to the left of the mora adjacent to the final foot. Although candidate (52w) violates IO-Faith-x_ω by shifting the primary stress to the penult, it falls within the window established by the higher-ranked constraints and emerges as the winner. Note that the accent's position on the penult rather than the ultima is due to x_ω-LEFT, which, as we shall see just below, actually ranks below IO-FAITH-x_ω.

(52) iskhuuróotatoon	WGHT-TO-HD	FIN-WIN-μ	IO-FTH-x_ω
x x x xx x x xx ☞ w. is khuu ro ta toon			1
x x x xx x x xx a. is khuu ro ta toon		1 W	L
x x x xx x x xx b. is khuu ro ta toon	1 W		L

To complete the analysis, it is necessary to determine the rankings that allow an underlying primary stress to maintain its position on the surface when it occurs within the basic window. The necessary ranking is IO-FAITH-x_ω >> x_ω-LEFT >> FIRST-μ. Consider the derivation of *boteér* 'herdsman.' Since the form contains a heavy ultima, the accent window extends only through the final mora of the penult. As (53) indicates, ranking IO-FAITH-x_ω above x_ω-LEFT prevents the latter from shifting the inherent primary stress as far to the left as possible within the window, in this case, shifting it from the ultima to the penult, as in (53b). Ranking IO-FAITH-x_ω above FIRST-μ prevents the inherent primary stress from shifting to a syllable-initial mora, in this case, from the final to the initial mora of the ultima, as in (53a). Candidate (53w), where the primary stress maintains its underlying position, emerges as the winner.

(53)

boteér	IO-FAITH-x_{ω}	x_{ω}-LEFT	FIRST-μ
x x x xx ☞ w. bo teer		1	1
x x x xx a. bo teer	1 W	1	L
x x x xx b. bo teer	1 W	L	L

The rankings necessary for creating and enforcing the accent window in AG are summarized in (54).

(54) WEIGHT-TO-HEAD, FINAL-WINDOW-μ >> IO-FAITH-x_{ω} >> x_{ω}-LEFT >> FIRST-μ

Ranking WEIGHT-TO-HEAD and FINAL-WINDOW-μ above IO-FAITH-x_{ω} and x_{ω}-LEFT confines primary stress to an accent window at the right edge of the word, whether the accent is inherent or recessive. The window consists of a single foot plus an adjacent mora, but the size of the foot can vary, due to WEIGHT-TO-HEAD, depending on the weight of the final syllable. When the final syllable is light, the final foot can be disyllabic, and the primary stress can occur as far to the left as the final mora of the antepenult. When the final syllable is heavy, however, the final foot must be monosyllabic, and the primary stress can only occur as far to the left as the final mora of the penult. While FIRST-μ determines the default location for accent within a heavy syllable, it can be violated to preserve the position of inherent stress or to ensure that the accent actually falls within the accent window.

6.4 A Morphology-Based Window

Window effects can also arise from opposite-edge RSA constraints applying to other types of categories, opposite-edge alignment of morphological or syntactic categories. In verb second languages, for example, the verb must appear just to the right of the leftmost constituent. In

Wackernagel phenomena, much the same restriction is placed on clitics: the clitic must occur just to the right of the leftmost base. Both verb second and Wackernagel phenomena can be analyzed in terms of a window effect. In infixing languages, restrictions on the depth of infixation are also suggestive of window effects. Rather than reviewing each of these possibilities here, I will instead focus on the accent window established by enclitics in Ancient Greek. While the enclitic window resembles the foot-based window discussed just above, a careful examination reveals that it is a distinct window effect.

6.4.1 The Enclitic Window in Ancient Greek

In Ancient Greek, when an enclitic is added to a base form, a new accent window emerges, and this can result in the appearance of an additional high tone in certain cases. When the original high tone of the base falls to the left of the base-final syllable, a second high tone may occur on the final syllable of the base or the final syllable of a disyllabic enclitic. The preference seems to be for the new high tone to fall on the final syllable of the base, as in (55), and it will do so unless it would be on the mora adjacent to the original high tone, as in (56a), would occur on a heavy base-final syllable, as in (56b), or both, as in (56c). In these situations, the new high tone occurs on the second syllable of a disyllabic enclitic.

(55)	a.	óikós tis	'some house'
	b.	óikós tinos	'someone's house'
	c.	eépeirós tis	'some continent'
	d.	eépeirós tinos	'someone's continent'
	e.	ángelós tis	'some messenger'
	f.	ángelós tinos	'someone's messenger'

(56)	a.	phílos tinós	'someone's friend'
	b.	phóiniks tinós	'someone's phoenix'
	c.	daímoon tinós	'someone's god'

In general, there are two situations where no new high tone is added. The first is when the original high tone falls on the base-final syllable, as in (57). The second is when the enclitic is monosyllabic and the new high tone cannot be positioned on the base-final syllable, as in (58). The circumstances in which a new high tone cannot occur on a base-final syllable are the same as those mentioned above. The new high tone would be on the mora adjacent to the original high tone, as in (58a); the new high tone would occur on a base-final heavy syllable, as in (58b); or both, as in (58c). Unlike the situation with disyllabic enclitics, however, a new high tone cannot occur on a monosyllabic enclitic, so the second high tone is absent altogether.

(57)	a.	phóos tis	'some light'
	b.	phóos tinos	'someone's light'
	c.	hodós tis	'some road'
	d.	hodós tinos	'someone's road'

(58)	a.	phílos tis	'some friend'
	b.	phóiniks tis	'some phoenix'
	c.	daímoon tis	'some god'

The enclitic window differs from the trisyllabic window discussed in Section 6.3.3 both in the category that defines the maximum size of the domain between accent and edge and in the category that defines the position that counts as adjacent to that domain. Where the foot defined the maximum distance between stress and edge in the trisyllabic window, via its head syllable, and the mora defined the relevant adjacent position, the enclitic defines the maximum distance in the enclitic window and the syllable defines the relevant adjacent position. In terms of the RSA approach, then, the enclitic window consists of the enclitic and the syllable adjacent to the enclitic.

When the enclitic is disyllabic a second high tone may be added if the original falls to the left of the final three syllables. ("e" denotes an enclitic syllable in (59) and the next several examples.)

(59) Ancient Greek enclitic window: disyllabic enclitic

Original high tone within the window

σσσ́ ee

Original high tone outside the window

σσ́σ eé

σ́σσ́ ee

When the enclitic is monosyllabic, a second high tone may be added when the original falls to the left of the final two syllables.

(60) Ancient Greek enclitic window: monosyllabic enclitic

Original high tone within the window

σσσ́ e

Original high tone outside the window

σ́σσ́ e

The RSA constraint responsible for establishing the enclitic window is ENCLITIC-WINDOW, given in (61).

(61) ENCLITIC-WINDOW: $*\langle x_\omega, Enc, \sigma\rangle$ / $x_\omega \ldots \sigma \ldots Enc$

'Assess a violation mark for every $\langle x_\omega, Enc, \sigma\rangle$ such that x_ω precedes *Enc* with σ intervening.'

Since ENCLITIC-WINDOW is violated whenever a syllable intervenes between the primary stress and an enclitic to its right, the maximal gap between primary stress and the right edge of the base + enclitic form depends on the size of the enclitic. When the enclitic is disyllabic, as in (62), the maximal gap between stress and edge is also disyllabic, and ENCLITIC-WINDOW allows the primary stress to occur on any one of the final three syllables. To emphasize how the window is established, only the head foot is shown in (62) and (63).

(62)

...σσ ee	ENCLITIC-WINDOW
x (on final e) x ☞ a. σ σ e e (head foot: final e)	
x (on first e) x ☞ b. σ σ e e (head foot: e e)	
x (on second σ) x ☞ c. σ σ e e (head foot: σ e)	
x (on first σ) x d. σ σ e e (head foot: σ σ)	*!

When the enclitic is monosyllabic, as in (63), the maximal gap is also monosyllabic. ENCLITIC-WINDOW allows the primary stress to occur on either of the final two syllables.

(63)

...σσσ e	ENCLITIC-WINDOW
☞ a. σ σ σ e (x x over e; e linked)	
☞ b. σ σ σ e (x x over final σ; σ linked to σ and e)	
c. σ σ σ e (x x over penultimate σ; σ linked to σ and σ)	*!

6.4.2 *Establishing the Enclitic Window*

A key assumption of the proposed analysis of base + enclitic combinations is that the addition of a second high tone indicates a shift in the position of the word-level stress. The prosodic word-level grid entry shifts from its original position, leaving the original high tone in place, and the undominated constraint x_{ω}-HIGH-TONE ensures that a new high tone accompanies the word-level stress in its new position. The constraint that is violated when the prosodic word-level gridmark shifts from its original position is the output-output faithfulness constraint OO-FAITH-x_{ω}, repeated in (64).

(64) OO-FAITH-x_{ω}
Every x_{ω} in the base form occurs in the same position in the derived form.

Main stress shift is triggered when the original main stress falls outside the enclitic window, indicating that ENCLITIC-WINDOW dominates OO-FAITH-x_{ω}. To illustrate, consider the derivation of *ángelós tinos* 'someone's messenger' in (65). The base form, *ángelos,* has its primary stress on its antepenultimate syllable, placing it two syllables outside the enclitic window when *tinos* is attached. The candidate that maintains the primary stress in its original position in the base + enclitic form, candidate (65l), violates ENCLITIC-WINDOW and is excluded. Candidate (65w) shifts the primary stress to the innermost syllable of the enclitic window. Though it violates OO-FAITH-x_{ω}, it satisfies the higher-ranked ENCLITIC-WINDOW and emerges as the winner.

(65) Base output: ángelos Derived output: ángelós tinos

angelos tinos	ENCLITIC-WINDOW	OO-FAITH-X$_{\omega}$
x x x ☞ w. an ge los ti nos		1
x x l. an ge los ti nos	2 W	L

When main stress shift occurs, as in (65), the high tone of the original main stress is preserved in its original position and a new high tone accompanies the new main stress. Preservation of the original high tone is due to an undominated output-output faithfulness constraint, OO-FAITH-σ_{HD}-TONE, which requires that head syllables present in the base form maintain the same tones in the base + enclitic form.

(66) OO-FAITH-σ_{HD}-TONE

Every σ_{HD} in the base form maintains the same tonal specification in the derived form.

Though the constraint enforcing the foot-based window discussed in Section 6.3.3 is still active in base + enclitic forms, main stress does not necessarily shift when its original position lies outside the foot-based window. It only shifts if it lies outside the enclitic window. While ENCLITIC-WINDOW must dominate OO-FAITH-X$_{\omega}$, then, OO-FAITH-X$_{\omega}$ must in turn dominate FINAL-WINDOW-μ. Consider a case of the failure of stress shift in (67). The primary stress in the base form, *phóos,* occurs on the ultima, meaning that it occurs on the antepenult when *tinos* is attached. While each of the candidates satisfies ENCLITIC-WINDOW, candidates (67a,b) shift their primary stresses to satisfy FINAL-WINDOW-μ, as well, candidate (67a) to the final mora of the base and candidate (67b) to the final syllable of the enclitic. Both candidates are excluded because they violate the higher-ranked OO-FAITH-X$_{\omega}$, and candidate (67w), which preserves the primary stress in its original position, correctly emerges as the winner.

(67) Base output: phóos Derived output: phóos tinos

phoos tinos	ENC-WINDOW	OO-FAITH-x_ω	FIN-WIND-μ
x x ☞ w. phoos ti nos			1
x x a. phoos ti nos		1 W	L
x x x b. phoos ti nos		1 W	L

To this point, then, we have seen that primary stress can shift from its original position in base + enclitic forms to bring itself within the enclitic window but not to bring itself within the foot-based window. This is due to the ranking ENCLITIC-WINDOW >> OO-FAITH-x_ω >> FINAL-WINDOW-μ. Note, however, that there are additional reasons that main stress shift fails to occur. As we shall see in Section 6.4.4, even if the original main stress falls outside the enclitic window, there are restrictions on where main stress can shift within the window and the shift will not occur if these cannot be met.

6.4.3 Determining the Position of Stress Shift

When the original position of the accent in a base form falls outside the enclitic window in a base + enclitic form, the preference is for primary stress to shift to the final syllable of the base. As (68) illustrates, the preference is due to the requirements of x_ω-LEFT. When the addition of an enclitic to a base form locates the original primary stress outside the enclitic window, ENCLITIC-WINDOW is violated if the primary stress does not shift to a position inside the window, as in candidate (68b). Once it is confined to the enclitic window, x_ω-LEFT prefers that the primary stress occur as far to the left within the window as possible. Because the primary stress of candidate (68a), which occurs on the final syllable of the enclitic, could recede further without violating ENCLITIC-WINDOW, (68a) loses to candidate (68w), where the primary stress occurs on the final syllable of the base.

(68) Base output: ángelos Derived output: ángelós tinos

angelos tinos	ENCLITIC-WINDOW	x_ω-LEFT
x (los) x (an) x (los) x x x x x ☞ w. an ge los ti nos		2
x (nos) x (an) x (nos) x x x x x a. an ge los ti nos		4 W
x (an) x (an) x x x x x b. an ge los ti nos	2 W	L

Despite the preference for primary stress to shift to the final syllable of the base, there are two circumstances, discussed just below, that can prevent it from occurring in this position. In forms with disyllabic enclitics, the main stress shifts instead to the final syllable of the enclitic. The main stress shifts to the final syllable, rather than the initial syllable, due to a constraint whose preferences supersede those of x_ω-LEFT in this context. The constraint, x_ω-ENCLITIC-RIGHT, aligns the prosodic word-level grid entry with the right edge of the enclitic when it happens to occur within it.

(69) x_ω-ENCLITIC-RIGHT: $*\langle Enc, x_\omega, \sigma\rangle$ / $[\ldots x_\omega \ldots \sigma \ldots]_{Enc}$
'Assess a violation mark for every $\langle Enc, x_\omega, \sigma\rangle$ such that x_ω precedes σ within *Enc*.'

RSA's ability to restrict the alignment requirement to a prosodic word-level grid entry that occurs within the enclitic is crucial in this context. When the prosodic word-level entry is able to occur on the base-final syllable, as it is in the cases discussed just above, it can occur outside the enclitic itself. x_ω-LEFT is free to locate the main stress in this position, so that it never becomes subject to x_ω-ENCLITIC-RIGHT. When the prosodic word-level entry cannot occur on the base-final syllable, however, it must fall within the enclitic itself, and it then becomes subject to x_ω-ENCLITIC-RIGHT. x_ω-ENCLITIC-RIGHT can then position it on the enclitic-final syllable.

The first situation in which main stress cannot shift to the base-final syllable arises, as illustrated in (70), when the supporting foot-level grid entry of the shifted stress would be in clash with the foot-level entry left in its original location.

```
(70)        x
          x x
      *phi los ti nos
```

The constraint that enforces faithfulness to the original foot-level entry is OO-FAITH-x_F, given in (71).

(71) OO-FAITH-x_F

Every x_F in the base form occurs in the same position in the derived form.

For forms with disyllabic enclitics, then, clash can be avoided by shifting the main stress to the final syllable of the enclitic. The ranking responsible is OO-FAITH-x_F, *CLASH, x_ω-ENCLITIC-RIGHT >> x_ω-LEFT. As (72) demonstrates, OO-FAITH-x_F eliminates a candidate like (72c), which shifts primary stress to the base-final syllable without leaving behind its original foot-level entry. *CLASH eliminates a candidate like (72b), which shifts primary stress to the base-final syllable, resulting in a clash with the foot-level entry left in the primary stress's original position. This leaves candidates (72w, a), where primary stress shifts to a position within the enclitic itself. Candidate (72a) is disqualified by x_ω-ENC-RIGHT, because it does not occur as far to the right within the enclitic as possible, and candidate (72w) emerges as the winner.

(72) Base output: phílos Derived output: phílos tinós

philos tinos	OO-FTH-x_F	*CLASH	x_ω-ENC-R	x_ω-L
☞ w. (phi los) (ti nos) x x x x x (phi) x (nos) x (nos)				3
a. (phi los) (ti nos) x x x x x (phi) x (ti) x (ti)			1 W	2 L
b. (phi los) (ti nos) x x x x x (phi) x (los) x (los)		1 W		1 L
c. (phi los) (ti nos) x x x x x (los) x (los)	1 W			1 L

The second circumstance where main stress cannot shift to the base-final syllable is when the final syllable happens to be heavy. Heavy syllables are necessarily head syllables as required by the WEIGHT-TO-HEAD constraint. Since the head syllables of the base cannot change their tonal specifications, due to OO-FAITH-σ_{HD}-TONE, and main stress must be associated with a high tone, due to x_{ω}-HIGH-TONE, main stress cannot shift to a base-final heavy syllable. Just as the stress shifts to the final syllable of a disyllabic enclitic, then, when shifting it to the final syllable of the base would result in clash, it shifts to the enclitic-final syllable when the base-final syllable is heavy. The necessary ranking is x_{ω}-HIGH-TONE, OO-FAITH-σ_{HD}-TONE, x_{ω}-ENCLITIC-RIGHT >> x_{ω}-LEFT.

In (73), the final syllable of the base form, *phóiniks*, is heavy, and it must be a head syllable. In the base output, however, it does not support the primary stress, so it must be associated with a low tone. OO-FAITH-σ_{HD}-TONE excludes a candidate like (73b) since it shifts primary stress to the base-final syllable where it must be associated with a new high tone. In the remaining candidates, primary stress shifts to a position within the enclitic itself. x_{ω}-ENC-RIGHT excludes a candidate like (73a) because the primary stress does not occur as far to the right as possible within the enclitic. Candidate (73w), where primary stress occurs on the enclitic-final syllable, emerges as the winner.

(73) Base output: phóiniks Derived output: phóiniks tinós

phoiniks tinos	OO-FTH-σ_{HD}-TONE	x_{ω}-ENC-R	x_{ω}-L
x (nos) x (phoi) x (nos) xx xx x x ☞ w. phoi niks ti nos			3
x (ti) x (phoi) x (ti) xx xx x x a. phoi niks ti nos		W 1	L 2
x (niks) x (phoi) x (niks) xx xx x x b. phoi niks ti nos	W 1		L 1

In this section, we have examined how the target location for stress shift is determined in base + enclitic forms. The preference is for primary stress to shift to the final syllable of the base, the leftmost syllable in the enclitic window. When stress cannot shift to the base-final syllable, and must occur within the enclitic instead, it emerges on the enclitic-final syllable. The circumstances in which stress shift must avoid the base-final syllable are when locating primary stress in this position would result in clash or when it would mean replacing a low tone from one of the base's head syllables with a high tone. As we shall see in the next section, these same circumstances actually prevent stress from shifting at all when the enclitic is monosyllabic.

6.4.4 Failure of Stress Shift

As mentioned above, stress shift fails to occur when the original main stress already falls within the enclitic window. There are two circumstances, however, where stress shift fails to occur even when the original main stress falls outside the enclitic window. These closely parallel the cases described above where stress shifts to the second syllable of a disyllabic enclitic, except they arise instead with monosyllabic enclitics. In other words, when stress cannot shift to the final syllable of the base, either because it would result in clash or result in a change in tone for one of the base's head syllables, the shift fails to occur at all when the enclitic is monosyllabic.

The central issue in this situation is why the stress cannot shift onto the monosyllabic enclitic itself. One possible answer is simply that enclitics prefer not to contain head syllables.

(74) *ENCLITIC-σ_{HD}
No enclitic contains a σ_{HD}.

When an enclitic is disyllabic, as in the examples analysed above, Weak Bracketing's non-violable exhaustive parsing requirement makes it impossible to satisfy *ENCLITIC-σ_{HD}. Disyllabic enclitics must contain a head syllable in order for parsing to be exhaustive. When an enclitic is monosyllabic, however, it can satisfy *ENCLITIC-σ_{HD}. It can avoid containing a head syllable by sharing the foot into which it is parsed with the final syllable of the base. The final syllable of the base is the head syllable and the single syllable of the enclitic is the non-head. It is the ability of monosyllabic enclitics, then, to avoid containing a head syllable that prevents them from hosting a shifted primary stress.

Consider, first, the situation where stress shift fails to occur in the context of a potential clash. The ranking necessary to account for the failure of stress shift in this case is OO-FAITH-x_F, *CLASH, *ENCLITIC-σ_{HD} >> ENCLITIC-WINDOW. Consider the tableau for the output *phílos tis* in (75). First, OO-FAITH-x_F eliminates candidate (75c), in which primary stress shifts to the base-final syllable without leaving behind its original foot-level grid entry. Next, *CLASH eliminates candidate (75b), which shifts primary stress to the base-final syllable, resulting in a clash with the foot-level entry remaining in the stress's original position. Finally, *ENCLITIC-σ_{HD} excludes candidate (75a). Because it shifts stress to the monosyllabic enclitic, the enclitic is the head of a foot. Candidate (75w), where stress shift fails to occur at all, emerges as the winner.

(75) Base output: phílos Derived output: phílos tis

philos tis	OO-FTH-x_F	*CLASH	*ENC-σ_{HD}	ENC-WIND
x x x x x ☞ w. phi los tis				1
x x x x x x a. phi los tis			W 1	L
x x x x x x b. phi los tis		W 1		L
x x x x x c. phi los tis	W 1			L

Next, consider the situation where stress shift fails to occur in the context of a potential tone change for a heavy base-final syllable. To account for the failure of stress shift in this context, the necessary ranking is x_ω-HIGH-TONE, OO-FAITH-σ_{HD}-TONE, *ENCLITIC-σ_{HD} >> ENCLITIC-WINDOW. In (76), for example, the final syllable of the base form is heavy. It was a head syllable in the base output, and it was associated with a low tone in the base output. OO-FAITH-σ_{HD}-TONE excludes candidate (76b) since it shifts primary stress to the base-final syllable where it must be associated with a new high tone. Next, *ENCLITIC-σ_{HD} excludes candidate (76a), where the primary stress shifts to the monosyllabic enclitic, forcing it to be a head. Candidate (76w), where stress shift fails to occur at all, emerges as the winner.

(76) Base output: phóiniks Derived output: phóiniks tis

phoiniks tis	OO-FTH-σ_{HD}-TONE	*ENC-σ_{HD}	ENC-WIND
x x xx xx x ☞ w. phoi niks tis			1
x x x xx xx x a. phoi niks tis		1 W	L
x x x xx xx x b. phoi niks tis	1 W		L

To summarize, the analysis of the AG enclitic window applies the ENCLITIC-WINDOW constraint to AG forms consisting of a base + enclitic combination. When the original primary stress of the base falls outside the enclitic window, the primary stress may shift to a position within the enclitic window. In forms with disyllabic enclitics, the primary stress will shift to the final syllable of the base, due to the preferences of x_ω-LEFT, unless it would result in clash or fall on a heavy syllable. In these cases, it must shift within the enclitic itself, occupying the final syllable due to the influence of x_ω-ENCLITIC-RIGHT. In forms with monosyllabic enclitics, primary stress will shift to the final syllable of the base, unless it would result in clash or fall on a heavy syllable. If it cannot shift to the final syllable of the base, the shift does not occur at all. This is attributed to the preference to avoid making monosyllabic enclitics the head syllables of feet.

6.5 Summary

In this chapter, we have seen how opposite-edge RSA constraints produce window effects. Rather than producing Midpoint Pathology effects, opposite-edge RSA constraints have the effect of confining one aligned category to a domain at the edge of a form defined in terms of the second aligned category and the separator category. In trisyllabic accent windows, for example, accent is a confined to a domain at the edge of a form consisting of a foot and an adjacent syllable (full windows) or a foot and an adjacent mora (truncated windows).

In examining trisyllabic accent windows, we saw that the RSA constraints provide a general and uniform approach. They account for full accent windows such as those found in Macedonian and Maithili, and they account for truncated accent windows such as those found in English, Latin, and Ancient Greek. While alternatives based on non-finality, extended lapse avoidance, or weak local parsing are able to account for accent windows in some circumstances, they fail to produce the appropriate accent window in key cases and, thus, fail to provide a general approach.

We also saw that window effects can arise in other contexts. They can apply to other categories besides accents, and they can be constructed from morphological and syntactic categories as well as prosodic categories. The discussion focuses on the enclitic window in Ancient Greek to demonstrate how an accent window can be constructed from a morphological category.

7 Conclusion

The prosodic hierarchy, the metrical grid, and the constraints that produce directional parsing effects are all closely intertwined in the theory of metrical stress. In this book, I have argued for a specific approach to each of these key components. First, I argued that directional parsing effects are the result of Relation-Specific Alignment constraints, which prohibit misalignment only when the aligned categories occur in a specific structural relationship. Second, I argued that relationships between categories in the prosodic hierarchy are governed by the Weak Bracketing approach to prosodic structure. Weak Bracketing requires that all categories on one level of the prosodic hierarchy be parsed into categories on the next level higher (Strict Succession), but it allows categories on the same level to overlap (Improper Bracketing). Finally, the Weak Bracketing approach to prosodic structure requires a different approach to the relationship between prosodic categories and the metrical grid. Where the standard assumption is that the relationship between feet and stress is one-to-one and non-violable, I argued for an Optimal Mapping approach, where violable constraints govern the relationship between feet and stress. It is possible for feet to emerge without a stress, and it is even possible for two overlapping feet to share a stress.

7.1 Relation-Specific Alignment

The Relation-Specific Alignment approach to parsing directionality posits three schemas for alignment constraints, repeated in (1). In each schema, the set of categories to the left of the slash is prohibited from occurring in the configuration to the right of the slash. The schema in (1a) promotes left-edge alignment by prohibiting a separator category from preceding one of the aligned categories within the other aligned category. The schema in (1b) promotes right-edge alignment by prohibiting a separator category from following one of the aligned categories within the other aligned category. Finally, the schema in (1c) promotes opposite-edge alignment by prohibiting a separator category from intervening between one aligned category and another that follows. Each of the schemas is relation specific in that violations for misalignment are assessed only when the aligned categories occur in the specific relationships indicated, *containment* in the same-edge schemas, (1a) and (1b), and *precedence* in the opposite-edge schema, (1c).

(1) RSA constraint schemas

a. Left-Edge: *⟨*ACat1, ACat2, (SCat)*⟩ / [... *SCat* ... *ACat2* ... $]_{ACat1}$

'Assess a violation mark for every ⟨*ACat1, ACat2, (SCat)*⟩ such that *SCat* precedes *ACat2* within *ACat1*.'

b. Right-edge: *⟨*ACat1, ACat2, (SCat)*⟩ / [... *ACat2* ... *SCat* ... $]_{ACat1}$

'Assess a violation mark for every ⟨*ACat1, ACat2, (SCat)*⟩ such that *ACat2* precedes *SCat* within *ACat1*.'

c. Opposite-edge: *⟨*ACat1, ACat2, (SCat)*⟩ / *ACat1* ... *SCat* ... *ACat2*

'Assess a violation mark for every ⟨*ACat1, ACat2, (SCat)*⟩ such that *ACat1* precedes *ACat2* with *SCat* intervening.'

Although evaluation of RSA constraints is always categorical – only one violation mark is assessed per locus of violation – RSA constraints can be either distance-sensitive or distance-insensitive, depending on the definition of the locus of violation. When the locus of violation includes the separator category, assessment is distance-sensitive. When the locus of violation includes only the two aligned categories, assessment is distance-insensitive.

The primary motivation for the RSA approach is to correct certain deficiencies in the behavior of constraints formulated under the standard Generalized Alignment approach. The primary deficiency of GA constraints is that they have the ability to produce Midpoint Pathology effects. For example, they have the ability to draw categories to the center of a domain, as ALIGN (σ, L, F, L, σ) draws a foot to the center of the prosodic word in the tableau repeated in (2).

(2)

	ALIGN (σ, L, F, L, σ)
a. [(σσ)σσσσσ]	c ff fff ffff fff!ff fffff
b. [σ(σσ)σσσσ]	p c ff fff ffff ff!fff
c. [σσ(σσ)σσσ]	pp p c ff fff ffff!
☞ d. [σσσ(σσ)σσ]	ppp pp p c ff fff
e. [σσσσ(σσ)σ]	pppp ppp pp p c ff!
f. [σσσσσ(σσ)]	ppppp pppp ppp p!p p c

Midpoint Pathology effects arise from the combination of two characteristics of GA constraints. The first is that they are distance-sensitive. In (2), ALIGN (σ, L, F, L, σ) assesses a number of violation marks for each pair of misaligned left syllable and foot edges in proportion to their degree of misalignment. The second characteristic is that GA constraints are relation-general. ALIGN (σ, L, F, L, σ) assesses violation marks for each pair of misaligned left syllable and foot edges regardless of whether the foot contains the syllable, the foot precedes the syllable, or the foot follows the syllable.

The effects of the Midpoint Pathology are not limited to contrived cases like the example in (2). Midpoint Pathology effects arise under constraints standardly adopted in OT analyses, such as ALIGN (F, L, ω, L, σ), which is employed to produce left-oriented directional parsing. When ALIGN (F, L, ω, L, σ) evaluates forms with multiple prosodic words, the expected leftward orientation emerges in the final prosodic word, but a bidirectional pattern emerges in non-final prosodic words.

(3)

	ALIGN (F, L, ω, L, σ)
a. [(σσ)(σσ)(σσ)σ] [(σσ)(σσ)(σσ)σ]	[cc ccc!c][cc cccc]
☞ b. [(σσ)(σσ)σ(σσ)] [(σσ)(σσ)(σσ) σ]	[cc ff][cc cccc]

GA constraints, then, cannot reliably produce the essential directionality effects that are their primary purpose.

Eliminating either characteristic of GA constraints, distance-sensitivity or relation-generality, is sufficient to eliminate Midpoint Pathology effects. Although previous treatments (Eisner 1997, Kager 2001, McCarthy 2003, Buckley 2009) have argued that distance-sensitivity must be abandoned, I argued in Chapter 2 that abandoning relation-generality is the better approach. The primary reason is simply that distance-sensitivity is crucial in producing alignment's essential directionality effects. Distance-sensitivity is crucial in producing conflicting directional orientations like that required for bidirectional parsing patterns in Weak Layering accounts. For example, distance-sensitivity is required to ensure that the medial foot in the Spanish forms in (4) is oriented towards the right edge rather than the left.

(4) Bidirectional parsing in Spanish

a. (bùro)cra(tìza)(ción)
b. (gràma)ti(càli)(dád)
c. (mate)ma(tìci)(dád)
d. (nàtu)ra(lìza)(ción)
e. (ràcio)na(lìza)(ción)

Distance-sensitivity is also crucial for producing directional parsing effects between heavy syllables in quantity-sensitive languages and in producing foot extrametricality effects. In the Banawá forms in (5), for example, distance-sensitivity is necessary to ensure that the head foot is rightmost nonfinal foot rather than a foot further to the left.

(5) Foot extrametricality in Banawá

a.	(abá)(rikò)	'moon'
b.	(mètu)(wási)(mà)	'find them'
c.	(tìna)(ífa)(bùne)	'you are going to work'

Because they abandon relation-generality and maintain distance-sensitivity, RSA constraints avoid Midpoint Pathology effects but are still able to perform the essential functions that the theory requires of alignment constraints. In examining the predictions of RSA constraints in the context of the Symmetrical Alignment approach, for example, we saw that the RSA formulation predicts the same set of patterns (minus the Midpoint Pathology effects) as the GA formulation, although with slightly different rankings. Distance-sensitive RSA constraints established general directional orientations, resulting in unidirectional parsing patterns in both under-parsing and exhaustive parsing systems, and distance-insensitive constraints created exceptions to general directional orientations, resulting in bidirectional parsing patterns in under-parsing systems.

Though the most critical result of the RSA formulation is the ability to maintain distance-sensitive evaluation while avoiding Midpoint Pathology effects, additional support for the RSA formulation comes from its ability to provide a natural, general account of window phenomena. It is often the case that some type of linguistic structure finds itself confined to a certain space, or window, at the edge of a form. Opposite-edge RSA constraints can account for such situations because they can have the effect of confining one of their aligned categories to a window at the edge of a form established by their other aligned category.

The most familiar examples of window phenomena are languages with trisyllabic accent windows, languages that confine accent to a form's initial three syllables or final three syllables. As an example, irregular accent in Macedonian confines a lexical accent to one of the final three syllables of a form. If suffixation would push the accent to the left of the final three syllables, the accent returns to the antepenult by default.

(6) Macedonian irregular pattern

a.	citát	'quotation'	b.	romántik	'romantic'
	citátot			romántikot	
	citáti			romántici	
	citátite			romantícite	

The opposite-edge RSA constraint responsible for an accent window like that found in Macedonian is FINAL-WINDOW-σ, repeated in (7).

(7) a. FINAL-WINDOW-σ: $*\langle x_{\omega}, \sigma_{HD}, \sigma\rangle \ / x_{\omega} \ldots \sigma \ldots \sigma_{HD}$

'Assess a violation mark for every $\langle x_{\omega}, \sigma_{HD}, \sigma\rangle$ such that x_{ω} precedes σ_{HD} with σ intervening.'

By prohibiting a primary stress from preceding a foot with a syllable intervening, FINAL-WINDOW-σ confines primary stress to the final three syllables of a form. The constraint is satisfied when primary stress occurs on the antepenult (adjacent to the final foot) or when primary stress occurs on the penult or ultima (within the final foot). If it occurs further to the left than the antepenult, one or more syllables intervene between the primary stress and the final foot, violating FINAL-WINDOW-σ.

(8)

	FINAL-WINDOW-σ
x (σ4) x (σ4) x x x x ☞ a. σ σ σ (σ)	
x (σ3) x (σ3) x x x x ☞ b. σ σ (σ σ)	
x (σ2) x (σ2) x x x x ☞ c. σ (σ σ)(σ)	
x (σ1) x (σ1) x x x x d. (σ σ)(σ σ)	*!

In addition to windows, like trisyllabic accent windows, that can be established using prosodic categories, we also saw that windows can be established using morphological and syntactic categories. In Chapter 6, I focused on the accent window established by clitics in Ancient Greek. In Ancient Greek, accent on a base form can shift if it falls further to the left than the syllable adjacent to an enclitic. The appropriate window is established using an opposite-edge RSA constraint that prohibits primary stress from preceding an enclitic with a syllable intervening.

7.2 Weak Bracketing

The second component of the proposed account is the Weak Bracketing approach to prosodic layering. The Weak Bracketing approach is a significant departure from the standard Weak Layering approach. Under Weak Layering, the leftover syllable in an odd-parity form can be dealt with in two ways: it can be left unparsed, as in (9a), or it can be parsed as a monosyllabic foot, as in (9b).

(9) Layering irregularities under Weak Layering

a. Unfooted syllable

```
σ σ  σ σ  σ σ  σ
 \/   \/   \/
 F    F    F
```

b. Monosyllabic foot

```
σ σ  σ σ  σ σ  σ
 \/   \/   \/  |
 F    F    F   F
```

Under Weak Bracketing, there are also two options: the leftover syllable can be parsed as a monosyllabic foot, as in (10a), or it can be parsed into a disyllabic foot that overlaps another disyllabic foot, as in (10b).

(10) Layering irregularities under Weak Bracketing

a. Monosyllabic foot

```
σ σ  σ σ  σ σ  σ
 \/   \/   \/  |
 F    F    F   F
```

b. Overlapping feet

```
σ σ  σ σ  σ σ σ
 \/   \/   \/\/
 F    F    F F
```

A significant portion of the book was devoted to contrasting the predictions of Weak Layering accounts to those of the Weak Bracketing account. The discussion focused on the relative abilities of the two approaches to avoid the Odd-Parity Input Problem. The OPIP is a set of problematic predictions that arise from the combination of the requirement that all syllables be parsed into feet and the requirement that feet contain at least two moras.

For odd-parity inputs, there are three ways to satisfy the parsing and minimality requirements simultaneously. First, if the odd-parity input contains a heavy syllable in an odd-numbered position, as in (11a), the heavy syllable can be parsed as a monosyllabic foot with the remaining syllables parsed into disyllabic feet. Second, the odd-parity input can be converted into an even-parity output, as in (11b), either through insertion of a single syllable or deletion of a single syllable, so that each syllable in the output can be included in a disyllabic foot. Finally, the leftover syllable from an odd-parity input can be included in a disyllabic foot that overlaps another disyllabic foot, as in (11c).

(11) Exhaustive binary parsing for odd-parity inputs

a. Odd-numbered H foot

σσHσσσσ → (σσ)(H)(σσ)(σσ)

b. Convert to even-parity

σσσσσσσ → (σσ)(σσ)(σσ)(σσ) *or* (σσ)(σσ)(σσ)

c. Overlapping feet

σσσσσσσ → σ σ σ σ σ σ σ
\/ \/ \/\/

The options in (11a,b), the only choices available under Weak Layering, are the options that lead to the OPIP. The OPIP can be usefully divided into two-sub-problems. The Odd Heavy Problem is a peculiar, and unattested, type of quantity-sensitivity that arises when the option is (11a) is employed. Only in odd-parity forms, a single odd-numbered heavy syllable is parsed as a monosyllabic foot. The Even Output Problem is the systematic, and unattested, conversion of odd-parity inputs to even-parity outputs. It arises when the option in (11b) is employed.

As we saw in Chapters 3 and 4, the OPIP is so pervasive under Weak Layering that it is impossible for Weak Layering accounts to predict a reasonably accurate typology of binary stress systems. The first of the Weak Layering accounts examined was the Symmetrical Alignment account of McCarthy and Prince (1993a). The most important characteristics of Symmetrical Alignment are its reliance on alignment constraints to produce basic directional parsing effects and the relative non-involvement of clash and lapse avoidance. Under Symmetrical Alignment, alignment constraints are formulated in right-oriented and left-oriented pairs.

Of the Weak Layering accounts, the manifestations of the OPIP are arguably least exotic under Symmetrical Alignment. Symmetrical Alignment suffers the effects of the OHP in rankings that produce both under-parsing patterns and exhaustive parsing patterns, though it can also produce exhaustive parsing patterns without OHP effects. When the OHP emerges, as (12) indicates, a single odd-numbered heavy syllable in odd-parity forms is parsed as monosyllabic foot. The single heavy syllable parsed in this fashion is either the leftmost or the rightmost, depending on which of the foot alignment constraints is higher ranked.

(12) The OHP in Symmetrical Alignment

A heavy syllable *H* is parsed as a monosyllabic foot *iff*

a. *H* occurs in an odd-parity form; *and*

b. *H* is odd-numbered; *and*

c. *H* is the heavy syllable conforming to (a,b) that is closest to the preferred edge of general foot alignment.

Symmetrical alignment suffers the effects of the EOP under both under-parsing and exhaustive parsing rankings.

Pruitt's (2008, 2010) Iterative Foot Optimization account is similar to Symmetrical Alignment in that it employs the same set of alignment constraints and does not make significant use of clash and lapse avoidance to produce basic directional parsing effects. It is different, however, in that it is implemented within the framework of Harmonic Serialism. In the course of the derivation of an output form, several evaluations are performed. The first evaluation takes the underlying form as its input, considers candidates with at most one difference from the input form, and arrives at an optimal output. The next evaluation takes the output of the previous evaluation as its input, considers candidates with at most a single difference from the input, and arrives at an optimal output. The evaluations continue in this fashion until the output is the faithful candidate. Iterative Foot Optimization suffers the effects of the OHP in under-parsing rankings only. The particular manifestations of the OHP are different, however, than those found under Symmetrical Alignment. Under Iterative Foot Optimization, as (13) indicates, an odd-numbered heavy syllable is parsed as a monosyllabic foot in odd-parity forms only if it is the last syllable in the course of the derivation to have its parsing status settled. Depending on the ranking of the alignment constraints, the last syllable might be the initial syllable, the post-peninitial syllable, the antepenult, or the ultima.

(13) The Odd Heavy Problem in Iterative Foot Optimization

A heavy syllable *H* is parsed as a monosyllabic foot *iff*

a. *H* occurs in an odd-parity form; *and*

b. *H* is odd-numbered; *and*

c. *H* is the last syllable in the derivation to have its parsing status settled.

Iterative Foot Optimization also suffers from the effects of EOP, exhibiting an even wider range of manifestations then those found under symmetrical alignment. The wider range of manifestations is due to its serial derivational perspective.

The manifestations of the OHP become increasing exotic under the Asymmetrical Alignment (Alber 2005) and Rhythmic Licensing (Kager 2001, 2005) accounts, where alignment constraints play a less central role in creating directional parsing effects. Under Asymmetrical Alignment, alignment constraints are not necessarily formulated in right-oriented and left-oriented pairs. Of the distance-sensitive alignment constraints that establish a general directional orientation for foot parsing, for example, only the left-oriented constraint, ALL-F-LEFT, is included in the Asymmetrical Alignment account. Asymmetrical Alignment relies on the rhythmic well-formedness constraints, *CLASH and *LAPSE, to produce directional parsing configurations that cannot be produced by ALL-F-LEFT.

Three versions of the OHP emerge under Asymmetrical Alignment. In the first, an odd-numbered heavy syllable in an odd-parity form is parsed as a monosyllabic foot only if it is in a position to avoid clash.

(14) Asymmetrical Alignment OHP version 1

A heavy syllable *H* is parsed as a monosyllabic foot *iff*

a. *H* occurs in an odd-parity form; *and*

b. *H* is odd-numbered; *and*

c. parsing *H* as a monosyllabic foot would not result in clash.

In the second version, the odd-numbered heavy syllable closest to the left edge in an odd-parity form will be parsed as monosyllabic foot. The left edge is the preferred of edge of alignment for Asymmetrical Alignment's only foot alignment constraint, ALL-F-LEFT.

(15) Asymmetrical Alignment OHP version 2

A heavy syllable *H* is parsed as a monosyllabic foot *iff*

a. *H* occurs in an odd-parity form; *and*

b. *H* is odd-numbered; *and*

c. *H* is the heavy syllable conforming to (a,b) that is closest to the left edge.

The final version of the OHP under Asymmetrical Alignment is a combination of the previous two. An odd-numbered heavy syllable in an odd-parity form is parsed as a monosyllabic foot if it occurs in a position to avoid clash. If no heavy syllable is in a position to avoid clash, the odd-numbered heavy syllable nearest the left edge is parsed as a monosyllabic foot.

(16) Asymmetrical Alignment OHP Version 3

A heavy syllable *H* is parsed as a monosyllabic foot *iff*

a. *H* occurs in an odd-parity form; *and*

b. *H* is odd-numbered; *and*

c. parsing *H* as a monosyllabic foot would not result in clash; *or*

d. if there is no heavy syllable that meets (c), *H* is the heavy syllable conforming to (a,b) that is closest to the left edge.

While Asymmetrical Alignment can produce the majority of its patterns without OHP effects, each of the predicted patterns can also emerge with one or more of the versions of the OHP in (14–16). Patterns produced with bidirectional parsing configurations – the iambic and trochaic internal lapse patterns – cannot be produced without OHP effects.

The most important characteristic of the Rhythmic Licensing account is that it abandons distance-sensitive foot alignment constraints altogether, relying instead on rhythmic well-formedness constraints to establish general directional orientations for foot parsing. Like Asymmetrical Alignment, Rhythmic Licensing is susceptible to three distinct versions of the OHP. In the first, an odd-numbered heavy syllable is parsed as a monosyllabic foot in odd-parity forms, only if it is in a position to avoid clash.

(17) Rhythmic Licensing OHP version 1

A heavy syllable *H* is parsed as a monosyllabic foot *iff*

a. *H* occurs in an odd-parity form; *and*

b. *H* is odd-numbered; *and*

c. parsing *H* as a monosyllabic foot would not result in clash.

In the second version, an odd-numbered heavy syllable is parsed as a monosyllabic foot in an odd-parity form if it is in a position to avoid clash. If there is no heavy syllable in a position to avoid clash, an odd-number heavy syllable in a position to create a peripheral clash is parsed as a monosyllabic foot.

(18) Rhythmic Licensing OHP version 2

A heavy syllable *H* is parsed as a monosyllabic foot *iff*

a. *H* occurs in an odd-parity form; *and*
b. *H* is odd-numbered; *and*
c. parsing *H* as a monosyllabic foot would not result in clash; *or*
d. if there is no heavy syllable that meets (c), parsing *H* as a monosyllabic foot would result in a peripheral clash.

In the final version of the OHP under Rhythmic Licensing, a heavy syllable will be parsed as monosyllabic foot in an odd-parity form, if it occurs in a position where it can avoid clash. If no heavy syllable is in a position to avoid clash, an odd-numbered heavy syllable in a position to create a peripheral clash is parsed as a monosyllabic foot. If no heavy syllable is in a position to create a peripheral clash, an odd-numbered heavy syllable in a position to create an internal clash is parsed as a monosyllabic foot.

(19) Rhythmic Licensing OHP version 3

A heavy syllable *H* is parsed as a monosyllabic foot *iff*

a. *H* occurs in an odd-parity form; *and*
b. *H* is odd-numbered; *and*
c. parsing *H* as a monosyllabic foot would not result in clash; *or*
d. if there is no heavy syllable that meets (c), parsing *H* as a monosyllabic foot would result in a peripheral clash; *or*
e. if there is no heavy syllable that meets (c) or (d), parsing *H* as a monosyllabic foot would result in a non-peripheral clash.

While the majority of patterns predicted under Rhythmic Licensing can emerge without OHP effects, all but the iambic final lapse pattern can also emerge with one or more of the versions of the OHP in (17–19). Patterns produced with bidirectional parsing configurations – the iambic and trochaic internal lapse patterns – cannot be produced without OHP effects.

In contrast to the Weak Layering accounts, the Weak Bracketing account avoids the OPIP altogether. In allowing feet to overlap, as in (11c), Weak Bracketing allows odd-parity strings to achieve exhaustive binary parsing using only disyllabic feet. There is never a need to resort to the option of parsing an odd-numbered heavy syllable as a monosyllabic foot, as in (11a), the option that leads to the emergence of OHP effects in Weak Layering accounts, and there is no need to resort to the option of inserting or deleting a syllable, as in (11b), the option that leads to the emergence of EOP effects in Weak Layering accounts.

7.3 Optimal Mapping

While the Weak Bracketing approach to prosodic structure allows the Weak Bracketing account to avoid the OPIP, it does not guarantee that the account predicts an accurate typology of quantity-insensitive stress patterns. To predict a reasonably accurate typology, an account needs to capture the three generalizations repeated in (20). The first concerns perfect alternation patterns, patterns that contain neither clash nor lapse. As indicated in (20a), perfect alternation patterns are symmetrically attested in mirror-image pairs. The trochaic version is attested, and the iambic mirror-image is also attested. The second generalization concerns patterns that depart from perfect alternation, patterns that contain either a clash or a lapse. As (20b) indicates, patterns that depart from perfect alternation are asymmetrically attested or symmetrically unattested. If the trochaic version of a pattern with clash or lapse is attested, its iambic mirror-image is unattested; if the iambic version of a pattern with clash or lapse is attested, its trochaic mirror-image is unattested. It is the asymmetrically attested mirror-image pairs that create iambic-trochaic asymmetries in the stress typology.

(20) a. In mirror image patterns with neither clash nor lapse, both members of the pair are attested.

b. In mirror image patterns with either clash or lapse, at most one member of the pair is attested.

c. Attested patterns with clash or lapse always have stress on the initial syllable, always leave the final syllable stressless, or both.

The final generalization concerns the reasons that arrhythmic configurations like clash or lapse arise. As (20c), indicates, when a clash or lapse arises, it arises near a form's left edge to accommodate an initial stressed syllable or near its right edge to accommodate a final stressless syllable. Since iambic patterns are typically incompatible with initial stress and final stresslessness, it is most often the iambic patterns that are unattested in iambic-trochaic asymmetries.

To capture the generalizations in (20), the Weak Bracketing approach to prosodic layering must be implemented in conjunction with the Optimal Mapping approach to constructing the metrical grid. The structural assumptions of Weak Bracketing require a revision of assumptions about the relationship between prosodic categories and entries on the metrical grid. Where the standard approach assumes a non-violable one-to-one correspondence, the Optimal Mapping approach allows for a more flexible, violable relationship. The violable MAP-TO-GRID constraints simply require that a grid entry occur within the domain of each prosodic category. Because the constraints are violable, it is possible for a foot to emerge without a stress on the surface as in (21a). Because the MAP-TO-GRID constraints only require that a grid entry occur within the domain of each category, and do not require that the relationship be unique, it is possible for overlapping feet to share a stress as in (21b).

The ability to employ overlapping feet in gridmark-sharing configurations to deal with the leftover syllable in odd-parity forms is a crucial factor in the Weak Bracketing account's restrictiveness. Gridmark-sharing configurations can never result in clash, and alignment constraints always prefer that they occur in positions where they avoid lapse.

The only constraints able to introduce clash or lapse under Weak Bracketing and Optimal Mapping are the asymmetrically formulated INITIAL-GRIDMARK and NON-FINALITY constraints.

When INITIAL-GRIDMARK and NON-FINALITY are low-ranked the result is perfect alternation. As (22) and (23) indicate, the Weak Bracketing account predicts each of the four perfect alternation patterns. It predicts both the trochaic and iambic minimal alternation patterns, and it predicts both the trochaic and iambic maximal alternation patterns.

(22) Minimal alternation patterns

a. Trochaic: Attested

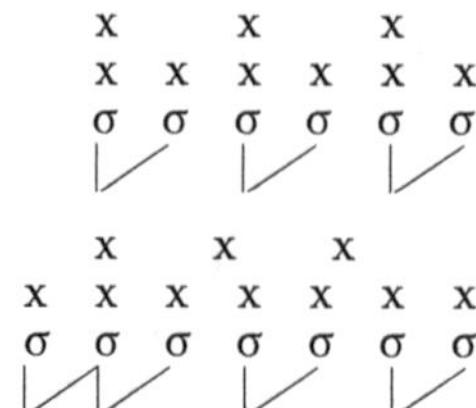

b. Iambic: Attested

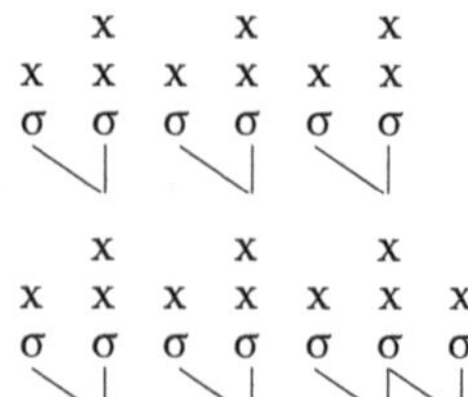

(23) Maximal alternation

a. Trochaic: Attested

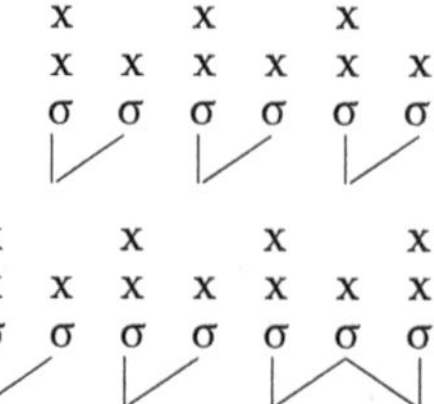

b. Iambic: Attested

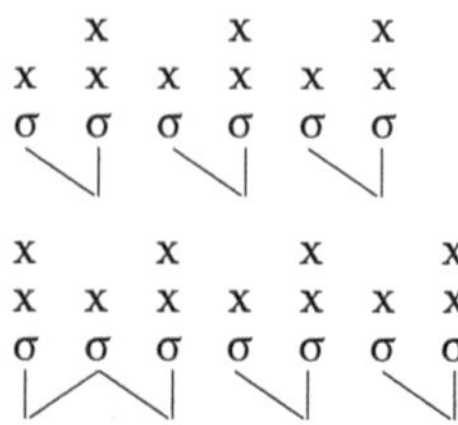

In predicting the perfect alternation patterns in mirror-image pairs, the Weak Bracketing approach captures the generalization in (20a) that perfect alternation patterns are symmetrically attested.

Patterns that depart from perfect alternation emerge when INITIAL-GRIDMARK or NON-FINALITY is high-ranked. The asymmetrical formulation of the two constraints is the key factor in predicting iambic-trochaic asymmetries. Because INITIAL-GRIDMARK can introduce clash or lapse near the left edge but not the right edge, it cannot create variations on perfect alternation in mirror-image pairs. Only the version with the variation at the left edge is predicted. Similarly, because NON-FINALITY can introduce clash or lapse near the right edge but not the left edge, it cannot create variations on perfect alternation in mirror-image pairs. Only the version with the variation at the right edge is predicted.

As indicated in (24) and (25), a high-ranking INITIAL-GRIDMARK allows the Weak Bracketing account to produce the trochaic initial clash and initial dactyl patterns without also producing their unattested iambic mirror-images.

(24) Trochaic initial clash: Attested

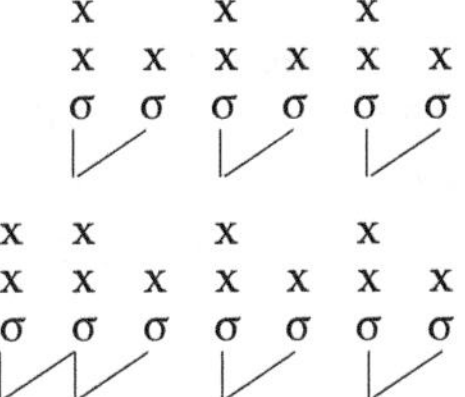

(25) Trochaic initial dactyl: Attested

```
    x       x       x
    x   x   x   x   x   x
    σ   σ   σ   σ   σ   σ

x           x       x
x   x   x   x   x   x   x
σ   σ   σ   σ   σ   σ   σ
```

As (26) and (27) indicate, a high-ranking NON-FINALITY constraint allows the Weak Bracketing account to produce the trochaic final dactyl and final amphibrach patterns without also producing their unattested iambic mirror-images.

(26) Trochaic final dactyl: Attested

```
x       x       x
x   x   x   x   x   x
σ   σ   σ   σ   σ   σ

x       x       x
x   x   x   x   x   x   x
σ   σ   σ   σ   σ   σ   σ
```

(27) Trochaic final amphibrach: Attested

```
x       x       x
x   x   x   x   x   x
σ   σ   σ   σ   σ   σ

x       x           x
x   x   x   x   x   x   x
σ   σ   σ   σ   σ   σ   σ
```

Finally, as (28) and (29) indicate, a high-ranking NON-FINALITY also allows the Weak Bracketing approach to produce the iambic final lapse and iambic reversal patterns without also producing their unattested trochaic mirror-images. While a high-ranking NON-FINALITY also allows the Weak Bracketing approach to produce the unattested iambic double lapse pattern in (30), it does not allow it to produce the unattested trochaic mirror-image.

(28) Iambic final lapse: Attested

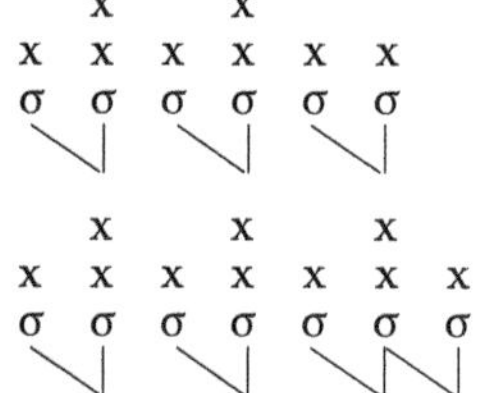

(29) Iambic reversal: Attested

```
   x     x  x
x  x  x  x  x  x
σ  σ  σ  σ  σ  σ

   x     x     x
x  x  x  x  x  x  x
σ  σ  σ  σ  σ  σ  σ
```

(30) Iambic double lapse: Unattested

```
   x     x
x  x  x  x  x  x
σ  σ  σ  σ  σ  σ

x     x     x
x  x  x  x  x  x  x
σ  σ  σ  σ  σ  σ  σ
```

Overall, then, the Weak Bracketing approach predicts a very accurate typology of binary default patterns. It predicts all of the attested patterns and only one unattested pattern. While the Weak Bracketing account predicts one unattested departure from perfect alternation, it successfully captures the generalization in (20b) that attested departures from perfect alternation have unattested mirror-images. In the case of the single unattested pattern, the account falls short in that it predicts one member of a mirror-image pair that is symmetrically unattested. The account also captures the generalization in (20c) that attested departures from perfect alternation emerge due to the requirement of initial stress or final stresslessness.

7.4 Directions for Future Research

Having addressed both the key representations and the constraints that produce directional parsing effects in a way that eliminates the most significant difficulties confronted by alternative approaches, the Weak Bracketing account provides a solid foundation for the theory of metrical stress. There are many issues, however, that have yet to be addressed in the context of Weak Bracketing. The most obvious, perhaps, is the issue of quantity-sensitivity.

While the Weak Bracketing approach eliminates the pathological quantity-sensitivity of the OHP, it is still necessary to address attested varieties of quantity-sensitivity. There are two basic types. In the first type, stress avoids light syllables. This is the type responsible for iambic and trochaic lengthening, weight-sensitivity in word-final syllables, and weight-sensitivity in unbounded stress systems. Significant progress has already been made in this area with the OT framework. The relevant phenomena can be effectively analyzed in terms of the PEAK PROMINENCE constraint (Prince and Smolensky 1993/2004, Walker 1997) the STRESS-TO WEIGHT constraint (Hammond and Dupoux 1996, Lorentz 1996, Crosswhite 1998) or syllable- and foot-internal nonfinality constraints (Hyde 2003, 2006, 2007b), and it is a relatively simple matter to implement the analyses in the context of Weak Bracketing.

The second type of quantity-sensitivity is the type where heavy syllables attract stress. This is the type of quantity-sensitivity associated with quantity-sensitive parsing in binary systems. The central issue in this connection is the different treatment of heavy syllables in iambic and trochaic systems. In left-to-right trochaic systems, the next stress to the right of a heavy syllable occurs on the immediately following syllable, as in (31b).

(31) Left-to-right trochaic systems

a.	*(x)(x)	b.	(x)(x)
	...H L L L...		...H L L...
	⟶		⟶

In right-to-left iambic systems, the next stress to the left of a heavy syllable skips the immediately preceding syllable, as in (32a).

(32) Right-to-left iambic systems

a. (x)(x)
...L L L̲ H...
←

b. *(x)(x)
...L L̲ H...
←

The difference in the resumption of the stress pattern indicates that quantity-sensitive trochaic languages parse heavy syllables as monosyllabic feet while iambic languages incorporate heavy syllables into disyllabic feet. The asymmetric foot inventories of Hayes (1995) and McCarthy and Prince (1986), for example, and the Foot Form constraints of Prince (1991) are among the approaches put forward to account for the difference. It has yet to be determined whether these types of approaches can be effectively implemented in the context of the Weak Bracketing account.

Another issue that has yet to be fully addressed is the issue of window phenomena. Although Chapter 6 presented a preliminary picture of how Relation-Specific Alignment constraints can be used to capture window restrictions based on both prosodic and morphological categories, it did not address the full range of phenomena that might be analyzed in terms of window restrictions. It remains to be demonstrated that the RSA analysis can be extended to account for the position of the verb in verb second languages, for example, for the position of Wackernagel clitics, or for restrictions on depth of infixation.

While the Weak Bracketing approach offers the best alternative among recent proposals for overcoming the Odd-Parity Input Problem, then, and for predicting and appropriate range of binary default patterns, there are several key areas within metrical stress theory where the effectiveness of the approach has yet to be fully explored.

References

Akinlabi, Akinbiyi. 1996. "Featural affixation." *Journal of Linguistics* 32 (02): 239–89. http://dx.doi.org/10.1017/S0022226700015899.

Alber, Birgit. 2005. "Clash, lapse, and directionality." *Natural Language and Linguistic Theory* 23 (3):485–542.

Árnason, Kristján. 1980. *Quantity in historical phonology: Icelandic and related cases. Cambridge Studies in Linguistics 30.* Cambridge: Cambridge University Press.

Árnason, Kristján. 1985. "Icelandic word stress and metrical phonology." *Studia Linguistica* 39 (2): 93–129. http://dx.doi.org/10.1111/j.1467-9582.1985.tb00747.x

Abaurre, Maria, Charlotte Galves, Arnaldo Mandel, and Filomena Sandalo. 2001. The Sotaq optimality based computer program and secondary stress in two varieties of Portuguese. ROA-463, Rutgers Optimality Archive, http://roa.rutgers.edu/

Austin, Peter. 1981. *A grammar of Diyari, South Australia. Cambridge Studies in Linguistics 32.* Cambridge: Cambridge University Press.

Ariste, Paul. 1968. *A grammar of the Votic language.* Bloomington: Indiana University Press.

Beckman, Mary. 1986. *Stress and non-stress accent.* Dordrecht: Foris. http://dx.doi.org/10.1515/9783110874020

Beckman, Jill. 1998. Positional Faithfulness. Ph. D. dissertation. University of Massachusetts, Amherst. ROA-234, Rutgers Optimality Archive, http://roa.rutgers.edu/

Birk, D.B.W. 1976. *The Malakmalak Language, Daly River (Western Arnhem Land).* Canberra: Australian National University.

Blake, Barry. 1969. "Pitta-Pitta." In *Handbook of Australian languages,* vol. 1, ed. R.M.W. Dixon and Barry Blake, 182–242. Amsterdam: John Benjamins.

Blanc, Haim. 1970. "The Arabic dialect of the Negev Bedouins." *Proceedings of the Israeli Academy of Sciences and Humanities* 4 (7): 112–50.

Blight, Richard, and Eunice Pike. 1976. "The phonology of Tenango Otomi." *International Journal of American Linguistics* 42 (1): 51–7. http://dx.doi.org/10.1086/465386

Boxwell, Helen, and Maurice Boxwell. 1966. "Weri phonemes." In *Papers in New Guinea Linguistics,* vol. 5, ed. Stephen A. Wurm, 77–93. Canberra: Australian National University.

Breen, Gavan. 1973. *Bidyara and Gungabala: Grammar and vocabulary.* Linguistic Communications 8. Melbourne: Monash University.

Brown, Herbert. 1986. *A comparative dictionary of Orokolo, Gulf of Papua.* Canberra: Australian National University.

Buckley, Eugene. 1992. Theoretical aspects of Kashaya phonology and morphology. Ph.D. dissertation, University of California, Berkeley. Published 1994, CSLI Publications, Stanford University.

Buckley, Eugene. 1994. "Persistent and cumulative extrametricality in Kashaya." *Natural Language and Linguistic Theory* 12:423–64.

Buckley, Eugene. 2009. "Locality in metrical typology." *Phonology* 26 (03): 389–435. http://dx.doi.org/10.1017/S0952675709990224

Buller, Barbara, Ernest Buller, and Daniel L. Everett. 1993. "Stress placement, syllable structure, and minimality in Banawá." *International Journal of American Linguistics* 59:280–93.

Bye, Patrik. 1996. "Scandinavian "level stress" and the theory of prosodic overlay." *Nordlyd* 24:23–62.

Capell, Arthur. 1962. *Some linguistic types in Australia. Oceania Linguistic Monographs 7.* University of Sydney.

Chafe, Wallace L. 1977. "Accent and related phenomena in the Five Nations Iroquois Languages." In *Studies in stress and accent, Southern California occasional papers in linguistics 4,* ed. Larry Hyman, 169–181. Los Angeles: Department of Linguistics, University of Southern California.

Chen-Main, Joan. 2006. On the generation and linearization of multi-dominance structures. Ph.D. dissertation. Johns Hopkins University.

Chomsky, Noam. 2001/2004. Beyond Explanatory Adequacy. In *MIT Occasional Papers in Linguistics 20.* Cambridge, MA:MIT (2001). Also in *Structures and beyond,* ed. A. Belletti. Oxford: Oxford University Press. (2004).

Cohn, Abigail. 1989. "Stress in Indonesian and bracketing paradoxes." *Natural Language and Linguistic Theory* 7:167–216.

Cole, Jennifer and Charles Kisseberth. 1995. Nasal harmony in Optimal Domains Theory. Ms, University of Illinois. ROA-49, Rutgers Optimality Archive, http://roa.rutgers.edu/

Cooper, Grosvenor, and Leonard Meyer. 1960. *The rhythmic structure of music.* Chicago: University of Chicago Press.

Crosswhite, Katherine. 1998. "Segmental vs. prosodic correspondence in Chamorro." *Phonology* 15 (3): 281–316. http://dx.doi.org/10.1017/S0952675799003619

Crowhurst, Megan. 1996. "An optimal alternative to conflation." *Phonology* 13 (03): 409–24. http://dx.doi.org/10.1017/S0952675700002694

Crowhurst, Megan J., and Mark Hewitt. 1995. "Directional footing, degeneracy, and Alignment." *Natural East Linguistic Society* 25 (1): 47–61.

Crowley, Terry. 1981. "The Mpakwithi dialect of Anguthimri." *Handbook of Australian languages,* vol. 2, ed. R.M.W. Dixon and Barry Blake, 146–94. Amsterdam: John Benjamins.

Crowley, Terry. 1998. *Ura.* München: Lincom Europa.

Dayley, Jon. 1989. *Tümpisa (Panamint) Shoshone Grammar. University of California Publications in Linguistics 115.* Berkeley: University of California Press.

de Lacy, Paul. 1999. "Morphological haplology and correspondence." In *University of Massachusetts occasional papers in linguistics 25: papers from the 25th reunion,* ed. Paul de Lacy and Anita Nowak, 51–88. Amherst: Graduate Linguistic Student Association.

Dench, Alan Charles. 1998. *Yingkarta.* München: Lincom Europa.

Derbyshire, Desmond C. 1985. *Hixkaryana and linguistic typology. SIL Publications in Linguistics 76.* Dallas: Summer Institute of Linguistics.

Donohue, Mark. 1999. *A grammar of Tukang Besi*. New York: Mouton. http://dx.doi.org/10.1515/9783110805543

Dresher, B. Elan, and Aditi Lahiri. 1991. "The Germanic foot: Metrical coherence in Old English." *Linguistic Inquiry* 22:251–86.

Dubert, Raymond, and Marjorie Dubert. 1973. "Biangai phonemes." In Alan Healey (ed.) *Phonologies of Three Languages of Papua New Guinea*, 5–36. Ukarumpa, Papua New Guinea: Summer Institute of Linguistics.

Dunn, Leone. 1988. *Badimaya, a Western Australian language. Papers in Australian Linguistics 17, Pacific Linguistics A71.*, 19–49. Canberra: Australian National University.

Echeverria, Max S., and Heles Contreras. 1965. "Araucanian phonemics." *International Journal of American Linguistics* 31:132–5.

Eisner, Jason. 1997. What constraints should OT allow? Talk handout from the Annual Meeting of the Linguistic Society of America, Chicago. ROA-204, Rutgers Optimality Archive, http://roa.rutgers.edu/

Ellison, Mark T. 1995. *Phonological derivation in Optimality Theory. Ms.* University of Edinburgh.

Everett, Daniel L. 1988. "On metrical constituent structure in Pirahã phonology." *Natural Language and Linguistic Theory* 6:20–46.

Everett, Daniel L. (1996), Prosodic levels and constraints in Banawá and Suruwaha. Ms., University of Pittsburgh. ROA-121, Rutgers Optimality Archive, http://roa.rutgers.edu/index.php3

Everett, Daniel L. 1997. "Syllable integrity." *West Coast Conference on Formal Linguistics* 16:177–90.

Everett, Daniel L. 2003. "Iambic feet in Paumari and the theory of foot structure." *Linguistic Discovery* 2 (1): 22–44. http://dx.doi.org/10.1349/PS1.1537-0852.A.263.

Everett, Daniel L., and Keren Everett. 1984. "On the relevance of syllable onsets to stress placement." *Linguistic Inquiry* 15:5–11.

Flierl, W., and H. Strauss. 1977. *Kâte dictionary*. Canberra: Australian National University.

Foster, Michael. 1982. "Alternating weak and strong syllables in Cayuga words." *International Journal of American Linguistics* 48:59–72.

Furby, Christine. 1974. *Garawa phonology. Pacific Linguistics, Series A*. Canberra: Australian National University.

Goddard, Ives. 1979. *Delaware verbal morphology*. New York: Garland.

Goddard, Ives. 1982. "The historical phonology of Munsee." *International Journal of American Linguistics* 38:1–5.

Gordon, Matthew. 2002a. "A factorial typology of quantity-insensitive stress." *Natural Language and Linguistic Theory* 20:491–552.

Gordon, Matthew. 2002b. "A phonetically-driven account of syllable weight." *Language* 78 (1): 51–80. http://dx.doi.org/10.1353/lan.2002.0020

Gordon, Matthew. 2011. "Stress: Phonotactic and phonetic evidence." In *The Blackwell Companion to Phonology*, ed. Marc van Oostendorp, Colin J. Ewen, Elizabeth Hume, and Keren Rice, 924–48. Oxford: Blackwell.

Granberry, Julian. 1993. *A grammar and dictionary of the Timucua language.* Tuscaloosa: University of Alabama Press.

Green, Thomas. 1993. Configurational constraints in a generalized theory of phonological representation. Ph. D. dissertation, MIT, Cambridge, Massachusetts.

Green, Thomas. 1995. The stress window in Pirahã: a reanalysis of rhythm in Optimality Theory. Ms, Massachusetts Institute of Technology, Cambridge. ROA-45, Rutgers Optimality Archive, http://roa.rutgers.edu/

Green, Thomas, and Michael Kenstowicz. 1995. The Lapse constraint. Ms. Massachusetts Institute of Technology, Cambridge. ROA-101, Rutgers Optimality Archive, http://roa.rutgers.edu/

Halle, Morris, and Jean-Roger Vergnaud. 1987. *An essay on stress*. Cambridge, Massachusetts: MIT Press.

Hammond, Michael, and Emmanuel Dupoux. 1996. "Psychophonology." In *Current trends in phonology: models and methods*, vol. 1, ed. Jacques Durand and Bernard Laks, 274–97. Salford: ESRI.

Hansen, Kenneth C., and L.E. Hansen. 1969. "Pintupi phonology." *Oceanic Linguistics* 8 (2): 153–70. http://dx.doi.org/10.2307/3622818

Harris, James. 1983. *Syllable structure and stress in Spanish: a nonlinear analysis*. Linguistic Inquiry Monograph 8. Cambridge, Massachusetts: MIT Press.

Hayes, Bruce. 1985. "Iambic and trochaic rhythm in stress rules." *Proceedings of Berkeley Linguistics Society* 13:429–46.

Hayes, Bruce. 1987. "A revised parametric metrical theory." *North East Linguistic Society* 17:274–89.

Hayes, Bruce. 1995. *Metrical stress theory: principles and case studies*. Chicago: University of Chicago Press.

Heinz, Jeffrey. 2007. The inductive learning of phonotactic patterns. PhD dissertation, University of California, Los Angeles.

Hercus, Louise A. 1982. *The Bagandji language*. Canberra: Australian National University.

Hercus, Louise A. 1986. *Victorian languages: A late survey. Pacific Linguistics B77*. Canberra: Australian National University.

Hercus, Louise A. 1999. *A grammar of the Wirangu language from the west coast of South Australia*. Canberra: Pacific Linguistics.

Hermans, Ben. 2011. "The representation of word stress." In *The Blackwell Companion to Phonology*, ed. Marc van Oostendorp, Colin J. Ewen, Elizabeth Hume, and Keren Rice, 980–1002. Oxford: Blackwell.

Hewitt, Mark S. 1994. Deconstructing foot binarity in Koniag Alutiiq. Ms., University of British Columbia, Vancouver. ROA-12, Rutgers Optimality Archive, http://roa.rutgers.edu/

Hintz, Diane. 2006. "Stress in South Conchucos Quechua: A phonetic and phonological study." *International Journal of American Linguistics* 72 (4): 477–521. http://dx.doi.org/10.1086/513058

Hualde, José I. 1998. "A gap filled: postpostinitial accent in Azkoitia Basque." *Linguistics* 36 (1): 99–117. http://dx.doi.org/10.1515/ling.1998.36.1.99

Hung, Henrietta. 1993. Iambicity, rhythm, and non-parsing. Ms, University of Ottawa. ROA-9, Rutgers Optimality Archive, http://roa.rutgers.edu/

Hung, Henrietta. 1994. The rhythmic and prosodic organization of edge constituents. Ph. D. dissertation, Brandeis University, Waltham, Massachusetts. ROA-24, Rutgers Optimality Archive, http://roa.rutgers.edu/

Hyde, Brett. 2001. Metrical and prosodic structure in Optimality Theory. PhD dissertation, Rutgers University. ROA-476, Rutgers Optimality Archive, http://roa.rutgers.edu/

Hyde, Brett. 2002. "A restrictive theory of metrical stress." *Phonology* 19 (3): 313–59. http://dx.doi.org/10.1017/S0952675703004391

Hyde, Brett. 2003. Nonfinality. Ms., St. Louis, Missouri: Washington University. ROA-633, Rutgers Optimality Archive, http://roa.rutgers.edu/

Hyde, Brett. 2006. "Towards a uniform account of prominence-sensitive stress." In *Wondering at the natural fecundity of things: essays in honor of Alan Prince*, ed. Eric Bakovic, Junko Itô, and John McCarthy, 139–83. Linguistics Research Center, University of California, Santa Cruz, http://escholarship.org/uc/item/4hp8s98w

Hyde, Brett. 2007a. "Issues in Banawá Prosody: Onset Sensitivity, Minimal Words, and Syllable Integrity." *Linguistic Inquiry* 38 (2): 239–85. http://dx.doi.org/10.1162/ling.2007.38.2.239

Hyde, Brett. 2007b. "Non-finality and weight-sensitivity." *Phonology* 24 (02): 287–334. http://dx.doi.org/10.1017/S0952675707001212

Hyde, Brett. 2008a. Alignment continued: distance-sensitivity, order-sensitivity, and the Midpoint Pathology. Ms., St. Louis, Missouri: Washington University. ROA-998, Rutgers Optimality Archive, http://roa.rutgers.edu/

Hyde, Brett. 2008b. The Odd-Parity Parsing Problem. Ms., St. Louis, Missouri: Washington University. ROA-971, Rutgers Optimality Archive, http://roa.rutgers.edu/

Hyde, Brett. 2009a. A closer look at Iterative Foot Optimization and the case against parallelism. Ms., St. Louis, Missouri: Washington University. ROA-1062, Rutgers Optimality Archive, http://roa.rutgers.edu/

Hyde, Brett. 2009b. "The rhythmic foundations of INITIAL GRIDMARK and NONFINALITY." In *Proceedings of the North East Linguistics Society* 38, Volume I, 397-410.

Hyde, Brett. 2011. "The Iambic-Trochaic Law." In *The Blackwell Companion to Phonology*, ed. Marc van Oostendorp, Colin J. Ewen, Elizabeth Hume, and Keren Rice, 1052–77. Oxford: Blackwell.

Hyde, Brett. 2012a. "Alignment constraints." *Natural Language and Linguistic Theory* 30 (3): 789–836. http://dx.doi.org/10.1007/s11049-012-9167-3

Hyde, Brett. 2012b. "The Odd-Parity Input Problem in Metrical Stress Theory." *Phonology* 29 (03): 383–431. http://dx.doi.org/10.1017/S0952675712000218

Hyde, Brett, and Brooke Husic. 2012. "Ancient Greek Accent Windows." *Revista Letras e Letras* 28:29–58.

Hyde, Brett and Bethany McCord. 2012. The inadequacy of a faithfulness-based approach to Spanish secondary stress. Ms, Washington, University. ROA-1154, Rutgers Optimality Archive, http://roa.rutgers.edu/

Itô, Junko, and Armin Mester. 1992. *Weak layering and word binarity*. Ms. Santa Cruz: University of California.

Itô, Junko, and Armin Mester. 1994. "Reflections on CodaCond and Alignment." In *Phonology at Santa Cruz*, vol. 3. ed. Jason Merchant, Jaye Padgett, and Rachel Walker, 27–46. Santa Cruz: University of California.

Jha, Subhadra. 1940–1944. "Maithili phonetics." *Indian Linguistics* 8:435–59.

Jha, Subhadra. 1958. *The Formation of the Maithili Language*. London: Luzac.

Kager, René. 1989. *A Metrical Theory of Stress and Destressing in English and Dutch. Linguistic Models 14*. Dordrecht: Foris.

Kager, René. 1993. "Alternatives to the iambic-trochaic law." *Natural Language and Linguistic Theory* 11 (3): 381–432. http://dx.doi.org/10.1007/BF00993165

Kager, René. 1994. Ternary rhythm in alignment theory. Ms, Research Institute for Language and Speech, Utrecht University. ROA-35, Rutgers Optimality Archive, http://roa.rutgers.edu/

Kager, René. 1995. "Review article." *Phonology* 12 (03): 437–64. http://dx.doi.org/10.1017/S095267570000258X

Kager, René. 2001. Rhythmic directionality by positional licensing. Handout from the Fifth Holland Institute of Linguistics Phonology Conference, University of Potsdam. ROA-514, Rutgers Optimality Archive, http://roa.rutgers.edu/

Kager, René. 2005. Rhythmic licensing theory: an extended typology. *Proceedings of the 3rd Seoul International Conference on Phonology*, 5-31.

Kakumasu, James. 1986. "Urubu-Kaapor." In *Handbook of Amazonian languages*, vol. 1. ed. Desmond Derbyshire and Geoffrey Pullum, 326–406. New York: Mouton. http://dx.doi.org/10.1515/9783110850819.326

Kálmán, Bála. 1965. *Vogul Chrestomathy*. Bloomington: Indiana University.

Kaye, Jonathan. 1973. "Odawa Stress and Related Phenomena." In *Odawa Language Project, Second Report*, ed. G.L. Piggott and J. Kaye, 42–46. Centre for Linguistic Studies, University of Toronto.

Keating, Patricia, Taehong Cho, Cécile Fougeron, and C. Hsu. 2003. "Domain-initial strengthening in four languages." *Laboratory Phonology* 6:145–63.

Kenstowicz, Michael. 1983. "Parametric variation and accent in the Arabic Dialects." *Chicago Linguistic Society* 19:205–13.

Kenstowicz, Michael. 1995. "Cyclic *vs.* non-cyclic constraint evaluation." *Phonology* 12 (03): 397–436. http://dx.doi.org/10.1017/S0952675700002578

Kenstowicz, Michael, and Kamal Abdul-Karim. 1980. "Cyclic stress in Levantine Arabic." *Studies in the Linguistic Sciences* 10(2).

Kerek, A. 1971. *Hungarian Metrics: Some Linguistic Aspects of Iambic Verse*. Indiana University Publications, Uralic and Altaic Series 117. The Hague: Mouton.

Kettunen, Lauri. 1938. *Livisches Wo"rterbuch mit grammatischer Einleitung*. Helsinki: Suomalais-Ugrilainen Seura.

Key, Mary. 1968. *Comparative Tacanan phonology with Cavinena phonology and notes on Pano-Tacanan relationship*. The Hague: Mouton.

Knudson, Lyle M. 1975. "A natural phonology and morphophonemics of Chimalapa Zoque." *Papers in Linguistics (Edmonton)* 8 (3–4): 283–346. http://dx.doi.org/10.1080/08351817509370404

Kouwenberg, Silvia. 1994. *A grammar of Berbice Dutch Creole*. New York: Mouton de Gruyter. http://dx.doi.org/10.1515/9783110885705

Kucera, Henry. 1961. *The Phonology of Czech*. Berlin: Mouton.

Ladd, D. Robert and Roca, Iggy. 1986. "Secondary stress and metrical rhythm." *Phonology Yearbook* 3:341–70. http://dx.doi.org/10.1017/S0952675700000683

Laidig, Carol. 1992. "Segments, syllables, and stress in Larike." In *Phonological studies in four languages of Maluku*, ed. Donald Burquest and Wyn Laidig, 67–126. Dallas: Summer Institute of Linguistics.

Lawrence, Wayne P. 1997. Haplology and vowel underspecification. Report of the special research project for the typological investigation of the languages and cultures of the east and west, 381–388.

Leer, Jeff. 1985. "Toward a metrical interpretation of Yupik prosody." In *Yupik Eskimo Prosodic Systems: Descriptive and Comparative Studies*, ed. Michael Krauss. Fairbanks, 77–134: Alaska Native Center.

Lehrdahl, Fred, and Ray Jackendoff. 1983. *A generative theory of tonal music.* Cambridge, Massachusetts: MIT Press.

Leskinen, Heikki. 1984. "Über die Phonemsystem der Karelischen Sprache." In *Studien zur Phonologischen Beschreibung uralischer Sprachen,* ed. Péter Hajdú and László Honti, 247–57. Budapest: Akadémiai Kiadó.

LeSourd, Philip S. 1993. *Accent and syllable structure in Passamaquoddy.* New York: Garland.

Liberman, Mark. 1975. The intonational system of English. Ph. D. dissertation, MIT. Published 1979, New York, Garland.

Liberman, Mark, and Alan Prince. 1977. "On stress and linguistic rhythm." *Linguistic Inquiry* 8:249–336.

Lieberman, Philip. 1960. "Some acoustic correlates of word stress in American English." *Journal of the Acoustical Society of America* 32 (4): 451–4. http://dx.doi.org/10.1121/1.1908095

Lichtenberk, Frantisek. 1984. *Toabaita language of Malaita, Solomon Islands.* Auckland: University of Auckland.

Lorentz, Ove. 1996. "Length and correspondence in Scandinavian." *Nordlyd* 24:111–28.

Lunden, Anya. 2006. Weight, final lengthening and stress: a phonetic and phonological case study of Norwegian. Ph.D. dissertation, University of California, Santa Cruz. ROA-833, Rutgers Optimality Archive, http://roa.rutgers.edu/

Lynch, John. 2000. *A grammar of Anejom.* Canberra: Australian National University.

MacDonald, Lorna. 1990. *A grammar of Tauya.* New York: Mouton de Gruyter. http://dx.doi.org/10.1515/9783110846027

Manning, Margaret, and Naomi Saggers. 1977. "A tentative phonemic analysis of Ningil." In *Phonologies of Five Papua New Guinea Languages,* ed. Richard Loving, 49–71. Ukarumpa, Papua New Guinea: Summer Institute of Linguistics.

Matteson, Esther. 1965. *The Piro (Arawakan) language. University of California Publications in Linguistics 22.* Berkeley: University of California Press.

McCarthy, John J. 2003. "OT constraints are categorical." *Phonology* 20 (1): 75–138. http://dx.doi.org/10.1017/S0952675703004470

McCarthy, John J. 2007. *Hidden Generalizations: Phonological Opacity in Optimality Theory.* London: Equinox.

McCarthy, John J. 2008. "The serial interaction of stress and syncope." *Natural Language and Linguistic Theory* 26:499–546.

McCarthy, John, and Alan Prince. 1986. Prosodic morphology. Ms, University of Massachusetts, Amherst, and Brandeis University, Waltham, Massachusetts.

McCarthy, John, and Alan Prince. 1993a. "Generalized alignment." In *Yearbook of Morphology 1993,* ed. Geert Booij and Jaap van Marle. Dordrecht: Kluwer. http://dx.doi.org/10.1007/978-94-017-3712-8_4

McCarthy, John, and Alan Prince. 1993b. Prosodic Morphology : constraint interaction and satisfaction. Ms, University of Massachusetts, Amherst and Rutgers University. ROA-482, Rutgers Optimality Archive, http://roa.rutgers.edu/

McCarthy, John, and Alan Prince. 1994. "The emergence of the unmarked : optimality in prosodic morphology." *North East Linguistic Society* 24:333–79.

McDonald, M., and A. Stephen Wurm. 1979. *Basic Materials in Wangkumara (Galali): Grammar, Sentences, and Vocabulary. Pacific Linguistics* B65. Canberra: Australian National University.

Mellander, Evan. 2003. "(HL)-creating processes in a theory of foot structure." *Linguistic Review* 20 (2-4): 243–80. http://dx.doi.org/10.1515/tlir.2003.010
Menovshchikov, G.A. 1975. *Iazyk naukanskikh eskimosov*. Leningrad: Nauka.
Michelson, Karin. 1988. *A comparative study of Lake-Iroquoian accent*. Dordrecht: Kluwer Academic Publishers. http://dx.doi.org/10.1007/978-94-009-2709-4
Miller, Wick. 1996. "Sketch of Shoshone, a Uto-Aztecan language." In *Handbook of American Indian Languages*, vol. 17. ed. Ives Goddard, 693–720. Washington: Smithsonian Institute.
Miyaoka, Osahito. 1985. "Accentuation in Central Alaskan Yupik." In *Yupik Eskimo Prosodic Systems: Descriptive and Comparative Studies*, ed. M. Krauss, 51–75. Fairbanks: Alaska Native Language Center.
Nelson, Nicole. 2003. Asymmetric Anchoring. Ph.D. dissertation, Rutgers University, New Brunswick. ROA-604, Rutgers Optimality Archive, http://roa.rutgers.edu/
Nespor, Marina, and Irene Vogel. 1986. *Prosodic phonology*. Dordrecht: Foris.
Nicklas, Thurston Dale. 1972. The elements of Choctaw. Ann Arbor, Michigan: University of Michigan dissertation.
Nicklas, Thurston Dale. 1975. "Choctaw morphophonemics." In *Studies in Southeastern Indian Languages*, ed. James M. Crawford, 237–50. Athens: University of Georgia Press.
Oller, D.K. 1973. "The effect of position in utterance on speech segment duration in English." *Journal of the Acoustical Society of America* 54 (5): 1235–47. http://dx.doi.org/10.1121/1.1914393
Orgun, C. Orhan, and Ronald Sprouse. 1999. "From MPARSE to CONTROL: deriving ungrammaticality." *Phonology* 16 (2): 191–224. http://dx.doi.org/10.1017/S0952675799003747
Osborn, Henry. 1966. "Warao I: phonology and morphophonemics." *International Journal of American Linguistics* 32:108–23.
Parker, Steve. 1997. "An OT account of laryngealization in Cuzco Quechua." Work Papers of the Summer Institute of Linguistics, University of North Dakota 41:1–11.
Payne, David L. 1981. *The Phonology and Morphology of Axininca Campa*. Arlington: Summer Institute of Linguistics and University of Texas.
Payne, David. 1990. "Accent in Aguaruna." In *Amazonian linguistics: studies in lowland South American languages*, ed. Doris L. Payne, 161–84. Austin: University of Texas Press.
Phinnemore, Thomas. 1985. "Ono Phonology and Morpho-phonemics." *Papers in New Guinea Linguistics* 22:173–214.
Piggott, Glyne. 1980. *Aspects of Odawa morphophonemics*. New York: Garland.
Piggott, Glyne. 1983. "Extrametricality and Ojibwa stress." *McGill Working Papers in Linguistics* 1: 80–117.
Piñeros, Carlos-Eduardo. 2001. "Segment-to-syllable alignment and vocalization in Chilean Spanish." *Lingua* 111 (3): 163–88. http://dx.doi.org/10.1016/S0024-3841(00)00029-2
Prince, Alan. 1980. "A metrical theory for Estonian quantity." *Linguistic Inquiry* 11:511–62.
Prince, Alan. 1983. "Relating to the grid." *Linguistic Inquiry* 14: 19–100.
Prince, Alan. 1991. "Quantitative consequences of rhythmic organization." In *Proceeding of the Chicago Linguistic Society 26-II: Papers from the Parasession on*

the Syllable in Phonetics and Phonology, ed. Karen Deaton, Manuela Noske, and Michael Ziolkowski, 355–98. Chicago: Chicago Linguistics Society.

Prince, Alan. 2002. Arguing Optimality. Ms., Rutgers University. ROA-562, Rutgers Optimality Archive, http://roa.rutgers.edu/

Prince, Alan, and Paul Smolensky. 1993/2004. Optimality theory: constraint interaction in generative grammar. Ms, Rutgers University and University of Colorado, Boulder. Published 2004. Malden, Mass. and Oxford: Blackwell.

Pruitt, Kathryn. (2008), Iterative foot optimization and locality in stress systems. Ms. University of Massachusetts, Amherst. ROA-999, Rutgers Optimality Archive, http://roa.rutgers.edu/

Pruitt, Kathryn. 2010. "Serialism and locality in constraint-based metrical parsing." *Phonology* 27 (03): 481–526. http://dx.doi.org/10.1017/S0952675710000229

Reesink, Ger P. 1999. *A grammar of Hatam*. Canberra: Australian National University.

Rice, Curt. 1992. Binarity and ternarity in metrical theory. PhD dissertation, University of Texas, Austin.

Rice, Curt. 2006. "Norwegian stress and quantity: the implications of loanwords." *Lingua* 116 (7): 1171–94. http://dx.doi.org/10.1016/j.lingua.2005.05.008

Rubach, Jerzey, and Geert Booij. 1985. "A grid theory of stress in Polish." *Lingua* 66 (4): 281–320. http://dx.doi.org/10.1016/0024-3841(85)90032-4

Saelzer, Meinke. 1976. "Fonologia provisória da língua Kamayura." In *Série Linguística* 5, ed. Loraine Bridgeman, 131–70.

Sapir, Edward. 1930. "Southern Paiute, a Shoshonean language." *Proceedings of the American Academy of Arts and Sciences* 65 (1): 1–296. http://dx.doi.org/10.2307/20026309

Selkirk, Elisabeth O. 1980. "The role of prosodic categories in English word stress." *Linguistic Inquiry* 11: 563–605.

Selkirk, Elisabeth O. 1984. *Phonology and syntax: the relation between sound and structure.* Cambridge, Massachusetts: MIT Press.

Selkirk, Elisabeth O. 1995. "The prosodic structure of function words." In *University of Massachusetts occasional papers in linguistics 18: papers in Optimality Theory*, ed. Jill Beckman, Suzanne Urbanczyk, and Laura Walsh, 439–70. Amherst: Graduate Linguistic Student Association.

Starke, Michal. 2001. Move dissolves into Merge. Ph.D. dissertation. University of Connecticut.

Stell, Nelida Noemi. 1972. *Fonologia de la Lengua Alulaj*. Buenos Aires: Universidad de Buenos Aires.

Steriade, Donca. 1988. "Greek accent: a case for preserving structure." *Linguistic Inquiry* 19: 271–314.

Street, Chester S., and Gregory P. Mollingin. 1981. "The phonology of Murinbata." In *Australian phonologies: Collected papers*, ed. Bruce Waters, 183–244. Darwin: Summer Institute of Linguistics.

Tauberschmidt, Gerhard. 1999. *A grammar of Sinaugoro: an Austronesian language of the Central Province of Papua New Guinea*. Canberra: Australian National University.

Tryon, Darrell T. 1967. *Nengone grammar*. Pacific Linguistics B6. Canberra: Australian National University.

Tryon, Darrell T. 1970. *An introduction to Maranungku*. Pacific Linguistics B15. Canberra: Australian National University.

Tyhurst, James J. 1987. Accent shift in Seminole nouns. In Pamela Munro (ed.) Muskogean linguistics. *UCLA occasional papers in linguistics* 6, 161–170. Department of Linguistics, University of California, Los Angeles.

van de Vijver, Ruben. 1998. *The Iambic Issue: Iambs as a Result of Constraint Interactions*. The Hague: Holland Academic Graphics.

Vaysman, Olga. 2009. Segmental alternations and metrical theory. Ph.D. dissertation, MIT. ROA-1011, Rutgers Optimality Archive, http://roa.rutgers.edu/

Voegelin, Charles. 1935. "Tübatulabal Grammar." *University of California Publications in American Archaeology and Ethnology* 34(2), 55–189.

Voorhoeve, C. 1965. *The Flamingo Bay dialect of the Asmat languages*. Gravenhage: M. Nijhoff. http://dx.doi.org/10.1163/9789004286740

Walker, Rachel. 1997. Mongolian stress, licensing, and factorial typology. Ms, University of California, Santa Cruz. ROA-171, Rutgers Optimality Archive, http://roa.rutgers.edu/

Wightman, C.W., S. Shattuck-Hufnagel, M. Ostendorfand, and P.J. Price. 1992. "Segmental durations in the vicinity of prosodic phrase boundaries." *Journal of the Acoustical Society of America* 91 (3): 1707–17. http://dx.doi.org/10.1121/1.402450.

Zoll, Cheryl. 1996. Parsing below the segment. Ph.D. dissertation, University of California, Berkeley. ROA-143, Rutgers Optimality Archive, http://roa.rutgers.edu/

Index

www.ingramcontent.com/pod-product-compliance
Lightning Source LLC
LaVergne TN
LVHW021126110826
R19582500001B/R195825PG844660LVX00010B/17

* 9 7 8 1 8 4 5 5 3 0 8 9 1 *